By the Light of Burning Dreams

Also by David Talbot

Between Heaven and Hell: The Story of My Stroke

The Devil's Chessboard: Allen Dulles, the CIA,
and the Rise of America's Secret Government

Season of the Witch: Enchantment, Terror,
and Deliverance in the City of Love

Brothers: The Hidden History of the Kennedy Years

Also by Margaret Talbot

The Entertainer: Movies, Magic, and My Father's
Twentieth Century

David Talbot and Margaret Talbot

with Arthur Allen

By the Light of Burning Dreams

The Triumphs and Tragedies
of the Second American Revolution

HARPER

An Imprint of HarperCollins*Publishers*

HarperCollins books may be purchased for educational, business, or sales promotional use. For information, please email the Special Markets Department at SPsales@harpercollins.com.

FIRST EDITION

Library of Congress Cataloging-in-Publication Data has been applied for.

ISBN 978-0-06-282039-6

21 22 23 24 25   LSC   10 9 8 7 6 5 4 3 2 1

*To our children—Joe Talbot, Nat Talbot, Ike Allen,
and Lucy Allen—and Jimmie Fails, and the other members
of their generation who are fighting the good fight.*

Contents

Introduction   *1*

The Purity of Protest and the Complexity of Politics:
Tom Hayden, Jane Fonda, and the Red Family   *15*

Revolution Has Come, Time to Pick Up the Gun:
Bobby Seale, Huey Newton, Eldridge Cleaver,
and the Black Panthers   *61*

Sisterhood Is Blooming: *Heather Booth*
and the Women of Jane   *109*

The Martyr Complex: *Cesar Chavez, Dolores Huerta,*
and the Righteousness of La Causa   *157*

Liberation Day: *Craig Rodwell and the Making of Pride*   *191*

We All Shine On: *John Lennon, Yoko Ono, and the*
Politics of Stardom   *235*

The Great Escape: *Dennis Banks, Madonna Thunder Hawk,*
Russell Means, and the Warriors of Wounded Knee   *281*

Acknowledgments   *331*
Notes   *335*
Index   *377*

Introduction

The first American Revolution was a glorious but abortive enterprise. Martin Luther King Jr.—who must be crowned the leading protagonist of the second American Revolution—sang the praises of the country's origin story in his final speech, extolling "those great wells of democracy which were dug deep by the Founding Fathers in the Declaration of Independence and the Constitution." The first revolution took the "puny" offspring of an empire, "a collection of disparate colonies huddled along the Atlantic coast [with] less than two million monarchical subjects," in the words of historian Gordon S. Wood, and turned "America into the most liberal, democratic, and modern nation in the world."

Successive waves of radical dissent—from the nineteenth-century abolitionist movement to the populist uprisings of the Progressive Era to the labor militancy of the 1930s to the sweeping social and cultural transformation of the 1960s and '70s that we are calling the second American Revolution—would keep the unfinished work of US democracy alive. King, like all those who fought heroically in the second War of Independence, knew how far short the nation fell from the ideals of its hallowed founding documents. It would take a second American Revolution to expand the "dream" he prophesied so that it included (or at least strove to include) those left orphaned by the Founding Fathers—African Americans, Native Americans, women, exploited workers of all races and ethnicities, gays and lesbians.

The civil rights movement—which won its greatest victories in the first half of the 1960s—ignited the second American Revolution. Inspired by civil rights and Black Power activism, a string of other liberation movements caught flame that decade and the next—including the Vietnam antiwar struggle, the United Farm Workers union, the American Indian Movement, women's liberation, and the gay and lesbian uprising. Together these upheavals—which were often linked by mutually supportive activists and shared goals—forged the nation's most daring interpretation of freedom and justice since the first American Revolution.

This second revolution forced the country to change its assumptions about race, war and peace, gender, sexual orientation, reproductive rights, labor justice, consumer responsibility, and environmental protection. Almost all of these movements grounded their claims at one time or another in the rights to life, liberty, and the pursuit of happiness—compelling America to be true to its stated ideals in the Declaration of Independence and the Bill of Rights. Like the great African American poet Langston Hughes, the activists whose stories we tell here wanted America to be America again—or was it for the first time? As Hughes wrote, "America never was America to me," and yet the longing and the faith that it could be remained real to him.

The nation's founding betrayal—the first and most profound way in which it failed to make true its promise—was the perpetuation of slavery, which George Washington himself called a "foul stain of manhood." While the soaring idealism of the original American Revolution inspired widespread hopes, and moved many slaves and economically dispossessed to join Washington's Continental

Army, only a small minority of enslaved African Americans (who made up one-fifth of the infant nation's population) won their freedom after the war. Indeed, a majority of the men who signed the Declaration of Independence were slave owners—including Washington, Thomas Jefferson, and James Madison. And those who opposed slavery in principle—like John Adams and Benjamin Franklin—never took decisive action on behalf of the nascent abolition movement.

Washington's young French general—Marquis de Lafayette, who was like a surrogate son—tried but failed to convince the father of the nation to free the men and women held in bondage on his Mount Vernon plantation. Lafayette later summed up the betrayal of the Revolution's ideals with bitter eloquence: "I would never have drawn my sword in the cause of America if I could have conceived thereby that I was founding a land of slavery."

If men like Washington, Jefferson, Madison, Franklin, and Adams had risen to the brilliance of their language and followed through on the "grand experiment" (in Lafayette's words) to liberate all of King George III's subjects, then America would have been spared history's terrible reckoning. But as the historian Gary B. Nash ruefully noted, "Eighty years later, more than 600,000 American lives were lost accomplishing the goal of emancipation, roughly one for each of the slaves in the new United States as of 1785."

The first American Revolution abandoned not only its enslaved population. During the War of Independence, Native American tribes—including even those who sided with the Patriots against the British—came under relentless onslaughts from white frontiersmen, militias, settlers, and even regiments of Washington's army. In a genocidal pattern that would be widely repeated for the next two hundred years, peace-minded tribal chiefs were ambushed; villages torched; men, women, and children massacred; treaties falsely made and soon broken.

Women, too, were disappointed by the expectations the American Revolution raised and dashed. Many of them had aided the Patriots' cause in various ways, with socially established women gathering funds for the perennially ragged Continental Army and the wives and lovers of soldiers serving as unsung camp followers, nursing their wounds, washing their uniforms. One of the liveliest ongoing debates over women's emancipation took place in the Massachusetts home of John Adams, where his wife, Abigail, kept up a constant drumbeat for America's leaders to "remember the ladies." Women must be allowed to at least have a voice in lawmaking, argued Abigail Adams, since "all Men would be Tyrants if they could," she wrote her husband in 1776. But Adams generally deflected his wife's political advice, believing in the sovereignty of elite white male leaders like himself.

John Adams worried that the Revolution had left colonial society's lower orders unconstrained, and he was not alone in his anxiety. In 1776, he wrote from the Continental Congress in Philadelphia: "We have been told that our Struggle has loosened the bands of Government every where. That Children and Apprentices were disobedient—that schools and Colledges [sic] were grown turbulent—that Indians slighted their Guardians and Negroes grew insolent to their Masters."

Adams fretted, "There will be no End of it. New Claims will arise. Women will demand a Vote. Lads from 12 to 21 will think their Rights not enough attended to, and every Man who has not a Farthing will demand an equal Voice with any other in all Acts of State." America's future second president ardently wished for the "Whirlwind" unleashed by the Revolution to be calmed by "more Serenity of Temper."

But over the next two centuries, that whirlwind would come howling free again and again. During the increasingly fractious years before the Civil War, Frederick Douglass—the great orator of African American liberation—often invoked the broken pledge of 1776 in his speeches and writing, on no occasion more powerfully than his famous Independence Day address delivered in Rochester, New York, on July 5, 1852. "The fathers of this republic," Douglass acknowledged to the nearly six hundred white abolitionists packed into Corinthian Hall that day, were "brave men" and even "great men" and their "great deeds" demanded universal admiration. And yet, Douglass declared, he could not join in the national celebration of freedom because "the great principles of political freedom and of natural justice embodied in that Declaration of Independence" were still not extended to men and women of his skin color. "The rich inheritance of justice, liberty, prosperity and independence, bequeathed by your fathers, is shared by you, not by me. The sunlight that brought life and healing to you, has brought stripes and death to me. This Fourth [of] July is yours, not mine. You may rejoice, I must mourn."

The postwar Reconstruction Abraham Lincoln had promised was short-lived, and emancipated Black Americans were soon plunged into another century of disenfranchisement and terror during the reign of Jim Crow. Meanwhile, women's struggle to vote—which began as early as the Revolution and received a full articulation at the Seneca Falls Convention in 1848—picked up momentum after the Civil War. But when two-thirds of the states ratified the Nineteenth Amendment in 1920 granting women the right to vote, racist voter suppression laws meant that it was chiefly white women who benefited—even though lesser-known Black suffragists like Mary Church Terrell, Ida B. Wells, Frances E. W. Harper, and Sojourner Truth helped drive the movement that became synonymous with white leaders like Susan B. Anthony, Elizabeth Cady Stanton, and Alice Paul.

Native peoples had to wait even longer for the right to vote—until the Indian Citizenship Act of 1924, passed in deference to the many tribes' members who had volunteered to fight in World War I. But the law remained hollow until Natives fought state by state for suffrage, with Utah becoming the last state to give its Indian people the right to vote, in 1962. It would take the American Indian Movement in the late sixties and seventies, inspired by the armed courage of the Black Panther Party, to demand full justice.

Throughout American history, up to the current Black Lives

Matter movement and the protests that swept the nation after the police killing of George Floyd in May 2020, it's been the great surges for freedom and justice led and bled by Black men and women that have propelled the nation toward the arms of its better angels. At any given time, the United States' success as a "shining city upon a hill" can be judged by the way it treats its African American citizens, those men and women forced to build the nation but systematically deprived of its bounty.

THE EXQUISITELY SENSITIVE, the visionary ones, could see the second American Revolution coming from far away. James Baldwin could feel the shimmers of fire in the 1950s. "Well, I am tired," the gay Black writer admitted even then, after a lifetime of scorn and abuse. "I don't know how it will come about. I know that, no matter how it comes about, it will be bloody. It will be hard. I still believe that we can do with this country something that has not been done before." There it was, in succinct expression—the weariness, the realism, and the battered hope that would compel a generation of revolutionaries.

Our book tells pivotal stories from this second American Revolution. Each chapter focuses on climactic events or turning points in the lives of radical leaders who knew they were driving the country far beyond the "Serenity of Temper" that Adams hoped would prevail over the "Whirlwind" of change. Nearly two centuries later, that "serenity" meant only disenfranchisement and poverty for millions of the nation's citizens. Civil rights leaders fought for and finally won the full rights of citizenship for African Americans through legislation like the 1964 Civil Rights Act and the 1965 Voting Rights Act. Black Power leaders went further than that, demanding relief from police harassment and violence in their communities and full and equal access to employment, education, housing, health, and nutrition.

Inspired by the nonviolent resistance of Martin Luther King and his followers, Mexican American labor leaders in the farm fields of California began a crusade combining politics and spirituality that not only forced agribusiness executives to the negotiating tables but employed the same moral force to launch a trailblazing wave of consumer boycotts.

Native American nations, after suffering two centuries of genocidal violence and government treachery, also began to resist. Galvanized by the Black Panthers, Indian leaders started fighting back against predatory police and sheriffs, ultimately taking a stand on tribal land, at the site of a historic massacre of their people.

Demoralized by assassinations of liberal and radical leaders and subjected to relentless harassment by federal and police agencies, the most prominent activists in the Vietnam peace movement became increasingly militant. But while some even went underground to fight a war of terrorism against Washington, others outlasted the reactionary Richard Nixon administration and mobilized the political forces of heartland America to finally squeeze off US funding for the war, enabling a North Vietnamese victory.

Inspired and dispirited by their experiences in the civil rights and antiwar movements, women embraced the power of sisterhood, creating a network of reproductive rights organizations, childcare campaigns, and consciousness-raising groups that made feminism the strongest force for change in 1970s America.

Emboldened by the rebellions of the 1960s, the gay and lesbian liberation struggle also burst from the closet. Again, it was police persecution that finally lit the fuse, but the freedom fighters against heterosexual hegemony would go far beyond battling cops and smashing windows to demand their place in American society.

Finally, radical celebrities demonstrated that they could harness their star power to shine a light on urgent causes and mobilize mass dissent. This was especially true of major rock musicians who could tap the almost sacramental power they wielded with a multitude of fans. Socially conscious entertainers were vulnerable to government reprisals as well as to left-wing opportunism. But in a media-dominated society, popular artists who were grounded in strong networks could become surprisingly effective at raising money and public awareness.

Our account of the second American Revolution invokes the sweeping power of this history, but zeroes in on the leaders at the heart of these movements. We do not subscribe to the "great man" theory of history because historical change is wrestled forward by countless great individuals, some working in obscurity. But we do believe that good leadership makes a profound difference, and that the most successful movements for major change, for *lasting* change, are usually helmed by charismatic and courageous leaders whose goals and motivations are intertwined with those they lead.

All of the activists profiled here shared a willingness to take legal and physical risks, to put their bodies on the line, at moments when they calculated that it would make a critical difference—in, for example, the armed Indian occupation of Wounded Knee, the fasts undertaken by Cesar Chavez, or the clandestine abortions carried out by outlaw feminists. They also shared, to varying degrees, a belief in simultaneously working *outside* of the system, creating alternative and sometimes underground institutions—and *within* it, pushing for changes in the law and making demands of elected officials. In Tom Hayden's case, and briefly that of Bobby Seale, they even became politicians, hoping to advance their radical agendas through elective office.

Revolutionary movements often have contentious relationships with those who lead them. The deep distrust of leaders felt by the current generation of activists is more widely held and articulated today, but even during the 1960s young radicals often invoked Bob Dylan's skeptical lyric from "Subterranean Homesick Blues": "Don't follow leaders, watch the parkin' meters." Iconic heroes who emerged from the nation's basement in those years sometimes proved reckless, vain, power-hungry, sexually predatory, drug-addicted, or even insane. Being subjected to constant government harassment and police violence also destabilized many insurgent leaders in the sixties and seventies. By infiltrating radical groups with agents and provocateurs, authorities sowed discord and paranoia within even disciplined organizations. Leaders on the left were also sometimes targeted for assassination by government agencies, which further eroded people's trust in the charismatic path to deliverance. *We know what happens to leaders—they kill them.* This was a tragic refrain, passed down through generations of sorrow, too often expressed by young protesters on the streets of Minneapolis, Portland, and Louisville during the uprisings of 2020.

Perhaps the history-making movements we chronicle in this book could have made their epic impact without inspired—and inspiring—leadership. These leaders were flawed men and women; they made mistakes; they fell victim to their own egos or to a lacerating quest for ideological purity; they often were defeated. But they were also catalysts for change much greater than common wisdom held possible—or advisable. They made a revolution whose shock waves are still shaking the pillars of American power. And a new generation of movers and shakers can learn from their triumphs as well as their tragedies.

THE LEADING PLAYERS in our book are a dynamic cast of characters. Dennis Banks, Madonna Thunder Hawk, and Russell Means of the American Indian Movement took a brave stand at Wounded Knee, proclaiming that Native peoples would long endure. Bobby Seale, Huey Newton, and Eldridge Cleaver spearheaded the rise of the Black Panther Party, the most dramatic expression of the Black Power movement. Tom Hayden and Jane Fonda mobilized the antiwar ardor of heartland America while other peace movement leaders were burning out, succeeding in slashing congressional funding for the Vietnam War and helping to finally end it. Heather Booth was the driving force behind the Jane Collective, an underground feminist abortion clinic in the years before *Roe v. Wade.* Cesar Chavez and Dolores Huerta created the

United Farm Workers movement, bringing dignity to essential but often scorned laborers. Craig Rodwell's unsung role in commemorating the Stonewall uprising helped pave the way for the triumph of gay pride. And John Lennon and Yoko Ono, the powerfully symbiotic couple, leveraged their celebrity to try to stop a war and bring down an American president.

We capture these revolutionary leaders at critical moments, exploring how the decisions they made and the actions they took changed not only their lives but the course of American history. What drove Seale and Newton to risk their lives by going into the streets of Oakland with guns to confront the notoriously violent and racist police officers of their city? And what were the consequences of those hair-trigger confrontations? What impelled Chavez to push himself to the brink of martyrdom with his marathon fasts? And how did his sanctification both elevate and hobble the farmworkers movement? Why did Booth risk imprisonment as a young mother in Chicago by setting up an illegal abortion service for desperate women of all races and classes? How did Banks, Thunder Hawk, and Means manage to build a resilient community of men, women, and children in a forlorn tribal outpost for seventy-one days under withering, warlike gunfire from President Nixon's forces?

Martin Luther King once told his young aide Andrew Young that only "certain people" were "crazy" enough "to do what I do." To take on the federal government; to confront violent cops, sheriffs, and counterprotesters; to organize disruptive actions that upset the majority of Americans. All of the men and women in this book were crazy—or courageous—enough to put themselves at the front of movements that made them targets for government surveillance, stiff prison sentences, or even assassination. King himself is not included in these profiles, but his presence is felt throughout the book. With his prophetic vision, brilliant oratory, and personal bravery, King looms over the second American Revolution.

Martin Luther King was a much more radical figure than the gatekeepers of American history generally allow. He sided with the poor and powerless against the wealthy elite and mourned a country heading toward "spiritual death" because it spent more money on war than on "programs of social uplift," as he declared in his famous antiwar speech at New York's Riverside Church on April 4, 1967, exactly one year before his assassination. On April 4, 1968, the day he was gunned down in Memphis, King phoned his church in Atlanta with the title of the Sunday sermon he never delivered: "Why America May Go to Hell."

One of the reasons that FBI director J. Edgar Hoover considered King to be "the most dangerous Negro" in America was his sweeping vision—and power—to unite all the radical movements of America into one mighty movement. In the last months of his life, King tried valiantly to forge a grand unity of resistance that only he could attempt.

King became more deeply involved in the peace movement after delivering his Riverside Church sermon. That fierce speech against US militarism and imperialism was almost universally denounced by the mainstream press—and even by some Black newspapers and civil rights leaders—with the *New York Times* calling it "facile" and "slander" and warning that "to divert the energies of the civil rights movement to the Vietnam issue is both wasteful and self-defeating." But King was used to brushing aside such handwringing. In his 1963 "Letter from a Birmingham Jail," King had condemned "the white moderate, who is more devoted to 'order' than to justice" as a greater impediment to Black freedom than even "the White Citizen's Council-er or the Ku Klux Klanner."

King never gave up on his dream of creating a multiracial movement powerful enough to end the war and divert spending to essential domestic needs. This was his goal when he began organizing a mass Poor People's March on Washington, aimed at occupying the nation's capital in summer 1968 and forcing Congress to prioritize peace over war. The nation's most prominent civil rights leader was building a surprisingly broad coalition to revolutionize US politics. Among those profiled here to whom King reached out was Bobby Seale. The militant leader, who deeply respected King, enthusiastically agreed to reinforce the Poor People's March with ranks of uniformed Black Panthers. It would have been an unprecedented and audacious show of militant unity.

"Martin was preparing to not just march on Washington with a half million people in 1968," said William Pepper, who helped inspire the civil rights leader to come out against the Vietnam War, "but to occupy the city with an encampment and to hound Congress into ending the war and spending those resources instead on social programs and fighting poverty. The [Lyndon] Johnson administration and the military were terrified—they didn't think they could put down that kind of massive disruption in the nation's capital."

Instead, after King's assassination, Washington was set aflame by furious protesters, one of over a hundred cities devastated by riots in the greatest wave of social unrest since the Civil War. The insurgency lasted four days in the capital and came within two blocks of the White House, where President Johnson called up army soldiers from the 3rd Infantry for protection while marines mounted machine guns on the steps of the Capitol.

The Poor People's March went ahead without King, but the occupation of the capital withered without his leadership, as did the dream to build one powerful movement of dissent. Some revolutionary leaders, like Seale and Newton, still promoted the goal of "intercommunalism," as the Black Panthers called their solidarity campaign, but they lacked King's majestic pulpit.

Nevertheless, this book underlines how the different "tribes" within the second American Revolution often did cross paths, reinforce one another's critiques, or deliberately work in unison. The opposition to the Vietnam War united nearly all of them—from Black Power leaders to women's and gay liberationists. Like King, this rainbow spectrum of activists saw the war as a drain on America's resources and *soul*, and explicitly linked US imperialism abroad to racism and authoritarianism at home. Unlike earlier labor and socialist movements in the United States, radicals of this era placed a high value on direct, participatory democracy—on the activism and example of rebellious young people, and on personal liberation and authenticity. They also tended to value "emotional and moral plain-speaking," as the historians Michael Kazin and Maurice Isserman note, over the mastery of theory.

While still in college, Tom Hayden was inspired to become an activist after meeting Martin Luther King on a picket line. Hayden later found himself as a codefendant with Bobby Seale in the stormy Chicago Eight trial. Feminist hero Heather Booth first tested her courage with other young civil rights volunteers from the North during the bloody 1964 Freedom Summer in Mississippi, and her husband Paul Booth was a cofounder of Students for a Democratic Society with Hayden. Dennis Banks and his fellow warriors were greatly helped during the long, violent siege at Wounded Knee by movie star Marlon Brando and by antiwar leader Bill Zimmerman, who piloted an intrepid relief squadron to the embattled Indians— and later served as Hayden's campaign chief in the New Left leader's first run for public office. John Lennon and Yoko Ono were recruited and guided during their year of living dangerously in Greenwich Village by radical leaders like Seale and his fellow Chicago Eight defendant Jerry Rubin, and befriended Kate Millett, a leading women's liberation intellectual. This cross-pollination of ideas and personnel between insurgencies was common, even though these protest leaders never realized King's dream of one righteous, revolutionary movement.

We fully acknowledge the failures and imperfections of the men and women profiled in this book. While achieving most of their social and cultural goals, they fell far short of taking control of the government or economy. And yet their legacy is immense— from demonstrating the efficacy of disruptive street protests, sit-ins, and boycotts to sparking a thorough reimagination of gender roles. In general, and to the chagrin of many moderates, such activists have often spurred liberalism to more daring leaps toward a truly egalitarian society. As the writer Jamelle Bouie has argued, "Simply put, an ambitious, active left is one that widens the scope of reform. It's a left that, even if you disagree with it, helps clear the pathways for action. It brings energy and urgency to liberal politics. And if nothing else, it's a foil against which moderates can triangulate and make the case for more than marginal change, should they want it."

Some of the leading players in our book were already dead by the time we began our research, a few died after we interviewed them, the rest are old and gray. But their stories still shine through time. Madonna Thunder Hawk, one of the American Indian Movement leaders revered as a "Red Giant," looks back at her thunderous history with a cold, no-bullshit clarity. But her words are still stirring and they lay down a challenge for the next generations:

"Someday soon, I'll be gone. And we're only responsible for our life span, what we do while we're here. We did the hard work, we stood our ground like our ancestors. And now it's your turn, your time—our children and grandchildren. We had our time. We did the best we could. They can read about me in your book. And then they'll go, 'Here's what she did—now what should *we* do?'"

The Purity of Protest and the Complexity of Politics

Tom Hayden, Jane Fonda, and the Red Family

Tom Hayden was disowned twice in his youth. Once by his
father—an abusive, alcoholic Irish Catholic veteran of World
War II who was repelled by his son's emergence as a leader of the
radical New Left in the 1960s. And once by the New Left itself,
when in Berkeley in 1971 he was voted out of the Red Family, a
two-house commune that was not just the center of radical activism in the Bay Area but also Hayden's emotional nest. Hayden's
ejection from the Red Family was especially traumatic for him because it was engineered by his angry lover, a beautiful and strong-
willed militant named Anne Weills, with whom he'd been raising
her young son, Christopher, and to whom he had proposed marriage. Hayden was not only evicted from the Red Family and from
the only intact nuclear family he'd ever known, he was also exiled
from all of Berkeley, with Weills and his housemates communicat-
ing to the city's febrile radical network that his egotism and sexism
made him also unfit for membership in the wider community.

Tom Hayden was the most brilliant strategist produced by the
New Left, the radical Thomas Jefferson who, in 1962, had written

the first draft of the idealistic and influential manifesto known as the Port Huron Statement. A declaration of independence from Cold War orthodoxy for the student generation coming of age in the 1960s, the statement rejected racism and militarism and called for a revival of "participatory democracy." It would help define the tone and the mission for the New Left and the movements that emerged from it, especially women's liberation. Even living in the "wealthiest and strongest country in the world," Hayden wrote, Americans had "unfulfilled capacities for reason, freedom, and love."

As privileged as his generation was, wrote Hayden, he and his peers had not been able to evade two realities: "First, the permeating and victimizing fact of human degradation, symbolized by the Southern struggle against racial bigotry, compelled most of us from silence to activism. Second, the enclosing fact of the Cold War, symbolized by the presence of the Bomb," which "brought awareness that we ourselves, and our friends, and millions of abstract 'others' we knew more directly because of our common peril, might die at any time." The reckoning that Hayden's manifesto called for was personal as well as political—which was fitting for a man whose politics would be so wrapped up, all his life, with his romantic relationships.

Hayden was a founder of Students for a Democratic Society (SDS), the nationwide youth group that led the growing campus rebellion against the Vietnam War—and for which the Port Huron Statement was a blueprint. He directed an SDS antipoverty project in Newark, New Jersey, trying to unite the civil rights and peace movements, and later chronicled the Black community's uprising in his 1967 book *Rebellion in Newark*. (Hayden was also one of the most gifted writers of his activist generation.) He sided openly with the declared enemies of United States imperialism, making trips to Hanoi and Eastern Europe to forge solidarity with North Vietnamese officials. And he was arrested for "conspiracy" and "inciting to riot" for helping to plan antiwar protests at the 1968 Democratic

National Convention in Chicago, which turned into a shocking melee when Mayor Richard Daley's police went on a club-swinging
rampage against demonstrators, reporters, convention delegates,
and anyone else who got in their way.

Hayden's propulsive evolution through the sixties mirrored
that of his protest generation. He had embarked on his life of activism after interviewing a "courteous, gentle" Martin Luther King
Jr. on a picket line outside the 1960 Democratic convention in Los
Angeles. The civil rights leader suggested that Hayden, who was
writing for his college newspaper, "shut [my] notebook" and join
the protest.

Hayden was one of the few youthful New Left leaders who was
able to cross political boundaries and confer with government officials and Establishment fixtures. As a student leader at the University of Michigan in Ann Arbor, he authored a letter to John F.
Kennedy during his 1960 presidential campaign urging him to
launch an alternative to military service, which later became the
Peace Corps. And he was invited to the Kennedy White House by
presidential adviser Arthur Schlesinger Jr. to discuss the visionary
goals of the Port Huron Statement. Later, Hayden came to know
Senator Robert F. Kennedy, as the younger Kennedy sought advice
about the growing antiwar movement and how he could become an
effective voice for peace.

For Hayden, the early 1960s was a "golden age" that glowed with
the heroism of the civil rights protests in the South, bonding young
Black and white activists on the front lines of racial liberation. As a
Freedom Rider, he was beaten in Mississippi and jailed in Georgia.
Despite the bloody turmoil, the new generation of protesters believed they could win, believed they could profoundly change the
country. But like many other members of the sixties generation,
Hayden was deeply shaken by the assassinations of the Kennedy
brothers and Reverend King. These three epic blows "permanently
derailed what remained of the hopes that were born at Port Huron," Hayden later wrote. "Whether one thinks the murders were

conspiracies or isolated accidents, the effect was to destroy the progressive political potential of the sixties and leave us all as 'might-have-beens,' in the phrase of the late [journalist] Jack Newfield."

Forced out of the political mainstream by the growing belligerence of the US Establishment and by the escalation of the Vietnam War, New Left leaders like Hayden became increasingly radicalized. They never intended to become alienated militants, Hayden declared, but the hardening of the system—what he called "the crisis of the elders"—shoved youthful protest to the violent margins. Hayden ended up in Berkeley, the far left of America, at the end of the sixties, flirting with political violence and deeply in love with a woman who was convinced that America teetered on the brink of revolution. And then even this sanctuary was ripped from him.

The story of how Tom Hayden was exiled from "the movement"—his political and personal home and hearth throughout the sixties—and was forced to redefine himself in the 1970s is not only a compelling drama. It contains important lessons about how radical leaders can insert themselves into the political mainstream without sacrificing their values—lessons that most comrades of Hayden rejected at the time and were not widely embraced by younger progressives until the next century.

IN 1970, WHEN Tom Hayden settled in Berkeley after the tumultuous spectacle of the Chicago Eight trial concluded—with Hayden and four other defendants convicted of inciting to riot at the 1968 Democratic convention—he was not only a haunted political figure, free on appeal while facing at least five years in federal prison; he was a nationwide radical celebrity. Hayden and his codefendants—including Black Panther leader Bobby Seale, until his courtroom protests provoked the aging, quick-tempered Judge Julius Hoffman to chain and gag him and then sever him from the case—turned the proceedings into a raucous forum about the Vietnam War and American justice. The Chicago Eight (later Seven) tried to read aloud antiwar statements, recite poetry, and even chant "Hare Krishna" in a dramatic effort to position the trial in its broader political context. But Judge Hoffman only kept slapping more and more severe contempt citations on the defendants—at one point even sentencing their lead attorney, William Kunstler, to four years in prison for denouncing Hoffman's courtroom as "a medieval torture chamber."

During the chaotic trial—which dragged from September 1969 to February 1970 in the oak-paneled, twenty-third-floor courtroom of downtown Chicago's Dirksen Federal Building—Hayden and his codefendants became regulars on the TV networks' nightly newscasts, with the trial evolving into a pageant of cross-generational conflict about the future of the country. The harsh prosecution, which carried the full weight of the Nixon administration in its effort to decapitate the protest movement, also forced Hayden to engage in dark introspection. Did the Chicago Eight trial mark the beginning of America's slide into fascism? Could he endure a long incarceration in some federal dungeon?

Hayden had grown up as a patriotic young American in a white-flight suburb of Detroit. His parochial-school priest was Father Charles Coughlin, famed for his radio tirades against Jews and Franklin Roosevelt's New Deal. Even Hayden's transformation into a college student dissenter was motivated by a devout belief in America's ideals, not by "foreign orthodoxies." Speaking of his early inspirations, Hayden always cited homegrown populists like Henry David Thoreau and C. Wright Mills, rebellious iconoclasts like Albert Camus, and generational free spirits like Bob Dylan (who attended one or two early SDS meetings) and even the creators of *Mad* magazine—not Marx, Bakunin, or Lenin.

But by the end of the 1960s, America was no longer recognizable as the country of Kennedys and King. Hayden and his Chicago Eight codefendants feared that President Nixon was turning the US into a police state, with his authoritarian deputy attorney general Richard Kleindienst labeling protest leaders "ideological criminals."

During the trial, Anne Weills had come from Berkeley to live with Hayden in the small South Side Chicago railroad apartment that he shared with Leonard Weinglass, a young lawyer on his defense team. While in Chicago, Hayden and Weills became friendly with the twenty-one-year-old, charismatic leader of the city's Black Panther chapter, Fred Hampton. In a December 4, 1969, predawn raid on Hampton's apartment by a heavily armed police squad, the Panther leader—who had been drugged the night before by an undercover agent—was shot to death in his bed, as he slept next to his pregnant wife. The brazen assassination of Hampton—who had been building a rare, multiracial coalition of Black, Puerto Rican, and white radicals in Chicago—seemed to signal an escalation of violent repression in America, with the raid carried out by a kill team under the direction of Cook County's top law enforcement official and the FBI.

"Tom and I went to Fred's apartment the next morning," recalled Weills years later. "I was just crying. You could still see the blood and the bullet holes. I had met Fred at the trial, I had hung out with him. We heard him speak in the park. He was like the Pied Piper—he was the most brilliant, young, radical male and the most ebullient person, excited and happy and joyful. And yet he was deadly serious about what he was fighting for. And he was only twenty-one. I mean they killed everybody in my lifetime."

Weills—horrified by the US government's escalating violence at home and in Vietnam, which she had visited earlier in 1968 with a peace delegation to bring home American prisoners of war—was drawn to the siren call of the Weather Underground, the SDS faction that began preaching armed revolution. While in Chicago, she participated in the Weather-organized Days of Rage, the spasm of hit-and-run street protests that attempted to incite disaffected teenagers as a militant vanguard and strike a direct blow against American institutions.

"I was part of what was called the 'women's action'—we tried to take over this federal building in downtown Chicago," recalled

Weills. "Some people were supposed to set fires in the women's bathrooms . . . but my job was to fly the NLF [the Vietnamese National Liberation Front] flag, and we were successful.

"We were driven [by the times]—not mad, but we were in a state of mind where we were willing to die. Like I never thought we'd live beyond forty. We were in a war—our own war against the State, fighting alongside the Vietnamese against the United States and its imperial policy."

Hayden had his own flirtation with the Weather Underground. During the riotous battle over Berkeley's People's Park in spring 1968, he had spent one night with the group's cofounder Bernardine Dohrn, the miniskirted femme fatale who used her sexual appeal as much as her fiery intellect to build her terrorist cadre. As Hayden was gravely considering the future of political activism in Nixon's America in the midst of the Chicago Eight trial, Dohrn tried to convince him to go underground with Weather leaders. "You are going to jail at the end of this trial," she bluntly warned Hayden. "What I really think is that you should split before it's over. Fascism is what's happening."

Weather Underground cells began planning a nationwide bombing campaign aimed at police officers and military personnel, with the goal of "bringing the war home." Hayden understood the group's "sinister attraction," as he later put it, and he and Weills both felt their movement teetering on the edge of a terrible abyss.

To be with Hayden, Weills had left her marriage to radical journalist Robert Scheer—who co-edited *Ramparts*, the leading left-wing magazine of the sixties, with the equally brilliant iconoclast Warren Hinckle. Hayden had also abandoned an early marriage, to the widely respected civil rights activist Casey Hayden. For Anne Weills, Tom's passionate engagement with the raging battles of their day was a deep part of the attraction that bound them together as a romantic couple.

"Anne and I were not the same people," Scheer observed a half century later. "I still love Anne and respect her enormously. But I never felt that I was a revolutionary in the sense that she is. I grew up in New York [in the 1940s and '50s] fearing revolution. I felt my parents were victims of the left. My mother had fled Russia because she was suppressed by the left. My father was basically a German anarchist."

By contrast, Weills was the daughter of a phone company executive and had lived in Paris as a college student. She had been radicalized by her family's Marin County neighbors, the brawling pack of six sons presided over by radical San Francisco defense lawyer Vincent Hallinan and his equally outspoken wife, Vivian. Weills's increasingly revolutionary politics seemed to spring from a sense of entitlement, as if her America had been stolen from her generation by a greedy and war-hungry power elite.

Hayden's more humble upbringing—his hard-drinking father was an accountant, his mother a librarian—didn't give him the same sense of birthright. But his quick ascendancy as a New Left leader, with its access to Democratic Party power circles and the liberal intelligentsia, gave Hayden the confidence that he deserved a commanding position in the US someday. Weills recalled watching with Hayden *Wild in the Streets* (1968), an outlandish, futuristic movie about a young rock star who is elected president. "He just totally identified with it—he wanted to be president."

Hayden decided not to go underground with Dohrn and her small army, despite the shadow of prison hanging over him and other protest leaders. He still believed there was a political path for him and the New Left, though it was growing gloomier and narrower under Nixon. "The fatalist in me sensed that [Dohrn] was right," Hayden wrote in his 1988 memoir, *Reunion*. "It was not my belief in the system, but my fear of the unknown, that kept me going through the motions [of the Chicago Eight trial] each day. The rationalist (or was it the dreamer?) in me, on the other hand, could not accept the inevitability of domestic fascism."

Weills remained under the spell of the Weather Underground until she and Hayden attended the group's "war council" in Flint,

Michigan, in late December 1969. Held in a dingy auditorium in a labor town already in decline, the conference brought together about four hundred young militants, most of whom were convinced that the American power structure was violently opposed to reform and could be brought down only by a wave of lethal bombings aimed at creating urban chaos and forcing a lethargic working class into finally taking revolutionary action.

The Flint gathering was feverish with its embrace of death, another example of how the poison of the Vietnam War and police repression at home was infecting a movement once dedicated to peace. One side of the auditorium was decorated with the images of revolutionary heroes—Marx, Lenin, Castro, Ho Chi Minh, and a late addition, the recently assassinated Fred Hampton. On the other side were displayed reactionary enemies, including Nixon, FBI boss J. Edgar Hoover, and, bizarrely, Sharon Tate, the wife of director Roman Polanski and a recent victim of the Charles Manson family's murder spree.

At one point, Dohrn whipped the crowd into a frenzy by celebrating the Manson family's Benedict Canyon bloodbath. "Dig it, they murdered those pigs and then ate dinner at their dining table and then stuck a fork in their bellies! Wild!" The Weather leadership's revelry over Manson mayhem and other savage assaults on bourgeois America were too much for Weills. "The whole thing was sort of like a freak show on some level to me."

The Weather Underground conference also made it clear that children would not be welcome at the coming revolution. One-year-old Christopher—Weills's son by Scheer—was one of the only kids at Flint, and she decided it would be wrong to subject him to the underground life.

Meanwhile, Hayden was proving to be a very dutiful and loving surrogate father to Christopher. By the time that he, Weills, and the boy resettled in Berkeley in 1970, Hayden was intent on creating the kind of tight family he had never enjoyed. But even though he and Weills had decided not to follow Bernardine Dohrn into

Weather's dark catacombs, they still were in the grip of revolutionary fervor in Berkeley.

BY THE EARLY 1970s, much of Berkeley's radical population—in a sprawling network of loosely connected East Bay residential communes and work collectives—was preparing for the revolution. Steve Wasserman, a Berkeley High School student at the time and a teenage inductee into this apocalyptic world, later recalled the guns and ammunition stored in the closets of communal houses. "My high school mates cut each other with knives in order to practice sewing up the wounds we were sure would be inflicted upon us as we mounted the barricades," wrote Wasserman years later after a long career as a book publisher and editor. "We went to nearby rifle ranges to practice with the M-1 carbines and shotguns we thought we would need to defend ourselves against the savageries of the nation's police and *agents provocateurs*."

Wasserman recalled Hayden as a gifted teacher and mentor, offering free classes to teenage militants in the backyard of the Ashby Avenue stucco house he shared at the time with two fellow radical leaders—the couple Stew Albert and Judy Gumbo. Discussing books like Mills's *The Power Elite*, Hayden riveted his outdoor classes. "He had a way of breaking down complex arguments, often offering up an analytical taxonomy that almost always had three components, out of which he'd forge some more compelling approach," Wasserman recalled. "And it was all delivered in a voice that evinced the deliberate, rather flat affect of his midwestern origins. A southpaw, he held his ubiquitous coffee mug in a wraparound embrace which, for reasons that elude me, was utterly captivating."

Despite his maturity and intelligence, "Tom was not immune" to the end-of-the-world feelings of despair that prevailed in radical Berkeley, observed Wasserman. Hayden himself later commented that "everything around me continued to decay" at the time, with "our lives spiraling toward some personal and political abyss. I felt something akin to what the psychiatrist Robert J. Lifton terms *death immersion*."

Even today, Weills is reluctant to speak about some of the dangerous activities in which she and Hayden engaged at the time. But after deciding to have a child with Hayden, she lost the pregnancy, and later explained, "We were involved in some serious things that I think triggered my miscarriage—because of all the stress."

Anne Weills had a passionate—and infuriating—relationship with Tom Hayden. On one hand, he was the radical action hero of her dreams. Hayden was no movie star, with his pockmarked face from a florid case of adolescent acne and his potato nose. Still, he moved through life with self-assurance and a rumpled, boyish charm.

"One of the things I loved most about him was his risk-taking, his fearlessness about power," she recalled. "And the sense that he belonged there." The two would talk in bed late into the night about political strategy and ideas. "All my life, when I really fall in love with someone, it's this intense physical and emotional but also intellectual bonding. Being in sync with somebody in that deepest sense."

Weills accompanied Hayden when he met with Bobby Kennedy in San Francisco and Los Angeles hotel rooms during the senator's 1968 run for president, which ended in a pool of blood on the greasy floor of the Ambassador Hotel pantry after RFK won the California primary. "I've never been a big electoral politics person. But we really felt that Bobby could end the war," she said. "Plus, he was very charismatic. Even as a college student, I had a big picture of Bobby Kennedy in my room."

But Hayden's constant need to be at the center of action became increasingly annoying to Weills, who resented riding in his sidecar. On the May Day 1970 weekend, Weills flew with Hayden to New Haven, Connecticut, for a rally to demand the release of Black Panther leaders Bobby Seale and Ericka Huggins, who'd been jailed on charges of arranging the murder of a suspected informer. Weills found herself both impressed and appalled by the smooth way that Hayden huddled with Yale University's patrician president Kingman Brewster Jr. and law enforcement officials to negotiate the conditions for a peaceful protest, on the eve of a volatile event that unnerved local authorities by drawing as many as twenty thousand demonstrators to the campus.

"You could tell that he really saw his role as a wheeler-dealer, as the man with the portfolio, the one that everyone in the room would acknowledge as the man to deal with the heavies. Look, somebody had to do it—and he did a good job. I suppose we were helping to protect the demonstrators. But it was just the ego part of it. In my later years, I've concluded that Tom was deeply narcissistic."

Weills began noticing the demons inside Hayden as early as the Chicago Eight trial, when she saw him and a comrade polish off pints of bourbon at night. "I didn't fully realize it then, but he was an alcoholic like his father. He never smoked pot. He didn't do drugs. He was afraid of them. Just alcohol. He thought drugs would fuck with his brains—that was his expression."

Hayden could also be very possessive, even locking Weills in their bedroom the night before the Days of Rage actions because she was becoming close to Terry Robbins, a handsome and reckless leader of the Weather Underground. In March 1970, the twenty-two-year-old Robbins, whom Hayden later labeled "a fanatic dreamer," blew up himself and two other members of the Weather Underground while trying to make a bomb in the basement of a Greenwich Village townhouse. The intended targets of the Townhouse Collective were military couples at a dance event scheduled on the Fort Dix, New Jersey, army base.

If locking up his lover was an extreme measure, Hayden was wise to steer Weills away from the doomed Robbins. But she resented the way he tried to control her life, just as she had bridled when her husband, journalist Robert Scheer, had tried to keep her away from protests that were risky confrontations with the cops.

Weills felt that strong men had been blocking her way all her life, beginning with her corporate executive father, who sternly warned her when she was a teenager that she was "so obstinate no man is ever going to want you."

"Of course, I didn't believe him," she added, finding that her generation of men were often very attracted to strong-minded women. Especially ones with Weills's swagger and physical appeal. She had an idyllic blond beauty in that free-spirited California way. In any case, by the early seventies, Berkeley was a center of the rising radical feminist movement. And Weills felt even more strongly that she didn't have to be an appendage, even to a New Left legend like Hayden.

Floating on a cloud of celebrity after the Chicago Eight trial, Hayden returned to the college-town environs of Berkeley as a larger-than-life hero. He and his fellow defendants, including the media-savvy Yippies Abbie Hoffman and Jerry Rubin, plotted launching a new radical group, propelled by their fame, called The Conspiracy. But Weills and her feminist circle dismissed the idea as a male vanity project that was way out of sync with the surging feminist mood in Berkeley.

"They decided to do this just as women in the antiwar movement were becoming more powerful and influential—this group of white male celebrities. We were like, 'What are you guys thinking?' I actually wrote an article in the *Berkeley Barb* pointing out how absurd it was and 'who do these men think they are?'—and that was the end of their idea."

Hayden was headed not just for a collision with radical feminism, but with the love of his life.

THE RED FAMILY COMMUNE—a group of men, women, and children who sprawled over two ramshackle houses on Hillegass Avenue and Bateman Street in Berkeley—was the nerve center of the city's radicalism, including antiwar actions, a battle to subject the local police force to community control, and a campaign to win seats on the city council. The Red Family also was famous for being "Hayden's collective."

But Hayden was not the only alpha male in the group. The Red Family, surprisingly, also housed Weills's ex-husband, Bob Scheer. In fact, it was Scheer, through his friendship with progressive Los Angeles benefactor Stanley Sheinbaum, who was able to secure a loan and acquire the Berkeley property. Somehow, in a testament to the social imagination of the era, Weills and the two closest men in her life found a way to live together in relative harmony and all take turns looking after young Christopher. "I don't think Bob ever really loved Tom or liked him. But I think he respected him," mused Weills.

The "complexity" of human relations, particularly in retrospect, "is always denied," commented Scheer himself. The reality, according to the progressive journalist, is that he once saved Hayden's life. Visiting Black Panther headquarters in Oakland together one day, Scheer was stunned to witness Panther leader David Hilliard furiously lunge at Hayden and choke him. "It had something to do with how Hilliard felt Hayden had betrayed Bobby Seale at the Chicago trial. I saw the life draining away in Tom. So I had to jump in and save his life! And I'm not the biggest, strongest guy in the world, but I had some prestige with these folks because I was friends with Eldridge Cleaver"—the ex-convict who became a *Ramparts* staff writer and Panther spokesperson with the publication of his bestselling memoir *Soul on Ice*.

The Red Family's ability to house both Hayden and Scheer also demonstrated the alpha female power of Anne Weills and the growing strength of the women's movement. The commune came increasingly under the influence of Weills and her Red Family sisters. The women spent long hours in feminist consciousness-raising sessions and the men were consigned to their own "criticism/self-criticism" meetings, designed to root out years of sexist programming. Hayden found these meetings to be "torture sessions," in which the men flagellated themselves for their "ego trips" and explored how by doing more housework and surrendering their male privilege they could empower the women in their lives.

Hayden found work in the commune's nursery, where the men were assigned, much more to his liking. But even Blue Fairyland, as the childcare center was called by the kids, was not immune to the radical social reengineering of the day. When Scheer and the other men used trips to a nearby ice cream store to reward good behavior and potty-trained the kids ("whose parents subscribed to the idiotic view that they would do it on their own time, like animals in the wild"), the commune erupted in debates over politically correct child-rearing.

Radical communes like the Red Family were supposed to elevate relationships between the sexes by breaking down the traditional patriarchal roles in families. And life in these experimental houses could indeed be filled with daily joys and epiphanies, as men and women learned new ways of living together and loving one another. But they often exacerbated underlying problems between couples by politicizing personal disagreements. Tensions between lovers could quickly go public, where they were subject to adjudication at heated house meetings.

The friction between Hayden and Weills was growing before they moved into the Red Family complex. But it reached combustion in the commune's hothouse atmosphere.

In his memoir, Hayden was honest about how difficult it was for him to downshift his leadership drive. On antiwar platforms across America, he had grown into a masterful speaker, bringing his sharp, Jesuit-honed analytical skills to dissecting the Establishment and its bankrupt case for the Vietnam War. The news media was inevitably attracted to Hayden, with his shaggy, youthful looks and his always quotable eloquence. Nevertheless, he had seen other movement leaders burn out after flying too high into stardom, like civil rights leader Bob Moses of the Student Nonviolent Coordinating Committee (SNCC), who had changed his name and fled

Mississippi and then the United States altogether in an attempt to remake his life. "I was drawn to the Berkeley collective," Hayden wrote, "as a possible place to change my behavior and to be more cooperative and less alienating to others, but I was not ready to abandon my basic nature as"—he added, with heavy irony—"a 'counterrevolutionary.'"

Despite Hayden's avowed commitment to lowering his media profile, to Weills and other Berkeley feminists, he still seemed addicted to the spotlight. "There was his whole thing of wanting to be the great white hero," she said, sighing.

Hayden's shrewd political instincts grew particularly grating for Weills. He could walk into a room, she recalled, and "he would be talking with you, and within a few minutes of conversation, he would be intuiting all of your hidden strengths and weaknesses. It was one of his skills, I guess. And then he would exploit that knowledge. Sometimes it was flattery—with women it was a more seductive thing."

To Weills, Hayden's "real genius for manipulation of people" was a "cynical" art. Others would call it a rare political skill on the left, where strategic expertise was in short supply. It's a battle over the proper kind of leadership that still rages in progressive circles today. The current generation's profound skepticism about charismatic leaders, especially if they are white men, echoes the sentiments of Weills and her Berkeley sisters fifty years ago. This is probably why the American left has not produced another Tom Hayden in the past half century.

"Tom really believed that individual agents make history—the great man theory," Weills recalled. "And coming out of the women's movement, we thought that you must have collective leadership. And you have horizontal, not top-down organization."

The irony is that beneath the rhetorical fireworks, Hayden and Weills, who had been intimately bound for three years and were now coming apart, were engaged in a power struggle over control of the Red Family, and by extension, Berkeley's radical community at large. It was a personal and political duel between the dominant man in the house and the dominant woman. And this time, Hayden was out-organized.

Hayden's final Red Family drama played out one evening in 1971, when he returned to Berkeley after an East Coast speaking engagement. Walking into the living room, he was surprised to see the entire commune sitting in a prearranged circle in anticipation of his arrival. The confrontation with Hayden had been organized by Weills, who felt their relationship was now finished. The end of their union was driven home for her when she discovered that Hayden had slept with one of her closest friends in the commune while he was away. But Weills didn't bring up this personal betrayal during the Hayden tribunal—following her lead, the group focused on his political crimes and took turns denouncing his sexism, arrogance, and manipulative ways. One commune member sneeringly denounced Hayden as a "politician," which was a dirty word on the Berkeley left in those days, even though the Red Family itself had dipped into local electoral politics under Hayden's leadership. His housemates—including Weills—announced that Hayden must not only leave the Red Family, he was being excommunicated from Berkeley as well.

Hayden "reacted angrily and defensively," he later wrote. How could the group eject him without any warning or a trial period? "What about Christopher?" he asked, looking at Weills. Was he supposed to leave the small boy "without explanation and never see him again?" But Weills and the rest of the circle just looked at him with "glazed unanimity."

"Finally, as the tension became unbearable, I got up and left," Hayden recalled. "My chest was on fire. I felt stunned that the collective, so recently a circle of friends, had drifted into a cult, away from what I considered reality. It was attempting to purge and purify itself of all that was wrong with the world." And Hayden, who had achieved celebrity status in that world, was now seen as the embodiment of its evil.

None of the Red Family collective spoke in defense of Hayden, even though Scheer also believed in electoral politics, and in fact had run for an East Bay congressional seat in 1966 against the Democratic incumbent, who was too timid to oppose President Lyndon Johnson's escalation of the Vietnam War. Though Scheer would roll up 45 percent of the primary vote on an early antiwar platform, Berkeley radicals were skeptical of Scheer's plunge into Democratic Party politics, with many denouncing the *Ramparts* editor as a "sellout"—the same left-wing scorn that would dog Hayden for much of his life.

Weills took a special pride in banning Hayden not only from her bed, but from Berkeley. "We even made a document that I found years later," she said. "It was like a proclamation stating that you, Tom Hayden, believe that people like you are the agents of history, and the collective believes that the masses make history. And because you can't conform to that, you're out."

His forced separation from the Red Family—and from Berkeley, the capital of American radicalism—was the most traumatic event of Tom Hayden's young life. At age thirty-one, he was hurled, unprepared, into a hostile world, Richard Nixon's America, with no political cocoon to protect him. The expulsion left him unmoored and humiliated, with his identity as a New Left leader shattered. He also lost the most important woman in his life, as well as the boy he had grown to love as a son.

In the next five years, Hayden would rebuild himself, becoming even more celebrated and entering a political stage where New Leftists rarely dared venture. His trajectory would expose the "self-imposed failures" of his radical generation, in his words, as well as his own.

FLEEING BERKELEY, HAYDEN drove south in his battered, 1957 Volkswagen Beetle to Los Angeles, the city of exiles and broken dreams. He moved into a seedy, $110-a-month oceanfront apartment in Venice, a neighborhood populated by underground artists, Hollywood has-beens, junkies, undocumented workers, and the other flotsam and jetsam of demimonde LA. He floated numbly in the isolation of his new life, suffering what he later called a nervous breakdown. "I didn't want to be bothered with being Tom Hayden to my neighbors," he later wrote. "I didn't want their curiosity, and I wanted to remember what it was like being anonymous again, to see what it felt like to live without fame. I took to reading history on the beach, changed my diet to vegetables and brown rice, studied martial arts and acupuncture, and pondered what to do."

FBI agents still dogged his steps, grilling his landlord about Hayden's activities. But there wasn't really anything to report. Hayden's stumbling search for a new life mirrored a broader confusion and self-immolation on the left. Back in Berkeley, the Red Family's ascendant sisterhood soon expelled Bob Scheer for the same crime of being a dominant, white male. He too would find his way south, where, building on his skills as an aggressive *Ramparts* journalist, he became a nationally prominent reporter for the *Los Angeles Times*.

Meanwhile, Anne Weills exulted in her new, strong independence. She didn't miss Hayden at first. "It was like the monkey is off my back! I was liberated! But then about three months into it, it really did kick in. Because Tom and I had been so close and so intimate on so many levels for at least three years, it was difficult. I guess I got really depressed for a while. I'm such a serious, tough female that I did start going out with [Red Family housemate] Bruce Gilbert for a time. But he was too submissive, too intimidated by me. And I liked him, I loved him, and I still care about him, but it just didn't work."

As the Red Family fell apart, Gilbert, drawn like other New Left comrades by Hayden's magnetism, would also end up in Los Angeles, where he broke into Hollywood as a producer for Jane Fonda. But Weills remained fixed in the Bay Area's radical firmament, drifting into what Hayden later described, with barely concealed bitter satisfaction, as "a tiny Marxist splinter group" and working in a factory. She later became a radical lawyer, collaborating with her equally militant husband Dan Siegel on prison reform cases. Eventually she and Hayden would find a way to join arms together again, but that was not until many years later.

During his days in Venice Beach exile, Hayden explored his Irish roots, for a time adopting the name of his maternal grandfather, Emmett Garity, who had died in a 1920 industrial accident. He began reading deeply about white America's genocidal war against Native people, eventually writing a book, *The Love of Possession Is a Disease with Them* (from a speech by Sitting Bull) that drew a provocative comparison between the US government's Indian Wars and its extermination policies in Vietnam. But like many radicals in the early 1970s, as President Nixon withdrew US ground troops from Vietnam while escalating the air war, Hayden was struggling to find a new role for himself. The peace movement was also wrestling to redefine itself as Nixon "Vietnamized" the war, and many first-wave antiwar leaders descended into revolutionary suicide.

Visiting his old comrade and Chicago Eight codefendant Rennie Davis, who was living in a small cabin in the dense northern Virginia woods, Hayden found that he too had lost his "mooring" after the traumatic trial, carried away by violent political fantasies. Davis tried to convince Hayden to cofound a radical supergroup in Washington with him, but Hayden told him it was "too late" and the combination of their "two powerful personalities in a single unit" would not only be widely condemned on the left, but would also attract more "surveillance and harassment" from the FBI and local police.

Hayden knew that his own name was still toxic in radical circles, especially among feminists, after his vocal denunciation by the Red Family. When he began dating a left-wing lawyer in Los Angeles named Joan Andersson, enjoying walks on the beach and talking about the knotted relations between women and men, he found her "an ideal friend in my time of retreat." But their relationship came under sharp scrutiny by Andersson's radical legal collective, Bar Sinister. Her women law partners warned Andersson that she was "backsliding" from feminism by sleeping with Hayden, and that he was "not only a disagreeable male chauvinist but not even a Marxist." Their sexual relationship did not last long, but a friendship eventually survived.

Hayden's long, dark night of the soul stopped short of remaking his basic identity. In the end, he decided that he was happy with his personal ambition and political drive. "No matter how hard and honest I tried to be toward myself, I felt no loathing of who I was," he later acknowledged. "No matter how much Anne [had] criticized my male chauvinism, I felt no guilt about gender. I wished to correct my faults, but more basically, I wanted to continue making a mark on my times."

Understanding that public action was an essential part of who he was, Hayden began rejoining the outside world within months of his traumatic flight to Los Angeles. He did this not by trying to return to the increasingly cloistered and doctrinaire corners of the radical left, which in any case were largely closed to him now, but by going back to his earliest days as a college activist, when he believed that the American people were capable of being politically awakened. The Weather Underground—and much of the broader left, including Hayden's revolutionary Berkeley comrades—had written off nearly all of white America as a hopeless cause, beneficiaries of the rotten fruit of US empire and captives of Cold War ideology. But Hayden was coming to a deeper realization: the majority of Americans clearly rejected the growing militancy of the antiwar movement, but they now largely embraced its fundamental antiwar message.

It was the explosive publication of the Pentagon Papers in June 1971 that reinfused Hayden with a belief in America. The trove of secret government documents, which exposed the futility of the Vietnam War and the duplicity of its architects, was stolen from the RAND Corporation, a think tank in Santa Monica (near Hayden's apartment), by two national security consultants, Daniel Ellsberg and Anthony Russo, who leaked them to the *New York Times*. It was now clear to Hayden that years of government deception and peace activism were shattering the US elite's consensus about the war and disillusioning most Americans. In fact, national polls taken only one month after the Pentagon Papers publication showed that a decisive majority of the country thought the Vietnam War was "immoral" and favored total withdrawal.

Hayden befriended both Ellsberg and Russo, reaching out to his Chicago Eight attorney Leonard Weinglass and recruiting him to join the Pentagon Papers legal team after the two whistleblowers were indicted in December 1971 on theft, conspiracy, and espionage charges (which could have resulted in a 105-year prison sentence for Ellsberg). The growing relationship between Hayden, one of the smartest leaders of the antiwar movement, and Ellsberg, who had been one of the war's sharpest, combat-experienced intellectuals, revealed the new contours of political activism in America. Before the Pentagon Papers trial began, Hayden took a hike in the Santa Monica mountains with Ellsberg, who told him in detail how he had come to lose faith in the war and the men leading it. It was as if the "haunted" Ellsberg, as Hayden described him, was making a confession: the antiwar radical had been right all along.

Hayden returned to his activist roots, teaching a course about the history of the Vietnam War at Immaculate Heart—a liberal Catholic college in downtown Los Angeles—and recruiting his students to create an antiwar media campaign. Hayden also pored over the massive Pentagon Papers, which totaled 7,000 pages encased in 47 volumes, and reduced them to a pamphlet for the public, distributing over 100,000 free copies during Nixon's 1972 reelection campaign. (The following year, a federal judge dismissed all charges against Ellsberg and Russo, after the growing Watergate scandal began contaminating the prosecution's case, including the revelation that Nixon's "plumbers" had broken into the office of Ellsberg's psychiatrist.)

By 1972, reflected Hayden, "I had come full circle, scarred but surviving, back to what I did best. I could lead by writing, teaching and local organizing in the mainstream—instead of distilling myself into a hardened revolutionary. I could work on being more human myself—and try to outgrow or avoid male power rivalries. I could feel better about America—instead of resigning myself to an alienated war against the system."

And at that point in his life, Hayden added, "I met a woman who changed my life again."

TOM HAYDEN HAD actually met Jane Fonda for the first time on an antiwar stage in Ann Arbor, Michigan, in February 1971, where they were both speaking. A latecomer to the heated world of radical politics, Fonda was unsure of how to use her celebrity. The daughter of an American icon, actor Henry Fonda, and the sex-kitten wife of French director Roger Vadim, who perversely flaunted her nudity in his ironic, soft-core space opera *Barbarella* (1968), Fonda was still trying to mold her own identity at the time, after a lifetime of "men defining me." She was politically inexperienced, but full of outrage about the tragic trajectory of America, after returning home from France to "be with my people, my country, and try to make this right"—like a Henry Fonda hero in a Hollywood classic. She was also a nervous wreck, after long bouts with anorexia and bulimia stretching back to her childhood, when her mother had slashed her own throat with a razor blade. Fonda was still starving herself with methamphetamine diet pills.

Hayden's initial encounter with Fonda was not auspicious. He found her "shrill . . . skinny" and taut with "the tensions of constant motion" onstage that night. But a year later, when he saw her present a slide show against the war at the Embassy Theater in Los Angeles, he thought her "an accomplished speaker." Visiting her backstage, he told her he too had developed a multimedia antiwar presentation with his Immaculate Heart students, and she invited him to her Laurel Canyon house to show it to her.

Hayden's slide show was less politically stiff than Fonda's, and its photos of Saigon sex workers who had undergone plastic surgery to turn themselves into objects of Western desire for their GI clients made Fonda begin to cry. She had just turned in an Oscar-winning performance as a call girl in the movie *Klute* (1971), and from her street research for the film and her own feminine-mystique programming, the actress felt the plight of the Vietnamese women in a deep way. As Fonda cried softly, Hayden thought to himself, *Maybe I could love someone like this.*

The romance between Hayden and Fonda—which evolved into a marriage the following year and one of the most effective political unions in the history of the American left—is often portrayed as another Pygmalion chapter in the actress's life, with Hayden politically directing her. But the reality is they shaped each other, working closely together to draw out the fullest version of themselves.

When Hayden showed up backstage at the Embassy Theater in 1972, Fonda later recalled, "He was a movement hero—I was extremely intimidated." But, of course, she had her own star power, and was soon determined to remake his image. "I must have been a strange sight" that night, mused Hayden. He was still deeply enthralled by the Native American narrative and his hair was long and gathered in a braid. Fonda remembered that he was wearing rubber sandals made from the tires of a US warplane shot down in Vietnam.

Hayden, like Fonda, was also unsure of navigating the labyrinth of male-female relations, after his parents' broken marriage and his own emotionally volatile experiences. Watching *Klute* at a movie theater before he became involved with Fonda, he found himself strangely identifying with Bree, her prostitute character, as she talked in a scene with her therapist about "the comfort of being numb" and about shielding herself from emotional intimacy.

Even as he grew closer to Fonda, Hayden still seemed to be in love with Anne Weills. His Berkeley ex-lover represented a deeply familial—in the sense that the movement was Hayden's true family—and yet dangerous time in his life that he would never again experience. When Fonda became pregnant with Hayden's son, he still felt he had to inform Weills of this new development in his life.

"Tom came to see me in Berkeley after Jane got pregnant, and because of the miscarriage that he and I had, he wanted to give me advance notice," Weills remembered. "And it was very kind and sweet. He said, 'I just want to tell you that Jane and I are going to have a baby.' And he talked about her like she was more of a friend than someone he was in love with. He said, 'I really like her—she really loves me.'" Weills laughed at the memory. "And that was it. Who knows? But it was a kind gesture."

But if Hayden still mourned his breakup with Weills, he was taking his political activism much further with Fonda than he ever could while living in the Red Family. The Berkeley left was a backwater that Hayden had to leave to fully engage the battle for power in America. Getting excommunicated from the radical community, as painful as it was, proved to be the rocket blast he needed.

Fonda and Hayden got married shortly after she became pregnant, deciding not to add "smashing monogamy" to their list of crusades. They were both determined to "come back to America," as they put it. The antiwar actress was widely reviled as "Hanoi Jane" for visiting North Vietnam in July 1972, where she was photographed as she peered through an antiaircraft gun and made radio appeals to US pilots to stop bombing civilian targets. She had been the object of a relentless harassment campaign by the Nixon administration; arrested on trumped-up drug-smuggling charges in November 1970 in Cleveland, where she was jailed overnight; and smeared by the FBI as a dangerous terrorist because of her support for the Black Panthers, Native American activists, and other militants. That same year, FBI chief J. Edgar Hoover tried to discredit

Fonda by authorizing a fake letter to *Variety* gossip columnist Army Archerd, alleging that Fonda had led a "refrain" at a Panther rally about killing President Nixon and "any other [obscenity] who stands in our way."

Fonda was also the target of press vituperation, political condemnation, hate mail, and death threats. Conservative publisher and commentator William F. Buckley recoiled at her "red-guard face," linking her to Mao's zealous enforcers in China. Legislators called for her execution as a traitor. She should never have read some of the letters, which haunted her long afterward with their grisly, misogynistic detail. "One man wanted to hang me upside down, to sink a hook . . ." she told a reporter in 1978, unable to complete the sentence. "She choked," observed the reporter, "and made a swinging motion between her legs."

But Fonda would turn the tables on the Nixon administration and the manufactured hate with Hayden's help, repositioning herself as a Hollywood celebrity with a common touch. "It was Tom's idea to go to the grassroots and speak to the silent majority," she said.

In fall 1972, as President Nixon coasted to reelection, Hayden was feeling oddly optimistic about his American future. A federal court of appeals reversed his Chicago conspiracy conviction, a movie star was pregnant with his baby, and public opinion had shifted dramatically against the war. Hayden and Fonda embarked on a barnstorming tour of ninety cities called the Indochina Peace Campaign, featuring speeches by Fonda and other celebrity friends, Hayden's multimedia presentation about the war, and protest music by the folk singer Holly Near. He would no longer be smothered by the "paranoia" and fatalism of the self-marginalized left. He would take the antiwar case directly to middle America, mobilizing churchgoers, farmers, veterans, and other average Americans to reinvigorate the faltering peace movement and finally terminate the war.

"Rather than withdrawing into personal happiness," Hayden

later reflected, Fonda and he "decided that our only meaningful course was to hurl our personal relationship into the center of public life and resume antiwar work as a team, pregnant and all." From this point on, Hayden and Fonda must be mainly understood as a political partnership, dedicated to using his strategic vision and her celebrity to make as big an impact on the nation's course as possible. It was Hayden's brains and Fonda's body, sneered their growing army of critics on the left and right, but the relationship was much more complex than their media image.

Hayden and Fonda took leadership of the campaign to end the war in Southeast Asia at a moment when Nixon's reduction of US troops in Vietnam and end of the draft rendered the antiwar movement anemic and aimless. Most of the big-name movement leaders had drifted away from the war by 1972, weary and demoralized by years of seemingly fruitless struggle. Hayden's long-time friend Rennie Davis, whom he respected more than any other antiwar leader, had veered into Eastern mysticism, devoting himself to Guru Maharaj Ji, the teenage self-proclaimed divinity who gathered an ardent following in the early seventies. Other close movement friends also began exploring spiritual enlightenment or political occultism, journeys that took them far away from the combat lines with US power, where Hayden had reenlisted with his new wife and political partner.

In later years, the media often delighted in spotlighting the "selling out" of radical celebrities like Jerry Rubin, who turned himself into a stockbroker and entrepreneur in the 1980s, declaring that "wealth creation is the real revolution." But many leading activists continued to live by their leftist values, including other members of the Chicago Eight. Bobby Seale and David Dellinger remained militant political activists, speakers, and educators into old age. (Coauthor David Talbot and Dellinger led a peace tour of Europe during the nuclear freeze movement in 1983, during which they both slipped into East Berlin, still under Communist control, to secretly meet with a Lutheran activist. When they arrived at the minister's apartment, his tearful wife informed the Americans he'd recently been arrested by the Stasi secret police.) Abbie Hoffman had a more tumultuous afterlife following his 1960s Yippie adventures, going underground in 1974 after being arrested for selling cocaine. (He insisted that Nixon drug agents had set him up.) He later reemerged on the public stage, still radical, getting arrested in 1986 for protesting against CIA recruitment on the University of Massachusetts–Amherst campus and putting the spy agency under scrutiny during his trial. Even Hoffman's 1989 death, ruled a suicide by the coroner, became controversial, with some former comrades like Dellinger alleging he'd been assassinated.

After returning from their national peace tour in late 1972, Hayden and Fonda continued their ambitious plan to activate middle America against the war. They settled down in Santa Monica, in a house Hayden purchased for $45,000. The antiwar leader was proud of owning his first home, a sagging two-story, wood-shingle bungalow one block from the ocean. It was a big step down from the palaces of Hollywood royalty for Jane, but she adapted to the funkier lifestyle, as they both turned their Wadsworth Avenue home into the West Coast nerve center of a revived antiwar movement. Activists crashed on the floor of their enclosed porch and others drifted in and out for meetings, including Bruce Gilbert and a couple of other former Red Family housemates whom Hayden had forgiven. One visitor remembered a Fourth of July gathering, as fireworks exploded over the nearby beach. Hayden, taking a phone call, suddenly ordered the lights turned off and everyone to hit the floor. Somebody was threatening to open fire on the home of the notorious "traitors." The couple's young son, Troy Garity (who later followed his mother into acting, taking the name of his paternal grandmother), recalled the homeless man whom his parents allowed to move into the Wadsworth Avenue basement. "I would come home [from school] sometimes, and he would be dressed in my parents' clothes."

Wadsworth was reminiscent of the Red Family's communal

whirlwind, but the house was clearly under the command of "Tom and Jane" and though the meals were equally wholesome and unimaginative—lots of stir-fry and organic takeout from the nearby pizzeria, Wildflour—nobody confused it with a radical Berkeley collective. Under the direction of the left's leading celebrity couple, the antiwar movement suddenly jerked to life—an epic achievement beyond the power of outposts like the Red Family and America's increasingly insular radical left.

Hayden's goal was to finally stop the war by defunding it. And between early 1973 and April 1975, when Saigon fell to North Vietnamese and National Liberation Front troops, that's what the Indochina Peace Campaign did, mobilizing a grassroots network throughout the country and running an increasingly effective lobby in Washington, DC. The lobbying efforts by IPC to cut off congressional funding of the war met with growing success as the Nixon presidency collapsed in scandal and Capitol Hill was infused with a new wave of post-Watergate legislators after the 1974 elections.

Hayden later looked back on the evening when the coalition assembled by his group—including seven major religious denominations, the United States Conference of Mayors, the United Auto Workers, and even the moderate Republican Ripon Society—succeeded in killing a key supplemental military aid provision to the South Vietnamese army. The spending bill was defeated after a long, bitter debate on the floor of the House—the beginning of the end for the US government's puppet regime in Saigon. After cheering the vote from the House balcony, Hayden and his IPC comrades "walked into a starry Washington night, thanking the heavens for our trust in the process."

In later years, it would become conventional wisdom in the media—and in liberal as well as conservative circles—to dismiss the Vietnam antiwar movement as ineffectual, as a lot of "sound and fury" that never amounted to anything politically decisive. But as Hayden wrote in his final book, *Hell No: The Forgotten Power of the*

Peace Movement, it was the unsung labors of that movement—the largest protest movement in US history—that finally turned public opinion against the carnage and squeezed off the war's Washington lifeline. Minimizing the historic significance of the Vietnam peace movement allowed future presidents to keep repeating the same mistakes. But, Hayden cautioned, "We need to resist the military occupation of our minds."

With the war that had defined his entire youth finally coming to an end, Hayden was now free to redefine himself. He had been expelled from the political mainstream, as well as from the radical left. And his wife had been effectively blacklisted in Hollywood because of her outspoken denunciation of the war. But working as a team, they refused to be sidelined. Hayden now decided to plunge directly into electoral politics, the arena considered off-limits by nearly all radical activists and yet the main stage of American power. And Fonda, with Hayden's encouragement, would attempt to revive her movie career—on her own terms this time.

IT WASN'T REALLY about winning when Tom Hayden challenged Senator John Tunney in the 1976 Democratic primary race in California. Hayden surely wouldn't win, but by running against incumbent Tunney—who had a reputation as a liberal, but was a shallow playboy and a bagman for corporate interests—the challenger would set himself up for a career in Democratic Party politics. That was the advice that Hayden got one evening in May 1975 as he huddled in a Washington, DC, apartment with some friends and party insiders, including Daniel Ellsberg and Robert Shrum, an aide to Senator George McGovern and a consummate Democratic player. Contemplating his political future after Vietnam, Hayden was immediately intrigued by how a Senate campaign "would allow me to change my status and, by implication, that of the sixties activists, from outsiders to mainstream participants in national politics."

For another participant in the Washington meeting, Bill Zimmerman, a Hayden Senate run also promised exciting strategic possibilities. "I thought that a Senate campaign would impose a discipline on us—that we'd be forced to understand more about our own country and our own people, after being focused for so long on Southeast Asia. We had been following leaders and idols like Ho Chi Minh and Che Guevara."

But the main goal of a Senate race in California must be to build a grassroots movement that would move politics in the groundbreaking state to the left. That's what legendary United Farm Workers leader Cesar Chavez strongly advised Hayden when he later sought his counsel. "We've seen many candidates come and go," Chavez told Hayden. "It would be a waste of time and money unless you build something lasting, like a machine. Not like [Chicago] Mayor Daley has, but a machine for people. That would interest us."

Hayden recruited some of his Port Huron–SDS collaborators, including Dick and Mickey Flacks and Paul Potter, and began hammering out a Senate campaign manifesto that ballooned to 278 pages. *Making the Future Ours* was a vast wish list of New Left goals updated for the 1970s. The major theme of the campaign was to be "economic democracy"—because the country was still deeply in the throes of the Cold War, it was too soon to reclaim the word "socialism." The Hayden campaign envisioned a society in which workers, consumers, and citizens all played an active role in directing the private sector and the country was ruled by a "Government of the People" instead of a "Government of the Corporations."

Hayden and his team began drawing on the organizing skills they'd learned in the antiwar movement. They opened twenty-two field offices throughout the state and deployed about two hundred paid campaign workers who fanned out in cities every evening to knock on doors and spread the word about Hayden.

Zimmerman was tapped by the candidate to run the campaign, even though "none of us knew shit about electoral politics. I figured I didn't know anything about running a campaign and Tom didn't know anything about being a candidate, but we had about a year before the actual election [in June 1976], and we could learn."

Zimmerman—who had grown up in a working-class, Jewish family in Chicago—was one of the American left's movers and shakers, popping up in many of the most iconic episodes of the era. In 1963, he traveled to Mississippi as a college student to work with SNCC leaders Bob Moses and James Forman on the front lines of the civil rights movement. He marched through the streets of Chicago in 1966 with Martin Luther King Jr. as a furious mob of white counterdemonstrators showered them with rocks, bottles, and racist insults. He helped lead numerous antiwar actions, including the 1971 Mayday protest, which tried to mobilize a street-fighting army and shut down Nixon's Washington. It was the failure of that demonstration, which could not raise enough militants to take the capital, that convinced Zimmerman that the antiwar movement had become estranged from the American people and needed to find less violent ways of expanding public opposition to the war. He then helped organize Medical Aid for Indochina, opening chapters across America and raising money to send medical supplies to North Vietnam. Zimmerman was invited to join the 1972 Hayden-Fonda antiwar tour of middle America, using his spot onstage to pitch the need for medicines and equipment to offset the terrible damage of the US onslaught.

Zimmerman was still a risk-taker, a quality that Hayden continued to admire in fellow activists, even as he himself trimmed his hair, bought business suits, and announced his Senate race. While working with the medical aid group, Zimmerman had secretly carried a new type of penicillin that didn't require refrigeration to the North Vietnamese embassy in Paris. The antibiotic, which could be administered to wounded Vietnamese soldiers in the field, was used to save countless "enemy" lives in the war. Zimmerman went ahead with the mission, even though he knew he could be arrested and tried for treason. And later, in 1973, Zimmerman led a small squadron of Piper Cherokee planes on a daring relief mission over

Wounded Knee, South Dakota, defying the Nixon administration's militarized siege of the Native American encampment there.

Zimmerman had driven from Boston to Los Angeles in his own aging VW after accepting Hayden's offer to help run his antiwar organization, arriving on the Fourth of July 1974. He soon found himself at the center of the Hayden-Fonda whirlwind, moving into a house next door on Wadsworth that Jane had secured for him and plunging into a relationship with Hayden's ex-girlfriend, Joan Andersson, who later became his wife. Even in exile from the Berkeley left, Hayden still had a knack for re-creating its incestuous bonds.

Hayden's Senate campaign was staffed by other antiwar movement heroes, including Fred Branfman, who was hired to oversee communications and research. As a young international aid worker in Laos in the late 1960s, Branfman witnessed the horrific casualties of the secret US air war in that military "sideshow." He escorted foreign officials and journalists to bombed villages and traumatized refugee camps, and after returning to the US in 1971, he lobbied Congress to cut off financing for the war and testified before a Senate committee. (Like Zimmerman, Branfman was another left-wing Zelig, popping up throughout his political career at memorable moments. In 1994, he was walking across Wilshire Boulevard in Los Angeles with Jerry Rubin when the Yippie turned yuppie was struck by a motorist, later dying in a hospital.)

Despite the campaign's assemblage of movement luminaries, Hayden was the undisputed star. Branfman later wrote unabashedly of his excitement at being invited to join the campaign. "[Tom] was doing something impossibly brave and visionary: he was our Moses, leading all of us 'lefties' who had become marginalized for opposing the war into the Promised Land of electoral politics."

But Fonda was very much the costar of Hayden's Senate race. She drew essential media coverage and money to the campaign, recruiting celebrities like Warren Beatty, Groucho Marx, and Linda Ronstadt to cohost fundraising parties and perform at benefit concerts. She even persuaded her father, Henry, who was more associated with flag-waving causes, to appear in a TV ad for Hayden. When Zimmerman urgently needed more funds for the campaign's expensive TV barrage, Fonda contributed her own money, including the $200,000 she was paid by Columbia Pictures to appear in a fluffy comedy opposite George Segal called *Fun with Dick and Jane*. The studio saw the light film as a box office test that Fonda had to pass before Hollywood would allow her to resume her career. Fonda passed the test, with the movie making over $13 million in the US and Canada and becoming Columbia's third-highest-grossing movie of 1977.

After Hayden first announced his Senate candidacy, an authoritative Field Poll taken in June 1975 showed he had the support of 12 percent of California's Democratic electorate. Novices in the trenches of electoral politics, Hayden and his top campaign officials were convinced he could rise in the polls with a grassroots strategy of statewide door-knocking. But eight months later, even after an army of young activists had joined the campaign, another Field Poll in February 1976 found that all of this grunt labor had moved Hayden up only one point to 13 percent. In frustration, Zimmerman went outside his activist circle and consulted with Peter Hart in Washington, DC, who was emerging as a savvy political pollster. Hart convinced him the campaign needed polling to select the three primary issues among Hayden's cornucopia that would most resonate with voters—which turned out to be national health insurance, getting big money out of politics, and transitioning from oil to solar energy. He also persuaded Hayden's campaign director that in a state the size of California, TV advertising must be a top priority.

Hayden proved to be too stiff on camera to shoot traditional campaign ads, but when Zimmerman's crew filmed him in question-and-answer mode, he connected with the audience. To listen today to recordings of Hayden on the stump in California—forty years before Bernie Sanders started translating the same issues into major topics of national conversation—is a lesson about his vanguard role in American political history. Hayden is animated and articulate about America's need for deep reforms, and cutting and sarcastic about the crushing power of the corporate establishment. There is something thrilling about how Hayden opens the doors of campaign politics to radical ideas that had been dismissed as the marginal demands of campus protesters and Black militants.

In late February 1976, Hayden and Fonda appeared at a San Francisco Democratic club event held in a warehouse called the Space. The crowd was quiet until a few minutes into his speech, when Hayden began hitting his applause lines, invoking the Bicentennial celebration fervor being marketed across the country that year. "A lot of people say I'm too radical," Hayden reminded the crowd in a rising voice. "[But] is there any question that what I'm saying is more radical than what Thomas Jefferson or Tom Paine said? It's probably a little more moderate. . . . The great point to stress here is that the Declaration of Independence and the Constitution and the Bill of Rights were not written by bureaucrats, were not written by a lot of soft people. They were written by people who were willing to pursue life, liberty, and the pursuit of happiness at whatever expense in terms of their reputation and their life. They were willing to do anything. They were people who gave up their lives, their fortune and their sacred honor, as they put it, to secure democracy in these United States."

Hayden was romanticizing the Founding Fathers' devotion to democracy for political effect. But he skillfully used their rhetoric to make his case for economic democracy. The Bill of Rights, he declared, must be extended to the economy. "The right of workers to have some control over their jobs. The right of consumers to have some power over prices. The right of people in their neighborhoods in cities like this to have some power over the downtown interests. . . . These are the bill of rights that should be posted on the doors of every big corporation in the United States. And it's going to take a very militant movement for economic justice to make these demands be heard. Because it's these big corporations today that are the modern equivalent of the king."

Finally, he invoked the moral passion of the radical movement that had made him a leader. "The power we have is in us . . . but that power has to come out. It's a spiritual power, a power of conviction, a power that propelled the labor movement at its best, the women's movement, the peace and civil rights movements. Those movements in the sixties were successful against all odds because those movements were full of people who were willing to live and even die for something beyond themselves. That's the kind of movement we have to create in 1976."

As Hayden concluded his rousing speech, the crowd burst into cheers. The former revolutionary—once branded a thought criminal by the Nixon administration—was brilliantly using the Spirit of '76 to transform himself into an America patriot, in the mold of those earlier Toms, Paine and Jefferson. Meanwhile, as Hayden frequently pointed out during the campaign, a number of those Nixon officials who had tried to imprison him were themselves now behind bars.

After Zimmerman flooded the TV airwaves in California with campaign ads—including a folksy spot featuring actor Will Geer, the beloved grandpa on the popular TV show *The Waltons*—Hayden's poll numbers quickly shot upward to 33 percent in late March. "Big bump, and my brain exploded," Zimmerman later exclaimed. "Suddenly I saw the way, and from that point on, we were in it to win. I realized that the left had never really used TV, the most powerful communications system that exists in the country. With the spike in the polls, we started raising money very seriously, and Jane really used her Hollywood connections because by then everybody could see we had a chance to win."

Alarmed by Hayden's surge in the polls, the Tunney camp mobilized to beat back the threat on its left. Dark money from the energy, agribusiness, real estate, and entertainment industries came pouring into Tunney's campaign. The massive cash infusion allowed Tunney to buy most of the available TV time, pushing the Hayden ads off the airwaves. Meanwhile, despite Hayden's swelling campaign, California's dominant media institution, the *Los Angeles Times*, refused to devote any serious coverage to his insurgent effort.

"I covered Tom's Senate campaign for the *LA Times*, and I could see how charismatic he was to his audiences," recalled veteran journalist Narda Zacchino, who became an admirer of Hayden's California political career despite the mixed feelings about him held by the man she had married, none other than Bob Scheer. "After watching Tom speak, I would go back to the *Times* and I'll never forget the conversation I had with the political editor. I told him, 'You know, I really think Hayden could give Tunney a hard time.' And he said, 'No, he doesn't have a chance—it's not worth our time to cover him.' So this was the biggest newspaper in the state, and they wouldn't give Hayden any play or serious consideration. . . . It was an ideological decision."

It became clear to Branfman, a newcomer to electoral politics, that "in challenging John Tunney, Tom Hayden had not simply taken on a sitting senator. He had challenged an entire Establishment of rich and powerful figures." Hayden was painted inaccurately by Tunney's attack machine as a radical "big spender" and "soft on Russia." Overwhelmed by his opponent's enormous campaign spending and largely ignored by the mainstream media, Hayden hit an electoral ceiling. On election night, he went down to defeat, with Tunney winning 54 percent of the vote and Hayden nearly 37 percent. Still, the former New Left leader's showing at the polls was impressive enough to gain national media coverage and to forge an alliance with Governor Jerry Brown, with Hayden representing the left wing of the California Democratic Party.

The lessons gained from this New Left debut in mainstream politics should have also riveted the attention of progressives across the country. How do you campaign for major offices on a radical platform? How do you use celebrity power to attract media coverage and money? How do you build an army of grassroots activists to counter the torrent of corporate campaign spending? Zimmerman found his longtime network of activists strangely uninterested in discussing campaign strategy and mechanics, and even "dismissive" of the Hayden race. "They said things like, 'You can't replicate this anywhere else. You had a celebrity wife and you still couldn't get 40 percent of the vote. You guys are sellouts.' It was not a reasoned response—kind of immature, very snarky."

Tom Hayden's 1976 Senate race was in some way the zenith of his political career, though he would go on to try unsuccessfully for other high offices and settle into a long tenure as a California state legislator. It was also a lost opportunity for the American left, which—failing to build on Hayden's example—wandered aimlessly for decades outside of the electoral arena. The reluctance of strong left-wing Democrats, independents, and socialists to run for office in the years after Hayden's 1976 race is a major reason the New Left fell far short of taking political power in America, while winning most of its social and cultural agenda.

There were other radical insurgents who broke into political office in the 1970s, including feminist Bella Abzug, raised a socialist in the South Bronx and hailed as the first Jewish woman in Congress when she was elected in 1970. Described as an "intersectional" feminist by biographer Leandra Ruth Zarnow, Abzug fought to make connections between women's liberation, racial justice, organized labor, antipoverty programs, and the Vietnam peace movement. But she served only three terms in Congress and lost her subsequent bids for the Senate and the New York mayor's office. Brooklyn congresswoman Shirley Chisholm advocated much of Abzug's bold agenda, but didn't come close to winning the Democratic presidential nomination in 1972. In California, Black Panther leader Bobby Seale shook up Oakland politics with his vigorous but unsuccessful race for mayor in 1973, and Harvey Milk rode the rising wave of the gay movement into office as a San Francisco supervisor in 1977. But Milk was assassinated the following year by a conservative political opponent, and Seale's political base collapsed with the destruction of the Black Panther Party. Tom Hayden was one of the era's few radical leaders who ended up grinding out a long career in electoral politics.

The Hayden Senate campaign mounted a celebration in a Los Angeles theater on election night in June 1976, treating their showing as a victory. As the crowd around the candidate began to thin out, Branfman approached Hayden in his usual guileless way, a tall, shambling man with an innocent spirit no matter how much political experience he would accrue in life. Branfman enthusiastically congratulated Hayden, who was never without guile, but that night replied in a heartfelt way. "I will never forget his answer," Branfman recalled years later. "He looked at me and responded simply. 'You're right, it's true. I behaved far better than I ever have before. I hope I can keep it up.'"

FOLLOWING HIS PATH-BLAZING run for Senate, Hayden proved a flawed leader. And the by-now-splintered New Left never lived up to his—or its—political ambitions. Immediately after the June 1976 primary, Hayden and Zimmerman's close alliance broke apart over their strategic disagreements. Zimmerman believed that they should convert Hayden's statewide campaign machine into an issues-driven operation. He wanted the Hayden-Fonda organization to spearhead California ballot initiatives that could build a wider popular base, such as the drive to regulate the auto insurance industry, which was notoriously gouging its customers at the time.

Zimmerman had worked briefly on producing TV commercials for a ballot measure on behalf of Cesar Chavez's farmworkers union, and he was excited about the possibility of bypassing California's powerful special interests and passing legislation directly by statewide votes. "I was not from California and none of the states I had lived in before had these popular initiatives," Zimmerman said. "So I was very impressed—you can go around the governor and legislature and write your own laws!"

But Hayden rejected Zimmerman's proposal to grow California's progressive movement by campaigning for ballot measures. He wanted to build his political machine instead by running a wave of progressive candidates for state and local offices. Zimmerman suspected Hayden's true motive was to advance his own political career. And that is what the Campaign for Economic Democracy essentially became, a platform for Hayden's moderately successful career, which topped out with winning campaigns for the state assembly and senate.

Meanwhile, Hayden's most intelligent and experienced radical comrades drifted away from his increasingly personality-dominated organization. Zimmerman started his own successful political consulting firm, eventually winning the drive to regulate the California auto insurance industry, among other victorious ballot measures. But ironically, it was the right that exploited California's initiative process more effectively than the left, when conservative Howard Jarvis's tax rebellion won overwhelming passage of Proposition 13 in 1978, a curb on public spending that would diminish the state's education system and other essential social services for decades to come. "Jarvis proved the potential for that strategy," said Zimmerman. "He just gave it to the right instead of the left."

Fred Branfman went to work in Governor Jerry Brown's brain trust, focusing on efforts to harness economic development to the solar future—a "Jobs from the Sun" concept that originated with Hayden's Campaign for Economic Democracy, but wouldn't get national recognition until the next century's Green New Deal campaign. By the time they parted company with Hayden, Zimmerman and Branfman no longer regarded him so heroically. Both realized, for instance, that Hayden's drinking, held in check during the early stage of the US Senate campaign, worsened under the stress of its final weeks.

"Tom would control his heavy drinking until the evening hours—but he would be drunk by eight or nine at night," Zimmerman recalled.

Hayden's campaign director also witnessed Hayden's growing resentment at being eclipsed by his more famous wife, a shadowed existence to which he'd subjected other intimates like Anne Weills but which he'd never before experienced. "I think Tom was affected by the attention that Jane got during the Senate campaign," Zimmerman said. "He was the candidate, but *she* was the celebrity. And whenever they went anywhere, she got more attention than he did. That bothered him a lot."

Zimmerman and Branfman—who both grew to enormously respect Jane Fonda and admire how she shed her Hollywood pedigree to work tirelessly for progressive causes, including her husband's political career—also came to resent Hayden's mistreatment of her. Branfman had been "in awe" of "Jane of Arc" since her antiwar days, he wrote near the end of his life, because of her "courageous" refusal to "turn a blind eye to the mass murder" in Vietnam. He was also deeply impressed by her "refusal to back down in the face of enormous hatred, countless death threats, and a campaign of vilification to which I do not believe any American public figure has ever been subjected."

Branfman also appreciated the way that Fonda shrewdly reassembled her Hollywood career, taking more control of the creative process and making overtly progressive movies that succeeded in back-to-back years at the box office, like *Coming Home* (1978), *The China Syndrome* (1979), and *Nine to Five* (1980). In fact, Fonda's career was soaring as Hayden's hit a political ceiling.

Interviewed in the cluttered living room of her family's Santa Monica house in 1977, Fonda—who had formed her own production company with Bruce Gilbert—was poised and articulate as she described her strategy for taking power in Hollywood and beyond.

"We're not interested in being protesters for the rest of our lives. We're talking about running candidates for public office. We're talking about sponsoring legislation. And we're talking about making progressive movies, because it's important to open up people's minds. . . . But you can't do that unless you have power."

But even as she reveled in her new strength as an actress and producer, Fonda still took pains to defer to Hayden, crediting him with being "the first person on the left I had ever met who really took movies seriously." Hayden, for his part, seemed to take pleasure in disturbing the interview by playing loudly with the couple's kids in the same room. Friends and coworkers noted how he often felt compelled to denigrate his wife in front of others.

Branfman cringed to watch Hayden belittle Fonda. "To put it simply," he recalled, "Jane was kept in her place within our world. Tom frequently disparaged her, subtly or crassly, dismissing her opinions when she dared to offer them. He was clearly in control of the relationship, making all decisions big and small. I remember being shocked when Jane would ask him what to do on even such matters as feeding Troy."

Branfman and others in the Campaign for Economic Democracy circle were also deeply troubled by Hayden's womanizing, which grew more reckless as the years went by and as his drinking got worse. Hayden aggressively propositioned female staffers in his own organization—women whose paychecks came from Fonda's generosity, as Branfman observed. While he was still in charge of CED communications, Branfman heard that Hayden had "pounced" on the girlfriend of a close colleague. Another day, Branfman recalled, "I received a call from a colleague in Sacramento [saying] I should tell Tom that a newspaper report was coming out in which a young woman—the daughter of a well-known Democratic donor—was claiming that Tom stuck his hand up under her dress under the table."

Fonda later remarked that "neither Tom or I were very big on talking about our feelings." But Hayden was remarkably candid in analyzing their marriage's failure, in a televised interview with, of all people, celebrity hound Barbara Walters. "You're living with someone who has studios and publicity companies working night and day to make her larger than life and it becomes artificial," he told Walters. "The house becomes a prop, the children are props.

Where's life? She felt the call of Hollywood and that was very jarring to me. I was drinking and womanizing. I wasn't ready to be the husband of somebody who was preoccupied with being an actress."

In the end, it was all too much for Fonda to tolerate or forgive. In February 1989, the couple announced their separation and at year's end their divorce. In their publicity statement, Hayden and Fonda vowed their disunion was "amicable" and insisted they would remain political partners. But once again, Hayden was on his own, disconnected from the movement that sheltered his turbulent youth and the celebrated marriage that helped launch his Democratic Party career.

IT TOOK HIS DEATH, but all the disparate elements of Tom Hayden's life reunited for his memorial service at UCLA's Royce Hall in February 2017. The tribute to Hayden—who died the previous October at seventy-six after a lengthy illness, including a stroke and heart trouble—drew over a thousand political leaders, activists, entertainers, and other friends and admirers from his crowded life. The memorial was arranged by Jane Fonda—who not only demonstrated the durability of her relationship with Hayden, but the longevity of her organizing skills at age seventy-nine— and Barbara Williams, the lesser-known actress whom Hayden had married after divorcing Fonda. Dolores Huerta, the sainted icon of the farmworkers movement, eulogized Hayden, as did Bobby Kennedy Jr. and also Bonnie Raitt, who sang Sam Cooke's "A Change Is Gonna Come" in his honor.

In the years after Hayden's memorial, Fonda escalated her activism as she advanced into her eighties, speaking out against Donald Trump's presidency and getting repeatedly arrested at the "Fire Drill Fridays" civil disobedience demonstrations she led at the Capitol in Washington, DC, to protest Big Oil's fueling of the climate crisis. As the country exploded in street protests following the police murder of George Floyd in May 2020, the actress went on CNN in a black beret and sweater—an apparent nod to the Black Panther Party, which she had supported decades earlier—denouncing "white privilege" policies, including redlining and other racist banking practices.

But there was a melancholy mood that afternoon in 2017, as many of Hayden's old 1960s comrades filled the campus auditorium in his honor. With Trump's recent presidential inauguration hanging over the service, there was a palpable sense of "what if" in the air. What if leaders like Hayden could have brought the rest of the New Left into the electoral arena with them? What if Hayden could have moderated his dominating ego and allowed the powerful women in his life to fully share his spotlight, or even eclipse him? What if the Democratic Party could have been infused with more progressive values and candidates after the Vietnam War? A President Sanders could have been sitting in the White House instead. And perhaps a Senate majority leader Fonda. But Hayden and the New Left had failed to synchronize their ambitions and fully throw open Democratic Party doors.

Todd Gitlin, a former SDS president who had become a prominent sociologist, was among those attending Hayden's memorial. He put the blame for the New Left's political failure on the movement itself, not on Hayden. "There were few people in the New Left who were as serious as Tom about taking and wielding power," he said. "I've always thought the difference between the right and the left is that they believe in power, while we're ambivalent about it. It's the difference between the Tea Party and the Occupy movements."

Several of the speakers praised Hayden for his long, unsung service in Sacramento, where he tirelessly worked for environmental and consumer protections, labor rights, and criminal justice reforms. But working for sixteen of his eighteen years in the California legislature under Republican governors, Hayden seldom got much publicity as the years went by. The public service itself became enough for Hayden, to his credit.

Before his own death, two years before Hayden's, Fred Branfman came to forgive his former political mentor's failings. "I still
feel I owe him a great deal for all I learned during my years with
him," Branfman wrote in an unpublished memoir, "and still respect
him more than any other political figure I encountered during my
years in politics. His influence on the '60s was seminal and his
subsequent political career has overall been one of honor and de-
cency. If he fell short of my projections, he has not fallen short in
comparisons with any political figure of the postwar era. That even
so seminal a figure as Tom Hayden could fail in his quest to create
a socially just society is, in the end, more of a commentary on the
bankruptcy of American politics than on him."

Some of Hayden's sixties comrades at the memorial service
were not happy with the afternoon's narrative as scripted by Fonda,
with its emphasis on Hayden's rebirth as a mainstream political
player after he married the movie star. At an Indian restaurant in
Santa Monica that evening, Bob Scheer and Anne Weills—still
close friends after all the years—complained about how Hayden's
Berkeley years had been written out of his life story. "What was
effective about Tom was his life of protest," said Scheer, objecting
to how the memorial seemed to suggest that Hayden's militance
was nothing more than a youthful phase out of which he needed to
grow. Late in life, Hayden himself was fond of quoting a line from
Italian novelist Ignazio Silone's *Bread and Wine*: "What would happen if men remained loyal to the ideals of their youth?"

Weeks after the memorial, sitting in her sunshine-filled law
office in a downtown Oakland tower, Weills acknowledged that
Hayden did remain true to his youthful values in the end. In 2013,
she was representing inmates who were engaged in a lengthy hunger strike at Pelican Bay, the notoriously cruel California state
prison near the Oregon border. Protesting the use of long-term
solitary confinement at Pelican Bay, the hunger strikers' campaign
quickly spread throughout the massive California penal system.
Even though Hayden was no longer a state legislator, Weills asked

him to intervene with progressive former colleagues in the state capitol, which he did. Thanks in part to Hayden's involvement, California lawmakers finally negotiated an end to the two-month strike before any prisoners died, by promising to hold hearings on prison conditions.

"It took Tom and I years to get friendly again, and that's never happened to me with other friends or boyfriends," Weills said. "[After our breakup], he got ensconced in the Democratic Party and all that, and he moved to the center, and that just added fuel to the fire [for me]."

But in the end, they found a way to come together again, through political struggle, which had always been their common passion. Hayden had worked with Los Angeles gang members, "and some of them were my clients," said Weills. The two had a lot to talk about when they got together again at an Oakland restaurant. One was still a crusading outsider, while the other had pushed the political system from within as far as he could. Between them was still a spark of youthful militance.

When Weills next heard from Hayden, it was a message on her voice mail. He was calling to tell her he'd suffered a heart attack. "He said I just want to let you know that I'm OK," but she could tell from his voice he was weaker.

"I called him back and left a message for him—I'm not sure I talked with him directly—wishing him well and just saying the nice things you would say. That I cared about him—not that I loved him, I wouldn't say that again. But, you know, he was my comrade, he was my . . . he was part of my family, he was like an old comrade."

Revolution Has Come, Time to Pick Up the Gun

Bobby Seale, Huey Newton, Eldridge Cleaver, and the Black Panthers

B obby Seale was comfortable with guns. His daddy gave him a .30–30 Winchester rifle when he was twelve and by the time he was thirteen, he was an expert shot. The two would go on hunting trips to Mount Shasta, driving from their family's crowded Berkeley, California, public housing apartment to the majestic peak near the Oregon border that had inspired a rich history of Native American legends. They hunted bear, mule deer, redtail deer, rabbits, squirrels, and pheasants. Bobby enjoyed roaming the wilderness with his father, but their relationship was fraught. George Seale was a skilled carpenter, but he couldn't get into the racist union. His father had beaten him as a boy, and he sometimes did the same to Bobby. The older man's temper was volcanic. Bobby never forgot the brutal beating he got when he was only six years old. Writing about it years later, he called it "unjust." That's the word he used. Bobby Seale grew up hating bullies.

At age sixteen, Seale began hanging out with Steve Brumfield, another African American teenager in his housing projects, who taught him how to get in shape. They would run for miles into the Berkeley Hills, all the way to Grizzly Peak, then down into Tilden Park, before circling back home. Steve was heavily muscled and could wrap bull snakes around his arms, but Bobby learned that strength came from stamina, not bulk. They shared an interest in Indian history and tattooed "Sioux" on their arms with needles, before they learned it was the French word for "cutthroat" and that the tribespeople called themselves Lakota. They started practicing lance fighting on the big lawn next to their projects. They read how General Custer "got his ass kicked" by the Lakota, as Seale put it. They hopped a train and lit out for Lakota country but only got as far as Sacramento. Bobby grew strong enough to stand up to his father and tell him he would no longer work on his carpentry jobs for free. When George Seale was growing up, he'd taken the same defiant stand with his own father.

Bobby Seale never went for the Black separatist mumbo jumbo. "I had more sense than that," he declared later in life. He always knew that his own blood was as mixed as America's. His grandmother on his mother's side was half Native American and her husband was half Irish, with light skin and blue eyes. His father's mother was born a slave and she and her husband took the name Seale from the prominent white family on whose Texas plantation they toiled. As a teenager in Berkeley, Seale knew more about American Indian history than about his African roots.

Seale got away from his father by enrolling in the US Air Force in 1955. He trained to do structural repair work on aircraft and in 1958 was stationed at Ellsworth Air Force Base in South Dakota. He was finally living in Lakota country, near the tribe's sacred Black Hills, but his military regimen prevented him from visiting the nearby Pine Ridge Reservation. Steve Brumfield was no longer in his life; he ended up killing himself.

Seale's air force service in South Dakota—where race lines between whites, Blacks, and Indians were strictly enforced—was tempestuous. A sergeant trying to block Seale's promotion from the rank of corporal set him up one day, calling him a "little black nigger," prompting him to lose his cool and begin beating the white airman with a piece of heavy aluminum. The incident cost Seale thirty days in the stockade, his promotion, and his corporal stripes.

Later, Seale had a run-in with the colonel who commanded the air force base. Before being transferred to Ellsworth, Bobby had bought a $600 drum kit on installments in Oakland and begun playing in a jazz band. At the air base, he played weekend gigs but fell behind on drum payments and the squadron's commanding officer, who happened to be related to the owners of the collection agency, began riding him hard to pay his bills. By then, Seale felt increasingly pressured and mistreated and demeaned by military life on the base. Summoned one more time into his CO's office to be browbeaten for not making his payments, Seale finally exploded and began "cussing out" the colonel. He was manhandled outside by two sergeants but kept heaping abuse on the CO all the way to the stockade. After Seale was court-martialed, the colonel told him he would never get a civilian job and then gave him five minutes to get off the base—less than two months before his four-year enlistment was over.

Looking back on his aborted air force service years later, Seale sounded surprisingly positive. He had learned a technical trade, the need to control his temper, how a disciplined organization was run, and a strong sense of how proud Black men were treated in America.

Despite his CO's threat, Seale found work at the Kaiser Aerospace Electronics plant near Oakland as a metals tester on the Gemini missile project. After six months on the job, he was confronted by a manager who discovered that he'd lied about his bad conduct discharge. "If you want to fire me, fire me," Seale bluntly told him. "If you don't want to fire me, forget it and I'll do the work." Seale was too good to fire so he kept his job. But fifteen months later, he quit "because the [Vietnam] war was going on and I felt I was aiding the government's operation."

By the early 1960s, Seale was becoming politically aware. A couple of years before, during his court-martial, he'd been asked what he thought about the civil rights movement. "I was stupid," Seale later recalled, "and I said, 'Well, the Communists are leading it, ain't they?'" But roaming around Los Angeles and the Bay Area after his discharge from the air force, Seale was identifying more and more with the rising civil rights movement. He began working as a standup comedian in Oakland clubs and at private parties. "I think comedians know a hell of a lot," he later wrote. "They know a lot of things that are oppressive and wrong."

On December 28, 1962, Seale went to hear the Reverend Martin Luther King Jr. speak at Oakland Municipal Auditorium on the hundredth anniversary of President Abraham Lincoln's announcement of the Emancipation Proclamation. Over seven thousand people crowded into the cavernous hall (since renamed the Henry J. Kaiser Convention Center), cheering King's call for a second proclamation to end the tyranny of Jim Crow racism over African Americans and open equal opportunities for all. Seale had long since stopped going to church—"I got tired of all the hell and damnation every Sunday and decided I haven't got time for that." But King's sermon that day was electrifying and even when Seale was over eighty years old, he still enjoyed recalling the minister's performance, using his powers of mimicry to resurrect the long-dead leader.

"Right now, in the San Francisco Bay Area, Langendorf Bread Company and Kilpatrick's Bread Company will not hire people of color," Seale orated, invoking King's robust pulpit voice. "And all across America, I say Wonder Bread will not hire people of color. I say we're going to have to boycott them and we're going to have to boycott them so consistently and so profoundly that we'll make Wonder Bread wonder where the money went!"

"I've never forgotten that," recalled Seale, still thrumming with King's magnetism. "The audience hit the roof. And I'm totally inspired by this man."

But didn't the Black Panthers come to denounce Martin Luther King as a "sellout" and an "Uncle Tom"? "I know people said that, but no, I never agreed with that," Seale stated in old age. "I was inspired first by Martin, and I kept being inspired by Martin."

The Nation of Islam's dogma of racial separatism held no attraction for Seale, but after Malcolm X broke from the organization and began charting a more secular, inclusive path toward Black liberation, the other great African American leader of the time widened his appeal among young activists, Seale included. When Malcolm was gunned down by a team of hit men during a speech in Harlem's Audubon Ballroom in February 1965, Seale immediately suspected government treachery—an impression confirmed years later when the assassination was exposed as a clandestine operation involving Nation of Islam leaders and FBI officials. In a blind fury, Seale became a "one-man riot" and started "throwing bricks at big, fancy cars with white guys driving. Only those cars. I considered them the enemy. While I was wrong, that was my emotion."

After his rage was spent, Seale retreated into the Berkeley Hills, where he and Steve Brumfield had trained as teenagers to become warriors. During the week he spent in the Berkeley wilderness, he had an epiphany. "While Dr. Martin Luther King was also my civil rights real hero, I was determined to make a Malcolm X out of my own self. I would fight for constitutional, democratic, civil, human rights. . . . I decided that I needed to start a new organization."

Seale enrolled at Merritt College—a commuter school in Oakland with a diverse, urban student body—and began organizing a multiracial coalition of students to demand a Black history course; by September 1965 the class was listed in the campus curriculum. The following year, he transformed his Black studies group into the Soul Students Advisory Council, a militant organization that won official campus recognition. Seale was already scouting for other Merritt students who shared his courage and vision, deriding many of his fellow campus activists as all-talk-no-action intellectuals.

There was one young man who loomed above all others. His name was Huey P. Newton.

NEWTON SEEMED TO leap out of the pages of one of Seale's most dog-eared books of the time, *The Wretched of the Earth*, the searing anticolonial manifesto by Frantz Fanon, who had died in 1961, the same year his book was published. The brilliant political philosopher and psychiatrist—who grew up in Martinique, the French Caribbean colony—had resurrected the lumpenproletariat, Marx's scorned underclass, as a potential force for revolutionary change. White colonial rule could be overthrown only through the liberating power of violence, wrote Fanon, and the criminals and hustlers who made up the lumpenproletariat had a special capacity for brute force. By aligning lumpen types with radical intellectuals, he theorized, this violence could be given revolutionary direction.

Newton was a complex young man—magazine-cover good-looking, but tightly wrapped; streetwise and trigger-tempered, but with intellectual aspirations. Semi-literate when he graduated from high school, Newton made up for his late start by voraciously reading volumes of political theory, history, and poetry. Taking classes at Merritt, he was also enrolled in law school at night. But Newton came from an Oakland family that sometimes earned its money and respect the hard way. He was not afraid to use his fists, or to pull a gun. He had already done time for stabbing a man with a steak knife at a party.

Newton initially rejected Seale's offer to join his radical student group. It was too hard to organize Black people, Newton told him, because they "don't know enough about their history." But when Newton showed up at a Soul Students rally at a Merritt auditorium packed with hundreds of students, he told Seale that he wanted in.

In his 1970 memoir, *Seize the Time*, Seale gushed about Newton's charismatic swagger and political brilliance. "Huey was something else. Huey was out of sight. He knew how to do it. He was ten motherfuckers." Seale gleefully narrated their farewell meeting with the Soul Students Advisory Council, which had been taken over by "jive college intellectuals" and "cultural nationalists." Seale strode into the campus meeting with a 9 mm pistol and meanwhile "Huey had called up his boys—the thugs off the block," including a nephew. "They don't like to do much of anything but fight, and they liked Huey and they respected Huey's ideas."

"These [Soul Student] niggers think they're bad," Newton told his street army. "We're going to show them if they're bad."

The other student leaders at the meeting were understandably cowed by Seale and Newton's show of force. They were no doubt relieved when the two men announced they were resigning from the group's "ivory-walled towers" and going into the streets of Oakland to organize "the Black liberation struggle."

Later in life, however, Seale expressed a much different view of Huey Newton, the brother-in-arms with whom he's been forever linked. When they completed the ten-point platform that was the founding document of the Black Panther Party for Self-Defense on October 22, 1966, it was Seale's thirtieth birthday and Newton was six years younger. Yet it was not only age but temperament that separated them. Newton was certainly brave, Seale acknowledged, but his "bravery was sometimes just spontaneous and stupid. . . . He'd never been in an organization where he could learn discipline."

In Seale's memory, Newton's street gladiator reputation was the thrilling allure behind the Black Panthers' rise, but also a knife-edge act that always invited disaster. Newton "didn't believe he could die," Seale remarked, which gave him a manic self-confidence. Seale was the older, wiser mentor, constantly pulling Newton back from the "revolutionary suicide" that the younger man courted.

Seale recalled the time he had to physically restrain Newton from lunging at an openly racist Oakland bus driver. "I ran up behind Huey as he was charging this bus driver and grabbed him from behind and pulled him back. I yelled, 'Stop the goddam bus!'

and I pushed him out." Outside, on the street, Seale told Newton about his own experience in the air force, and how beating up a racist only landed him in the stockade. "We fight back by organizing." That's what he told Huey that day.

But Newton always strained against Seale's leash. He was tantalized by the idea of funding the revolution through armed force. One day he asked Seale to meet him on a corner in downtown Oakland. "See that Bank of America over there," Newton said, pointing. "If we knock off this bank, we could get half a million dollars and that would support the revolution."

Seale was aghast. "Are you out of your fucking mind?" he erupted. "You don't know what the hell you're talking about. You guys will be mowed down. When they ring the alarm, how would you come out of there?"

It's about seizing political power by organizing the community and winning elections, Seale instructed his young protégé. Oakland city managers controlled budgets much larger than a half million bucks, and if they took control of the city, they would have ample resources to uplift the impoverished Black population.

HUEY NEWTON, DISSUADED from knocking over the bank, became obsessed with the idea of picking up guns and confronting brutal, racist cops on the streets of Oakland. Unlike Newton's Bank of America scheme, this was a brash act of political street theater that immediately appealed to Bobby Seale, who saw the tactic's larger potential for seizing the Black community's attention. Newton had read about Robert F. Williams, the former leader of the National Association for the Advancement of Colored People (NAACP) chapter in Monroe, North Carolina, who advocated armed self-defense against white vigilante violence. Ku Klux Klan terrorists were often entwined with local law enforcement agencies in the South, so Jim Crow lynchings frequently had official protection if not involvement. On the night of October 5,

1957, Williams organized a group of men, many of them World War II veterans armed with automatic weapons, to guard the home of his NAACP chapter's vice president against a feared KKK raid. When the Klansmen motorcade arrived, Williams's men opened withering fire on them from behind sandbag fortifications, shooting in a disciplined fashion to run off the hooded marauders but not to kill them.

Williams, who became a controversial figure within the civil rights movement, argued the case for his armed self-defense strategy in the September 1959 issue of the left-wing magazine *Liberation*. While Martin Luther King Jr., the icon of nonviolent resistance, was "a great and successful leader of our race," Williams acknowledged, Blacks in the South were often forced to confront white supremacists' "savage violence" with violence of their own. "I wish to make it clear that I do not advocate violence for its own sake, or for the sake of reprisals against whites," explained Williams. "Nor am I against the passive resistance advocated by Reverend Martin Luther King and others. My only difference with Dr. King is that I believe in flexibility in the freedom struggle."

Responding to Williams in the magazine's next issue, King conceded that "when the Negro uses force in self-defense, he does not forfeit support—he may even win it, by the courage and self-respect it reflects." Even King, the American civil rights movement's embodiment of the Gandhian philosophy of nonviolent resistance, had a flexible view of guns. A Black Mississippi farmer had prophetically warned King in 1964, "This nonviolent stuff ain't no good. It'll get ya killed." But, in fact, the civil rights leader—who was subjected to countless death threats before his assassination in April 1968—kept so many guns in his family home in Atlanta, "just for self-defense," that a movement colleague described King's parsonage as "an arsenal."

The militant Robert F. Williams was fired in 1959 by the NAACP's more cautious executive director, Roy Wilkins, who derided him as "the Lancelot of Monroe," and the organization's counsel and future US Supreme Court justice Thurgood Marshall even recommended that the FBI investigate Williams. In 1961, Williams, under intense legal harassment, was forced to flee overseas with his wife, spending the rest of the 1960s in Cuba and China. But his ideas about armed resistance continued to influence the Black liberation movement. Newton was one of many young activists who absorbed Williams's 1962 book *Negroes with Guns*.

As journalist Charles E. Cobb Jr., a former Student Nonviolent Coordinating Committee (SNCC) field secretary in Mississippi, has written, the young Northern Freedom Riders who ventured into the embattled Deep South in the 1950s and '60s to politically mobilize African Americans were often defended by Black gunowners in rural communities despite the young activists' idealistic pacifism. "The claim that armed self-defense was a necessary aspect of the civil rights movement is still controversial," Cobb wrote. "However, wielding weapons, especially firearms, let both participants in nonviolent struggle and their sympathizers protect themselves and others under terrorist attack for their civil rights activities. This willingness to use deadly force ensured the survival not only of countless brave men and women but also of the freedom struggle itself."

In 1966, as he and Seale were contemplating their Oakland debut as militant organizers, Newton also read about the Lowndes County Freedom Organization (LCFO) in Alabama—brave voter registration activists in a violence-ridden community that was 80 percent Black but where African Americans were kept home on Election Day with a reign of fear and intimidation. Newton was impressed by the bold black panther logo of the new political party in Lowndes County, where many Black citizens felt the need to arm themselves against white law enforcement officers and vigilantes. Outside a rural grocery store, a deputy sheriff had fired his shotgun at two white priests who were working with SNCC, killing one and seriously wounding the other. (The deputy sheriff was later acquitted of all charges.) In a 1966 interview, LCFO chairman John

Hulett explained the symbolism of the black panther, an animal that "moves back until it is cornered, then it comes out fighting for life or death. We felt like we had been pushed back long enough and that it was time for Negroes to come out and take over."

That fall, SNCC's Stokely Carmichael—the charismatic, young champion of the rising "Black Power" movement—was announced as the keynote speaker at a University of California–Berkeley conference to highlight the armed resistance of "bloody Lowndes County." A few days after reading about the October conference, Newton later recalled, "while Bobby and I were rapping, I suggested that we use the panther as our symbol." Soon after, the two men officially founded the Black Panther Party for Self-Defense.

Point number seven in their ten-point party platform called for "an immediate end to POLICE BRUTALITY and murder of black people" and urged that "all black people . . . arm themselves for self-defense." Newton considered urban police forces to be "occupying armies" that repressed African American citizens, often robbing them of their freedom, dignity, and even their lives. The Oakland police force, in fact, was notoriously racist and vicious, composed overwhelmingly of white officers in a city that by 1960 was nearly one-quarter African American.

"There was absolutely no difference in the way that police treated us in Mississippi than they did in California," recalled Black Panther Party member William Calhoun years later. "They may not have called you 'nigger' every day, but they treated you the same way they did in Mississippi."

By 1966, the racial cauldron in Oakland was so hot that the white mayor, John Reading, summoned the city council to his office to warn that if communication did not improve between city hall and impoverished Black citizens, Oakland would become "another Watts." That Black district in Los Angeles had exploded in August 1965, with nearly fourteen thousand National Guard troops reinforcing the infamously violent LAPD, and thirty-four deaths, before the fiery rebellion was crushed.

Reading the August 1966 issue of the SNCC newspaper, Newton was inspired to learn that Watts activists had begun monitoring police activities in their community after the rebellion, driving behind LAPD squad cars and documenting on notepads cases of police abuse. But members of the Community Alert Patrol complained that police so often harassed them, they were left with only one option, "to get our guns and start shooting."

When Newton urged that the fledgling Black Panthers arm themselves and start their own police patrols in Oakland, Seale was equally excited. But, he cautioned Newton, the operation had to be highly disciplined and law-abiding. He told Newton, who'd been studying law at Merritt College and San Francisco State College, to read everything he could about gun laws. Seale also suggested that his young partner spend time in the little law library at the North Oakland Anti-Poverty Center, where he worked as a youth counselor. He had secured a job for Newton at the center, along with several other "brothers on the block," like teenager Bobby Hutton, so they wouldn't have to keep pursuing dead-end careers as street criminals. Several of these young poverty workers, like Hutton, would become the first members of the Black Panther Party.

Bobby Seale still thought of himself as an organizer, not a revolutionary. He'd taken the title "chairman" of the Black Panther Party, while Newton was "minister of defense." He was the one with the broader vision. The Panthers were advocating not armed aggression, stressed Seale, but self-defense. Their police patrols were not an end in themselves, but a first step in a campaign to take political power in Oakland and perhaps in other cities across America. As Seale later put it, "We're not just doing self-defense for its own sake. We're doing it so I can capture the imagination of the people. And if we can do that, I can organize a political, electoral machine."

What better way to electrify Black men and women in cities like Oakland than to stand up to abusive cops with the power of guns and the law? Oakland was a powder keg of smoldering resentments, with African Americans locked out of educational opportunities, good jobs, unions, city government—and with violent white cops keeping a heavy boot on the city's lid. Black citizens were fed up with being pulled over, stopped, shaken down, humiliated, threatened, beaten up, jailed, and sometimes shot by the armed occupiers in their community. But they had no one to call for help.

That's when the Black Panthers rolled up on Seventh Street.

THE BUSTLING RETAIL and entertainment corridor along Seventh Street in West Oakland competed with the Fillmore District across the bay in San Francisco for the title "Harlem of the West." African Americans, fleeing the Jim Crow terrorism of the Deep South, began settling in the area in the 1920s and '30s, with many finding work as Pullman porters on the trains that terminated their runs near the Oakland wharves. After a long, hard-fought union drive, the all-Black Pullman porters workforce became the basis for a rising middle class in the area. Black-owned businesses— beauty salons, butchers, ice cream parlors, clothes stores, furniture dealers—sprang up along Seventh Street to cater to local families. During World War II, the neighborhood's population boomed as more African Americans poured into the area to work in the shipyards that were building floating fortresses for the US Navy and in the port from which thousands of soldiers and sailors were embarking each month for the war in the Pacific. At night the war workers and GIs blew off steam in the bars and nightclubs that lined both sides of the street.

Before, during, and after the war, Slim Jenkins Café—situated near the railyards, at the corner of Seventh and Wood Streets— reigned as the premier nightspot, drawing well-dressed couples for white-tablecloth dining and entertainment, featuring top performers like Duke Ellington, the Ink Spots, Billie Holiday, Nat King Cole, Earl "Fatha" Hines, Sarah Vaughan, and B.B. King. And by the early 1960s, other popular Seventh Street clubs were competing for dominance with Jenkins, including Esther's Orbit Room, run by a former Jenkins waitress named Esther Mabry, whose lounge featured a new generation of acts, like Etta James, Aretha Franklin, and Al Green.

By 1967, Oakland's Harlem of the West was under stress, as the railroads and shipyards shed jobs and urban renewal bureaucrats targeted the area for redevelopment. The neighborhood had already been bisected by the towering, two-tier Cypress Freeway, and beginning in 1960, a once vibrant twelve-square-block area south of Seventh Street, including four hundred Victorian homes, was razed to accommodate a sprawling new US Postal Service distribution center. Finally, in the midsixties, construction also began on the West Oakland station and tracks for the Bay Area Rapid Transit monorail—whose looming shadow and loud racket would eventually doom Seventh Street.

But during the early months of that year, as the Black Panthers were opening their first office and beginning their street patrols, Seventh Street was still the place to step out on a Saturday night. Well-dressed African American couples dined, drank, and danced in the many venues whose neon signs lit up the street. The entertainment district was also a magnet for cruising Oakland Police Department cops, who were quick to jump on any perceived infraction or even display of exuberance.

It was about nine o'clock on a Saturday night when a small fleet of vehicles carrying fourteen Black Panthers, including one woman, approached the wide, busy boulevard. Seale spotted an Oakland police car blocking traffic on Seventh Street, with a white cop placing a Black man under arrest. Grabbing his walkie-talkie, Seale barked at Newton, who was riding in another car, "Huey! Huey! A block away, a police car is on the right. We should park—park!"

The pack of Panthers all exited their cars and began marching in formation toward the police car. They were all armed, some with rifles, some wearing handguns. Newton was carrying an M-1 military rifle and Seale had a .45-caliber pistol. "I had to give [Huey] credit—he had done his homework [on California gun law]," Seale recalled. They knew that by law their guns could not be concealed and that long guns had to be pointed straight up or at the ground, while handguns had to be holstered. "Everyone was trained how to hold their guns. I trained them—I was military."

The Panther patrol was also in uniform, with each member wearing a black beret, leather jacket, slacks, and blue shirt—a look created by Seale, who had seen Newton wearing a similar outfit one day on the Merritt campus, minus the beret. "That came from us watching an old World War II movie about the French underground," Seale said. "The French resistance fighters wore black berets."

A crowd of thirty or more men and women from the clubs and bars began gathering, staring in wonder at the spectacle of young, armed, neatly uniformed African Americans surrounding a white policeman. Leaving a liquor store, an elderly man marveled aloud at the sight before him: "What the heck is this here? What they got, sticks in their hands?"

"Them ain't no sticks, Jimmy," a tall, Black man told him. "Them goddam guns, man."

It was at this point that the Oakland cop looked up from his seat in the car and noticed his dilemma. The crowd began to disperse, sensing that the policeman would quickly assert his authority. But Newton spun around and addressed them. "No one leave. You have a right to stand here. We've checked the law." They had a right to observe "police officers who've been brutalizing our people in the community. So no one leave. The law is on your side."

Newton was the designated speaker that night. He and Seale realized that in high-tension confrontations like this, only one person should speak for the group. It would be different at rallies, where Seale would emerge as the one to fire up the crowds. He was comfortable in the spotlight, and he had a strong, rat-tat-tat delivery, whereas Newton's voice was high-pitched and his public speaking stiff and didactic. "I would pace around, I was going to keep your attention," said Seale. "Not only had I been a stand-up comedian, I'd been a jazz drummer—I knew how to be on a stage, I knew about this, how to communicate with people. I'm theatrical, I integrate the intellectual with the emotional."

But in potentially explosive situations like this one on Seventh Street, Huey Newton could be surprisingly focused and self-controlled. Even his voice sounded more firm and commanding.

By now the Oakland cop seemed more angry than afraid. In a loud voice he growled at Newton, "You have no right to observe me." But Newton was prepared to cite the law with precision. The police officer was wrong, Newton informed him. "A California State Supreme Court ruling states that every citizen has a right to stand and observe a police officer carrying out their duty as long as the citizen stands a reasonable distance away."

Seale recalled Newton's effect on the crowd—a handsome, fit, young Black man in a slick outfit boldly asserting his legal rights, with a rifle in his hands. "Some sister was standing on the sidewalk, watching all this, and she says, 'Well, go ahead and tell it!' She was a well-dressed woman coming out of one of those nightclubs down there, like Slim Jenkins." Seventh Street was hopping, and the Black Panthers were quickly becoming the main act.

The cop was still locked in his verbal duel with Newton. "Is that gun loaded?" he asked.

"If I know it's loaded, that's good enough," Newton shot back, citing another court ruling. "You cannot remove my property from me . . . so step back," he sharply ordered, sensing the cop was about to make a move toward him. "You cannot touch my weapon."

Again, the policeman asked if Newton's rifle was loaded.

In reply, Newton jacked a round into his weapon's chamber, still making sure to keep it pointed at the ground. "Like I said, if I know it's loaded, that's good enough."

"Man," exclaimed the tall man in the crowd, "what kind of Negroes are these?"

When Newton cocked his gun, Seale recalled, "so does everybody else with long guns, about seven more people—clack, clack, clack, clack, clack, clack."

The cop knew he had to retreat. He carefully loaded his arrestee into the rear of his patrol car, making sure to protect his head, and then sped off.

Now it was Bobby Seale's turn to speak. While several of his soldiers passed out copies of the party's ten-point platform, Seale addressed the astounded crowd. "Ladies and gentlemen, my name is Bobby Seale and I'm chairman of the Black Panther Party. This is my friend Huey Newton—he's the minister of defense of the Black Panther Party. We are organizing in the community and we're going to have voter registration programs. We're meeting tomorrow at our North Oakland headquarters, at 5624 Grove Street. You come there tomorrow at 2 p.m. and we can explain more to you about the Black Panther Party."

To this day, Seale insists that the Panthers' intensely dangerous street confrontations with police were meant to raise their community's consciousness, to inspire Black Americans to take political action, not to incite a bloodbath. "We were not thugs—we knew our law," he stated. "And I knew our political goal and our strategy was that if we could capture the imagination of the people, then I could organize them and unify people—register people to vote and take over the city government."

But like guns introduced in a stage play, firearms assume their own inevitable logic in political life. As dramatist Anton Chekhov advised, "One must never place a loaded rifle on the stage if it isn't going to go off. It's wrong to make promises you don't mean to keep."

Among the twenty or so people who showed up at the Black Panthers' office the day after the Seventh Street showdown, only about three or four joined the party, recalled Seale. "You don't have to carry a gun to be a member of the Black Panther Party," Seale stressed to the newcomers that day. "It's not about that." But some people were still afraid to get involved. "It was dangerous—because we were out there with guns," acknowledged Seale in retrospect.

Conversely, others who came into the storefront headquarters were too gung-ho about the Panthers' display of firepower. "Anybody who walked into the office talking about wanting to shoot white people, I'd say, 'Sit down!' And I'd start educating them. One guy came in and said, 'The white man's the devil!' And I said, 'That's totally unscientific. . . . The Nation of Islam is over there.' My ideology was more the Declaration of Independence and the Constitution of the United States of America."

But the Black Panthers' willingness to wield guns on city streets—to directly confront violent, abusive police officers with their own arsenal—did indeed capture the Black community's imagination. Seale knew the Panthers couldn't start electing more Black officials and forcing America to live up to its principles unless they were willing to risk their lives. It was strictly legal when the Black Panthers began their armed self-defense patrols. But it was a combustible tactic in 1967 Oakland—a declaration of war as far as the city's racist, hair-trigger police department was concerned.

There were other occasions throughout the Black Panthers' brief but action-packed history when Huey Newton engaged in similar high-wire confrontations. In another early incident outside the party headquarters, the minister of defense faced off with a belligerent group of Oakland cops, while several other Panthers—including Seale—observed the organization's rules of engagement and looked silently on. At one point in the rapidly escalating standoff, Newton, gripping his M-1, snarled, "If you try to shoot at me . . . I'm going to shoot back at you, swine." This showdown also ended, miraculously, without bloodshed. But Newton couldn't be controlled, and he told his partner that "we might not ever come back home one day."

Seale was the older and wiser and more grounded man. But he knew the Black Panthers had seized the time with Huey Newton's "crazy" courage. "I'm with you, Huey," he replied that day. "Fuck it, I'm with you."

IN LATE FEBRUARY 1967, the Black Panthers' daring reputation grew in the Bay Area as armed members of the organization
escorted Betty Shabazz, Malcolm X's widow, from San Francisco
International Airport to a meeting in the city with the editors of
left-wing *Ramparts* magazine. At one point in front of the magazine offices, Huey Newton again got into a chilling face-off with
a policeman. Gripping a shotgun, Newton walked directly up to a
menacing San Francisco cop, who had a hand on his gun. "OK, you
big, fat, racist pig—draw your gun," Newton challenged him, as the
other police officers fanned out of the range of fire. The cop finally
backed down, and since Shabazz had already been whisked away
by then, Newton and his armed entourage peacefully dispersed.

In April, the Panthers raised the stakes with police again when
they took up the case of Denzil Dowell, a twenty-two-year-old
construction worker who was shotgunned to death from behind by
a deputy sheriff in Richmond, a poor, heavily Black community a
few miles north of Oakland. A predominantly white jury ruled it
justifiable homicide because law enforcement authorities claimed
Dowell was in the process of committing a robbery. But Dowell's
family produced conflicting evidence that indicated the young man
was holding up his hands when he was shot in the back and head.
His mother called the shooting "murder" and the family summoned
the Panthers, who began organizing protest rallies against police
violence and protecting the dead man's relatives from harassment.

One Sunday afternoon, a lawman barged uninvited into the
home of Dowell's mother to interrogate her, an intrusion that was
not unusual for the grieving family. This time, however, Newton
was visiting, and when he saw the deputy push his way into the
house, he jumped up with his shotgun and confronted the tres-
passer. The officer beat a hasty retreat to his car and drove away.

The next month, the Black Panthers burst into the national spotlight with a brazen display of firepower at the California state capitol in Sacramento. With the Panthers' armed police patrols in mind, a Republican state assemblyman named Donald Mulford from the wealthy Piedmont district of Oakland had introduced a bill outlawing the carrying of loaded firearms in public. Legislators in California and across the nation had never expressed concern about heavily armed white militias, but when a militant Black group began displaying guns, lawmakers like Mulford flew into action. Realizing that the Mulford bill was a direct challenge to their core tactic, Black Panther leaders decided to pick up their guns and lobby state legislators.

On the afternoon of May 2, 1967, a caravan of thirty Black Panthers—twenty-four men and six women—cruised up to the majestic, domed capitol and marched into the building, carrying their guns in accordance with the law at the time. The armed group was led by Bobby Seale, who—doubting Newton's ability to keep his cool—had talked him into staying in Oakland "to handle any press in case something went wrong." A frenzied flock of newspaper reporters and TV camera crews quickly surrounded the Panther contingent, and the whole swarm of people barged onto the assembly floor instead of the spectator gallery where Seale thought they were headed. Security guards quickly pushed them back out again, but an agitated Assemblyman Mulford announced that a "serious incident has just occurred."

Standing outside the state assembly, surrounded by the media scrum, Seale realized it was also the Panthers' political moment. He delivered a powerful, prepared statement, charging that California legislators were trying to keep "Black people disarmed and powerless at the very same time that racist police agencies throughout the country are intensifying the terror, brutality, murder, and repression of Black people." Then, showing how far beyond the civil rights movement the Panthers had leapt—not just in their open display of loaded weapons but in their ideology—Seale connected the enslavement and Jim Crow brutalization of African Americans to "the genocide practiced on the American Indians . . . the dropping of atomic bombs on Hiroshima and Nagasaki, and now the cowardly massacre in Vietnam." These massive acts of violence grew from "one policy," Seale told the press huddle: the war waged by "the racist power structure of America" on "people of color."

Assemblyman Mulford won the battle when his bill passed the legislature and was signed into law by California governor Ronald Reagan, who had scurried away from a picnic with schoolchildren on the capitol lawn when the troupe of armed African Americans showed up that day. Newspaper headlines screamed, "The Capitol Is Invaded!" The "invasion" also drew breathless news reports on network TV. But the Black Panthers won the propaganda war in their community. For many young African Americans, the Black Panther action was inspiring. Party membership surged.

Interviewed by the *New York Times*, twenty-two-year-old Billy John Carr—once a Berkeley High star athlete and now scrounging to support his wife and child—explained why he joined the Black Panthers right after the Sacramento show of force. "As far as I'm concerned it's beautiful that we finally got an organization that don't walk around singing. I'm not for all this talking stuff. When things start happening, I'll be ready to die if that's necessary, and it's important that we have somebody around to organize us."

Loaded guns had made the Black Panther Party, but now they could no longer legally use them to challenge cops. Bobby Seale was not fazed by this new ban, because he knew they had already captured Black America's attention. Seale was ready to pivot to politically mobilizing the community. As for Huey Newton, he knew the law inside and out, but had never felt bound by it. In October of that year, Newton was jailed after what seemed increasingly inevitable—a shootout with Oakland police, back on Seventh Street, that left one officer dead and Newton seriously wounded. Facing the death penalty, Newton became the central cause of the

Black Panther Party, with "Free Huey" rallies spreading across the nation.

Newton's absence from Black Panther leadership should have been liberating for Seale, who no longer had to monitor his partner's unpredictable behavior. But by then, the Panthers had a third charismatic figure at the pinnacle of the party, an ex-convict and celebrity author. His name was Eldridge Cleaver.

ELDRIDGE CLEAVER ALREADY had a reputation as the next Malcolm X when he was released in December 1966 from the California state prison system, where the thirty-one-year-old had spent the formative years of his life educating himself in prison libraries. Evolving from a convicted drug dealer and rapist to a Black Muslim and finally a Marxist revolutionary, Cleaver had written a collection of searing essays behind bars that would become an instant bestseller when published as *Soul on Ice* in 1968. The book established Cleaver's reputation as that rare phenomenon, a rising star in the Black literary firmament with undeniable street credibility. It also added to his already iconic reputation at *Ramparts*, the radical, San Francisco–based monthly that had hired him as a staff writer directly out of prison.

Robert Scheer, who had his own reputation as a prominent Berkeley radical and *Ramparts* editorial overseer (with buccaneering, eye-patched Warren Hinckle), recognized Cleaver's writing talent and expected him to become a journalistic star for the magazine. But Cleaver knew he was destined to become a Black Panther as soon as he saw Huey Newton in action, backing down the trigger-happy cop in the *Ramparts* office. *Work out, soul brother!* Cleaver rejoiced in his mind. *You're the baddest motherfucker I've ever seen.*

Cleaver joined the party, though he had to keep it secret for a while because his parole restrictions prevented him from becoming a member of a gun-wielding organization. But he was soon being introduced as the Black Panther minister of information, and with Newton behind bars and Seale fighting his own legal battle stemming from the Sacramento demonstration, Cleaver found himself thrust into the spotlight.

Cleaver's public speaking skills rivaled those of Seale, and he was a major draw—as well as a target of authorities—on college campuses. Like the other Panther leaders, Cleaver opposed the racial confines of Black nationalism, appealing to a broad, young, multiracial crowd. He was a cocky champion of Black masculinity, writing in *Soul on Ice*, "We shall have our manhood. . . . We shall have it or the earth will be leveled by our attempt to get it." But he did his chest-beating with ironic style, even humor. In a speech at Stanford University, he challenged "sissy" and "coward" Governor Reagan to a duel with the weapon of his choice, even a marshmallow. "I'll beat him to death with a marshmallow," Cleaver crowed.

Onstage, the handsome, goateed Cleaver possessed a cool vibe. He had a jazzy type of delivery, sometimes closing his eyes as he spoke, like a musician blowing his horn. He had a silver stud in one ear, and he often wore shades. His father had been a piano player, and there were preachers in his family line.

Cleaver was a big, well-built man with the physical prowess of the boxer he'd been in prison. His wife, Kathleen Cleaver, and he made a very photogenic couple. The daughter of a foreign diplomat and a mathematician, Kathleen had been raised around the world and educated in elite liberal arts schools. Trained as an SNCC activist, she also knew how to work the media. She had a self-assured demeanor and looked like a model; with her Afro halo, hoop earrings, black turtleneck sweaters, and miniskirts, she cut a riveting figure at party press conferences. Only twenty-one and nearly ten years younger than Cleaver when she met him at a SNCC conference in Tennessee, Kathleen was immediately impressed by his physical stature and his aura. "He was like Richard Pryor as a Communist," she said, laughing, years later. "And he looked like Muhammad Ali."

Bobby Seale knew he couldn't write, and he relied on the word-smith Cleaver to craft the party's message, in speeches as well as the pages of the Black Panther newspaper. But Seale soon realized that Cleaver, like Newton, was a force beyond his control. Cleaver immediately recognized himself in Newton—the outlaw bravado that was more than just a pose. "Huey P. Newton was a gun-toting gangster." That's how Cleaver summed up the Black Panther co-founder many years later, not long before his death in 1998. "But that's not all he was."

The same could be said of Cleaver—a brilliant writer and speaker, with a strain of criminal madness. That's what it took to make a rev-olution, Cleaver and Newton both believed. Guns were more than just a stage device to them. They were not just props, but essential instruments of power.

Cleaver and Newton were the heroic realization of Fanon's dream, the fusion of lumpen lethality and intellectual prowess. But Cleaver also had a literary glamour that Newton lacked, hailed while still a prison writer by the likes of Norman Mailer. Cleaver was also a year older than even Seale, whom Kathleen Cleaver called "a father figure" to younger Panthers, who were mostly in their late teens and twenties. Seale soon realized he couldn't guide or lead Cleaver; he was a dark star beyond the chairman's reach.

Cleaver began threatening armed warfare in cities across Amer-ica if Newton, who was facing the death penalty for the murder of Oakland policeman John Frey, was convicted. Seale was incensed by Cleaver's escalating rhetoric. "He'd be writing things in the news-paper like, 'Pigs come into our community, 'cause we have some-thing for you.' And I'd say, 'Eldridge, we supposed to be taking defensive positions—not offensive.' He'd put out shit like, 'If you convict Huey Newton, the sky's the limit.' That [was] offensive to me."

When Newton was convicted of the lesser charge of volun-tary manslaughter on September 8, 1968, there was rage on both sides—among Oakland cops as well as Panthers. Expecting trouble that night, Seale ordered all party members to stay off the city's streets, waving away Cleaver's complaints about the peace edict. "And about midnight that night," Seale recalled, "two Oakland police got frustrated because the streets were clear and they shot up the window of the Black Panther Party headquarters. They couldn't help themselves. Because they were all ready to kill themselves some Black Panthers that night. I protected my party members. I didn't go around killing people or beating people up."

But Cleaver kept arguing for pushing the cops out of the Black community through armed force. And he found support from Newton, who was still behind bars while his manslaughter conviction was being appealed. According to Seale, "Eldridge wrote some executive mandate: 'From now on any party members with technical equipment, they must use it or leave the party.' He told Huey he wanted to do this and Huey said do it. I went to see Huey in jail and said, 'What are you talking about? [Our] principle is that if we get in a fight, we take the arrest, if we can take the arrest.' I was talking with him through the little window in jail. I said, 'I'm not going to organize people and then have them just jump up and start shooting.' So they got a shotgun and a motherfucking pistol—the goddamn power structure is armed enough to get all the motherfucking members killed."

Cleaver exuded danger, and his magnetism initially drew the admiration of celebrities, including Marlon Brando, who was not just a trendy revolutionary tourist, but a sincere supporter of African American and Native American liberation. Kathleen Cleaver recalled the day that Brando, seeking inspiration for a new movie role, visited their home—a large, one-room studio in San Francisco's Castro district.

"He was studying for his role in *Burn!*," a 1969 historical drama by Italian director Gillo Pontecorvo about a slave revolt on a Caribbean island. "We had a round table in our apartment and Eldridge was at one end and Marlon Brando was at the other end and there were some other Panthers. Brando was staring—I realized later he was studying a role. I just [thought] this is weird. It was like he was trying to inhale Eldridge. [By the way], I think the movie is brilliant. I've seen it many times. Most people who know Brando haven't seen this one, because it's about revolution."

Brando was a loyal financial supporter of the Black Panthers, Seale said, but Cleaver drove him away from the party. While in prison, Cleaver had become enamored of the dire philosophy of Russian anarchists and nihilists. Writing in the party newspaper, he drew heavily from one scorching manifesto, *The Catechism of a Revolutionary*, penned in 1869 by Sergey Nechayev (reportedly with input from leading anarchist Mikhail Bakunin). The opening lines of Nechayev's manifesto set the stark terms for the avenging angels of the revolution: "The revolutionary is a doomed man. . . . He is [the civilized world's] merciless enemy and continues to inhabit it with only one purpose—to destroy it."

Brando was appalled when he read these drastic sentiments in the Black Panther newspaper, as channeled by Cleaver. "One day Brando called me up," Seale recalled, "and said, 'Bob, what is this? You're talking about killing your family for the revolution? Killing your mother and father?' I said, 'What are you talking about?' 'Well it's in your *Catechism of a Revolutionary*. I'm not going to support any shit like this.'"

The movie star had been wiring thousands of dollars to the Panthers whenever Seale phoned him to request a donation—$5,000 here, $3,000 there. But the money stopped flowing from him after he read Cleaver's violent rhetoric.

Seale "bawled Eldridge out," but Cleaver was too committed to his violent revolutionary path to bend to the chairman's will. Seale thought differently of Kathleen. "She was a very stable sister, she knew what was happening. And she understood when I argued with Eldridge where I was coming from." But Seale's problems with Eldridge were nonstop. "Oh, my God—these are the headaches that I had."

The internal Panther conflicts came to a head around Martin

Luther King. Cleaver regarded the civil rights movement's fore-most leader as soft. "We saw ourselves as providing backbone that was missing from [King's] nonviolent movement," he later stated. But Seale had greatly admired the preacher from the day he saw him at Oakland Municipal Auditorium. In early 1968, the Rev-erend Ralph Abernathy, King's deputy in the Southern Christian Leadership Conference, made a surprising phone call to Seale.

"'I'm very honored that you're calling,'" Seale recalled telling Abernathy. "And he said, 'Well, Dr. King had me call you. We have put together more than a hundred Black community organizations in different cities all across America. And Dr. King wanted to know if you and the Black Panther Party would be willing to work with us . . . and to help organize for an upcoming Poor People's March that we're going to do later this year?' And I said, 'Yes, yes!'"

King was the nation's apostle of nonviolent change, but he was building a broad coalition for his march on Washington, including militant groups like the Black Panthers, to force the federal gov-ernment to stop the Vietnam War and divert funds to domestic social programs. The eagerness of leaders as different as King and Seale to work together on ambitious protest campaigns like the Poor People's March shows the potential for a much broader pro-gressive movement—for a dynamic turning point, anyway—before political assassinations and repression robbed these movements of much of their optimism.

Seale's warm feelings of solidarity with King were not shared by Cleaver, however. "Before he realized I [was building] this co-alition, Eldridge put Dr. King in our newspaper as a bootlicker! I said, 'Eldridge, you cannot be putting stuff like this about Dr. King in our newspaper.' And he said, 'Well, all that nonviolent stuff, blah, blah.' And I said, 'What you talking about? I got a coalition with him. The Black Panther Party is about defending our consti-tutional, democratic, civil rights—the right to peaceful protest is a constitutional, fucking human right. We defend that. So we defend Dr. Martin Luther King's rights.' I said, 'Eldridge, we got coalitions with white, left, radical organizations—and they have peaceful marches too.' And he says, 'Yeah, but that's different.' And I say, 'It's not different.'"

Despite his critical views of King, Cleaver felt compelled to take action against the police after the civil rights leader was assassinated in Memphis, Tennessee, on April 4, 1968. On the evening of April 6, as Cleaver was leaving the *Ramparts* office to drive across the Bay Bridge to Oakland, his editor, Bob Scheer—who by now also considered himself Eldridge's friend—warned him to remain a journalist that night and not get thrown back in prison. In the wake of King's assassination, dozens of cities were set on fire by outraged Black protesters, but Seale and his Panther deputies worked hard with civil rights leaders to make sure that San Francisco and Oakland stayed relatively peaceful. However, Cleaver again took the opposite line. He felt that unless the Panthers struck back against police—the front line of racial oppression in the US—the group would lose credibility with African Americans. Cleaver was able to rally about a dozen other Panthers to take up arms, including Bobby Hutton, the seventeen-year-old kid who was Seale's first Panther recruit.

That night, an Oakland police car came under withering fire while patrolling Union Street. Officer Richard Jensen was riddled with thirteen bullets and his partner Nolan Darnell was shot in the shoulder. Cleaver later maintained he had been ambushed by the cops, but it was he who had declared war that night. "Hell, I didn't even know who Eldridge Cleaver was!" Darnell later emphasized.

In 1980, a dozen years later, Cleaver publicly admitted for the first time—to Kate Coleman, a reporter for *New West* magazine—that he had ambushed the police car. "I believed in 1968 that it was necessary to drive the police out of the community with guns," Cleaver explained to Coleman, one of the few progressive journalists at the time willing to write honestly about the Black Panthers.

Police reinforcements roared into the neighborhood, and while Jensen and Darnell were rushed by ambulance to a nearby hospital,

Cleaver and Hutton took refuge in the basement of a house. The ensuing firefight turned West Oakland into a war zone, and looking back at the shootout near the end of his life, Cleaver still expressed a sense of exhilaration. "I will tell anybody that that was the first experience of freedom that I had," Cleaver stated in an interview with a producer for PBS's *Frontline*. "I was free for an hour and a half because during that time, the repressive forces couldn't put their hand on me because we were shooting it out with them for an hour and a half."

Finally forced to surrender by a tear-gas barrage, Cleaver stripped to his underwear and warned "Lil' Bobby" to do the same before he gave himself up, so the cops could see he had no concealed weapons. Hutton came out wearing only his pants and with his hands raised, but police immediately executed him, ripping apart the teenager's body with twelve shots. Cleaver miraculously escaped death that night. One cop later reminded the Panther leader that he had stuck his pistol against Cleaver's head. "I was already squeezing the trigger," the policeman recounted. "I was going to blow your head off because three officers had gotten wounded . . . [but] something told me not to do it."

In the police van afterward, two cops began severely beating Cleaver "and I have no doubt that they meant to kill me." But a superior officer listening over the police radio commanded them to stop. Cleaver was badly injured but he survived the battle that night. Freed on bail, and facing three counts of assault and attempted-murder charges, Cleaver fled to Cuba and then Algeria, where he was joined by Kathleen.

Young Bobby Hutton was canonized as a martyr by the Black Panthers and white radicals. Seale organized a military-like funeral for the murdered boy, followed by a rally near Oakland's Lake Merritt featuring a short, emotional speech by Brando, who still felt connected to the militant group. "That could've been my son lying there," the movie star told the crowd of about one thousand people.

But in his heart, Seale knew the Oakland shootout should never have happened. "There was no discipline [that night]," he said years later. "One thing for sure, you had a lot of people coming to the party and they didn't understand guns and weapons. They think it's just some power, baby, and acting the fool."

Meanwhile, the man who had led Lil' Bobby to his death was in exile. The Algerian government hailed Cleaver as a revolutionary hero, even giving him offices in Algiers to establish the first international headquarters of the Black Panther Party. Algeria still had the glow of its long liberation struggle against France, after finally winning independence in 1962. And revolutionary dignitaries from around the world, as well as journalists, came to Algiers to meet with Cleaver—among them Bob Scheer.

White radicals, a few of whom helped Cleaver flee the United States, generally held a worshipful attitude toward the Black Panthers, readily overlooking the brutal behavior of leaders like Cleaver and Newton. Some New Leftists, like the Weather Underground, went so far as to anoint the Panthers "the vanguard of the revolution." San Francisco Bay Area radicals like Scheer and Tom Hayden were less inclined to glorify the Panthers, in part because they worked more closely with them on political projects. But many still excused the behavior of charismatic figures like Cleaver, long after their cruelty and criminality were exposed by Bay Area journalists like Paul Avery and Kate Coleman. (The fact that David Horowitz—who edited *Ramparts* after Scheer and then skidded from the far left to the loony right—became an extreme critic of the Black Panthers didn't help the credibility of the group's adversaries.)

One of the most successful and astute journalists produced by the New Left, Scheer continues to defend Cleaver to this day. "I never saw the evil Eldridge," he said. "I never saw him pistol-whip anybody. He was very disciplined as a writer at *Ramparts*. I was Eldridge's editor and I came to be his friend, and I cared about his well-being. I worried about him going back to jail—and I did see him as a political prisoner, and I was fully convinced that he would be killed if he went back to prison.

"Look, I never believed that the Panthers and Eldridge were the vanguard of the revolution. I don't recall a time in my entire conscious life when I ever thought America was going to have a violent progressive revolution. I respected him—more as a writer. I certainly didn't respect him as a political organizer or leader. In a certain way, I didn't take his politics seriously."

On the other hand, Scheer went on, "taking those guns to the [California] legislature to challenge the double standard [about gun rights], standing up to the police—all that showed physical courage. I mean thuggery, violence—the whole ghetto life is laced with that. But I part company with those who see Eldridge as just a showman. Nobody had more real-life experience about oppression."

Scheer had recently seen *Whose Streets?*—the 2017 documentary about the Ferguson, Missouri, uprising over the police killing of eighteen-year-old African American Michael Brown. The seasoned journalist was wrestling to put Eldridge Cleaver in the context of Black people's long, agonizing struggle for equal rights.

"I think Eldridge thought that unless you create a situation of mayhem and chaos, the system that was inherently oppressive and uncompromising would win. And he wasn't the first person to believe that. I suspect that Huey felt similar. Eldridge thought that all this protest [in the 1960s] was going to disappear and they were just going to beat us down. And this comes up in this movie about Ferguson—*Whose Streets?* If we don't really push back, we're going to be betrayed."

At Black Panther rallies, the female party members would sing, "Revolution has come, time to pick up the gun," while the uniformed men, pumping their fists in the air, would respond, "Off the pigs!" Newton and Cleaver had tried to set off the revolution by engaging policemen in battle on the streets of Oakland. Now Newton sat behind bars in a California state prison in San Luis Obispo, and Cleaver was exiled in North Africa. Both men had woefully miscalculated the revolutionary moment. Cleaver's calls for armed revolution in the US from his Algerian compound sounded more and more forlorn as time passed.

Rid of the party's two most reckless leaders, Bobby Seale angrily mourned their loss in public. But he was now freed to pursue his own idea of revolution—a militant but peaceful confrontation with power that began with community mobilization.

BLACK PANTHER MEMBERSHIP surged again with the outrage in the Black community over King's assassination. No longer just a Bay Area phenomenon, party chapters sprang up in Los Angeles, Chicago, and New York, and in smaller cities across the country. "They killed the last chance for peace—I had no more use for them," recalled William Calhoun, who performed as a young man in a Black Panther soul band called the Lumpen.

Using his skills as an antipoverty organizer, Seale immediately began harnessing this new energy. With Newton still in prison and Cleaver a fugitive from justice, Seale now shifted the Panthers away from armed battle with the police to community programs designed to forge closer bonds with impoverished Black families. In September 1968, the party announced plans to launch a Free Breakfast for Children program in Oakland. Beginning operation in St. Augustine's Episcopal Church in January 1969, the breakfast program became an immediate success, feeding 11 kids on opening day and 135 by the end of the first week. By November, the Panthers reported they were feeding thousands of children a day in twenty-three cities across America, including Seattle, Chicago, Des Moines, Kansas City, and New York.

Although the Free Breakfast programs became the party's most prominent face of community assistance, Panther chapters in various cities also opened liberation schools, legal aid offices, free health clinics, housing cooperatives, and other social services. During this period, women took a larger role in operating the party, particularly at the grassroots level. "One of the ironies of the Black Panther Party," historian Clayborne Carson has observed, "is that the image is the black male with the [leather] jacket and gun, but the reality is the majority of the rank and file by the end of the sixties are women."

Ericka Huggins, a rising young Black Panther in the Los Angeles and then New Haven chapters, later recalled, "I was very young but I realized I had to step forward after so many people in the party were jailed or killed. We worked nineteen hours a day, but we were young. . . . My mind was expanding, my heart was opening. I was pushing my body to its physical limits."

Seale said he encouraged this growing female activism within the party. He recalled the time when visiting a Panther chapter, the men were served "steaming platters of fried chicken and soul food" by the women members, who "then stood along the wall while the men prepared to dig in."

Bobby stopped the feast, declaring "It wasn't right." He said to the women, "You did the work here, and these guys are going to eat the best parts of the chicken. I hereby declare that's over."

The golden era of the Black Panthers under Bobby Seale, however, was short-lived. In July 1969, FBI chief J. Edgar Hoover—the secret police commissar whose autocratic powers extended throughout ten presidencies—publicly declared that among all of the Black liberation groups, "the Black Panther Party, without question, represents the greatest threat to the internal security of the country." By then, Hoover had already unleashed the full powers of his clandestine counterintelligence program (COINTELPRO) against the group. In an internal FBI memo written by Hoover in September 1968, he revealed plans to "accelerate" the bureau's offensive against the Panthers. FBI field agents would be instructed to "thwart and disrupt" the party, creating "factionalism" and "suspicion" within party ranks and fomenting "opposition" to the group from the Black community at large.

Hoover's ruthless subterfuge had a murderous impact on the Black Panthers. In January 1969, John Huggins, the twenty-three-year-old head of the Panthers' Los Angeles chapter and Ericka's husband, was gunned down—along with fellow Panther leader Bunchy Carter—on the UCLA campus by members of the rival US Organization, a Black nationalist group that the FBI was inciting to violence.

Encouraged by the FBI and President Richard Nixon's administration, which took office the same month as Huggins's murder, police launched dozens of violent raids on Black Panther offices and homes throughout the country. The most notorious of these assaults took place in Chicago in December 1969, when young Panther leader Fred Hampton—the target of a COINTELPRO campaign—was shot to death in his bed early one morning by a death squad operating in conjunction with the Chicago police and the FBI.

By 1969, Bobby Seale was leading the Black Panthers away from armed struggle to community service. But Hoover was increasingly concerned about these peaceful projects. "No aspect of the Black Panther program was of greater concern to the FBI than the Free Breakfast for Children Program, which fostered widespread support for the Panthers' revolutionary politics," observed historians Joshua Bloom and Waldo E. Martin Jr. When the agent in charge of the FBI's San Francisco office suggested that the bureau should not attack the Panthers' community programs, Hoover tartly corrected him, writing, "You have obviously missed the point. . . . One of our primary aims . . . is to keep this group isolated from the moderate black and white community which may support it."

In August 1969, Seale was arrested and later driven by federal marshals across the country to Chicago, where he was to stand trial with other members of the Chicago Eight on conspiracy charges related to the 1968 Democratic convention antiwar protests. The Black Panthers had taken a strong antidraft and antiwar stand, but Seale had spoken only briefly during the Chicago protests and had not helped organize them. Still, the Nixon administration was trying to decapitate the radical resistance movements with one swing of the judicial scythe, so Seale was lumped together with white New Left leaders including Tom Hayden, Rennie Davis, Abbie Hoffman, and Jerry Rubin. After insisting on the right to have his lawyer, Charles Garry, in court, who was delayed in California for medical reasons, Seale ended up gagged and shackled on the orders of tyrannical judge Julius Hoffman—which evoked shocking national flashbacks to the slavery era—and was later severed from the case.

In 1970, Seale's legal ordeal continued in New Haven, Connecticut, where he was put on trial with Ericka Huggins and framed for ordering the torture and murder of a nineteen-year-old Panther named Alex Rackley. The execution-style killing had actually been orchestrated by a Panther whom party leaders suspected of being an FBI undercover agent—a man Seale believed he had thrown out of the party. Eventually the New Haven jury deadlocked, after leaning heavily toward acquitting Seale and Huggins, and in May 1971 the judge dismissed the case against both of them.

By then, the relentless FBI and police war on the Black Panthers had taken a heavy toll. "Never had I experienced so much death, month after month after month," Huggins later recalled. "The police and the government were bent on wiping us out. When you skirt that close to losing your life, you don't take any moments for granted. My husband and my best friend were murdered. Three months later I was arrested for a murder I didn't commit. I didn't get out for two and a half years. By then my child was three years old."

But it was not the vicious repression that finally broke the Black Panthers. It was bitter internal dissension. And at the heart of this madness was Huey Newton, Bobby Seale's brilliant and volatile brother—the Panther he'd never been able to tame.

WHEN BOBBY SEALE returned to Oakland in 1972 after nearly two years behind bars, he used the new fame and respect he'd acquired in the courtrooms of Chicago and New Haven to extend the Black Panthers' coalition with other movement groups. United Farm Workers union leader Cesar Chavez had already generated controversy by endorsing Seale's largely symbolic 1968 campaign for California State Assembly, as a way of encouraging the Panthers' shift to nonviolent politics. After his release from prison, Seale continued working with protest leaders—including some of his white codefendants in the Chicago Eight trial—to mount demonstrations against President Nixon at the 1972 Republican National Convention in Miami. And Seale began hanging out in New York with ex-Beatle John Lennon, who was becoming increasingly involved with radical causes.

Seale emphasized that the Black Panthers strongly believed in multiracial coalitions with other radical and progressive groups. "Abbie Hoffman and Jerry Rubin [the Yippie leaders on trial with Seale in Chicago] were great," the Panther leader recalled. "I liked Tom [Hayden] too—he was just more of an intellectual. I liked all of them.

"John [Lennon] got in touch with me and took me on the *Mike Douglas Show* [in February 1972]. He was cohosting the [afternoon talk] show for an entire week. So that's how I got to know him. After that, whenever I hit New York, I'd go by and see John Lennon. I must have visited him and Yoko Ono four or five times."

Despite Seale's rising national stature, he was no longer in control of his own party. By then Huey Newton was sitting alone on the Black Panther throne. Released from prison in August 1970, after an appeals court overturned his involuntary-manslaughter conviction, Newton was greeted by an ecstatic crowd outside the Alameda County courthouse. Stripping off his gray prison shirt to reveal his massive, sculpted torso, the party cofounder climbed on top of a parked car and shouted to the crowd, "You have the power and the power is with the people!" But over the next two years, Newton moved relentlessly to consolidate absolute power within the Black Panther Party.

For security reasons, Newton moved into the twenty-fifth-floor suite of a luxurious apartment building overlooking Lake Merritt and, ironically, the Alameda County jail, where he'd spent a long stretch of his thirty-three months behind bars. He was relentlessly stalked by the Oakland police and FBI, whose agents even moved into the apartment next door to his suite. He was targeted by an FBI disinformation campaign, designed to "demythicise [*sic*] Newton, to hold him up to ridicule and tarnish his image among BPP members . . . and insinuate he has been cooperating with police to gain his release." The bureau's counterintelligence officers sent the Panther leader numerous forged memos and letters alleging that his stature within the party was eroding and trying to amplify his feelings of paranoia.

Staying mostly in his penthouse, Newton grew isolated from rank-and-file Panthers, who continued serving free meals to the needy, testing uninsured patients for sickle cell anemia, distributing free clothes and shoes, and providing other essential services to the Black community—party efforts initiated by Seale and now given the dramatic title "Survival Programs" by Newton. Slipping into the role of revolutionary messiah, Newton displayed little interest in everyday members of his party. Instead, he met in his suite with a stream of wealthy donors, white celebrities, radical journalists, and prominent intellectuals who sought audiences with him. Newton ventured outside to engage in a series of recorded conversations with the famous psychiatrist Erik Erikson before an elite Yale University audience, but he insisted on finishing the dialogue in his Oakland penthouse.

Newton's public statements became increasingly oracular and eccentric. He fancied himself a revolutionary leader of the same stature as leaders in Cuba, China, and North Vietnam. He offered to send a regiment of Black Panther warriors to Vietnam to fight the forces of US imperialism. His overture was politely declined by the government in Hanoi. He sent letters to the capitals of Israel and surrounding Arab nations containing his Middle East peace plan, which involved toppling the governments in those countries. He flew to Beijing ahead of President Nixon's historic China mission, and was granted a meeting with Premier Zhou Enlai. Upon his return to the US, Newton grandly "acknowledged the progressive leadership of our Chinese comrades in all areas of revolution."

Meanwhile, Newton was establishing his own cult of personality in Oakland, surrounding himself with sycophants, adoring light-skinned African American women, and thugs from the streets. Still a struggling reader and never a fluent writer, Newton was nonetheless given to flashes of political brilliance that he would dictate to secretaries or speak into a tape recorder. His manic late-night meetings were fueled by endless supplies of cognac and Ritalin and lines of cocaine. "It appears Newton may be on the brink of mental collapse," boasted an FBI agent in early 1971. "We must intensify our counterintelligence."

Alternative journalists like David Weir developed a mixed view of Newton. "When he was sober, Huey Newton was brilliant," said Weir, who wrote about the FBI's clandestine war on the Panthers with Lowell Bergman for *Rolling Stone*. "He had a smart attitude about white people and great political analysis. But during my last interview with him, he threatened to kill me. I was writing about a botched hit on a witness in Richmond. He was drinking cognac.

"Some Panthers did devolve into thugs, but you can't tell one side of the story without the other," Weir continued. "The Panthers did a lot of historically significant things, including standing their ground against the cops and fighting police brutality, as well as organizing the Black community. Their service programs were extraordinary. But at the same time, they were unprepared to be the 'vanguard of the revolution' the way that many radicals wanted them to be. I remember in the course of our investigation for *Rolling Stone*, Lowell and I looked at each other and said, 'Oh my God, they did a lot of bad stuff.'"

Old friends of Huey Newton like the activist-actor Peter Coyote— whose Diggers street group distributed free food and clothing in

San Francisco before the Panthers launched their own program—
thought that Newton's psyche had deteriorated badly as a result of
his prison ordeal. "There was a big difference before and after he
went to jail," Coyote remembered. "Before jail, he was a completely
charismatic guy. I felt our causes were commensurate. Afterward I
had the feeling that his bodyguards were there as much to protect
people from Huey as the other way around. Something changed
when he went to jail. I'd get these calls from him and there was this
constant refrain: 'They're putting something in my food, man.' It
was making him feel crazy, like there were bugs crawling around
under his skin.

"Without a doubt, there was a personality change after he came
out of jail. One day we were singing songs together at [Diggers
founder] Emmett Grogan's wake. A Digger woman came up to him
and said, 'Hey, Huey, it's nice to see you, baby.' And he spun and
slapped her right across the face, and spat out, 'Don't call me baby.'
He just snapped. And I said, 'What the hell, Huey! You can't do
that.' And he said, 'Well I just don't like being called baby.'"

Following his release from incarceration, Newton proudly announced in public that prison authorities had been unable to break
him. But privately he told friends that his experience behind bars
had been harrowing. He estimated that he spent eleven months in
solitary confinement in the Alameda County jail before his 1968
conviction, and twenty-two more months in solitary afterward in
California state prisons in Vacaville and San Luis Obispo. He described "the hole" in San Luis Obispo as a "torture chamber." The
solitary unit in the Alameda jailhouse was known to prisoners as
the "soul breaker," and Newton confessed that his confinement
there "nearly killed me."

"The minute I stepped inside, I wanted to beg them to let me
out," he told Elaine Brown, one of his beautiful, light-skinned
lovers and a close Panther ally. "I was ready to do anything they
wanted me to do. I didn't care about being tough. I just wanted out.
I was shaking with fear."

English historian Joe Street, who has studied the US government war on the Black Panther Party, has written, "It is inconceivable that incarceration had no [psychological] impact on Newton," citing the substantial body of medical evidence since the Black Panther era on the destructive effects of enforced isolation on prisoners' psyches. "It is impossible to disentangle Huey P. Newton's later life from his prison experience, indicating that he, and possibly the entire African American radical political movement, lived in the shadow of the soul breaker."

While he did suffer a torturous experience behind bars and a psychological warfare campaign directed at him by law enforcement agencies, it is also true that Huey Newton had been known as "crazy" ever since his youth on the streets of West Oakland. "Niggers on the street don't like 'pretty niggers,'" Newton confided one day to Elaine Brown. "They called me 'pretty' and 'high-yellow nigger.'" Young Newton became such a target of neighborhood abuse that he was afraid to leave his house. A streetwise older brother set him straight. He had to make *others* fear *him*. "By the time I became a teenager, I was challenging the first fool who looked at me wrong, and walking around with an ice pick in a paper bag. . . . I earned a reputation as 'crazy.'" Later, it had taken this same insane courage for Newton to again and again confront racist cops on the streets of Oakland, until one such confrontation inevitably erupted in gunfire.

Now, ruling the Black Panther empire from his lofty lair, Newton suppressed his own rampant fears by snorting more lines of "the white witch" and making everyone fear *him*. Accused of going soft by Eldridge Cleaver, who from his remote outpost in Algiers was calling on radicals in America to become terrorists, Newton finally flew into a rage and expelled the international leader from the party in an outburst bizarrely captured on a cheery TV morning show in the Bay Area. Over the televised long-distance hookup in May 1971, Newton called Cleaver a "coward" and a "punk" for fleeing overseas, making clear who controlled the Black Panther Party.

The Newton-Cleaver split led to armed warfare between the Panther chapter in New York, which was aligned with Cleaver, and the party's Oakland headquarters. The bloody civil war spelled the end of the Black Panthers as a national force. In August 1971, the House Committee on Internal Security declared that the Panthers were no longer a threat, with their national organization "near disintegration." By 1972, the party had lost so many demoralized members around the country that it had again become a local organization, with Newton issuing a call for all Panthers to move to Oakland and make the city an organizational stronghold.

The FBI had employed its full subversive powers to sow discord and distrust within the Black Panther Party and its once wide support network, including the Black community and white radicals and liberals. But in the end, the party's own leadership tore apart the organization.

"Huey didn't want any other strong leaders in the party," Seale stated. "He got rid of Eldridge, and he got rid of [rising, charismatic] Geronimo Pratt in Los Angeles, and he got rid of [future congressman] Bobby Rush in Chicago. . . . I built that organization over several years, and Huey tore it down piece by piece."

IN 1972, WHEN Bobby Seale announced his campaign for mayor of Oakland, on a ticket with city council candidate Elaine Brown, it was the Black Panthers' last hurrah. Brown, still committed to the armed overthrow of the US government, saw the campaign as only a step toward revolution. But Seale, a lifelong believer in the possibilities of democratic change through the ballot box, threw himself passionately into the campaign. Seale campaigned for over a year against the white Republican incumbent, John Reading, forcing a runoff election in May 1973.

Brown, who had developed a worshipful relationship with Newton, despised Seale. Despite Seale's pro-feminist statements, Brown told a very different story in her 1992 memoir, *A Taste of Power*, about the besieged status of strong Panther women like her, although she eventually pushed her way to the top of the party with the backing of Newton. "You didn't get these [Panther] brothers from revolutionary heaven," Brown later wryly remarked.

Even formidable women within the party were sometimes subjected to predatory sexual behavior and violence disguised as political punishment.

Nonetheless, Brown was impressed by the political skill and determination of her running mate in the 1973 Oakland election. This was the pinnacle of Bobby Seale's political career, the closest he would come to achieving his long dream of taking power in his hometown. "At dawn every day, Bobby pushed us onto the streets. We might ride a bus on a gray morning to talk to people going to work an early shift. We might parade through a school or a hospital or a shopping mall with balloons and trinkets to give away, along with Panthers to register people to vote. . . . Every evening, we would walk the streets of Oakland, block by block, knocking on doors. At the end, Bobby would gather together all those party members working on the campaign to review his voter maps, to plan the next day, the next week, the next month."

Seale was electrified by the democratic process. This time he was wearing a business suit, not a leather jacket. And he was handing out campaign literature, instead of the Black Panthers' ten-point platform. But his message was the same. The Black people of Oakland deserved full employment, decent housing, good education, equal justice, an end to police brutality. It was nothing less than a campaign for self-determination, to empower a people who had always been disenfranchised despite now representing nearly half of the city's population.

Seale and Brown succeeded in producing a record African American turnout, but on Election Day they were both soundly defeated. Nonetheless, Seale declared "a people's victory"—and it was a triumph of sorts for a party widely condemned as lawless and a mayoral candidate who had been sitting behind bars the previous year.

Seale saw the contest as the auspicious beginning of the Black Panthers' entry into the electoral arena. He began plotting a mission to run party members for nearly every office in Oakland, including himself for city council. But by then, Huey Newton was a major impediment to Seale's plan to work within the political system. His Black Panther cofounder had become an Oakland crime lord, running a down-low business out of his faction's Lamp Post bar hangout, a racket that was built on drug-dealing, extortion, robbery, arson, beatings, and even murder.

Seale insisted he knew nothing about Newton's dark side—"He hid his shit from me"—even though he began embezzling money from the Panther organization. The $100,000 bail raised for the Panther 21 when they were charged in New York with plotting a series of bombings in 1969 never reached them, said Seale, who had helped raise the money. He suspected that the funds ended up in the pockets of Newton's people. "That's why the New York Panthers split from the party," Seale concluded. The New York defendants ended up spending months in notorious Riker's Island jail before being found innocent of all charges in May 1971.

After the 1973 mayoral race, Seale received a tip from Oakland police chief Charles Gain—a liberal cop with whom he'd developed a trusting relationship—that drug dealers were conspiring to put a hit on Newton. "Gain said he didn't want to see a shooting war develop in Oakland."

Seale was finally forced to confront Newton's criminality, but his partner—"snorting lines of cocaine and sucking up Rémy Martin"—waved away the warnings about his decline into addiction and crime. "While I was trying to build a mass organization, Huey was running a criminal gang of twelve or thirteen people," Seale said. "If I had won the mayor's race, I would've gotten rid of Huey. I would've had him arrested. He was a motherfucking drug dealer. He was ripping off the Panther organization."

Elaine Brown, a longtime Newton loyalist, would tell a very different story about the final falling-out between the two Black

Panther founders. One day in 1974, she wrote in her memoir, the Supreme Servant of the People—as Newton was now grandly calling himself—summoned Seale to his penthouse cockpit. Two of Newton's big, menacing bodyguards were there, and Brown later joined them.

Newton had a wild idea—all of his ideas were now like rockets into the sky. The Panthers would produce a Hollywood movie starring Bobby as a legendary ghetto gangster, Elaine would write the screenplay, and they would all make a fortune. The story meeting went on for hours, fueled by Newton's mounds of cocaine and bottles of cognac. And then deep into the marathon meeting, Brown saw the switch flip in Newton's brain before anyone else did. She knew when these rages would overtake him.

Suddenly, Newton turned on his partner of nearly a decade, whom only minutes earlier he was building up as a future movie star. Now Seale was "a punk" who didn't merit the title of party chairman. "You've been believing your own lies too long, Bobby, running around telling people you're the *cofounder* of the Black Panther Party. . . . But you are *not* the cofounder of the Black Panther Party!"

His rage growing, Newton ordered one of his bodyguards, a huge man known as Big Bob, to get his bullwhip and punish Seale with twenty strokes to his naked back. "With the ferocity of his four hundred pounds, Bob brought the tail of the whip down onto Bobby's back. Though a relatively thin man, Bobby bent only slightly with each lash, his head down, eyes tight, braced for the next crack." Brown, who claimed Seale had once ordered her to be whipped as a disciplinary measure, sat coolly smoking during Seale's ordeal. "My moment of pity for him lapsed as I recalled the lashes on my own back."

Brown wrote that she would inherit the title of Black Panther chairman after Newton stripped it from Seale and expelled him from the party and even from Oakland. But the title was now a poisoned honorific. Brown would sleepwalk for a few more years in the party, before Newton's brutality finally drove her out too. By then, the organization was an empty shell, a racket run by an increasingly volatile and strung-out leader.

Years after Brown's book was published, Seale dismissed her account of his humiliation as "pure bullshit." He insisted that he chose to leave Oakland on his own, after concluding that Newton had reduced the Black Panthers to ashes, settling first in Denver with his family and later in Philadelphia. "Huey and Elaine never threatened me—I'd crosshair you if you did that," he said flatly.

In any case, the bitter split between Bobby Seale and Huey Newton in 1974 marked the end of the Black Panthers as a political beast.

IN AMERICA, AFTER enough time passes, outlaws often become saints. And so it was with the Black Panthers, fifty years after the party was founded by two young Black revolutionaries, when the Oakland Museum of California mounted a glamorized historical exhibition of the Panthers, with a $100,000 grant from the Ford Foundation. The people of all ages and races who crowded into the October 2016 exhibit were able to sit in a replica of the wicker chair where Huey Newton, with a shotgun in one hand and a spear in the other, had posed for the iconic Panther photo. They could peer through the grating of an old jail door behind which Newton had sat, generously donated by the Oakland Police Department.

The curators of the "All Power to the People: Black Panthers at 50" exhibition made a point of connecting the Panthers' street resistance to the younger Black Lives Matter movement against police brutality. At a museum lecture, Charity Clay, a thirty-year-old professor at Merritt College, where Seale and Newton got their political start, complained that her students knew the Panthers only by their cool regalia, and not their ideology. "The young people know their style—the black leather coats, the berets, the dark glasses," Clay said, but they can't "run down the ten-point program."

A number of surviving party leaders wandered like celebrities through the museum crowds, speaking on panels, dining at a candlelit banquet, and signing posters in the lobby. There was Elaine Brown—still a striking figure at age seventy-three, surrounded by security, and wearing an all-white suit and black spike heels. "Black Lives Matter is a slogan, an idea, but it needs some substance to it," she told a museum audience. BLM protesters should take note of what the Black Panthers had done, added Brown. The Panthers had firmly declared, "No, the police ain't coming up in here." Three years later furious, nationwide protests over the police murder of George Floyd in Minneapolis would inject the notions of defunding, or otherwise rethinking, the police into the public conversation.

Most of the prominent Panthers at the museum festivities were women—Brown, Kathleen Cleaver, Ericka Huggins. The group's bloody history with police and FBI agents, as well as its own demons, had taken a toll on many of its male legends. Huey Newton was long gone—gunned down in 1989 at age forty-seven, on the streets of West Oakland by a young shooter who was trying to win the approval of a prison-based gang called the Black Guerilla Family. Newton, by then lost to his drug habit, could no longer defend himself against an ambitious twenty-five-year-old dealer who was competing for his crack-cocaine turf.

Eldridge Cleaver, too, was dead, having expired in a Southern California hospital in 1998 at sixty-two after a lengthy physical and mental decline. The Cleavers had returned from exile in 1975, dispirited by their travels in Communist and other dictatorial countries. "I'm telling you after I ran into the Egyptian police and the Algerian police and the North Korean police and the Nigerian police and Idi Amin's police in Uganda, I began to miss the Oakland police," Cleaver said the year before he died. Cleaver dismayed fellow Panthers by becoming a born-again Christian and expressing approval for an old adversary, Ronald Reagan, after he became president.

Dogged for years by reports that he was a wife-beater, Cleaver finally publicly acknowledged the truth to journalist Kate Coleman in 1980. Kathleen Cleaver "needed disciplining," he announced, including striking her in the face, going on to assert the institution of marriage was "fatally undermined" when a husband could not inflict "corporal discipline on his wife and children." Kathleen, a proud and intelligent woman, stayed in the abusive marriage, which produced two children, until the following year. She then resumed her undergraduate education at Yale University, later graduated from Yale Law School, and pursued a long legal career capped by teaching law at Emory University in Atlanta. Kathleen Cleaver, who has sat for many interviews about Panther history, has never been able to unravel the mysteries of her long marriage. In an interview during the Panther museum exhibition, she said only that Cleaver, whom she finally divorced in 1987, had suffered from bipolar disorder and his mood swings were exacerbated by drugs.

Like other prominent women in the party, Kathleen Cleaver never stopped believing in it. "The Black Panther Party appeared like a comet and it reverberates still," she declared in a curatorial statement released by the Oakland Museum.

Bobby Seale is the only surviving member of the triumvirate of charismatic men who led the Black Panthers. During the party's fifty-year celebration, he proudly took the spotlight, giving interviews to the press and signing copies of the handsomely published coffee-table book he had produced with former Panther photographer Stephen Shames.

Seale has remained politically engaged throughout his life, writing another memoir about his Black Panther life, *A Lonely Rage* (1978); working for the Congressional Black Caucus and Representatives Ron Dellums and John Conyers on Capitol Hill; developing a course on social responsibility for Temple University in Philadelphia; and finally returning with his family to the Bay Area, where he maintained a full schedule of public speaking events into his eighties. He talks about Black Panther efforts as early as 1969 to win voter support for placing the police under community control. Other demands in the party's ten-point platform seem equally relevant today, more than five decades after Seale and Newton wrote the document, including the calls for freeing Black Americans from prison bondage and dispensing reparations for slavery.

Now Seale is sitting with a visitor in a community center in East Oakland with old Black Panther posters on the wall, and going back in time. Still lean and spry, Seale is reliving that first armed showdown on Seventh Street with the Oakland police. He's out of his seat now, acting it all out. He's pulsing with adrenaline, leading his uniformed team again as they confront the cop in a show of disciplined force and run him out of the neighborhood. Bobby and Huey are together, armed and defiant. The people of poverty-plagued Oakland no longer need cower—the panther has pounced.

"Ladies and gentlemen, my name is Bobby Seale and I'm chairman of the Black Panther Party. This is my friend Huey Newton. . . ."

Sisterhood Is Blooming

Heather Booth and the Women of Jane

When Jeanne Galatzer opened the apartment door that afternoon in early May 1972, she was not expecting to see two
Chicago homicide detectives. The cops were tall and muscular, and
to Jeanne, who was twenty-one years old, five feet two, and slight,
they looked enormous. Jeanne was working "the Front" that day,
which meant that she was watching over an apartment full of boyfriends and sisters and kids of women who were getting abortions
over at the other apartment, a few miles away, which Jeanne and
her feminist coconspirators called "the Place."

In 1972, abortion was fully legal in just four states in the country. Sixteen other states allowed it only under carefully circum-
scribed conditions, such as if a pregnancy had resulted from rape
or incest or endangered the health of the woman. Illinois fell into
neither category, which meant that anyone performing an abortion
in Chicago could face prison time. Adults waiting at the Front for
friends and loved ones who'd been ferried away to an unknown
address got nervous and needed to be reassured. Kids got antsy and
needed to be entertained. Jeanne was a shy person and sometimes
felt like she was hosting an unusually tense all-day tea party.

When the women came back after their abortions, the Front

was supposed to be the place where Jeanne and the others in the underground abortion service talked to them about contraception, reiterating what had been said in earlier counseling sessions about how they might take control of their own bodies and lives. They made sure women had their antibiotics and Ergotrate, a medication that helps the uterus contract. They handed out copies of the newly published *Our Bodies, Ourselves*, the eye-opening, pass-it-along handbook from the Boston Women's Health Collective, which guided information-thirsty readers through subjects from avoiding sexually transmitted diseases to enjoying masturbation. One of the other women in the service joked that running the Front was like being a "stewardess with a radical feminist consciousness." You even handed out snacks. When the knock came at the door, Jeanne figured it was one of their own dropping off more Triscuits and apricot nectar.

That day was the beginning of the end for one of the most remarkable feats of grassroots activism—and sheer chutzpah—in the history of American feminism. The underground service known as Jane was founded by Heather Booth, a twenty-year-old college student who would go on to become a legendary progressive organizer. The Jane Collective would safely—and illegally—provide at least ten thousand abortions between 1965 and 1973, many of them performed by women with no medical background who trained one another. More directly and viscerally than any of the myriad alternative institutions the women's movement created in the late 1960s and '70s, Jane would deliver on the promise to make the personal political. And for the women who worked in it, the experience created a heady and indelible feeling of having transformed themselves into the heroes of their own lives.

Jeanne had been adrift when she joined the underground service a year and a half earlier. She was "Susan" in those days, but she never liked the name—it was so all-American, every high school cheerleading squad had at least one—and eventually she would start going by her middle name. After dropping out of school in her last quarter at the University of Chicago, confused about her future and mildly depressed, Jeanne had gotten a mind-numbing office job, coding for an insurance company. Her desk happened to be stationed right under the office Muzak speaker, and the recognizable rock tunes, rendered into flutey, anodyne instrumentals, were a frustrating daily reminder of the counterculture she was close to, but not quite a part of.

Women's liberation, the new movement she had been hearing about on campus, had begun speaking to her, or as she thought of it, shouting to her. Jeanne grew up in the steel mill town of Hammond, Indiana. Her father was a pharmacist and her mother was a housewife. In a community that was mostly Polish Catholic or Appalachian evangelical, her family stood apart. Her father's family were Jewish refugees from Russian pogroms, and Barney, her father, had lost a job in Chicago for refusing to cross a picket line of striking Black porters. Her mother was a cradle Catholic who'd been forced out of the church when she divorced her former husband after the first time he hit her. Still, though her parents were kind, and progressive in certain ways, they ran a household that was firmly divided by gender. Jeanne had two older brothers and they seemed to lead entirely different lives from her. Barney and the boys spent Sundays in the living room watching football or baseball behind a closed door, and it never occurred to them to ask her in.

Sports carried a lot of weight in the Galatzer household. The boys wrestled competitively, and the whole family looked up to Uncle Milt, an outfielder for the Cincinnati Reds and the Cleveland Indians. Jeanne was an avid swimmer, but in those years before Title IX, there was no girls' swim team at school. Like many young women in the 1950s, that era before women's liberation cracked open so many of the strictures of gender, Jeanne thought about the world of ambition and striving and success that seemed open to her brothers, and felt like a second-class citizen, even in her own family. In junior high, she found herself weeping when she confided in her dad how much she loved math. To his credit, he told her she could be a mathematician when she grew up, but she was sure he was wrong—only men could be.

And then there was the double standard when it came to sexuality. The Pill had been available since 1960, but generally only to married women. In college, when Jeanne went to her family doctor requesting it, he told her he "didn't believe in birth control. Like it was Santa Claus or something." She left his office embarrassed and empty-handed. A friend in whom she confided discreetly handed her a folded-up piece of paper with the name of an African American ob-gyn in Chicago who was willing to prescribe the Pill to single women. Jeanne went to see him—success! Still, she resented that she'd had to "crawl through broken glass, it felt like" to get ahold of something so simple and necessary.

In fall 1971, she heard about the underground abortion service known as Jane. It was, she'd learned, entirely run by women, mostly students and young stay-at-home mothers. Jeanne talked her friend Sheila Smith into going to a meeting with her. Like Jeanne, Sheila was a bright scholarship student from a lower-middle-class background. She'd grown up in a rent-controlled, prewar apartment in Forest Hills, Queens, that often felt much too small for her family of four. Her father, who died when she was sixteen, was an alcoholic, an accountant who was often out of work and who beat her mother, and sometimes Sheila and her brother, too. Sheila developed self-reliance early: "When people who should be in charge are kind of blowing it, and you can figure that out as a seven-year-old, or maybe a five-year-old, you tend to feel like you have to think for yourself and look out for yourself and you don't necessarily respect the supposed wisdom of authority."

Jeanne and Sheila had both marched against the war in Vietnam, and attended meetings and sit-ins organized by the campus left, but they were often frustrated with all the speechifying and theorizing. Both were drawn to the idea of doing something more hands-on and practical, especially if it helped women. For Sheila, "the whole issue of abortion really revolved around the rights of a woman to her own body, and also her ability to be economically self-sufficient, which can be harder if you can't control conception. Unless you're asexual—and most people who I knew at that time in their twenties were not!—this was going to be a big, big factor in your life."

In 1969, at an abortion speak-out in New York organized by the feminist group Redstockings, one woman bemoaned the prevailing attitude that "it was all right to be, you know, sleeping with somebody—that's fine!—but when you get pregnant, then there's something wrong with you, and all of a sudden you're some kind of *creature* and everybody's gonna look at you and whisper and say, '*She's* pregnant.'"

No contraceptive method was fail-proof. Sheila had known somebody who got pregnant with an intrauterine device (IUD) implanted. The same thing had happened to one of the women at the speak-out, who'd been fitted with an IUD at "a very fine clinic." But when the device malfunctioned, and she'd asked where she could get an abortion, she was told, "We can't do anything to help you, dear. It's your problem, dear." Then the unforgiving reality hit her. "There you are, you're a patient in a clinic, and all of a sudden you're a criminal," the young woman said. "You're one of the 2 percent, or you're one of the 10 percent, and that's your problem. You're a statistical error, and you're a criminal because you're a statistical error."

The Jane meeting was held in a big, old apartment in Hyde Park—the leafy Southside neighborhood surrounding the University of Chicago campus—and it was crowded, maybe thirty women packed into the living room, with the chairs pushed back against the walls. Women in jeans and sneakers, their hair tucked under bandannas, sat cross-legged on the floor. There was some trouble at first because Jeanne had brought Sheila along without asking ahead of time, which violated the group's security protocols and put everybody on alert.

The Janes were wary of potential spies. Chicago had a particularly zealous Red Squad, a police intelligence unit that monitored and infiltrated the activities of almost every group on the left, and which had stepped up its activities since the massive street demonstrations during the 1968 Democratic convention. FBI director J. Edgar Hoover had recently added women's liberation, which he referred to as WLM, to the antiwar, environmental, and Black Power movements the agency was targeting for discrediting and disrupting through its COINTELPRO domestic surveillance program. "It is absolutely essential," Hoover wrote in a memo, "that we conduct sufficient investigation to clearly establish subversive ramifications of the WLM and to determine the potential for violence presented by the various groups connected with this movement as well as any possible threat they may represent to the internal security of the United States." Hoover conjured a militant, disciplined, probably communistic insurrection, in lieu of the homegrown, freewheeling, consciousness-raising challenge to traditional gender roles that constituted the actual women's liberation movement. Seeing it through that lens justified seeding women's groups and communes with informants.

Sheila looked around the room, and with her granny glasses and her characteristically wry, intelligent gaze, took in the anxiety, verging on paranoia. Once a few of the women had grilled Jeanne and Sheila, the atmosphere calmed down. The newcomers were allowed to stay, and to hear how the enterprise worked.

A woman might see an ad in one of the local alternative newspapers or a flyer on a campus bulletin board: "Pregnant? Don't want to be? Call Jane at 643–3844." She'd dial the number and leave a message on the bulky two-reel answering machine the collective used. More than a hundred calls came in every week. Somebody compiled the messages every few hours and handed them off to a "call-back Jane," who phoned women that same day: "Hello, Brenda? This is Jane from Women's Liberation returning your call." She'd first assure the caller that the group could help her, then she'd ask how far along the pregnancy was and take a brief medical history. Sometimes the women were crying; sometimes they'd already tried on their own to induce an abortion, with knitting needles or caustic purgatives or scalding-hot baths.

Each woman would get written up on a three-by-five index card, with her name and phone number and a few notes about her situation. At their weekly meetings, the Janes would pass the cards around and pick the women they wanted to counsel. Later a "Big Jane" would make the calls setting up the time and place for the abortion, and scheduling the fellow Janes who'd be on duty. There were some women who came through the service and hardly wanted to be counseled at all about what to expect, physically and emotionally, from the experience; they'd hunch over on the edge of a couch with their coats still on, even when it was hot and stuffy in the room. And there were others who would sit up with the Janes all night in their kitchens when the counselors let them, drinking coffee, smoking cigarettes, laughing, weeping, sharing their life stories.

The service used paramedic abortionists—they weren't doctors, but they were experienced and good. Jeanne nodded—that sounded fine. But Sheila, who was a savvy reader of a room and of people, picked up on something that had been left unsaid. She told Jeanne later that she was sure some of the women were doing the abortions themselves, even though none were doctors or nurses or, for that matter, paramedics.

Jeanne was undeterred—she liked the work right away. She liked the feeling it gave her, of being competent and together. She liked the camaraderie with the other Janes. She liked how a woman came in with an overwhelming problem and she could help solve it there and then. Other political work could feel like such a slog, its palpable rewards long delayed. But at Jane, "We'd finish an abortion and a woman would look up and say, 'It's done?' And she'd be so relieved, and sort of incredulous." She had her life back, and all the possibilities she had imagined for it.

Jeanne knew what they were doing was illegal, of course, but she was twenty-one years old, and maybe a bit naively optimistic, or as she would say decades later, "I was really young, and everybody around me was doing this, and it did not occur to me I could get sent up."

Later, Jeanne would look back on what happened that day at the Front as her first real lesson in the consequences of actions, the abrupt end to a lingering, adolescent sense of invulnerability. Even in her relative obliviousness, though, Jeanne quickly registered who those towering men were at the door, and what she had to do. She walked at a clip down the long hall of the apartment, with the detectives in their trench coats and shiny black shoes following right behind. "These are the police," she told the thirty or so adults and children gathered in and around the living room. "You don't have to tell them anything." She had a moment to savor her surprise at her own breathless poise. Then the detectives clamped handcuffs on her wrists and arrested her.

Meanwhile, over at the Place, Jeanne's friend Sheila Smith had begun what was to be her first shift assisting a more experienced Jane with the actual abortions. She'd be sterilizing instruments, taking temperatures and blood pressure readings, holding women's hands during the procedures. Soon she'd be giving antibiotic shots and learning to insert a speculum, and eventually she'd be trained to perform an abortion by means of dilation and curettage, or a D&C, gently but thoroughly scraping out the lining of a woman's uterus, including the developing embryo. Only four or five of the hundred or so women who worked in the service ever acquired the skills to perform the abortions themselves, but Sheila hoped to be one of them.

Sheila would be graduating from the University of Chicago the next month, with a degree in anthropology, and she wasn't sure what she was going to do for a living. But she was clear on what she needed to do that day, and on how right it felt to be helping women who had nowhere else to turn. Within a few hours, she was arrested, snared in the same police dragnet that would catch Jeanne.

THE SAGA OF the Jane Collective began seven years earlier, in the winter of 1965, when Heather Tobis (she would be Heather Booth when she married a few years later) listened to a plea for help from a friend she used to date. His sister was pregnant and desperate to get an abortion, but she had no idea where to turn: Did Heather?

At first glance, Heather might not have seemed like the person to ask about anything quite so flagrantly illegal. She was a sopho-more at the University of Chicago, living in a dorm, as all female undergraduates at the university were required to in those days, and subject to a curfew that was stricter for women students than for men. A Jewish doctor's daughter from Long Island, Heather was soft-spoken and self-contained, with a natural, understated sort of elegance and a talent for speaking in full sentences. A friend described her style of relating to people as "inclusive, reasoned, humorous, and egalitarian." She had green eyes and long hair that she often wore in a single braid tossed over one shoulder. With her turtlenecks and neat, A-line skirts, she could have graced the cover of *Seventeen* magazine's annual back-to-school issue.

But Heather was tougher and more rebellious than she looked. Once she learned about an injustice, she was not the sort of person who could sigh, declare it a terrible thing, and put it out of her mind. At her big, suburban high school, she had quit the cheerlead-ing squad when she noticed that it never recruited any of the Black girls. She'd resigned from a high school sorority when she realized it didn't let in anyone who wasn't thin, clear-complexioned, and con-ventionally pretty. In the cafeteria, she put together a friends' table of all the people on the outs—"The people who were too this or too that." On weekends, she made her way to Greenwich Village to hang out in Washington Square Park and listen to folk music. She joined a picket line organized by CORE (Congress of Racial Equality) outside of a Woolworth's in Manhattan to protest segregated lunch counters in the South.

Though the campus left was still nascent in 1963, Heather got involved with it right away at the University of Chicago, joining SDS (Students for a Democratic Society) and the Friends of SNCC (Student Nonviolent Coordinating Committee). And she made the decision that would change her life. She applied and was accepted to be one of 650 mostly white, Northern students who would head to Mississippi in the summer of 1964, under the auspices of the dynamic, Black-led SNCC.

Since 1961, SNCC leader Bob Moses—a bespectacled former math teacher from Harlem with a graduate degree in philosophy from Harvard and an aura of almost saintly calm—had been seeking to get Black residents of Mississippi onto the voter rolls. By 1963, only about 6 percent of those eligible were registered. Black citizens who tried registering to vote and the activists who assisted them, including Moses, were regularly threatened, beaten, and jailed. (Local people who dared to exercise their constitutional rights suffered economic retribution, too: they'd suddenly have bank loans called in, or be summarily fired from their jobs.) In 1961, Herbert Lee, a Black farmer and father of nine who worked with the SNCC drive in Mississippi, was murdered by a white state legislator who claimed self-defense and was cleared in an inquest that same day. One of several eyewitnesses to the shooting, a Black army veteran named Louis Allen, eventually told federal authorities what he'd seen. He was gunned down on his front lawn two years later.

The strategy for what became known as Freedom Summer was hard-nosed and high-risk: the country might be able to ignore the persecution of Black civil rights activists struggling against brutal disenfranchisement, but if white college students were subjected to the same treatment, the national press would be compelled to pay attention and the federal government might intervene in the state. "These students bring the rest of the country with them," Moses maintained. "They're from good schools and their parents are influential." Their presence in the Deep South could force a political crisis: "Only when a metal has been brought to a white heat," Moses said, "can it be shaped and molded."

At the same time, the volunteers would organize and staff so-called Freedom Schools as alternatives to segregated education in Mississippi. In these classes—held in church basements or outside, in the shade of spreading trees—Black children and adults could acquire literacy skills and learn American and African American history. As Charles Cobb Jr. a SNCC field secretary in the state, described their purpose, it would be to fill "an intellectual and creative vacuum in the lives of young Negro Mississippians, and to get them to articulate their own desires, demands, and questions . . . to stand up in classrooms around the state and ask their teachers a real question . . . [and] challenge the myths of our society."

Throughout the winter and spring of 1964, staff and supporters of SNCC, including the comedian Dick Gregory and young activists like Julian Bond, toured college campuses recruiting student volunteers for Freedom Summer. In April, Casey Hayden, a SNCC organizer in Atlanta, who was then married to the New Left student leader Tom Hayden, spoke at the University of Chicago, and Heather went to hear her.

Like Heather, Casey Hayden had a force of character and a political vision that sometimes surprised people who had not bothered to look beyond the surface. Hayden, who had grown up in a small town in southeast Texas, had sorority-girl good looks (complete with cornflower-blue eyes and a honey-blond flip) and a penchant for picketing in high-heeled white pumps. But she knew what it was like to feel like an outcast. She and her sister had been raised by their grandmother, aunt, and twice-divorced mother in a time and place where a no-Ozzie-all-Harriet upbringing didn't help a girl's reputation. People in sultry, coastal Victoria, Texas, gossiped about her beautiful mother, Eula, not only because she was the lone divorced woman in town and supported her daughters herself, working as a secretary, but because she had, in Casey's words, "an independent and unbigoted turn of mind," not bothering, for instance, to hide her close friendship with a Mexican American man at work.

Casey Hayden had a warm, throaty laugh and a gift for sincere public speaking. In 1960, when she was twenty-two, she gave a thrilling address to a national convention of students in Minneapolis, urging them to support SNCC's sit-ins. In what one reporter called a "Southern voice so soft it would not startle a boll weevil," Hayden told the story of when Henry David Thoreau was jailed for civil disobedience, specifically for withholding taxes to protest the institution of slavery. His fellow transcendentalist Ralph Waldo Emerson went to see him, and asked, in dismay, "What are you doing in there, Henry?" Casey waited a dramatic beat, then, her voice throbbing, delivered Thoreau's reply: "What are you doing out there, Ralph? What are you doing out there?" After a moment of silence, the six hundred student delegates gave her a standing ovation.

Tom Hayden, then a student at the University of Michigan, was in the audience that day and interviewed her afterward for his student newspaper, impressed because she had been a leader of sit-ins in Austin, and because she "had the ability to think morally [and] express herself poetically." Their political commitments would outlast their commitment to each other—they were both young, and Tom wasn't ready for monogamous coupledom. (Despite his lifelong penchant for falling in love with strong, charismatic women, he never would be.) But for a time, he "idolized" her, and she was captivated by his intellectual intensity and his "funny face with the sad eyes."

Heather was an eighteen-year-old freshman when she heard Casey Hayden outline the plans for Freedom Summer. Hayden had initially shared some of the concerns of Black SNCC staff in Mississippi that an influx of white students would incite violence, not protect locals from it, and she was explicit about the dangers for everyone involved. She explained the practicalities, too: though volunteers would be living with Black families, who were taking considerable risk in housing them, each volunteer would have to pay for her own transportation, and minimal living expenses, about $150 a week. Nonetheless, Heather recalled how Hayden "just swept us up in her enthusiasm. This is what we had to do."

For the young volunteers, Freedom Summer was a crash course both in the exhilarating possibilities, and the sheer terror, of putting one's body on the line in the pursuit of social justice. In June, Heather attended a training session for the students held on the parklike campus of a women's college in Oxford, Ohio. There were moments of inspiration as students were immersed in "revolutionary nonviolence as a way of life," sang spirituals and protest anthems together, and had frank conversations across racial lines, often for the first time in their lives.

But there were also undeniable tensions. The idealistic white college students had a lot to learn, and their Black peers bore the burden of teaching them. One night, the Freedom Summer volunteers all watched a CBS News report in which a big, white sheriff with a thick drawl barred the entrance to a courthouse to prevent Black, would-be voters from registering. The white students saw him as a ridiculous caricature of Southern intransigence, and started laughing. Offended, six of the Black SNCC organizers got up and walked out. They knew that somebody who might look like a buffoon to white Northerners could still exercise lethal power.

The white and Black volunteers talked through that and other incidents, at length. One of the Black SNCC organizers told a white student, "We cried over you in the staff meeting because we love you and are afraid for you." But, he added, "Don't tell me that you are coming down here to help me, because you are saving yourselves."

On June 21, 1964, word arrived that three young organizers for the civil rights project, James Chaney, Andrew Goodman, and Michael Schwerner, who had set out together to investigate a church burning in Neshoba County, Mississippi, had gone missing.

Goodman was a white volunteer from Queens College who had attended the first of the two training sessions and arrived in Mississippi just a day before. Schwerner, also white, was a staff member of CORE and a Cornell graduate. Chaney was a twenty-one-year-old Black CORE staffer from Meridian, Mississippi. Schwerner's twenty-two-year-old wife, Rita, was still with the group training session in Ohio. She told TV reporters who came to interview her that if Chaney had been alone, "this case, like so many others that have come before, would have gone completely unnoticed."

Evidence exhumed from the red clay of Mississippi that summer would prove her point. While searching for Chaney, Goodman, and Schwerner, investigators would find the bodies of eight Black men—some mutilated, or with hands bound, one a fourteen-year-old wearing a CORE T-shirt—for whom the authorities had not been bothering to search. For Heather, that was perhaps the most devastating revelation of all—that Black lives could count for so little.

Heather talked with her parents on the phone the night before she was to leave for Mississippi. They were all badly shaken by the story of the three young men, whom by now most everyone presumed dead. Heather had two brothers and they were a close family, and a liberal one. Part of the SNCC strategy was to pull the white students' parents into the mission; SNCC leadership called on them to use their privilege and whatever influence they might have to demand federal protection for the voter registration campaigners in Mississippi. Heather's parents had given their permission for her to go—that was required for any of the volunteers under twenty-one—and they would sign on for that effort, writing to and visiting their congressman.

But on the eve of Heather's departure, her mother was crying so hard on the phone, Heather couldn't understand what she was saying. And her father, normally so gentle and calmly supportive, was almost as distraught. They asked her did she know "how much it takes to make a child?"

From Mississippi, Heather wrote to her younger brother Jon, "I thought of how much it took to make a Herbert Lee or many others whose names I do not know. I thought of how much it took to be a Negro in Mississippi twelve months a year for a lifetime. How can such a thing as a life be weighed?" In the same letter she admonished her brother to be "considerate to Mom and Dad"— please "don't go defending me or attacking them if they are critical of the Project." She understood how frightened they were for her.

Bob Moses spoke to Heather's group of Freedom Summer volunteers before they departed for Mississippi. He invoked the need to counter corrupt power with an unflagging commitment to advancing the good. He referred to Tolkien's *Lord of the Rings*—in 1964, more of a cultish obscurity, but one that resonated with some of the students—to describe how a hero "gains a means of ultimate power he does not want," but can't give up. Dressed, as he habitually was, in denim overalls, Moses looked down at his feet, and spoke in a voice so quiet the group had to listen intently to hear it. He told the students he felt terrible asking them to go. "Looking at us sitting in the same room where the 3 missing men had been last week," one volunteer wrote to his father, "Moses seemed almost to be wanting all of us to go home." Indeed, Moses stressed, anyone who wanted to should feel free to leave, and not be ashamed. They should know, though, that he wasn't asking them to risk anything he himself wasn't risking.

From the back of the room, a young woman began to sing: "They say that freedom is a constant sorrow." And gradually, voice after voice joined in until everyone in the room was singing, their arms wrapped around one another. No one left.

In Mississippi, Heather lived with people she would never forget. In Ruleville, her host was a midwife and moonshiner. In Shaw, a tiny town that was not too tiny to be segregated, she was housed by Andrew and Mary Lou Hawkins and their children. The Hawkinses were a remarkable family, brave in a way that somehow never made them famous. Andrew Hawkins was a carpenter, but in addition to supporting the SNCC campaign, he worked to de-segregate the local schools, and organized sharecroppers to get a little more per bale of cotton.

In 1969, Hawkins would become the lead plaintiff in a lawsuit alleging that the allocation of city services in Shaw violated the rights of its Black citizens to equal protection under the Constitution. The Black side of town lacked the paving, streetlights, and adequate sewage and water systems that the white side had. The lawsuit made it all the way to the federal court of appeals, which ruled in Hawkins's favor, establishing a precedent for holding cities to account for racial bias. But the Hawkinses' courage exacted a terrible toll. Their house was firebombed, killing one of their sons and two of their little granddaughters. In 1972, Mary Lou Hawkins was shot to death by Shaw's only Black policeman, who was tried and acquitted of manslaughter. To many who knew the Hawkinses, including Heather, the incident seemed to fall into a pattern of retribution against the family.

When Heather and other volunteers stayed with them, Andrew and Mary Lou gave up what Heather understood only later was their own double bed and slept on the couch. The Hawkinses kept a pig and a garden and had an outhouse in back. The family and guests shared meals of collard greens, chitterlings, and biscuits, and on Sundays took Heather and the other white students to the local Black revival church with them. At night they discussed politics, local and national. The family subscribed to the *Chicago Defender*, an African American newspaper, and Andrew wanted to talk Chicago politics with Heather, though she soon discovered that he knew more about them than she did.

On August 4, FBI investigators found the bodies of Chaney, Goodman, and Schwerner buried under an earthen dam. The two white men had been shot; Chaney had been horrifically beaten as well as shot. Neshoba County deputy sheriff Cecil Price, who had taken part in the murders, reassured the other perpetrators, fellow Klansmen, "Well, boys, you've done a good job. You've struck a blow for the white man. Mississippi can be proud of you. You've let those agitating outsiders know where this state stands."

The state of Mississippi declined to prosecute the men responsible, and a federal prosecution in 1967 resulted in sentences of under six years (and even less time served) for seven of those indicted.

In addition to the widely publicized murders of Chaney, Goodman, and Schwerner, there were numerous other acts of intimidation directed at the Freedom Summer volunteers. The historian John Dittmer would later tally over 1,000 arrests; 65 buildings bombed or burned, including 35 churches; and the beatings of at least 80 activists. Heather herself would be arrested and spend an afternoon in jail for carrying a sign about voter registration.

Throughout the summer, Heather remembered feeling "sad, angry, and guilty all at the same time." The realization came over her that the civil rights workers had only themselves to depend on. SNCC had some lines of communication open with the Justice Department, but Washington, DC, was a long way away from the Mississippi Delta. She'd grown up "believing that the police were your friends. They were the crossing guards, the place to call if you ran into trouble." Now she was learning a very different lesson. When she shared this observation with Victoria Gray, a Black local movement leader, Gray told her, "Well, dear, I never, ever thought of the police as my friends."

In a letter she wrote to her parents, Heather offered a glimpse of how tense the Mississippi nights could be. "Last night I was a long time before sleeping, although I was extremely tired," she wrote. "Every shadow, every noise—the bark of a dog, the sound of a car—in my fear and exhaustion was turned into a terrorist's approach. And I believed that I heard the back door open and a Klansman walk in, until he was close by the bed." Then she "rethought why I was here, rethought what could be gained in view of what could be lost." She breathed deep and, in her mind, said the words of the movement hymn, "We Shall Overcome."

"Anyone who comes down here and is not afraid I think must

be crazy as well as dangerous to this project where security is quite important," she wrote. But fear was only useful if it didn't immobilize you.

When she left Mississippi for Long Island at the end of the summer, something strange happened to her. As glad as she was to be reunited with her family, the contrast between the comfort and safety of home and the existential dangers and relentlessly high stakes of life on the front lines of the civil rights movement created a crisis for her. For several days, Heather found herself unable to speak at all.

In the short run, Freedom Summer didn't look like a political triumph. At the end of the summer, the activists behind it tried to replace the all-white Mississippi delegation to the 1964 Democratic National Convention in Atlantic City with an integrated, majority Black delegation representing what they called the Mississippi Freedom Democratic Party. Under pressure from President Lyndon Johnson, who didn't want to lose the Southern vote to Republican opponent Barry Goldwater, the convention's credentials committee refused to seat the freedom delegation. It was a bitter blow to the group, who had taken the bus up from Mississippi, high on righteous hope. Many of the Freedom Summer volunteers held a vigil outside the convention on the boardwalk, to which they had also brought the station wagon that Chaney, Schwerner, and Goodman had been driving when they were abducted, now a burned-out hulk.

But in the longer term the attention that Freedom Summer drew, and the outcry over the deaths of the three civil rights workers, helped create the momentum to pass the Civil Rights Act of 1964 and the Voting Rights Act of 1965. The Democratic Party adopted new rules that blocked segregated delegations at the 1968 convention. Freedom Summer trained legions of young Black activists who pushed the grassroots civil rights and Black Power movements forward. And among the white student volunteers, many went on to help create or lead other peace and social justice movements of the 1960s: Tom Hayden became a leader of the Vietnam antiwar movement; Mario Savio launched the Free Speech Movement in Berkeley; Marshall Ganz became a key figure in the United Farm Workers crusade; and Heather, and a number of other women who were part of Freedom Summer and other civil rights organizing, built the women's liberation movement.

The white women came away inspired by the leadership strengths of Black women organizers, particularly in SNCC, where they occupied a number of important positions. Diane Nash, a former beauty queen, was a cofounder of SNCC, an important strategist of nonviolent resistance, and, like so many in the movement, a veteran of numerous arrests and jailings. Ella Baker, a canny adviser to SNCC, identified the enormous potential of bringing student sit-in leaders to join the older, church-based figures who initially dominated the civil rights movement. Dorie and Joyce Ladner, sisters from Hattiesburg, Mississippi, were indefatigable organizers in voter registration and other civil rights campaigns. Fannie Lou Hamer, the youngest of twenty children born to Mississippi sharecroppers, was a legendary moral force in the movement. At a SNCC meeting in August 1962, Hamer had volunteered to go to the courthouse the next day and try registering to vote. "I guess if I'd had any sense, I'd a been a little scared," she said later. "But what was the point of being scared? The only thing the whites could do was kill me, and it seemed like they'd been trying to do that a little bit at a time since I could remember."

It was Hamer who made the case for the Mississippi Freedom Democratic Party before the credentials committee in Atlantic City. In her flowered dress, holding a white pocketbook, she spoke so powerfully and persuasively on national television that Lyndon Johnson hastily called an impromptu press conference so the networks would interrupt her testimony and focus on him instead. To Heather, who met her in Ruleville, Mrs. Hamer, as she was always known in the movement, was someone who "conveyed a moral core even in her everyday conversation."

White women like Casey Hayden and Heather Booth who were battle-tested by the civil rights movement would be among the architects of a new women's movement. In 1965, Hayden coauthored with Mary King one of the first pieces of writing suggesting that the left needed to address the oppression of women. The essay's title, "Sex and Caste: A Kind of Memo," captured the mood of a transitional moment for women, simultaneously bold and tentative.

Heather would forever be grateful for Freedom Summer, which launched her life as a political organizer. The civil rights movement was what stirred America awake, roused the left from the timidity and quiescence induced by Cold War McCarthyism. "The civil rights movement, as it burst forth, gave new courage to everything that came after," she said, including the women's movement. She had learned so much in Mississippi—"That if you organize, you can change the world—but only if you organize"; that you had to listen, really listen, to what people told you they needed in their lives. And she learned, in a visceral way that would never leave her, "There are sometimes unjust laws, and you need to stand up to the unjust laws and unjust authorities."

SO, FOR HEATHER, the story of Jane, like the story of her feminism and her lifelong political organizing, started with Freedom Summer. When her friend called her in 1965 to ask for help finding someone who would do an abortion, she quickly said yes. It wasn't that she knew anything, really, about abortion or how to get one, other than that it was illegal. But she knew how to take action.

Confronted for the first time by an unwanted pregnancy, albeit another woman's, it occurred to Heather that someone in the civil rights movement—her model for audacious efficacy in the world—might be able to help. She contacted the movement-affiliated Medical Committee for Human Rights and got a name: Dr. Howard. T. R. M. Howard turned out to be a prominent African American surgeon from Mississippi, who had been involved in investigating the lynching of Emmett Till in August 1955 and served as a mentor to civil rights leaders such as Mrs. Hamer and Medgar Evers. Howard had antagonized J. Edgar Hoover by publicly complaining that the FBI "can't find a white man when he kills a Negro in the South." In Mississippi, he'd lived in a heavily armed and guarded compound until deciding that the KKK death threats against him had become intolerable, and moved to Chicago in late 1955.

When Heather spoke to Dr. Howard on the phone, he agreed to do the abortion—he had discreetly provided them for years. Heather later heard back from her friend that it had gone fine.

Though Heather didn't tell anyone else what she had done, word got out and soon another young woman called, and then another, and another. The phone in her University of Chicago dorm was a communal one in the hall; to keep things anonymous and discreet, she tried to get the word out that women looking for abortion help should ask for "Jane." She could have guessed when it was a Jane call anyway—there was always a moment of silence, a hesitation, then an indrawn breath before the woman started speaking. At first most of the callers were students at her own university or other Chicago schools, then from schools throughout the Midwest. Heather was amazed by how many women needed abortions and how urgently.

After a while, it seemed to her that the women who called could use a little counseling, some preparation for what to expect. Dr. Howard handled the abortion arrangements like most underground providers did: An assistant picked the women up on street corners, blindfolded them, and brought them to undisclosed locations. Heather figured she could make the experience a little less alienating if she quizzed Dr. Howard on the phone to find out more about the procedure, and then began sharing that information with the women who called, and listening to them if they wanted to talk.

In 1966, Heather went to a campus sit-in against the draft. A lanky, rumpled guy named Paul Booth sat next to her. Though he was a hard-core New Left leader—the cofounder and national secretary of SDS—he had a lively sense of humor. An SDS colleague,

Alan Haber, once described him as a rarity in that argumentative, intellectually serious organization—a "cheerful spirit." To keep everybody alert and upbeat during the fractious final drafting of the Port Huron Statement in June 1962, he had sung songs and spun stories. Booth was known for spearheading a national campaign called "Build, Not Burn" to encourage draft resisters to devote themselves to national service rather than burning their draft cards. He took flak for it from more militant SDSers, but Paul, who was one of the first student radicals to try forging connections with labor unions, tended to dwell, as another SDS friend would say of him, on "the left wing of the possible."

The sit-in lasted three days and three nights, and Heather and Paul talked the whole time. By the end of it, he had asked her to marry him, and she had accepted, though she wanted to wait until she graduated a year later. They thought of themselves as in it for the distance—deeply committed to progressive politics, the painstaking work of hand-to-hand organizing, and each other. In 1968, they had their first son, Gene, and in 1970, their second, Dan, each named for an American socialist leader, Eugene Debs and Daniel De Leon.

As the Red Squad files on her attest, in the final years of the 1960s, Heather was not only a young wife and mother and a graduate student (in education at the University of Chicago), she was also an exceedingly busy activist and in-demand movement speaker. "The subject was present," as her vigilant Red Squad watchers noted, at meetings of the American Friends Service Committee, and at peace rallies in Grant Park. She attended an SDS national convention, spoke at a gathering in support of the 1968 Mexico City student uprising, was observed criticizing various left-wing panels for having all male speakers, and was pegged as a leader of a group called Teachers for Radical Change. She was heard expressing sympathy for a boycott to protest neglect of predominantly Black schools, and asking for "information on how much money the Board of Education spends on their policemen to patrol the schools."

Heather had leapt into the abortion referral business "because I was helping an individual person, and just wanting to do a good deed." Unlike much of what filled her days, it didn't feel at first like political work, because it wasn't public. But after a while she found herself asking, *Why is this secret? Why is it illegal? Why are women demonized for this?*

Heather's involvement in the burgeoning women's movement spurred her to ask a lot of questions she'd never asked herself before. In 1965, she attended an SDS convention where the "woman question" was supposed to be discussed. Women began sharing their experiences, but the men kept cutting them off, contradicting their accounts of their own lives. At one point, Jimmy Garrett, a Black SNCC organizer Heather had known in Mississippi, stood up and told the women "they needed to talk alone together and get their act together." At first Heather resisted the idea—she was dedicated to the vision of the beloved community, men and women of all races working together. But the discussion with the men continued to be frustrating, and it occurred to her that Garrett had a point.

The SDS women got together and talked all night, about "what made us what we are," Heather recalled, "and the ways we are not allowed to fulfill what we could be." In September 1967, Chicago hosted a gathering called the National Conference for New Politics to try launching a presidential ticket headed by Martin Luther King Jr. and the activist pediatrician Dr. Benjamin Spock. When the feminists Jo Freeman and Shulamith Firestone attempted to take the floor to discuss women's issues, one of the male conference organizers patted the brilliant Firestone on the head and told her, "Cool down, little girl," while the male comrades within earshot chuckled.

In January 1969, a feminist journalist named Marilyn Webb spoke at a counter-inaugural rally against incoming President Nixon in a big tent on the National Mall. "Women must take control of our bodies, we must define our own issues," she began. "We will take our struggle to our homes, to our jobs, to the streets." As the rock critic and feminist Ellen Willis, who was there, recalled, "The men went completely nuts," with some shouting "Take off your clothes!" and "Take her off the stage and fuck her!" Time after time, women on the left were hearing they had to wait in line behind other oppressed groups, and they were hearing it in patronizing and sometimes overtly misogynistic ways.

"Building an American women's liberation movement was a matter of survival for politically conscious and skilled women in the late 1960s," said Vivian Rothstein, a leftist community organizer and civil rights movement veteran who befriended Heather after moving to Chicago from her native California. "We were smart, we were dedicated, we had revolutionary ideas—but who besides ourselves gave a damn? We had hit the glass ceiling on the left and there was nowhere for us to go. We were hungry for political discussion with others who took us seriously, and we slowly began to find each other."

The New Left had distinguished itself from the old Communist Party–dominated left through an emphasis on direct democracy and personal fulfillment—a fresh spirit of rebellion against the conformism and repression of the 1950s. In that way it opened up the possibility of reexamining and recasting family relationships and women's roles. But in reality, as one man on the left recalled, the women "were always there and were respected, but it was always the guys who did the writing and position formulating." Moreover, women were often expected to be at once nurturing—to make the peanut butter sandwiches and clean up after the guys at SDS conventions, like fifties housewives—and also sexually free and available (not uptight!) like cool sixties chicks. (The Vietnam draft resistance movement blithely adopted the slogan "Girls Say Yes To Boys Who Say No.") It was in the gap between what the New Left promised to all, and what it actually delivered to women, that Second Wave feminism grew.

In fall 1967, Heather, Vivian, Amy Kesselman—a New Yorker

who'd moved to Chicago to do community organizing under the slogan "If the Machine shortchanges you, kick it"—and Naomi Weisstein, a playful, badass, neuropsychologist who later founded the Chicago Women's Liberation Rock Band—became the nucleus of a feminist collective they called the Westside Group. (Other intellectually gifted rabble-rousers soon joined, including Shulamith Firestone before she moved to New York and wrote the startling bestseller *The Dialectic of Sex*.) Radical feminist collectives were springing up all over the country—New York Radical Women, Redstockings, Cell 16, The Furies. People hitchhiked, and piled into drive-away cars, to go check out new women's liberation scenes in Ann Arbor or San Francisco or Washington, DC, crashing on one another's secondhand couches and poring over one another's mimeographed manifestos. Jo Freeman, another veteran of the civil rights movement who was a member of the Westside Group, credited Heather Booth with getting more of these new women's groups started than any other single person—she put the word out with startling efficiency on the New Left network.

"The best part of the group was that we all took each other seriously," Naomi Weisstein remembered. "We had become so used to the usual heterosexual chill that it was a giddy and slightly terrifying sensation to talk and have everybody listen. All of sudden we were no longer inaudible. I can hardly describe the joy! Unbelievable! The sound system had just been turned on."

The Westside women, Weisstein recalled, talked ecstatically and exhaustively about all kinds of previously unexplored or taboo subjects—whether they could consider "Jackie Kennedy our sister or our enemy and whether we were too middle-class, had too much 'white skin privilege' and were too well-educated to be complaining at all." (Not coincidentally, the Gang of Four, as Heather, Naomi, Vivian, and Amy called themselves, all came from progressive Jewish families where verbal and analytical skills were highly prized.)

They found that "when a movement starts, its force quickly becomes greater and more powerful than the social constraints we bring to it," as Naomi put it, "so after we had kicked around capitalist disaccumulation for a while, we zoomed back and talked monogamy, and our egalitarian, anti-hierarchical vision of utopia and community, and where children fit into our scheme." They talked about makeup and bras (did women have to wear them?) and orgasms (why didn't women have more of them?). They considered their experiences with street harassment and other forms of ogling—should the tables be turned on men?

At one point, they debated whether wearing uniforms would be a good way of helping women evade the clutches of the fashion industry. That was Vivian Rothstein's suggestion—her mother had been a seamstress in Los Angeles and Vivian had enough know-how to suggest a durable, no-iron fabric, and pockets placed for convenience. Not surprisingly, the proposal didn't get far. But it was an indicator of how fluid the possibilities seemed, how much the air crackled with wild ideas.

They wanted to build a radical movement that would encourage people to change their lives, but at the same time, in Weisstein's words, "steer a generous course away from denouncing women for the choices they made in their efforts to get through the day." Liberal organizations like the National Organization for Women (NOW) were doing good work trying to pass the Equal Rights Amendment and win equal pay for equal work, but the radical feminists were bolder, more utopian. Radical feminism bloomed alongside the influential, reformist variety, but it was like a wild, climbing rose, profuse and full of thorns, compared to the neat, productive plot the mainstream women's movement was tending.

Under the influence of radical feminism, even happily married Heather Booth, who was more pragmatic and less countercultural than some of her friends, delighted in performing "zap" actions inspired by the group WITCH (Women's International Terrorist Conspiracy from Hell). Dressed in pointy black hats and black thrift-store dresses, she and Kesselman invaded an all-male panel at the University of Chicago and hexed it, chanting, "Knowledge is power through which you control / Our mind, our spirit, our body, our soul / Hex!"

In 1967, when Vivian Rothstein was twenty-one, she traveled to Vietnam with a delegation of peace activists, including Tom Hayden (who was friends with both Paul and Heather Booth, and would remain so throughout his life). She appreciated that Hayden "was one of the few New Left men who took me seriously as an activist and a person," but it was actually the Vietnamese, not the American peace activists, who had insisted that women be included in the delegation. In Hanoi, Vivian became fascinated by the workings of the Vietnamese Women's Union, which included women-run schools and craft centers as well as political organizing groups. She took the idea home with her and it became the spark for the Chicago Women's Liberation Union, which launched in 1969 and grew into one of the most vibrant of the country's radical feminist organizations.

The women's union embraced a rich and heady array of projects including, at various points: the rock band (signature tunes included "Papa, Don't Lay That Shit On Me" and "Ain't Gonna Marry"), a graphics collective, a rape crisis hotline, a lesbian newsletter called *Blazing Star*, a group called Secret Storm that worked on getting women access to the sports teams and facilities at neighborhood parks, a pregnancy testing service, a campaign to support the female janitorial staff at city hall who were going up against Mayor Richard Daley's political machine, and a prison group that taught classes and worked to improve conditions for incarcerated women.

One of the union's biggest successes was the Liberation School for Women. It held classes such as "Readings in Women's Liberation" ("how we've been oppressed at home, at school, on the job, as sex objects"), "Women and their Bodies" (covering "birth control, abortion, female anatomy and physiology, medical situations"), a self-defense class, and a popular "fix-it" course ("in which we work together to overcome our ingrained fears of machines and electricity, and work with tools.")

The classes, often offered in church basements at night, cost just a few dollars, and there was childcare available. As a result, they attracted not only campus radicals, but also secretaries, cashiers, teachers, nurses, and homemakers. (In the words of one movement publication, they could learn such important distinctions as a "distributor from a carburetor," and "the clitoris from the vulva.")

Heather Booth thought it would be a good idea if Jane became a working group of the Chicago Women's Liberation Union, and in 1969, it did: it was now, officially (or as officially as a stealthy underground organization can be) the Abortion Counseling Service of Women's Liberation. By then there was a growing effort to legalize abortion, and the issue had become more politicized and less hidden than it had been in 1965. Some of the pressure came from medical groups and took a temperate, legalistic approach. But a lot of the energy, and the push to define access to abortion as a right, came from the radical feminist movement.

Women were daring to tell about their own abortions at speakouts like the one organized by the Redstockings in 1969, held at the Washington Square Methodist Church in Greenwich Village. They were loudly disrupting legislative sessions and panels on abortion at which only male speakers had been scheduled to testify. ("Gals Squeal for Repeal, Abort State Hearing" read a headline in the New York *Daily News*.)

Heather had been going around to various meetings of left-wing and women's groups, talking about abortion reform in the context of feminism, and about Jane work as a way to help women *right now*. Her pitch brought new women into the group to take over the day-to-day operations, allowing her to step away from Jane to work on other issues, including a campaign for childcare that ended up winning $1 million in Illinois state funding, along with reforms in licensing and the establishment of an oversight board made up of parents and providers.

Heather's new recruits wanted to wrest control of Jane from the professional abortionists. They wanted to know where the women were being taken, and what was happening to them there. They wanted to lower the price and drop the blindfolds. Heather agreed, but she had never even met Dr. Howard in person. It seemed clear that he would have no interest in working closely with a collective of radical women to create the new kind of abortion service they envisioned. She had, however, made contact with another abortionist—identified only as "Mike"—and he seemed like a promising candidate to take over from Dr. Howard.

Mike was wary at first—he'd agree to meet with only one of the women at a time because meeting with more than one would constitute a conspiracy, he explained. He was also intent on making a decent income for his troubles. Still, he was open to partnering more closely with the Janes. That was to his advantage too, he soon realized. When a Jane was present during the abortion to hold a woman's hand and explain what was happening, the woman was more likely to relax and the procedure to go more smoothly.

And then, at some point, the women realized that Mike had deceived them: he was not, in fact, a doctor. He'd learned his skills apprenticing under another abortionist who probably had an MD, but he himself did not. Members of the group's inner circle found out first. At a meeting where the information was made known to all of the Janes, some of them were appalled. But others saw it as an opportunity. Collective member Judy Pildes (later the writer and activist Judith Arcana), for example, remembered thinking, *If he can do this, and do it well, and he's not a doctor, that means we can do it.*

Soon several of the women had learned to do the abortions—and by the time of the arrests, Mike was out of the picture, and it was only Janes performing them. For a while, there had been no more blindfolds, no more motel-room abortions—and a lot more feminism.

IN 1970, THE state of New York legalized abortion, enabling some women elsewhere who could afford the travel and medical expenses to go there for a safe procedure. But women who lacked resources—mostly poor and nonwhite—continued to have few options in the early 1970s. They had risky "back-alley" practitioners in it for the money, compassionate doctors scattered here and there who believed in making abortion available to women in need—and Jane. (A few might be able go before a hospital committee to plead for a so-called therapeutic abortion that would save them from suicide or a breakdown—a humiliating ritual that, in any case, was generally only available to well-off white women with private insurance, and even for them in declining numbers by the late sixties.) Many of the women who came to the Jane Collective for help had children already. Some had partners who abused them. One Jane had counseled a young woman who'd sneaked away from home. She said her husband insisted she carry her pregnancy to term but got mad because the baby they already had "made too much noise." Mothers called on behalf of their pregnant daughters—on occasion, girls as young as eleven or thirteen who had been raped. The Janes tried to make eye contact and talk to the girls, but it was hard; often they had their faces buried in their mothers' sleeves.

On that fateful day in May 1972, Sheila Smith was glad that her mentor, Martha Scott, would be at the Place. It wasn't that she or any of the Janes knew what would go down that day. Sheila just felt more comfortable working with tall, calm, capable Martha, who was the anchor of the group in many ways. Martha was twenty-nine and had four children, the oldest a set of twins. Her husband, Norbert, who was considerably older than her, was a printer who worked nights, which gave Martha, a stay-at-home mother, time to counsel women in the evenings after she'd put the kids to bed. Norby Scott shared his wife's conviction that the abortion laws were unjust, and figured that if somebody needed to defy them, it might as well be his wife and her friends—in fact, it would be cool if it were his wife and her friends. Some of the younger Janes, especially the broke students, like Sheila, loved hanging out at the Scotts' house, playing with the kids, staying around long enough to sit down with the family for dinner.

The Place was in an eleventh-floor apartment the Janes had rented for the purpose a few months back in a nondescript high-rise on Chicago's South Shore Drive. A view of the lake made the apartment seem ritzier than it was. (The Fronts were set up in an ever-shifting array of apartments and houses lent by Janes and friends of Janes for a few days at a time.) The Janes made every effort to create an atmosphere at the Place that was homey and not antiseptically medical. To Jeanne, the time she and some of the others had spent fixing it up had felt a little like playing house. They'd had fun kitting the apartment out with Marimekko sheets and bright, pop-art-style posters silkscreened by the Graphics Collective of the Chicago Women's Liberation Union. A favorite was the one of a stylized red flower on a black background that said, "Sisterhood Is Blooming. Springtime Will Never Be the Same."

The décor of the Jane clinic reflected a philosophy. The Janes wanted to set their work apart from that of other underground abortionists in Chicago and elsewhere—mostly men who treated it as a way to make a quick, if risky, buck, and who sometimes had connections to the mob. Those abortionists often worked out of cheap motel rooms, offered little if anything in the way of counseling or follow-up, and not infrequently hit on the women who came to them desperate to end unwanted pregnancies.

With the departure of Mike—who originally had wanted to charge as much as he could, up to $500 (the equivalent of over $3,000 in 2020) for an abortion—the Janes lowered their price further, letting women pay what they could, which was sometimes nothing or next to it. One woman paid $36 in coins. When Jeanne Galatzer had the job of driving women from the Front to the Place, she'd pull over on a side street en route to ask for the money—often a crumpled wad of bills she didn't even count, just stuffed in the pocket of her jeans.

But if the Janes didn't want to resemble seedy, greedy, back-alley abortionists, they didn't want to re-create mainstream, male-dominated medicine, either. The abortion service was part of a new women's health movement that was emerging in the late 1960s and early '70s, out of radical feminism. The movement aimed to empower women by demystifying medical and anatomical knowledge, which included teaching them to do self-examinations of their vaginas and cervixes with plastic speculums. It tried to banish the feelings inculcated by puritanical misogyny and modern advertising that fundamental bodily functions such as menstruation were dirty or unseemly. It encouraged women to learn about their own capacities for physical pleasure and to approach sexual encounters with the expectation of reciprocity.

In 1970, when the radical feminist Anne Koedt published an essay, "The Myth of the Vaginal Orgasm," contradicting much of the prevailing medical and psychological dogma about female sexuality, it constituted a life-changing aha! for many people. "Frigidity has generally been defined by men as the failure of women to have vaginal orgasms," Koedt's essay began. "Actually, the vagina is not a highly sensitive area and is not constructed to achieve orgasm. It is the clitoris which is the center of sexual sensitivity and which is the female equivalent of the penis."

Self-help clinics animated by a feminist ethos were popping up all over the country. A self-help clinic "might be held at a women's center, with participants perched on shabby sofas below a poster of a raised fist clenching a speculum," wrote historian Michelle Murphy, or "in the privacy of a woman's home after her children and husband were safely sent away." In any case, they were in "nonmedicalized settings, with women examining themselves impromptu on couches, chairs, or pillow-topped tables. No sterile blue paper gowns or drapes here. Women wore their street clothes, taking off skirts, pants, and underwear, but casually leaving on socks and knee-highs."

In 1970, the Boston Women's Health Collective—like Jane, a group of women in their twenties and thirties who'd met through activism and were rethinking their lives—conducted their own research and published the first version of *Our Bodies, Ourselves* (originally titled *Women and Their Bodies*) in a 193-page, 75-cent newsprint edition from the New England Free Press. As a member of the Boston collective recalled, "People who had post-partum depressions worked on the post-partum chapter. People who had abortions worked on the abortion chapter. We always said the personal is the political, the political is personal, and there it was." Filled with practical information and with intimate, first-person testimony about sex and reproduction that neither objectified nor pathologized women, *Our Bodies, Ourselves*, which the Janes handed out in their offices, became a surprise bestseller, translated into thirty-three languages and still in print today (revised and updated every few years).

Meanwhile, historians influenced by the women's movement excavated a lineage of midwives and female healers. Such women had been persecuted as witches in the medieval period, and in the late nineteenth century were shunted aside in the drive to professionalize the practice of medicine—an effort that, not coincidentally, left it almost exclusively in the hands of men. Inspired by such forebears, the women's health movement defined its own approach against that of male doctors who talked down to women or discounted their descriptions of symptoms.

A pamphlet the Janes produced about their work emphasized that "abortion is a safe, simple, relatively painless operation when performed by a trained person in clean conditions," "less complicated than a tonsillectomy," which was true. "People hear about its horrors because desperate women turn to incompetent people or resort to unsafe methods." In person, the Janes explained everything about the procedure as clearly and thoroughly as they could. There were no stirrups on the beds and no white coats for the Janes on duty. They did not refer to women as patients. "Patient" was a word the medical establishment used—it implied a subject-object relationship—and "we always tried to get away from thinking of women as objects we were going to do something to," as one Jane put it. The Janes and the people who came to them for abortions were all in it together—"All partners in the crime of demanding the freedom to control our own bodies and our own childbearing."

The aim was for women to come out of the experience feeling listened to and respected, as well as physically and emotionally healthy. But the hope was that they would, if at all possible, also emerge with a heightened feminist consciousness. After talking with the Janes, a woman might see that her personal experience had a political dimension—she might be newly willing to think about what it really meant that abortion was illegal. If childbearing (and, in general, rearing) were a woman's work, why was the ability to decide whether or when to give birth denied her?

Not everybody who turned to Jane ended up liking the sisters-doing-it-for-themselves vibe. Lorry, a young Black woman who had an abortion through the service and was interviewed about it later, found the apartment setting too funky. The young white woman who performed the abortion wore jeans and a flannel shirt and had long, flyaway hair—a look that, to Lorry, did not inspire confidence. The whole antiprofessional atmosphere made her wonder if the Janes knew what they were doing, a concern exacerbated by the fact that the procedure was painful for her.

Jeanne recalled that she dressed on the job "like a twenty-year-old poor person. We wore what we wore. Jeans and a shirt. . . . We bent over so far backward not to come off as doctors, or act like doctors," because medicine was "so patriarchal in those days." But it was a leap of faith for women to come to the Jane Collective, she realized looking back, and maybe some of them would have been put at ease by a more professional mise-en-scène.

Still, many women who came to the service for help with their unwanted pregnancies found the whole homespun scene comforting and inspiring. And a few women who obtained abortions through the service actually ended up joining it, which was how many of the Janes had hoped things would go. They included "Lois," one of the few Black women in the group, a civil rights activist in her early twenties who had three children, and who decided to throw her lot in with Jane because she "wanted to be there for women to see. To me Jane was a movement and black women at that time were not interested in that movement because our movement was differ-ent. When people talked about the women's movement, they talked about women burning bras. We were trying to: one, deal with being black women; two, deal with prejudice; three, deal with the struc-ture, being single parents and staying alive. That was our struggle."

For some Black women on the left, the issue of reproductive rights was complicated by the fact that one strain of Black national-ist politics pushed women in the community to bear more children and to resist contraception as a genocidal white plot—writing as one woman did in the *Black Panther* newspaper that "[our] revolu-tionary strength lies in the fact that we outnumber the pigs."

The long history of white interference in the Black family still cast a shadow, as did the eugenics movement, and the legacy of pop-ulation control efforts that sterilized Black and Puerto Rican women at higher rates and often more coercively than white women. Nina Harding, a Black socialist and feminist in Seattle, who is credited with inventing the coat hanger as a symbol of the fight to legalize abortion, remembered that in the early seventies, "to raise the issue of abortion," as Harding insisted on doing, "was viewed as not be-ing supportive of the Black struggle." Still, leading Black feminists including the novelist Toni Cade Bambara, the Brooklyn congress-woman and future presidential candidate Shirley Chisholm, and the flamboyant lesbian lawyer Florynce Kennedy did become out-spoken proponents of the right to abortion, pushing back against the notion that it was solely a white women's issue.

To Kennedy, who in 1970 brought an important lawsuit chal-lenging New York State's ban on abortion, the call for women to have more babies for the revolution wasn't "too far removed from a cultural past where Black women were encouraged to be breeding machines for their slave masters."

The Janes were white hippie types for the most part, and person-ally, Lois favored a more polished, put-together style. Nonetheless, she could relate to her white sisters because they all had "big mouths, just like me." Lois appreciated the "laid-backness, the closeness of the one-to-one basis, the lack of the sterile scene and white walls. I didn't get the attitude that, I'm the doctor and you're the patient. I'd had a baby when I was sixteen. If I'd known Jane, I might not have had it. That's what I was thinking. Maybe the next sixteen-year-old doesn't have to have a child because she doesn't have an alternative."

WHEN THE DETECTIVES started casing the Front, Jeanne Galatzer had the impression they were looking around for some serious cash hidden somewhere. But the collective didn't have that much, and most of it, Jeanne could have told them, because she was treasurer at that point, was in a shoebox in her apartment. Another Jane had a wad of money in her freezer, behind the ice cream. Real criminal organizations, Jeanne mused, were probably more meticulous about how they stashed their gains.

Jeanne did not know it yet, but the detectives had already been to the Place, where they had arrested six of her colleagues—Sheila, Martha Scott, Abby Gollon, Diane Stevens, Madeline Schwenk, and Judy Pildes.

Judy was the driver that day, ferrying women back and forth between the Front and the Place, several at a time. Until a couple of years before, she'd been a high school English teacher in a middle-class township north of Chicago. But when she was twenty-seven, Judy was fired, along with two other young, liberal-minded teachers about whom a few parents had complained. Students would show up in her classroom waving around, say, Eldridge Cleaver's *Soul on Ice* and ask, "Can we read this?" And Judy would say, "Sure, we have to do what's in the curriculum first, but when we finish, we can." She wasn't all that political at that point, just eager to connect to the students, and excited about the material they got excited about.

Judy's marriage, to a lawyer named Michael, was faltering—they kept breaking up and getting back together. In the summer of 1970, when she was out of a job and nearly out of her marriage, she had a pregnancy scare, and somebody put her in touch with Jane.

The conversation she'd had with the Jane who counseled her—a former social worker named Ruth Surgal—had been so deep and honest that she found herself still thinking about it even after her ridiculously late period finally showed up.

The school board hearings about Judy's firing dragged on, several nights a week, for almost a year, airing outlandish claims about her and the two other teachers. It was exhausting and mortifying to sit through them. As long as she was being falsely accused of all this mutinous activity—fomenting Communist revolution while flouting the traditional canon and not taking attendance—she figured she might as well actually do something rebellious. Illegal abortion it would be.

The arrests took place on Judy's first day back on the job with Jane after her maternity leave. She and her husband were in one of their longer reconciliation phases, and six months earlier she had given birth to a baby boy, after a planned pregnancy. There had been heated debate about whether or not Judy and another counselor, a woman named Eleanor Oliver, should continue working with the service when they were visibly pregnant. In the end, though not everyone came around, a majority of the Janes voted to allow it. *As, of course, they should,* Judy thought fiercely: "We always said that women should have babies when we want them and abortions when we need them." Judy and Eleanor's pregnant bodies would show they meant it.

Judy was confident and articulate, with unruly, dark hair; strong features; and long legs, which she used to tuck up under her when she sat at a classroom desk to teach. Her very public firing from the school district and her covert work with Jane had endowed her with a bit of an outlaw swagger. When the cops started following her car that day, they lost her several times, because without even knowing they were on her tail, she'd been engaging in diversionary driving, darting down side streets and varying her routes between the two apartments. Still, when they finally caught up to her at the Place, Judy was the first to be arrested.

Once inside the apartment, where twenty-three women had undergone abortions already that day, with six to go, the detectives barged around, banging on doors and throwing them open. They kept asking, "Where's the doctor? Where's the *guy*?" In the bedroom where she was working, Martha hastily covered up the woman who was about to undergo her procedure. Sheila, who was determined to keep her mouth zipped, picked up a copy of *The Martian Chronicles* that somebody had left lying around and tried to concentrate on reading it.

The detectives sent the women who'd just had abortions to a hospital to be checked out. They handcuffed the seven Janes in a daisy chain and packed them into police wagons, then collected the thirty or so friends and relatives waiting back at the Front, and brought all of them—a roiling, motley bunch—to a precinct station. It was undoubtedly more than the cops had bargained for; usually when they raided an underground abortion business, they came away with a doctor of some kind; maybe a lone, sheepish assistant; and one frightened woman. This time they'd even scooped up boisterous little kids.

On the way to the station, the women had time to consider how they had fallen afoul of the police at last. The service had been functioning in more or less its present form for three years. It had provided thousands of abortions. Despite their worries about surveillance, the Janes had reason to believe that the Chicago police knew about their operation and turned a blind eye. Occasionally they noticed signs that their phones were tapped. Once or twice, when one of the group turned up at a march or rally, one of the Red Squad cops had uttered a sly, "Hi, Jane."

Eleanor Oliver had counseled a woman who warned her not to be alarmed when she called her work number—at the Chicago Police Department. The women in the group were fairly sure they had provided abortions for the wives, daughters, and girlfriends of police officers. The service was a kind of safety valve, as some of the Janes came to realize, taking the pressure off women—but also off men and families—when unintended pregnancy was so common and the law was so rigid.

Typically, the police arrested underground abortionists for one of a few reasons. Sometimes an abortionist who worked with the mob stopped paying protection money, and got ratted out. That obviously didn't apply to the Janes. Occasionally, a woman showed up at a hospital to be treated after a botched procedure, or even died, eliciting the attention of the police. But Jane had an impressively clean safety record. No death had been attributed to anything the abortion service did. There had been one sad incident that pushed some of the Janes to rethink their work with the group: a woman came to see them who had already made an attempt to abort her own pregnancy and developed a serious infection before the group performed her procedure. The Janes on duty told her to go to the hospital, which she did, but when they followed up, they learned she had died several days later.

At some point, the group had decided to do second-trimester abortions in which they assisted women to miscarry, after inducing labor, initially using an abortifacient called Leunbach's Paste, applied by a doctor who came in from Detroit. Some of the counselors had no interest in helping with such cases—they were morally ambivalent about late-term abortions and found them physically and emotionally draining. "We never resolved it as a group," Martha Scott remembered.

Often it was the younger, poorer women, mired in more harrowing life circumstances, who came in for later abortions—teenagers who hadn't recognized they were pregnant, for example—and the Janes found it hard to turn them away. The experience was risky and arduous for the women going through it, and for the Janes willing to assist them, too. Eleanor Oliver recalled that the doctor they relied on for such late-term abortions "never spent more than five minutes with his clients. Those that he treated who did not come through the service were entirely on their own after that five-minute encounter. Can you imagine going through a miscarriage entirely alone, not knowing what to expect next? The whole idea is barbaric. Yet that is what these women encountered. He usually did not even administer the procedure on a bed. He asked them to get up on the kitchen table—it was higher—and that is where he left them."

Still, even with these more challenging cases, the group's safety record remained solid. The Janes' willingness to stay with girls and women throughout an induced miscarriage, offering coaching and comfort, was probably key. And they were careful: they couldn't afford mistakes, even those that in a regular medical practice might be regretted but excused. In the early 1990s, a researcher who examined abortion-related deaths reported to the Cook County coroner in the years the service was active was unable to trace any to actions of the collective. "In fact," he concluded, "over the years of active practice, Jane's medical complications were comparable to those at licensed medical facilities in New York and California."

In the end, the arrests turned out to have been the result of bad luck they couldn't have predicted. Somebody at the Front that day turned out to be the anti-abortion sister-in-law of a woman scheduled for an abortion. She'd tipped off the police in her own neighborhood, not the Hyde Park neighborhood where the Fronts were usually located. The cops there hadn't heard of Jane and they responded with a stakeout at the Front, rather than letting the matter slide, as law enforcement likely had in the past. To her chagrin, Jeanne realized later that the nervous woman she had spent a good deal of time soothing that morning was the very woman who had turned her in.

Now they had to do their best to conceal the identities of the other women using the service that day. A few of the Janes had index cards on them bearing the names and phone numbers of these women. At first, they contemplated tearing them up and scattering them like confetti, only they didn't want to litter. Somebody said, "Chew them up and swallow them!" Linked together in the police wagon, they began to do just that. At some point Sheila calmly observed that they didn't need to macerate and ingest the entire cards—just the portions that were written on.

At the station, the Janes were defiant. The detective who was interviewing Judy said, "Oh, I see you used to be a high school teacher. I used to be a high school teacher, too. What made you go wrong?"

"What made *me* go wrong?" she spluttered. "You used to be a teacher—now you're a cop!"

When Judy and Diane Stevens found themselves in the bathroom at the same time, they realized they both still had cash on them that women had paid them that day. "What should we do with it?" Judy whispered. Diane said, "One thing's for sure—we're not letting them have it." They flushed the cash down the toilet.

The bust was a kind of high, but a hangover was coming. Judy, who was breastfeeding her baby, was starting to get extremely uncomfortable. And she was pissed at Michael, her husband. They had made a deal that he wouldn't go out of town for work while she was on duty with Jane, just in case she ever got arrested. But when she'd called her husband's office to say, OK, *this is it*, his partner had answered and told her Michael had flown to New York on business. One of the Janes was watching the baby, but Judy began to feel fearful. What if they took him away from her?

At one point, Sheila and another of the seven were left unattended in an office, and Sheila started prowling around, poking into desk drawers, where she found a stash of skin magazines. "When the cops came back in to ask us about Jane, I gave them a hard time about having pornography in the workspace." Despite her bravado, she was scared, though. "I was about to graduate and I thought, *Nobody is ever going to hire me.* I just saw my whole future crumbling in front of me."

Later that night, after the friends and relatives from the Front had all been sent home, the seven Jane women were taken in another police wagon over to the women's lockup at Eleventh and State Streets. A guard came to remove Judy from her cell; her husband's law partner and two other young lawyers were waiting to see her. Judy had been milking her engorged breasts over the dirty sink in her cell, and was worn-out.

The lawyers had a plan: They would take her before the night court judge, whose behavior they thought they could predict. He'd release her on her own recognizance. She was a married white lady, a nursing mother, no less, whose husband was an officer of the court. Then when the other six women went before a judge in the morning, he would have a hard time ordering a prohibitively high bail for them, since the terms of Judy's release would already have set a precedent. Judy didn't know what to do—she didn't want to desert the other six. She asked to go back to her cell, where she burst into tears. Then she realized she could shout to the other Janes in their cells nearby. She yelled out the plan and asked, "What should I do?" They told her to go.

The stratagem worked. The night court judge called her Mrs. Pildes and said things like, "Let's get you home to your baby." Bail for the other Janes was set at a not-impossible $2,500. Jeanne's roommate had produced the shoebox full of money from their apartment. Ruth Surgal, one of the Jane stalwarts and the woman who had first counseled Judy, felt guilty about not being arrested with the group, and immediately started chasing down the funds to free them. Suddenly, somehow, there was enough cash to spring the six Janes who'd spent the night in jail. Sheila's boyfriend and her roommate were waiting for her in the bright sunshine of a May morning. She'd never been so glad to see anybody.

Later that day, the Chicago Women's Liberation Union put out a statement that raised the political ante on the arrests. It invoked the 1969 murder of the Black Panthers Fred Hampton and Mark Clark by the Chicago police, aided, it was later revealed, by the FBI. "It is indicative of our 'system of justice,'" the statement read, "that law enforcement officials choose to consider abortion a crime, whereas the murder of black people in their communities by police, and the slaughter of revolutionary leaders like Fred Hampton and Mark Clark by the state go unpunished."

The lawyers who had helped spring Judy wanted to go out to a diner for a predawn breakfast to celebrate their clever scheme, which had, after all, paid off. Judy sat through the meal like a zombie. Back at her home at last, she stood over the crib where the baby was sleeping—just staring at him, drinking him in, not making a sound to wake him up. But he must have sensed she was there because he wriggled awake, and she nursed him. She felt the tension in her body seep away. Who knew what lay ahead? Maybe she'd get divorced. Maybe she'd go to prison. Maybe she'd set out on the road for destinations unknown. For now, though, she was home. Anywhere the baby was—that was home.

THE JANES WHO'D been arrested tried to hang together as a group after the bust. They had the backing of the Chicago Women's Liberation Union, and even the local chapter of NOW. Buttons started appearing on the street saying, "Free the Abortion 7." All that was encouraging. They got together to discuss the case over regular lunches at an old-fashioned German restaurant downtown. Once they all went away, with husbands, kids, and dogs in tow, for a weekend retreat in Door County, Wisconsin, at a farmhouse belonging to a friend of Judy's.

But these occasions could get tense. For one thing, after they were indicted, they had lengthy prison sentences hanging over them. For another, though they'd worked together so effectively, only a few of them were friends; a couple of them actively disliked each other. The women in the service were divided over whether Jane should continue doing clandestine abortions while the seven were awaiting trial. The seven themselves initially thought it was too risky, but others argued they couldn't leave desperate women in the lurch. A certain amount of guilt-tripping ensued. There had been 250 people on the waiting list the day of the bust, and the Janes now helped some of these women get to New York, or Washington, DC, where abortion was now legal.

In the end, Jane did start up again, within two weeks after the bust, run by Janes who had not been arrested. Astonishingly, the police did not pursue the matter. A few of the Abortion 7, including Judy, went back to work in the service, their charges still pending. Abby, who decided not to, thought those who demurred "were considered lesser feminists; we weren't radical enough to put our lives on the line again." She got involved with setting up a Planned Parenthood clinic in the suburbs, and felt good about her work making contraception more accessible: "Prevention is a hell of a lot easier than abortion."

The one thing they all agreed on was the lawyer they chose together. They had gone to fancy law firms where they sat at vast, gleaming conference tables and were turned down for representation. *Abortion and conspiracy to commit it? I don't think the partners would appreciate it if I took that on.* They had interviewed movement lawyers who supposedly had good politics but acted like sexist jerks, addressing them as "girls." And some seemed to want to turn their defense into a cause célèbre, which worried them. "We didn't want to be made into martyrs," Sheila recalled. "We wanted to get off."

They knew Jo-Anne Wolfson was the one the first time they met her. Dubbed the "Queen of the Hopeless," she was one of the very few women in Chicago or anywhere who practiced criminal defense law, and she was tough, brash, and wily. Wolfson's past clients included members of the Black Panthers, which earned her some cred with the Janes. (Not that she was all that politically punctilious: in the next few years, she would defend corrupt cops and a shady equestrian suspected of murdering a widowed candy heiress.) She appreciated how gutsy the Janes were—and gave them high marks for not having told the police anything they could use.

Judy never forgot Wolfson's courtroom outfit the day of the seven's arraignment: canary-yellow pants, a canary-yellow sweater, and a canary-yellow briefcase, all setting off a deep tan, television-ready makeup, and a pouf of auburn hair sprayed firmly into place.

Though the seven tried to neaten up for court appearances, "we looked positively Dickensian next to her."

Wolfson's strategy, aided by several delays on the part of the prosecution, was to drag the case out as long as possible. She knew that the Supreme Court had the case that would become *Roe v. Wade* on its docket, and if they could just wait for that ruling, hoping it would be favorable, they'd be set.

Indeed, on January 22, 1973, the court ruled 7–2 in *Roe v. Wade* that a right to privacy grounded in the Constitution granted women an unfettered right to abortion in the first trimester, and a limited one in the second trimester. The Janes had been practicing medicine without a license, but that wasn't what they'd been charged with—what they'd been charged with was no longer illegal anywhere in the country. The case against the Abortion 7 was dropped.

This was, of course, a triumph, and the Janes gathered to celebrate the *Roe* decision over cheese and bread at Martha Scott's house. But somehow the mood "was more subdued than jubilant"— and in a way, that was prescient. Three years later, Congress adopted the Hyde amendment, which barred federal funding to pay for abortions, making them inaccessible for many of the low-income women the Janes had been dedicated to helping. Abortion was legal, but it wasn't really in women's hands—almost from the beginning, the right guaranteed by *Roe v. Wade* was undermined by federal and state restrictions that often seemed to punish women for trying to exercise it. The Janes knew that all the sneaking around they'd been forced to do as illegal amateurs was far from ideal. Still, sometimes they missed what they had created in the feminist underground.

Meanwhile, the radical feminist movement was disintegrating around them. There were splits between politicos who identified as socialists and wanted to stay strongly connected to the wider left and feminists who wanted to chart a separatist path; between straight women and lesbians; between Black activists who wanted to foreground their issues and white women who thought they could be subsumed in an overarching sisterhood.

The attempt to transform so much of life at once, the personal as well as the political, had been overwhelming. Looking back, Vivian Rothstein thought radical feminism, like other left-wing movements of the time, attracted people who were searching for absolute truths, and "couldn't deal with the fact that there isn't one." The perfect became the perennial enemy of the good; the quest for ideological purity drove subtler thinkers and more pragmatic organizers out of the very groups they'd poured so much of themselves into creating.

Maybe most damaging to the women's liberation movement, though, were the twinned phenomena that Jo Freeman identified in two important essays as the "tyranny of structurelessness" and "trashing." Feminists of the era became so devoted to an egalitarian, nonhierarchical credo that they ended up shaming and ejecting their "stars"—women whose talents or leadership abilities raised their profiles too high above the parapets. Naomi Weisstein felt trashed for her intellectual authority as a professional scientist and even for her success as the parodically strutting leader of Chicago's women's rock band. "The rage against women who stood out in any way had reached monstrous proportions," she recalled.

Jane had avoided some of that. Not that there weren't women in the group who monopolized power and knowledge, and others who resented them for it. But their focus on legally risky, physically demanding and, above all, practical work saved them from the theoretical fights, sectarian backbiting, and endless personal recriminations that felled other groups, including eventually the Chicago Women's Liberation Union.

For her part, after 1972, Heather Booth decided the atmosphere in the Union was "so acrimonious that she no longer recruited other women to it." Her social justice work henceforth would be more inclusive, embracing local and national electoral politics. When she was fired from a part-time editorial job for encouraging her coworkers to organize, she sued, and in 1972, with the money from the settlement she got, founded the Midwest Academy, which trained thousands of labor, community, environmental, and other

organizers. She went on to serve as a chief strategist or field director for many campaigns from Harold Washington's successful run
to be the first Black mayor of Chicago to national get-out-the-vote
efforts for African American voters, to issue campaigns to generate
public support for the Consumer Financial Protection Bureau, the
Affordable Care Act, and marriage equality.

Heather and Paul—who had a long career in the labor movement, most prominently as a leader of the public services employees' union, AFSCME—were married for fifty years, until he died
in 2018 at age seventy-four. Much of the political work they each
did grew out of their partnership. The day he died, Paul Booth was
drafting an article, "Building an Enduring Democratic Majority," for
The American Prospect magazine, and had encouraged Heather to
attend a demonstration on Capitol Hill in defense of the Deferred
Action for Childhood Arrivals program. She was arrested while protesting. In their last conversation, Paul told her he was proud of her
act of civil disobedience. The couple who fell in love at a sit-in had
enjoyed "a deep romantic, social, political, and personal connection"
from the beginning, Heather recalled, and their shared intuition that
they had it in their power to make it last had proven true.

IN THE END, radical feminism's alternative visions and institutions left a powerful transformative legacy. Radical feminism
pioneered consciousness-raising; galvanized awareness of sexual
harassment and rape; contributed to a richer, more inclusive understanding of sexuality, marriage, and the family; created terms
like "sexism" and "male chauvinism"; and pushed liberal feminists
to incorporate some of its fervor and outrage. Jane, for its part, not
only safely provided thousands of abortions; it, like the rest of the
feminist health movement, helped catalyze an important cultural
shift toward empowering women and giving them more agency in
the medical system—more knowledge and control of their bodies,
their sexualities, and their gender identities. Though one in four

women will have an abortion in their lifetimes, the procedure remains politically contested and subject to constant legal challenges. In advocating for its importance as a linchpin of autonomy and equality, feminists today continue to draw on the arguments that feminists in the 1960s and '70s pioneered. And Jane itself prefigured some of the mutual aid groups active today, such as Women on Waves and Women on Web, which have responded to attacks on reproductive rights in countries around the world, including the US, by providing the abortion pills mifepristone and misoprostol, along with medical advice, directly to patients, allowing people to manage their own medical abortions at home.

Some of the Janes went on to train as nurses and doctors, but most did not. The decisions that their experience with the service emboldened them to make weren't always the obvious ones. When Jeanne began to feel more in charge of her own life, for instance, she realized that what she really wanted to do was have children and devote herself to raising them. After marrying a psychoanalyst named Robert Levy, to whom one of the Janes introduced her, she went on to have five, returning to school much later for a master's in biochemistry. For most Janes, the time with the collective was an episode in their lives that continued to burn brightly in their memories, though some kept it secret. "It was the single most intense period of our life," one remembered, "and when it stopped there was something missing."

Judith Arcana, as Judy has been known for decades, is a writer whose work often reflects on her experience with Jane. When she thinks of that time, she is sometimes reminded of a poem called "To Be of Use," by the feminist poet Marge Piercy:

The people I love the best
jump into work head first
without dallying in the shallows
and swim off with sure strokes almost out of sight. . . .

We were of use, thinks Judith. *And it was enormously important to our development—as humans, as conscious women.*

The Martyr Complex

Cesar Chavez, Dolores Huerta, and the Righteousness of La Causa

On the evening of February 13, 1968, in the third year of a bitter strike against the grape industry in California's Central Valley, Cesar Chavez, the leader of the United Farm Workers (UFW), sat down to supper with two movement activists, Ginny and Fred Hirsch, at the union's headquarters in Delano. Fred, once known as "Fred the Red" by his fellow workers in the plumbing business, was only a few days out of the hospital, where he'd been treated for a savage beating at the hands of twenty strikebreakers. A few weeks earlier, in the predawn hours, two men had tried to force their way into the home of Dolores Huerta, Chavez's top deputy, smashing windows and spraying her children with broken glass before driving off when neighbors appeared. The district attorney declined to press charges, which was not unusual. Every week, company thugs drove picketers off the roads around Delano; attacked them with knives, pipes, and baseball bats; and occasionally shot at them. The police seldom intervened except to arrest the strikers for illegal picketing.

Delano, an hour north of Bakersfield toward the bottom of the San Joaquin Valley, was the center of cultivation for table grapes, which grew in monotonously long, flat rows that matched the drudgery of the men and women who worked the fields at the whim of the growers. Chavez had chosen the town as his base to build a farmworkers union in 1962. The tenders of the grape were less migratory than some field laborers; about five thousand of them lived in Delano year-round, which made them good candidates for what would become the union's first big organizing drive. The thirty-eight thousand acres of table grapes around Delano required a lot of attention from skilled workers—tying, pruning, and girdling the vines (removing a strip of bark to keep nutrients flowing toward the maturing fruit), thinning and tipping (shaping) the grape bunches, and carefully harvesting them for attractive presentation to grocery shoppers.

Chavez's brother Richard lived in Delano, and Cesar's wife, Helen Fabela Chavez, had a brother and a sister there. The relatives could be counted on to help out with union business, financial struggles, and care for the couple's eight children while they put in their long days and weeks organizing workers up and down the valley. The UFW depended on extended family to stretch its limited resources—not just blood relatives, but a growing community of students, priests, church activists, and unionists who had left their homes around the country to answer the call of battle with Chavez and the farmworkers. Many of the same sorts of idealistic Americans who had headed to rural Mississippi for Freedom Summer now felt the pull toward California's Central Valley—some, in fact, were already veterans of the civil rights movement.

The UFW had little money but a good deal of solidarity. It was essentially a volunteer organization, out of necessity and because Chavez wanted it that way. "I like the whole idea of sacrifice to do things," he said. "If they are done that way, they are more lasting. If they cost more, then you will value them more." Chavez believed that a religious or moral attitude was key to the success of any movement for social change, and he didn't think you could serve poor people if you weren't living in poverty yourself. Besides,

Chavez didn't think of the union as simply a vehicle for winning better wages and benefits. He wanted to build a poor people's community that was spiritual at heart.

Chavez's philosophy—and the union's chronic shortage of funds—were evident in how UFW activists lived. People slept where there was room on a mattress or a couch or space on the floor, and they ate wherever a meal was offered. When they hosted Cesar on that February evening, Ginny and Fred Hirsch would recall, he had shown an unusually large appetite, consuming several bowls of pasta.

The next day, Chavez began a fast that lasted twenty-five days and changed labor history.

THE LEADER OF the most successful effort to organize agricultural workers in America was a diminutive vegetarian with alert brown eyes and lank, raven-black hair. He walked in beat-up shoes or was driven around in beat-up cars. He dressed in worn checkered shirts that made him look like a tough *cholo*, projecting the street attitude he had cultivated in scuffles with racist whites before transforming himself into a community organizer.

Soft-spoken, five feet six, with perpetual deep circles under his eyes from overwork and chronic back pain, Chavez was the undisputed leader of the nonviolent UFW movement, which by early 1968 had shaken the Central Valley to its core, inspiring thousands of workers and infuriating the agribusiness elite while sending ripples out to all the little towns and hamlets in America where the country's two million farmworkers—most of them Mexican Americans, Blacks, and Filipinos—stooped to weed and harvest crops and prepare the soil under the burning sun for a subsistence wage.

Chavez and many of his top lieutenants were men and women whose parents or grandparents had escaped to California and the Southwest during the Mexican Revolution. Most of the men, including Chavez, had served in the US military during or after

World War II. They were proud of their heritage and determined to force the United States to give them the kind of fair shake that white GIs got after the war.

Born in 1927, Chavez experienced a life-altering blow at age twelve when his father lost the family's ranch near Yuma, Arizona, to a predatory banker, forcing his family to pick up stakes and become migrant workers in California. As they traveled from melon patch to apricot orchard to broccoli field, Chavez, his parents, and his four siblings often went hungry and sometimes camped in tents in the woods during the winter.

The labor contractors who controlled access to jobs were often rapacious and deceitful. The racist landowners and growers dealt with the workers as if they were simpleminded children. "We lived in barracks, shacks, tents; sometimes we lived in our car for two or three days when we couldn't find a camp," the playwright and UFW activist Luis Valdez recalled. Children were barefoot and malnourished. There were no toilets in many of the fields, no clean water, no rest periods. Field-workers bathed in irrigation ditches and were poisoned with dangerous pesticides.

The kids joined the harvest and were lucky to go to school a few months in the winter, and usually in a new place, while their parents were reduced to begging or welfare. Chavez attended thirty or forty different schools and didn't get past the seventh grade. Valdez, who was thirteen years younger, had managed to graduate from high school and study theater at San Jose State College (later University) before returning to Delano to join Chavez in 1965. "You'd drive by these towns that had these neat, decent homes, well painted and with lawns, and you'd wonder, *Why can't I have that? What's wrong with me?*" Valdez said. "You get a very lost feeling."

Righting those wrongs and giving the farmworker some dignity was the UFW's central reason for being. Dignity meant a lot of things: more money, access to health care and decent housing, and a chance to hope for something better for one's children. It meant recognition of farm work as honest labor that entitled those who did it to equal treatment under the law.

The legal system was rigged against farmworkers, who were excluded from the 1935 National Labor Relations Act, which prohibited employers from firing a worker for joining a union. In principle the exception was intended to protect farmers and the nation's food supply chain from midharvest walkouts by striking workers. In fact, it rested on racial and political underpinnings. During the early 1930s, growers and police brutally crushed a series of strikes involving Mexican and Filipino workers. "The majority of farmworkers in the U.S. are minority groups," Chavez said. "If we'd all been Anglos that would have been a different thing."

CESAR CHAVEZ BUILT the United Farm Workers union from scratch, in part using methods he'd learned at the Community Service Organization (CSO), where he was recruited in 1952 by the legendary organizer Fred Ross, an associate of Saul Alinsky and his Industrial Areas Foundation. Ross had organized the labor camp that was the setting for John Steinbeck's novel *The Grapes of Wrath*. He'd engineered the first Chicano councilman's election in East Los Angeles; he got sidewalks built and police imprisoned for beating up Mexican Americans. Organizing, the way Ross presented it, "was so powerful I wanted to commit my life to doing it," said Dolores Huerta, who met Chavez while the two were enrolled at the CSO.

Chavez, whom Ross quickly identified as his most gifted pupil, rose to national director of the CSO by the time he left in 1962 to create the union. On first impression he seemed likable but ordinary—full of soft-spoken humor, warmth, and curiosity about everything. He lacked the oratorical gifts of the traditional leader, but his intelligence, determination, and indefatigability won people over.

Gilbert Padilla, who like Chavez grew up living rough in the fields and served in the military with little to show for it, remembered an encounter with a notoriously racist federal immigration inspector in Fresno in the 1950s, when the two men were working at the CSO to get citizenship papers for Mexican immigrants. When the two men handed the inspector a collection of application cards, he threw them on the floor and called Chavez a Communist. Most of the group backed off a few paces, but Chavez stood his ground. "Cesar said, 'You son of a bitch, pick them up! What did you call me?'" That impressed Padilla. "The others were scared but I liked that. This is good!"

Ross had developed a powerful organizing tool at the CSO—the house meeting—which Chavez perfected. A union activist would get himself invited to a worker's home for an informal talk to discuss grievances. In the process of learning what was on a small group of workers' minds, the organizer would enlist them in the movement to overcome those problems. The format was intimate enough for good communication but it multiplied the organizing message like a virus.

The meetings—conducted by Chavez, Huerta, Padilla, and a few others on the union's early team—went on night after night and year after year in the little towns along Route 99 from Bakersfield to Stockton. Chavez wasn't working in a vacuum. In 1959, a tough Filipino activist named Larry Itliong had created the Agricultural Workers Organizing Committee. Eventually, Chavez and Itliong's forces would merge with AFL-CIO backing, under the union flag designed by Chavez's cousin—the black Aztec eagle on a red background.

By 1964, Chavez's movement had more than a thousand members and a credit union with $25,000 in assets. For their $3.50 monthly dues the workers also got a life insurance policy, which the union took pains to cover. The wife of a worker who bought one of the first policies died of cancer a few weeks later, forcing the union to hold a big chicken barbecue dinner to raise the money to pay her settlement—and Cesar himself did a lot of the cooking.

Chavez turned down grants from progressive organizations, saying that the donations would compromise his movement by forcing it to produce immediate results. Eventually he did accept a $5,000 monthly contribution from the United Auto Workers. Activists trickled into the area, many from the Migrant Ministry, an arm of the ecumenical National Council of Churches. Chris Hartmire and Jim Drake, who were Protestant ministers, were key to the early organizing efforts. In 1965, LeRoy Chatfield left a Catholic religious order to join Chavez's fight. To believe in *La Causa* at this time was truly an act of faith, since Chavez and his organization were running on fumes. "I really thought Cesar was crazy," Drake wrote later. "They had so many children and so little to eat and that old 1953 Mercury station wagon gobbled up gas and oil. Everything he wanted to do seemed impossible." Chavez's only income was a $50-a-week salary. The Migrant Ministry paid for Drake's car and a gas station credit card so he could chauffeur Chavez around the valley.

Dolores Huerta, Chavez's second-in-command, was three years younger and grew up in more comfortable settings in Stockton, where her mother owned and operated a restaurant and later a hotel. Her parents were divorced but she remained in contact with her father, a labor organizer who went on to serve in the New Mexico state legislature. Before joining the CSO, Huerta graduated from community college and worked as a teacher in Stockton. After cofounding the union in scruffy Delano, however, she learned to live bare-bones like everyone else, even with her growing brood of children. She would sleep at night on a mattress on the floor with a pile of kids.

Huerta was tough. Valdez remembers picking her up early one morning at her small, crowded Delano home to chase scab grape trucks down the highway to the Los Angeles Produce Market. When they got to the market, the UFW picketers, led by tiny Dolores, climbed up on a loading dock to implore the brawny warehouse workers—members of the Teamsters, who were at war with the UFW—not to handle the grapes. "A goon came out of some-where and just picked her up and threw her off the dock," Valdez recalled. "She must have fallen four feet. Landed on her back with a thud. I was shocked. How could a man do something like that to a woman?" Huerta was stunned for a moment, then got right back on the dock to restrain Valdez and her other young men—who wanted to "jump the fuckers"—reminding them of their solemn commitment to nonviolence.

Huerta would also display her strength as a negotiator and lob-byist in the union's many confrontations and bargaining sessions with growers and legislators. She gave birth to eleven children by three men, the last of whom was Chavez's brother Richard. But Huerta was mother to many more, her overwhelming commitment to *La Causa* second only to Cesar's sacrificial devotion. Huerta's home life was folded into that of the UFW, and her children of-ten seemed to come second—a defiance of the traditional role of Latina women that horrified the paternalistic growers. But within the farmworkers movement, many viewed Dolores Huerta as a saint.

Chavez's leadership team included hardened veterans of farm labor struggles, religious apostles for the preferential treatment of the poor, clipboard-carrying collegiate types, and radicals of vari-ous stripes. The UFW's legal team was created and led by a brash lawyer named Jerry Cohen. Fred Ross joined his former pupil's fight in 1966 and gave the movement additional rigor, demanding strict accountability from field organizers.

In 1965, the union won a big raise for workers at a rose farm in Porterville (each worker had sworn on a rosary not to break the strike), and led a successful rent strike against the owners of a di-lapidated labor camp in Woodville. But the union's first big battle was not of its own choosing. On September 8 of that year, Larry Itliong—still operating separately—pulled Filipino grape workers out on strike during the Delano grape harvest. After some initial reluctance, Chavez decided to join the strike, and UFW members unanimously agreed at a mass meeting to throw in their lot with the Filipinos. The great grape strike had begun, with powerful significance for the farmworkers movement's future course.

AS THE STRIKE dragged on, the United Farm Workers sent emissaries to speak at churches and campuses around the state. The UFW crusade started attracting activists from the civil rights movement like Marshall Ganz, who had gone to high school in Bakersfield, where his father was a rabbi, and dropped out of Harvard to join the 1964 Freedom Summer in Mississippi. The movement gathered White, Black, and Chicano supporters; liberal church members and radical activists arrived in Delano with station wagons full of clothes and food. At gatherings led by Chavez and Huerta, they all joined in singing songs of struggle and heard inspirational stories from the farmworkers. When these activists went home, they spread the message of *La Causa* and enlisted others to return to Delano.

Some of the new recruits were hellraisers like Alfredo Acosta Figueroa of Blythe, California, whose family were Indian activists and radical mine workers who traced their ancestry to Joaquin Murrieta, the Mexican Robin Hood who fought a guerrilla campaign against Anglos during the California Gold Rush of 1849. In 1965, Huerta recruited Luis Valdez, who grew up in a migrant family in Delano before escaping to get his college education. For him, returning to Delano—"A place you try to get away from"—meant dealing with old ghosts. "I was able to go back and confront the past, a sense of humiliation, the powerlessness, the racism, frankly, but I was able to do it now as an activist." Like the civil rights movement, the farmworkers' struggle brought activists from around the country together with local people, and did its best to try to ensure that the former listened to the latter and were guided by them.

Up and down the state, the movement electrified workers like Maria Saludado Magana, who said that after joining the union, "I felt like I was a person." Even Allan Grant, a staunchly conservative leader of the growers, would later acknowledge that Chavez had "got the farm laborers to recognize that they are individuals with the same rights as any other individual in this country. They have the right to a voice and to say what they think about their treatment."

In Delano, Valdez created El Teatro Campesino, an exuberant theatrical troupe that not only entertained farmworkers but took the UFW message out to the larger world. Valdez and his creative partner, Agustín Lira, belonged to a new generation of Chicano activists who fought not only to secure economic gains but to proclaim the validity of their unique culture in white-bread America. Valdez and Lira were inspired partly by the early-twentieth-century radicalism of the International Workers of the World ("the Wobblies") and the class-conscious German playwright Bertolt Brecht, but their guerrilla theater presentations were proud displays of mestizo culture, with its mixed Indian, Spanish, Catholic, and Nahuatl heritage.

El Teatro shows were brash and brassy, with loud and clear calls for basic American justice. "There is no poetry about the United States," Valdez would say. "No depth, no faith, no allowance for human contrariness. No soul, no mariachi, no chili sauce, no *pulque*, no mysticism, no *chingaderas*." The radical troupe poked fun at the growers who long had demeaned the Mexican American worker as little more than a draft animal. It was low-budget, wisecracking theater, comfortably staged in a university auditorium, on the back of a one-and-a-half-ton truck during a political rally, or directly on a picket line.

By early 1966, the grape strike had gained enough national attention to bring a Senate subcommittee on migratory labor to Delano for a field hearing, where New York senator Robert Kennedy pointedly questioned Kern County sheriff LeRoy Gaylen. When the sheriff testified that he had the right to jail union activists on the mere suspicion they might violate the law, Kennedy tartly suggested "in the luncheon period that the sheriff and the district attorney read the Constitution of the United States."

The day after the hearing, while the press was still in town, Chavez began a 340-mile pilgrimage through the San Joaquin Valley to demand grower contracts with the union. Seventy-five marchers, carrying their black eagle flag and the Virgin of Guadalupe, the symbol of Mexicans' Catholic faith, set off from Delano on March 17. By the time they reached the statehouse in Sacramento on Easter Sunday the crowd was ten thousand strong. Governor Edmund "Pat" Brown wasn't there—he was playing golf with Frank Sinatra in Palm Springs—but the march helped cast a national spotlight on the movement.

As a result of the growing public pressure, the UFW won agreement from Schenley Industries, a major grape grower and producer of brand-name liquors such as Dewar's scotch, to recognize the union. A few months later, the UFW became the first agricultural union in US history to sign a major collective bargaining agreement when it settled a violent strike with DiGiorgio, the biggest agricultural producer in California. To win the DiGiorgio strike, Ross dispatched teams of organizers to fetch five hundred workers from Texas and Mexico so they could vote in the union election. The victories gave workers who'd felt cowed their whole lives a sense of power. "They can stop and shout at the cops," exclaimed Valdez, observing a standoff at a picket line in 1967. "When did farmworkers ever do that?"

AT THE CORE of Chavez's success in the early years of the UFW was his demand for utter commitment from union members. He believed that hard struggle and sacrifice, even in the face of bodily harm, strengthened solidarity. Chavez compared his forces to the Vietcong, fighting a guerrilla battle that employed flexibility and mobility. When a strategic opportunity opened up, "we just turn around and hit it. That's real organization. . . . When we see them make a mistake, we move right in." Such an opportunity presented itself in February 1968.

At this juncture, the farmworkers movement had stalled. The union hadn't signed a new contract in six months and Giumarra Companies, the largest table grape grower in the valley, was resisting the union's strike efforts. Meanwhile, DiGiorgio was ripping out its Delano vines, rendering moot its earlier agreement with the UFW, since it no longer was growing grapes. The day before Chavez had his final meal with the Hirsches, Giumarra's lawyer obtained a contempt citation against the union that accused the UFW of illegal picketing and trespassing, claiming that union members had hurled dirt clods and refuse at scab workers, and spread nails on their driveways and at the entrances to the grape fields. The citation named Chavez and an organizer named Epifanio Camacho, who was running a UFW picket line.

Legal trouble was nothing new for Chavez. He had been arrested or cited many times for violating laws or injunctions thrown up by a legal structure that favored the rich and powerful. But there was an element of truth to the Giumarra complaint that bothered him. After three years of fighting with little to show for it, the farmworkers were getting frustrated. Picketing was a largely thankless task. In the summer you stood for hours in the implacable valley sun, begging and scolding frightened strikebreakers—many of them poor, vulnerable, undocumented workers with families to support—not to cross the lines.

The weather that February felt equally hostile to the strikers' efforts, with the cold tule fog hanging like a shroud, donated coats and knit caps pulled down low on foreheads, breath condensing in the chill air. They were out there alone, at risk of violence from thugs and harassment from the sheriff's department. At best it was grueling work, changing one or two minds at a time. On lucky days, the picketers might win over a small group of workers. But no matter how many strikebreakers agreed to join the UFW, the new union members could easily be replaced by the company. Tensions were rising. Chavez was hearing reports about Camacho's picket—which he ran with fearless Mexican and Filipino compadres—that were starting to trouble him. (Camacho himself denied reports of picket violence.)

Nonviolence was an acquired behavior for Chavez. As a youth he sometimes battled the racists of the Central Valley with his fists; on one occasion, he brawled with a group of kids who tried to make him leave the "white" seats in a movie theater. His union members were not shy about committing acts of vandalism, and Chavez almost certainly knew about some of this activity, though he reportedly told one aide, "I don't want to know." There were packing sheds set on fire, sugar dumped into gas tanks, laxatives slipped into scab workers' food. The union sent "submarines" into the fields who worked undercover to agitate, slowing down and sabotaging production. Under instructions from Chavez's freewheeling cousin Manuel Chavez, Hirsch and other activists had posed as hoboes to smash or shoot up freezer units on freight trains leaving Delano, with the intention of spoiling their loads of cooled grapes. On the other hand, the violence by growers was much worse and more menacing—bombings, shootings, beatings, and tire-slashings of union cars were common.

That week, Chavez published an article in the union newspaper *El Malcriado* (*The Brat*) that reflected his spiritual crisis over the violence he saw rising around him. "The world already suffers from enough misery and bloodshed, without our adding fuel to the flames," the union leader preached. "Our only goal is to end the suffering and pain of the farm worker's life. . . . Even when we are brutally attacked, we do not reply in kind." The union was committed to nonviolence, he insisted, quoting the nineteenth-century Mexican president Benito Juarez, who stated that "respect for the rights of others is the essence of peace." Chavez went a step further: If any union members were guilty of violence against Giumarra, he wrote, "they must turn themselves in" to the union. "We abhor violence, we do not use it ourselves, and we do not wish it in any form."

Turning the other cheek had strategic value, helping to win over a public increasingly weary of ghetto riots, antiwar militance, and televised scenes of police brutality. In Vietnam, the Tet offensive was bringing the fighting to another climax. In the second week of February, 543 US troops died and 2,547 more were wounded, the war's bloodiest week for the American side. Meanwhile, the Chicano activist Reies Tijerina had just spoken at a rally in Los Angeles where Black Panther leader Stokely Carmichael encouraged guerrilla warfare in the cities of America, many of which would erupt in flames two months later after the assassination of Martin Luther King Jr. "Cesar was afraid that if we started using violence, then that violence would be used against us," Huerta said years later.

Violence was also growing in the fields as the farmworkers movement's momentum was slowing. Chavez decided things "had to be zoomed up," said Fred Ross.

The UFW was already embarking on a bold new strategy to take the struggle into the streets of America's volatile cities. In late 1967, Chavez began sending some of his best people—rank-and-file farmworkers and outside activists alike—to urban centers to join with labor, civil rights, and church supporters to organize consumer boycotts of Giumarra grapes. Like all the union's activities, the plan relied on smarts, hard work, and solidarity. Eliseo Medina, a Delano farmworker who had joined the movement in 1966, was put on a plane to Chicago with $100, the name of one supporter, and instructions to get Chicagoans to stop buying grapes. Marshall Ganz and twenty-one-year-old Jessica Govea, a farmworker whose father had worked with Chavez at the CSO years earlier, went to Toronto to organize the boycott there. Huerta would do the same in New York City.

As the boycott was getting underway, Chavez sought to draw some of the media's spotlight back to dusty Delano by offering up himself in a stunning act of personal sacrifice. Chavez would use his own body as a canvas on which to illustrate the struggle of farmworkers, as Mahatma Gandhi had done decades earlier to raise awareness about the independence struggle in India.

THREE DAYS AFTER Cesar's dinner with Fred and Ginny Hirsch, out-of-town visitors took him and his brother Richard to lunch at Abbati's, a favored dining spot. Cesar told Richard that he'd started a fast of penance for his own wrongs and any violence by union members. "He felt he was responsible as the leader of the union for all the acts of any of us," an aide wrote. It was not a hunger strike, launched with specific demands, like those that Irish nationalists had been staging in British prisons for decades, or British and American suffragists had engaged in during their final push for the vote. He had no specific demands, and insisted that his aims were personal and not tactical. Chavez had been reading Gandhi and settled on the idea of a penitential fast to recommit himself and his movement to a strategy of nonviolence. Chavez said the fast was private. If it became public, he said later, it couldn't be used as a bargaining tool in negotiations with the growers.

But the fast would have a powerful impact on the strike. It was one of the most brilliant acts of theater in the history of US social activism.

As word of the fast rippled through the UFW community, many reacted with shock or exasperation. Some supporters, like Chris Hartmire, who led the liberal-Protestant Migrant Ministry, immediately grasped the purpose and value of the fast. Others, such as the Reverend John Duggan, a radical Catholic priest, thought it would distract from the new boycott effort. Tony Orendain, the secretary-treasurer of the union and one of Chavez's earliest UFW comrades, was so upset that he turned his back on Chavez during meetings. Saul Alinsky said the fast was "embarrassing" to his organization. Bonnie Burns, the wife of UFW organizer LeRoy Chatfield, thought Chavez was manipulating the religious beliefs of farmworkers, but she came to accept it as a "spectacular pageant. I began to understand its value, realizing that all of us are influenced by drama that plays upon our emotions and elicits action."

In New York City, where he was leading a grape boycott training program, Fred Ross delivered the news to the union members and supporters. It hit Dolores Huerta like a punch in the gut. "I vomited, and I know the women in the boycotts in New York City broke down and started crying. I think I lost eight pounds the first week of his fast," she said. But Huerta quickly grasped the religious dimension of Chavez's sacrificial act, and she asked a priest to give a special mass the next Sunday. Those who were skeptical of Chavez's saintliness "just couldn't accept it for what it was," she said. "This is part of the Mexican culture—the penance, the whole idea of suffering for something, of self-inflicted punishment." Indeed, a pageantry of penitence takes place each December in Mexico City, when tens of thousands of Mexicans walk for days, some on their bleeding knees, to the shrine of the Virgin of Guadalupe.

On February 19, Chavez invited all union members to Filipino Hall, the cavernous meeting place where the strike vote had taken place in 1965. He told the crowd he was tired of paying lip service to nonviolence as a fundraising tool and meant to make it central to the union's philosophy. How was it possible to oppose killing in Vietnam but support rioting in the cities, he asked? He himself was guilty of condoning acts like throwing dirt clods at strikebreakers, Chavez admitted. It all had to stop.

The fast was a private religious matter and no one could argue with him about it, Chavez said. It wasn't a hunger strike, and if anyone should try to join his fast, "I would be ashamed." Chavez said he was retreating to Forty Acres, the desolate plot between the town dump and some radio transmission towers that the union had purchased for its headquarters with a donation from the United Auto Workers. Then he walked off the stage. Larry Itliong took the microphone and pleaded with Chavez to change his mind. While he had always followed Brother Cesar, Itliong said, he called instead for a petition pledging nonviolence. Manuel Chavez interjected that Cesar was a stubborn Indian and no one would change his mind.

The next day, Chatfield and Richard and Manuel Chavez cleared out the supply room of the half-built adobe gas-station building on Forty Acres. Out went machinery, motor oil, tires, and surplus clothing. In went a mattress, some chairs, and a heater. They hooked up electricity from a utility wire outside. Helen, Chavez's wife, and other women painted the windows to imitate a church's stained glass, with peace symbols and designs of Our Lady of Guadalupe. Around his neck, Chavez wore a mezuzah, the small, decorative container for Torah verses that Jews traditionally affix to the doorframes of their homes. Adorning and sanctifying the room were an altar arrayed with votive candles, along with pictures of Christ, crucifixes, and a huge union banner. Richard Chavez collected fresh cuttings from a nearby vineyard and twisted the vines into small crosses that were pinned above the door.

The Reverend Mark Day, the UFW's chaplain, organized daily masses for Chavez's fast. Day's presence at Delano itself owed a great deal to Chavez's persistence and the powerful influence his struggle was having on American consciences.

Local Catholic congregations, whose pews were full of prominent Croatian American and Italian American grower clans, saw UFW efforts as Communist subversion, and urged churches to blackball pastors who supported the strike. A few months earlier, Fresno's Roman Catholic bishop, Timothy Manning, had ordered Day to leave Delano, and sputtered with rage when the young priest appeared at his door asking if he could stay. As Day left the office, several UFW women, including Helen Chavez, marched in and sat down, announcing they would not leave until Bishop Manning changed his mind. Within a few hours, with tips from UFW members, the *Los Angeles Times* and other media outlets were calling to inquire about the dispute. It didn't take long for the shaken Manning, accustomed to worshipful obedience from Mexican American women, to reverse himself. Day would remain in Delano.

The episode came full circle in early March, when Bishop Manning himself came to Delano to pray for Chavez, saying he appreciated the UFW leader's commitment to nonviolence. As in many sectors of American life, the tide was slowly turning. The growers' red-baiting didn't work anymore. Their intransigence and demeaning language about the strikers pushed moderate church leaders toward the farmworkers' cause.

As Day built a stage and set up tents for pilgrims at Forty Acres, organizers headed out to the vineyards to explain the fast to farmworkers and invite them to the masses. Eventually, more than ten thousand people, mostly farmworkers but also Chicano militants, Catholic priests, Black ministers, and Filipino leaders, visited the shrine. Hundreds were invited into Chavez's room, where he spoke with them from his bed. In the past, death threats had often forced Chavez to sleep in a different house every night. The fast gave him a chance to stay in one place, to pause from day-to-day union business and talk to people. Strike leaders from Central Valley ranches came for intimate planning and strategy sessions. "I did more organizing out of this bed than I did anywhere," Chavez told the writer Peter Matthiessen.

Manuel Chavez, who "did the dirty work" for his cousin Cesar, stayed close to his side and poked gentle fun at him during the fast. "You can't come in, sisters," Manuel told a group of nuns at one point. "Cesar's eating right now." Everyone in the union knew Cesar's unstoppable commitment to the fast and to the cause. If the joke fed into the growers' hostile claims that Chavez was a Commie and a fraud, his enemies' stubbornness and humorlessness were proving to be their downfall. "For our adversaries, irony did not exist," Jerry Cohen said. The farmworkers enjoyed spraying a little playful bullshit—"*Chingaderas*," as Valdez put it—on their white overlords, in the manner of the famous Mexican comedian Cantinflas.

The fast generated a new zeal for the union. "As word went out across the valley and the state, more and more people kept showing up," Hirsch wrote later. "The movement was turning into a crusade, fueled with religious fervor. But for the pervasive Catholicism of it all, Mao would have been proud." Even the non-Catholics in the movement admired the spiritual—and political—power that Chavez was channeling. "Cesar was the only labor leader who studied Gandhi and Martin Luther King," recalled Cohen later. "Can you imagine George Meany fasting?" Meany was the longtime, conservative, cigar-chomping leader of the AFL-CIO, which had embraced the UFW the previous year, although he was leery of Chavez personally.

Chavez grew progressively weaker, but this wasn't his first fast and he knew what to expect. Fasts sharpened the mind, he said, "like when your ears pop as you cross over a pass." He had researched the fasts done by Gandhi and the Irish nationalists, and found that no one died before the forty-eighth day. There were leg cramps the first week, but "after six or seven days you begin not to be afraid of anything," he said. "After fifteen days you're not even afraid of death itself. It's very interesting. You're able to see and hear things you can't normally see and hear. Your senses get very strong." When he watched his children eat during the fast, Chavez said, "they looked like puppies."

On the thirteenth day of the strike, Chavez and Camacho were due in Kern County Superior Court to face the Giumarra complaint, and some three thousand farmworkers awaited them, crowding the yard and street in front of the courthouse, lining the stairs and the corridors of the building and filling the courtroom itself. As Cohen and Chatfield helped the weakened Chavez up the stairs and the escalator to the courtroom, the men and women in his path fell to their knees, one after another, to show respect. At the top of the escalator Chavez turned from the cameras and winked at Cohen—a message that "he hadn't lost his sense of humor or grown full of himself despite the national attention the fast was attracting," the lawyer said. A teenage girl who was staying with the Chavez family and happened to be standing on the other side of Cohen thought the wink was for her and took it as a gesture of friendly modesty at a triumphal moment.

The Giumarra lawyers tried to get Judge Walter Osborne to clear the court and the courthouse but he refused. "If I kick these workers out of this building, it will be one more example of goddamn gringo justice," he said.

From that moment, Cohen felt, the union became an undeniable force in Delano and in California in general. The valley's judicial system was normally under the control of the growers. But that "came into question when thousands of union-conscious farmworkers were drawn to Delano by the charisma of Cesar Chavez," Hirsch wrote later. Their powerful response was "a nonviolent assault on Kern County's citadel of agribusiness power." The judge postponed the proceedings, and Giumarra later dropped the charges. "The religious overtone just blew the court away," Cohen said. It also enabled Chavez to cement his control over the union's direction, converting sacrifice into power.

On the twenty-first day of the fast, Cesar met with his senior aides and agreed to end it the following Sunday, March 10. In New York, Huerta was in touch with Senator Robert Kennedy, who agreed to fly to Delano to break the fast with Cesar in Memorial Park. On Saturday, the day before the planned ceremony, an activist named Doug Adair saw Rudy Reyes, a member of Manuel Chavez's sabotage gang, making Molotov cocktails behind a boulder near the road out to Forty Acres. Reyes said he was following Manuel's orders. Adair and Dolores Huerta, who had returned to Delano for the event, ordered Reyes to get rid of the stuff—the place was crawling with reporters and highway patrolmen. Bad publicity would ruin the whole message of the fast. That night, Manuel banged on the door of Huerta's house, drunk and holding a gun, saying he was going to kill Adair. No one took him seriously.

The mass held to mark the breaking of the fast was "a spectacle of spectacles," one witness recalled. An enfeebled Chavez sat before a crowd of four thousand with a blanket over his knees at an altar on the back of a truck bed, with RFK on one side and Chavez's mother, Juana, and wife, Helen, on the other. Kennedy handed Chavez a small piece of *cemita*, the sweet, sesame-seed-covered roll that originated in Puebla, Mexico. At a photographer's request, Chavez gave it back to RFK so he could hand it to Chavez again. In a statement that others read for him in Spanish and English, Chavez said, "It is my deepest belief that only by giving our lives do we find life. I am convinced that the truest act of courage, the strongest act of manliness is to sacrifice ourselves for others in a totally nonviolent struggle for justice. To be a man is to suffer for others."

In his response, Kennedy gave a strong endorsement to the UFW. "The world must know that the migrant farmworker, the Mexican-American, is coming into his own right," he said. Then he fought through the crowd to the Chatfields' car for the ride back to the air-field. Surrounded by well-wishers on every side, Kennedy spontaneously jumped onto the hood, leaving a dent the Chatfield family would always treasure. "Should I run for president?" he asked the crowd. The answer was a resounding "*¡Sí!*" Kennedy announced his candidacy a few days later. The picture of him breaking bread with Chavez was on the front page of newspapers across the country.

The thirty-five pounds Chavez lost during the fast put a severe strain on his kidneys. The experience astonished believers and nonbelievers alike. Chavez "spent himself like coin in an effort to cement nonviolence into the Union's foundation," Cohen wrote. There had been a penitential aspect to the blistering march to Sacramento during the Lenten period of 1966. But "if the march was my introduction to Catholicism, the fast was a graduate degree," whose discipline and expressive power were "transformational," said Marshall Ganz.

Eliseo Medina, who had always respected the moral aspect of Chavez's leadership, also recognized the fast's organizational brilliance. "It was a turning point," he said. "It was a moment where the commitment of nonviolence could have fallen apart, three years into the strike, no end in sight. When he made that Gandhian sacrifice, it reawakened the depth of commitment that people had. And when Kennedy came out to join with Chavez, that put the movement back on the front pages at a key moment."

CESAR CHAVEZ'S CHARISMA was a vivid and powerful organizing tool. The fields of the Central Valley had become a "battlefield where the fight is not only for agricultural workers but the redemption of the whole country," as one writer put it. A multiracial, intergenerational, interfaith coalition, UFW seemed to offer the last great hope for peaceful change at a time when the movements for civil rights and peace were descending into violence and factionalism. The media loved Chavez. Peter Matthiessen, on assignment for the *New Yorker*, described him as "beautiful, like a dark seraph." He was leading a last-ditch fight against raw capitalism's exploitation of people and the land, Matthiessen enthused, and gained wide respect, even among the young and radical, because he was a true leader. "In an ever more polluted and dehumanized world . . . in a time starved for simplicity he is, simply, a man."

But nonviolence was becoming an increasingly perilous path to tread. As he ended the fast, Chavez received a congratulatory telegram from Martin Luther King Jr. A month later, the great civil rights leader was dead, assassinated in Memphis. On June 4, after the UFW threw all of its resources into a get-out-the-vote campaign in East and South Central Los Angeles, Bobby Kennedy won the pivotal California primary for the Democratic presidential nomination. Huerta was on the stage at Los Angeles's Ambassador Hotel for his victory speech; Chavez, still recovering from the effects of his fast, had turned in for the night. A few minutes after Kennedy finished his victory speech, while shaking hands with kitchen staff, he was shot and fatally wounded. With Kennedy's assassination, the farmworkers union lost its closest friend in politics.

The 1968 presidential election, bringing to power agribusiness ally Richard Nixon, was another dagger.

But the fight had to go on, and the UFW was finding new momentum in its grape boycott campaign. Originally aimed only at grapes grown by Giumarra, the union broadened its boycott to include all table grapes after the company struck a deal with forty other growers to ship its grapes under their labels. This had the effect of focusing the entire California farm industry's attention on the troublesome union.

Under the skilled leadership of Fred Ross and Dolores Huerta, who brought the campaign to New York City—the metropolitan area that accounted for nearly a quarter of Giumarra's market—the boycott spread across the nation. In New York, union activists began their day at 4:30 a.m., organizing picket lines at a Bronx produce terminal. The union drew support from churches, synagogues, and campus groups. The African American community was especially sympathetic because many Blacks had grown up doing brutal farm work in the South. Celebrities like Leonard Nimoy and Joan Baez were a common sight on picket lines outside supermarkets.

California, the union's home state, also became a primary battleground in the grape boycott. The National Farm Bureau, which enjoyed the vocal support of President Nixon, reportedly canceled a convention at the Cow Palace after San Francisco mayor Joseph Alioto embraced the UFW campaign. Fred Ross's son, Fred Ross Jr., was shot at by a security guard at a San Francisco market while leading a boycott action. On one foggy Saturday afternoon, a hundred recovering addicts and ex-cons from the city's Delancey Street Foundation rehab program marched in formation to an afternoon rally with Chavez at Dolores Park. But the group's support came with a price. Delancey's own charismatic leader, John Maher, was a former member of Synanon, an addiction recovery group turned cult that would come to have a sinister influence on Chavez.

The grape campaign leaders, who initially focused their limited resources on a few large cities, found that people were taking the boycott into their own hands, organizing protests in places like Burlington, Vermont, and Syracuse, New York. There were sympathizers everywhere.

"Boycott" became a household word. The campaign began going international. Longshoremen slowed the loading of grape shipments destined for overseas after the Pentagon tripled its grape purchases for the troops in Vietnam to undermine the boycott. "Don't patronize this store," a leafletter told Dolores Huerta as she was walking to a meeting in a fancy New York City neighborhood. "They have grapes and not only that, their caviar is spoiled."

As the campaign began hurting growers' profits, the atmosphere back in Delano grew more menacing. In early 1969, the union got wind of a plot by farm labor contractors to assassinate Chavez, and he acquired two German shepherds, named Huelga and Boycott, to beef up his unarmed security team. At the time, Chavez was in terrible pain and often conducted union business from a tiny bedroom with orange-pink walls, filled with a large hospital bed and a standing blackboard. The room had an electric blanket, a crucifix and votive candles, a statue of St. Francis, a huge picture of Gandhi and a smaller portrait of Robert Kennedy, and a woodcut of a family burying their dead. A black velvet poster bore the faces of the slain Kennedy brothers and Martin Luther King with one word in red letters, "Why?"

The grape boycott was a remarkable success. Some seventeen million Americans stopped eating grapes to support it, and by July 1970 table grape shipments were down 24 percent in the top ten North American markets, according to data gathered by the union. President Nixon and his attorney general John Mitchell tried unsuccessfully to get the Justice Department to declare the boycott illegal. California governor Ronald Reagan declared it "immoral." But sinking prices, evaporating markets, and bad publicity of every type eventually drove the growers to the bargaining table. To speed negotiations, Chavez again resorted to fasting for several days in July 1970.

On July 29, John Giumarra Sr. led a group of twenty-nine Delano-area growers out to Forty Acres to sign a contract that would end the boycott and provide benefits to sixty thousand California table grape workers. Chavez broke his fast with matzoh and Diet Rite Cola, his main nutrients on the go. After five years of struggle, the UFW had won a powerful victory. But there was no time to celebrate.

A WEEK BEFORE he signed the grape contracts, Chavez had sent telegrams to twenty-seven vegetable growers saying the UFW wanted to negotiate agreements with them. The growers, concentrated in the Salinas and Santa Maria Valleys a few hours' drive west of Delano, saw the writing on the wall and quickly devised a plan to keep the movement at bay. The very week that the grape growers were inking contracts with the UFW, the vegetable industry signed two hundred sweetheart deals with the Teamsters Union that covered crops like cauliflower and artichokes, and especially lettuce. "It was a roller coaster," recalled Marshall Ganz, who was the UFW's organizing director at the time. "The joy of getting those [grape] contracts and seeing the growers fall one by one after five years. Then you get a gut punch! So it's like, OK, we have to go to battle."

The vegetable industry's hasty move would backfire badly. "The growers brought down upon themselves exactly what they thought they were avoiding," Jerry Cohen noted. The union's success in the grape campaign electrified the vegetable workers. On August 2, 1970, the day after the grape contracts were signed, Chavez and Ganz drove from Delano over to Salinas, where thousands of workers converged on Hartnell College in Salinas with homemade banners identifying their companies and ranches, interspersed with American and UFW flags.

"It was a big deal! A Mexican guy kicking ass!" Ganz recalled. "That had all kinds of meaning for people. Holy shit, this isn't just a dream, this is real, look at the benefits! It was a fire on a dry plain that just ignited something. And that felt like a real movement that I had never experienced before. That experience in Salinas was just unbelievable."

The fight in the vegetable fields involved different actors, and required different strategy. While the grape industry tended to hire individual workers, the vegetable workers traveled the migrant labor circuit from Salinas to Fresno to the Coachella and Imperial Valleys in crews of twenty-five to thirty men. Vegetable growers paid by the piece, rather than the hourly wage typical of grapes, and that incentivized the crews to form skilled teams that could quickly pick, pack, and load the crops. "These were young men— rough-and-tumble guys who worked piece rate, had a work life expectancy of 10 years . . . worked hard, lived hard and partied hard," one observer wrote.

The vegetable growers were also better organized than their counterparts in grapes. The industry had banded together decades earlier to import Mexican braceros and deal with US Labor Department inspectors and immigration officials. The vegetable pickers hadn't received a raise in years and were eager for a fight. The growers, organized in advertising and marketing alliances, formed a united front against their workforce—they hired goons with attack dogs and brought in Teamster toughs from as far away as Los Angeles.

"I had to learn to incorporate the nonviolence practiced by Cesar. Let me tell you, this was not easy for a barrio dude like me!" recalled Rey Huerta, an engineering draftsman from East Los Angeles who joined the UFW as a volunteer in time for the Salinas battle. "To let the rednecks call us degrading names, to let them beat us, arrest us, then run over us—all these things were really stretching my commitment to the cause for justice."

On August 24, some five thousand farm workers rallied in Salinas to support a strike vote. Harry Bernstein, a longtime labor reporter for the *Los Angeles Times*, later told Ganz he'd never seen

Martin Luther King Jr. led a 1966 "March Against Fear" in Mississippi, flanked by civil rights leaders Floyd McKissick (*left*) and Stokely Carmichael. King increasingly reached out to militant leaders as he tried to build a coalition against war, racism, and poverty.

Tom Hayden, with Black Panther leader David Hilliard (*left*), came to New Haven, Connecticut, for a protest to free Panthers Bobby Seale and Ericka Huggins. Hayden saw himself as "the man with the portfolio," able to move smoothly between the power elite and radicals.

Hayden posed with Anne Weills during
a Richard Avedon photo shoot of the
Chicago Eight. Although he asked
Weills to marry him, Hayden later lost
out to the radical feminist when he was
purged from the Red Family collective.

Exiled from the Berkeley left, Hayden moved to Los Angeles, where he partnered romantically and politically with actress Jane Fonda. Hayden and Fonda's dynamic alliance helped revive the peace movement and cut off funding for the Vietnam War.

In 1975, Hayden and Fonda, photographed with their son, Troy, on the porch of their Santa Monica home, prepared for his U.S. Senate challenge. Hayden tried to bring New Left ideas into the electoral arena, while Fonda revived her acting career with politically charged films.

Black Panther Party chairman Bobby Seale spoke at a Free Huey rally in Oakland, California, in July 1968. Seale embraced armed self-defense as a constitutional right, but always envisioned the party moving into electoral politics. He ran for Oakland mayor in 1973.

Seale and Black Panther cofounder Huey Newton stood outside the party's national headquarters in Oakland in 1971. Seale publicly celebrated Newton's courage and charisma, but struggled to contain Huey's temper and later his substance abuse and criminality.

Kathleen Cleaver, pictured in 1968, won respect for taking over Black Panther press relations when the party's leadership was jailed or on the run from police. But later she joined her husband Eldridge in Algeria after he jumped bail and fled overseas.

Eldridge Cleaver was a riveting speaker and powerful writer, but Seale clashed with him over his incendiary rhetoric and behavior. Years after the organization splintered, Cleaver admitted he initiated a bloody shootout with Oakland police and also beat his wife.

Heather Booth's experience registering Black voters during the dangerous 1964 Freedom Summer in Mississippi helped turn her into a lifelong activist. Here she is (playing the guitar) with the legendary civil rights figure Fannie Lou Hamer.

As a University of Chicago student, Booth started the daring underground abortion service known as Jane. She went on to found or direct many other progressive organizations, including Citizen Action, where she's pictured in 1980.

On a sunny afternoon, some of the Janes took a break from their clandestine work. The risky nature of their mission helped the group cohere better than more fractious women's liberation groups. *From left to right*: Martha Scott, Jeanne Galatzer-Levy, Abby Pariser (Gollon), Sheila Smith, and Madeline Schwenk.

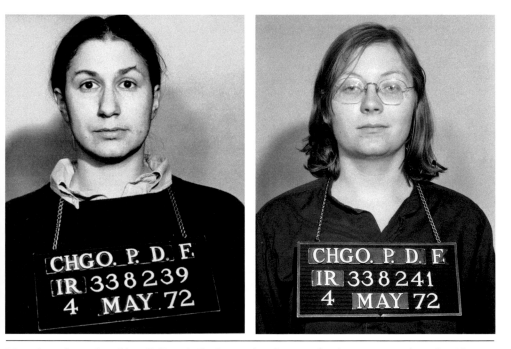

Mug shots for Judy Pildes (*left*) and Sheila Smith taken on the day in 1972 when the Chicago police arrested the Abortion Seven.

Cesar Chavez talked with farmworkers near Fresno, California, in 1975. He wanted to go beyond traditional labor organizing and build a poor people's movement based on spirituality.

Chavez ended his twenty-five-day fast in March 1968 by breaking bread with Senator Robert F. Kennedy. The farmworker leader's sacrificial hunger strikes wreaked havoc on him physically but, in the beginning, energized his movement.

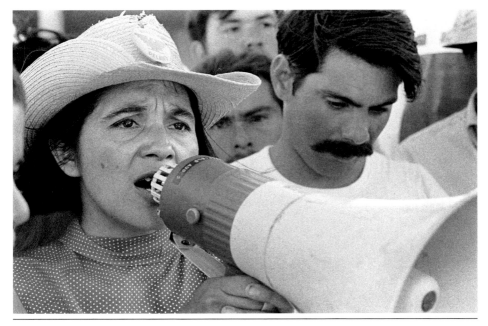

Chavez's essential partner, Dolores Huerta, was equally committed to his vision of militant nonviolence. Shown here at a 1969 rally in Coachella, California, she became a sainted figure within the United Farm Workers movement.

Progressive movement leaders often turned out for one another, as in this dual appearance by Huerta and Martin Luther King Jr.'s widow, Coretta Scott King (*left*), when Chavez was jailed in Salinas in 1970.

Craig Rodwell, an angry young man with charm, opened the first gay bookstore in the world and made it a hub of activism. He posed at his Oscar Wilde Memorial Bookshop, in New York, in 1970.

The 1969 Stonewall uprising might never have become a historic rallying symbol for the modern LGBTQ movement if it weren't for Rodwell. The Christopher Street Liberation Day parade, held a year later, in June 1970, became the first pride parade.

The lesbian activist Ellen Broidy *(second from left)* marched with friends at the Christopher Street Liberation Day parade. Like many in the New York streets that day, she woke up not knowing what to expect and ended the afternoon feeling inspired in a whole new way.

Martha Shelley, one of a new generation of gay activists with strong ties to the counterculture and the wider left, gave the "power to the people" salute at the Oscar Wilde Memorial Bookshop in 1969.

Casting off the burden of Beatledom, John Lennon and his wife, Yoko Ono, moved to a modest Greenwich Village apartment in 1971 and began a year of living dangerously, working with radical activists to bring down the Richard Nixon presidency and end the Vietnam War.

In the early morning hours of December 11, 1971, Lennon strode onstage at a University of Michigan stadium for his first solo performance in the U.S. He used the benefit concert for imprisoned activist John Sinclair to announce his radical plans: "We start again."

John and Yoko joined a protest march in 1971, as they ramped up their activism. The celebrity couple spoke out against U.S. and British imperialism, the mass killing of rebellious Attica state prisoners, the sexual exploitation of women, and other injustices.

Lennon inflated Ono's idea for street peace posters to a Beatles-size vision, with billboards in a dozen cities, from New York's Times Square to Tokyo. It was time to counter endless war propaganda, the musician declared: "Our product is peace."

American Indian Movement (AIM) cofounder Dennis Banks struck a contemplative pose on the South Dakota plains in 1974, the year after Native Americans took a stand at Wounded Knee against heavily armed officials and militia.

AIM leader Russell Means (in dark glasses) held a press conference after the occupation. "What Wounded Knee told the world was that John Wayne hadn't killed us all," he later stated.

Madonna Thunder Hawk sang at a ceremony during the Wounded Knee siege. "We women didn't need to make a big deal out of everything we did," said Thunder Hawk, who played a key role as a medic and leader.

Lenny Foster, a twenty-five-year-old Navajo, led Dennis Banks through the fortified encirclement on the final night of the occupation. Foster, holding his M-1 carbine in a beaded scabbard, was prepared to give his life for his "general."

Actress-activist Sacheen Littlefeather said she was "redlisted" in Hollywood after she delivered Marlon Brando's statement on behalf of American Indians at the March 1973 Academy Awards ceremony. But she never regretted the media protection she gave Wounded Knee warriors.

Bill Zimmerman (*left*), with Dennis Banks, personified the solidarity between protest groups. Zimmerman registered Black voters in Mississippi, helped organize the 1971 Mayday protest against the Vietnam War, led the airdrop over Wounded Knee, and chaired Tom Hayden's run for U.S. Senate.

anything like it. From King City to Salinas, a distance of fifty miles, "it was nothing but red flags all the way."

As the strike deepened, production of lettuce plummeted to a quarter of its normal level and the price doubled. The growers hired scab workers; Chavez responded with a lettuce boycott and was threatened with an injunction and arrest. After returning from a round of television appearances and speeches in New York City, Chavez was happy to report to jail, because it gave the union an opportunity to create a media circus rivaling the spectacle of the earlier court proceedings in Delano.

Escalating its rhetoric, the UFW drew a tenuous link between the lettuce grower Bud Antle and Dow Chemical, which was notorious for producing napalm, the incendiary agent being sprayed in Vietnam by US forces. Chavez told his followers, "Boycott Antle, boycott Dow, boycott the hell out of them!" After Chavez spent two weeks in jail, the California Supreme Court voted on December 23, 1970, to dissolve parts of the injunction against Chavez and ordered him released. Interviewed on the steps of the jail, the union leader described it as damp and leaky, like a labor camp, and suggested wryly that Monterey County should build a new one. He thanked Ethel Kennedy, Robert's widow, who had joined the vigil for his release. Then he was driven home to spend Christmas with Helen and their family in Delano.

This was a high point in the life of the UFW. There would be more victories, culminating in the Teamsters' withdrawal from California's fields in 1977. But by then, the UFW's visionary leader was well on his way to becoming more of a cult figure than a labor organizer.

A FEW MONTHS after his release from jail, Chavez decided to move his headquarters to a 187-acre compound called La Paz, a former tuberculosis sanatorium nestled in the Tehachapi Mountains, an hour south of Delano and four hours from Salinas. The decision, controversial among his advisers though not seriously challenged at the time, can be seen as the beginning of the end of the UFW as a powerful force in agriculture.

Chavez was a searching soul and autodidact, a voracious reader of books as a means of self-invention and self-improvement. He saw La Paz as a place to start fresh with the union, a community where he could train a generation of farmworkers in religious principles, healthy living, and collectivism. In Gandhi's autobiography, subtitled *The Story of My Experiments with Truth*, the Indian leader stressed that he had followed practices of simplicity, dietary restriction, celibacy, and nonviolence in the hope of opening himself to God's will during his well-publicized battles against racism and colonialism. Chavez read Gandhi's book many times, and he would forever elevate the idea of sacrifice as primal to *La Causa*. At times it would become a principle deployed to shout down more practical considerations.

Even in 1968, as he was beginning the fast that would lead to remarkable gains for the farmworkers, Chavez expressed a strong antimaterialism. "When the union began, nonviolence was at the center," he said. "Now we're more concerned with paid vacation and an extra dime an hour." As the union got closer to signing contracts in 1970, Chavez worried that organizers would create a labor elite with a lot of benefits surrounded by a world of suffering. "The only way to correct this is by organizing in the rural area on a broader scale," he wrote.

A fundamental split was developing within the UFW between those focused on the traditional union objectives of improving wages, working conditions, and representation of labor, and those who saw the union as a grander *Causa* with aims that included raising consciousness and building a poor people's party. One activist described the two camps as *"sacrificios"* and *"beneficios."* It was clear which avenue Chavez wanted to pursue. He had done more than perhaps anyone in US history to win material gains for farmworkers. But he was scornful of those who saw these gains as ends in themselves. It was a kind of otherworldly attitude, and eventually it would contribute to the union's collapse.

To be sure, no one would deny that sacrifice had been the essential element of the UFW's mold-breaking practices. Chavez and his cohort had demonstrated their absolute commitment to the cause through fasting, marching, subjecting themselves to violence and innumerable arrests, and living in abject poverty. (UFW activists, including most of the leadership, typically received $5 a week, plus room and board.) The missionary nature of their work, Chavez believed, was necessary to inspire the farmworkers to risk going on strike. And it was an essential part of the union's appeal to the millions of Americans who boycotted grapes and lettuce and marched on picket lines with striking workers. During Chavez's 1968 fast, the movement had distributed leaflets that read, "He sacrifices for us. And his sacrifice demands a response from each and every one of us."

In the view of Chavez and his deputies, the *beneficios* weren't possible without the *sacrificios*. Yet at times it seemed Chavez saw sacrifice as the main point. He became too much of a saint—a wisecracking one, to be sure, but his expectations of others grew ever more rigorous and excessive at a time when the union needed to expand and become more professional about its prime mission. Doug Adair, who was editor of *El Malcriado* in 1968, thought the transformation began with the fast that year—the rising passions around it had lifted Chavez onto a pedestal. He was no longer "Brother Chavez" but an "unapproachable father." Some saw an increased unwillingness to cede power and decision-making to field-level organizers who had risen to leadership from the base, as he had.

In 1971, Eliseo Medina returned from his boycott work in Chicago and found the union's fieldwork in disarray. One of the union's major demands in addition to better wages and benefits was the replacement of labor contractors, the middlemen who did the hiring for the growers, with a system in which work assignments would move through union halls. Many of the contractors—though not all—were known to play favorites and screw people out of their wages.

But creating an efficient hiring hall based on worker seniority, as the union sought to do, was complicated because of the long-standing relations among farms, contractors, workers, and their families. The diversion of the UFW's attention to the Salinas vegetable fields led to neglected administration of the grape contracts, including the hiring process. The union's rigidity infuriated rank-and-file members. In his new job running the union's operations in Calexico, on the Mexican border, Medina saw that the dispatching system was splitting up families and leading to bribery. The workers didn't want a revolution, as Medina saw it; they wanted a decent living and saw the union mainly as a means to that end.

Such problems no longer really engaged Chavez, who tended to lose interest in campaigns when there was no obvious corporate enemy in the crosshairs. He now focused on building La Paz, where roughly 250 people would live at any time. Under Chavez's direction, La Paz communards planted an organic garden, cooked in a community kitchen, and ate in a common dining area. He wheedled volunteers into staying on beyond their planned periods of service and resisted calls to start paying professional salaries to field organizers, which he saw as an opportunity for corruption.

By the mid-1970s, Chavez was hovering in air much more elevated, or eccentric, than that inhabited by workers in the field. In February 1977, the nine-member UFW board was asked to meet at a lodge in the Sierra foothills owned by Synanon, an increasingly shadowy organization that Chavez had apparently come upon through John Maher's Delancey Street. Synanon founder Charles "Chuck" Dederich Sr. had built a successful recovery and real estate empire. The organization's frighteningly disciplined internal structure appealed to Chavez, who felt oppressed by administrative problems and a not always competent staff. But by this time, Synanon was descending into a criminal and even murderous cultishness.

"We were greeted by people with shaved heads. Everybody's, like, super nice," Ganz recalled about the 1977 union board meeting. "There's no smoking, which made some of us crazy, but lots of food." Board members Medina and Ganz had prepared a presentation for the meeting that included ambitious plans for the union's future organizing among citrus and vegetable workers. "Before we could even get to that, Cesar presented the subject of who we were as a union, where we were going; did we want to be a business union or a movement?" Medina said. That ended any discussion about the union's future in the fields, and "that issue never came up seriously again."

Chavez would force the board to start playing "the Game," a mind-control technique that Synanon leader Dederich had originally developed as a way to break down bad habits in drug addicts. Participants in the Game would subject an individual to withering abuse for an hour or two, with the goal of exorcising harmful behavioral patterns. It was also a mechanism for Dederich, and in turn Chavez, to gather intelligence on their underlings' thoughts and weaknesses.

The Game proved to be poison for the UFW. The exercise fed Chavez's growing paranoia about conspiracies against his leadership. Increasingly isolated and obsessed with his own power, he took a six-day Silva mind control course in Los Angeles in 1978 and then announced he could cure ailments by laying on hands. When Chavez declared that he could read people's "auras," such was the abject state of many union members that they told one another they could see auras, too, including a heavenly one around Cesar's head.

When other union leaders resisted his unsound ideas, Chavez would threaten to quit. He opposed efforts to build up local chapters with their own elected leaders, and defeated renewed efforts to create paid organizing positions in the field. That crippled the development of leadership. Not many skilled organizers with families were willing to work for a few dollars a week, as Chavez continued to demand. "It was a question of control," Medina recalled. "That led to a lot of internal conflict and eventually led a lot of people to leave."

One by one, all the union leaders who had accompanied Chavez on the UFW's long march left the union—a long exodus of young, talented activists that had begun years before, when Chavez purged leftists and then drove out the talented Luis Valdez, whom he saw as threat to his reign. "Looking back, I find it ironic that we could negotiate contracts with growers, pacts with Teamsters, and a law with agribusiness, but we could not settle our internal disputes," Jerry Cohen wrote in 2009. He left the union in 1979 after Chavez fired the legal staff, who were vital to representing workers before the California Agricultural Labor Relations Board, and replaced them with inexperienced law students.

"We never found the solidarity or the courage to say 'Cesar, it's time for you to go,'" Ganz said. By 1981, the only remaining leaders were the ever-loyal Huerta, Chavez, and their mingled family members.

By the time that Chavez died in his sleep of a heart attack in 1993, United Farm Workers membership had sunk to about five thousand people. At sixty-six years of age, "the hunger artist"—as he came to be known by the media—had worn out his body with multiple fasts.

Over the years, Dolores Huerta had argued constantly with Chavez, and had been repeatedly fired by him, but each time she simply showed up for work the next day and life went on. But at critical times, Huerta had sided with her UFW cofounder, even taking part in the Game sessions when long-serving officials Medina and Ganz were accused of plotting to take over the union.

Reflecting years later on her relationship with Chavez, Huerta said simply, "I should have fought with him more."

The collapse of the United Farm Workers was a tragedy not only for the devoted organizers who worked with Chavez and the thousands of workers they tried to help, but for a broader society that is still struggling to honor its "essential workers." If the UFW had taken another direction, "I think we would have a big union of farmworkers in California, a powerful voice for farmworkers today and in the future," Medina remarked. "When you dedicate your life to something, and pour your heart and soul into it, and have it disintegrate, it's bad."

But not everything was lost in the collapse of the UFW. The movement pioneered new methods of organizing and trained cadres of activists who would go on to many other fights for social justice and workers' rights. The UFW showed the power of consumer boycotts and cross-cultural alliances, of voter registration drives and publicity campaigns. Above all, perhaps, the union demonstrated the transcendent appeal of integrating economic demands with calls to moral and spiritual conscience.

Veterans of the UFW campaigns would win better conditions for janitors, hospital and hotel workers, organize boycotts against repressive regimes in countries like El Salvador and apartheid South Africa, and register record numbers of Latino voters—giving Barack Obama a slogan for his 2008 presidential campaign: Yes, we can! (*¡Sí, se puede!*) Medina launched his own twenty-two-day hunger strike in 2013, at the age of sixty-seven, to demand immigration reform. "I learned so much and my life changed so much as a result of having been with the union that I don't regret a minute of it," he concluded.

After finally leaving the UFW in 2002, Huerta started the Dolores Huerta Foundation to train a new generation of organizers, modeled on the Community Service Organization, Chavez's and her alma mater. As she turned ninety in 2020, Huerta was still fighting the good fight. The previous year, she was arrested by Fresno County, California, sheriffs while demonstrating for livable wage increases for home care workers.

For thousands of men and women, life had no higher purpose until Cesar Chavez led them on a noble crusade. He failed only by not leading the farmworkers movement all the way to the holy land.

More than two decades after Chavez's death, *New Yorker* writer Nathan Heller offered an astringent reappraisal of his life—a sort of retort to the euphoric portrait of Chavez that Peter Matthiessen had written for the magazine during the UFW's rise. But Heller still had a hard time taking the farmworker leader off his pedestal entirely. "Chavez set out to be a moral leader, but, by the end of his life, that possibility had faded," wrote Heller, "and he had ended up something more interesting and compromised: an American hero."

Liberation Day

Craig Rodwell and the Making of Pride

The shop was everything Craig Rodwell had imagined, and his imagination had been everything when it came to the shop. In 1967, the year he opened it, there was nothing like his establishment in the United States—in the world, for that matter. To save up the $345 he needed for the first three months of rent on a storefront near Washington Square in New York, he had worked sixteen-hour days, two summers in a row, at a hotel on Fire Island frequented by gay men. That part would have been more than fine—Craig, who was twenty-five that first summer, was gay himself and proud of it. A working-class Chicagoan who had come to New York to study ballet and hang out in the neighborhood he hadn't known any better than to pronounce "Green-witch" Village, he had a dancer's lithe body, brown hair he wore neatly side-parted, and an angry-young-man intensity that belied his preppy good looks and drew people to him, if it didn't scare them off first. But one of Craig's duties at the hotel was loathsome to him. He had to sit on top of a tall ladder in the hotel bar and shine a flashlight on men who looked like they might dance together. Local authorities throughout the country allowed bars that catered to gay people to stay open, often under mob ownership and at the price of regular payoffs to the police. But they also exerted control over what went on inside, using laws against lewd behavior and disorderly conduct, for example, to prevent men from dancing with men or women with women. Sometimes pissed-off men would shake the ladder on which Craig or another employee was perched. Inwardly, he applauded them.

Outwardly, and uncharacteristically, Craig did as he was told. The Oscar Wilde Memorial Bookshop would be worth it, he thought, in part because it would be the spiritual opposite of that ladder in the bar and everything it symbolized. It would have nothing to do with the shame-inducing, exploitative spaces to which many queer people had accustomed themselves with varying degrees of alienation. Here, there would be no police raids, no blackmailing of closeted customers, no flashlights unless the power went out. Patrons could freely browse and converse and mingle, and, he hoped, organize.

Craig had been raised as a Christian Scientist, and though he no longer practiced the religion, the model of the Christian Science reading room inspired him. The bookshop he wanted to open would be a hangout, a community gathering place in a way that most bookstores weren't in those days. He would offer free coffee and cookies and tack political posters and meeting notices to the walls. It would be a store devoted to books by and about gay people; owned by a gay man; and unlike most gay bars, welcoming to women as well as men.

The store would not sell porn magazines, though over the years plenty of shoppers came in looking for them. In his private life, he was certainly no puritan. Craig was a habitué of the gay cruising scenes in Washington Square Park bordering McDougal Street; on the city's Upper West Side; and at Riis Park Beach in Queens. These cruising spots, colloquially known as "meat racks," were sexual banquets for a young man like Craig, reliable places to find willing partners for a hot, quick encounter, and sometimes more. He was also intimately familiar with the police harassment that went along with these pursuits—he'd been arrested more than once for curfew violations or other minor infractions of city codes, and the cops had knocked him around like he was "wanted for murder in Kansas or something."

A hookup with a man he met cruising on Central Park West and Eighty-Eighth Street in 1962 soon turned into a full-fledged love affair. Craig was twenty-two. The man was ten years older, jokey, Jewish, ardent, and urbane. A former navy diver and high school math teacher now working as a statistician for an insurance firm, he was, as Craig described him, "an enveloping kind of personality" given to ingenious romantic gestures. He introduced his younger boyfriend to the ethnic restaurants of New York—Ukrainian, Middle Eastern, Japanese; the man loved the richly varied fabric of the city and wanted to savor all of it, and for Craig to savor it with him. Craig was then a student at a ballet studio in Carnegie Hall, and poor as a cute gay church mouse. When he told his lover that he took his lunch break on a rock in Central Park every day, the older man gave him a tiny porcelain vase and a paper flower to adorn the picnic spot.

The man, whose name was Harvey Milk, was closeted and politically conservative—a Goldwater supporter in the 1964 presidential election. It would be fifteen years before he emerged, politically transformed, gloriously out, and famous as the first openly gay elected official in California. (In 1978, Milk would become a gay martyr, assassinated, along with San Francisco mayor George Moscone, by a fellow member of the San Francisco Board of Supervisors.) "In San Francisco in the 1970s," as the historian Lillian Faderman observed, Milk would run with "Craig Rodwell's groundbreaking ideas," but in the early sixties, when they were lovers, he "could not tolerate Craig's gay activism." Craig would push him: "Yes, Harvey, you've got a great job, a nice apartment, all the kitchenware a queen could ever dream of. Everything but the chance to be openly who you are, like a normal human being."

To Craig, being openly gay meant "being myself, being free,

being a whole person. Not being afraid." The other part of Christian Science faith that had stuck with him was the weight it put on telling the truth, whatever the risks. People told him he wouldn't get a job if he didn't keep his sexuality hidden, but after those summers on Fire Island, Craig knew he'd never work anywhere again where he couldn't both be out—that was a given—and support other people to be. Harvey protested that was not an option for him: "I can't let it out," he'd tell Craig. "It would kill my parents." He was appalled when Craig distributed homemade leaflets about a discussion group for homosexuals to all the apartments nearby that had two men's names on the mailboxes. "You shouldn't do that to people," Harvey chided his hotheaded boyfriend. "Getting those in mailboxes will make people paranoid that everyone knows about their being gay."

For all the energetic cruising Craig did in his wilder days, he always wanted there to be more gay venues where people gathered for "the simple and very human purpose of being with people like us and interacting with them on many levels—social, intellectual, cultural," not only sexual. A gay bookshop that wasn't selling skin magazines could serve that purpose. "I'm not a censor," he told a newspaper interviewer years later. "There are five places on the block where you can get that stuff. But not here." It was vital to him that the shop be a place where gay people "didn't feel they were being exploited either sexually or economically"—and that included being asked to overpay for a cellophane-wrapped magazine, the profits of which were likely enriching scuzzy, probably straight businessmen.

The Oscar Wilde Memorial Bookshop opened the day after Thanksgiving, 1967, in the ground-floor storefront of a brick apartment building at 291 Mercer Street, near Waverly Place. It had just twenty-five book titles in stock, three copies each, along with a selection of the few gay publications then around that Craig could countenance, such as *The Ladder*, the newsletter of the lesbian organization Daughters of Bilitis. His mother flew in from Chicago and they stayed up all night getting the store ready for its grand opening. The store was small—"cozy" might be a nice word for it— with just about ten shelves.

A profile of Craig from the 1972 book *The Gay Crusaders* noted, wonderingly, that the Oscar Wilde "looked like any ordinary book store, not like a porno shop with the shades drawn. The sunlight comes into this bookshop. So do customers under twenty-one." Craig had to defend his stance over and over again. "One salesman couldn't really believe Craig was giving hot porn the cold shoulder," wrote the book's activist authors, Kay Lahusen and Randy Wicker. "At last the man became livid, yelled 'Cocksucker!' at Craig, and stormed out of the shop."

There were some materials Craig wouldn't carry because they offended him, personally, politically, ethically—and hell, it was his store. In later years, he would stop stocking a Philadelphia gay newspaper because of a personal ad it ran that said, "No fats, no druggies, no addicts, no blacks." Craig told the writer Vito Russo, "That's just plain insulting and at the very least insensitive. . . . It's one thing to say GWM or GBM seeks the same. While we wish we lived in a world where people didn't regard race as a factor, it is a reality of living. People do. But to say no drug addicts, junkies, or Blacks, that's another story."

When the store first opened Craig and his mother had to spread the books out to fill the space. It would be decades before the full flowering of LGBT studies in the late 1980s and '90s, before queer-themed books could be found in almost any publisher's catalogue. Lesbian titles, fiction or nonfiction, were particularly hard to find. There were the pulp novels from the 1950s and early '60s with titles like *Strange Sisters* and *Odd Girl Out*—but many of them were out of print, and Craig had mixed feelings about them anyway. He avoided carrying "books with certain key words: third sex, twilight world, perversion—nothing about that. I wanted to depict homosexuality as basically good."

Lesbian pulp fiction was a godsend for many queer women,

giving them a glimpse of illicit satisfactions and a confirmation that other women like them at least existed—even if, as depicted in the books, they were mainly to be found in reform schools and sororities, clad in lingerie that just wouldn't stay put. But the books—and certainly their salacious covers—were often designed for the delectation of heterosexual male readers, Craig's women friends informed him, and the plotlines typically culminated in punishment (suicide, perpetual loneliness) for their sexy Sapphists. "There's just a lot more published for gay men than for gay women," Rodwell complained. "It's part of male chauvinism in our society." In a few years' time, he would be able carry two new lesbian novels: Isabel Miller's *A Place for Us* (later published as *Patience and Sarah*), based on the true story of a nineteenth-century painter and her female companion living in connubial bliss on a farmstead in upstate New York; and *Rubyfruit Jungle*, Rita Mae Brown's cheerfully explicit and agreeably literary 1973 debut. He threw himself into promoting both books.

For opening day, he had stocked a few weighty sociological studies that took a sympathetic view of homosexuality, such as *The Homosexual in America: A Subjective Approach* by (the pseudonymous) Donald Webster Cory, and *The Wolfenden Report*, the findings of the British government commission that recommended decriminalizing private, consensual sex between adult men. He would sell works by writers then generally known to have been gay and works by heterosexual writers who offered three-dimensional portraits of queer life: plays by the store's namesake, Oscar Wilde; poetry by Hart Crane; *Quatrefoil*, an achingly sincere 1950 novel about the love affair between two navy men; and the gritty Hubert Selby novel *Last Exit to Brooklyn*, with its wrenching chapter, "The Queen Is Dead," about a smart, lovelorn transgender woman who dies of a drug overdose. (The Smiths would later take the title for an album.)

It was possible to find these books in scattered libraries and bookstores, if you looked hard enough or were brazen enough to ask for them, but it was impossible to see them assembled in one place, testifying to a distinct cultural tradition. The opening of the Oscar Wilde Memorial Bookshop marked "the first time in American history," notes the historian Jim Downs, "that literature had been organized under the subject heading of 'gay culture.' The Library of Congress catalogued 'homosexuality' under the subheading 'criminality and medical abnormality' and had no subject heading for gay literature and culture. By placing just a few books and political pamphlets on a shelf, Rodwell, with his mother at his side, changed the world of letters' official definition of homosexuality. In his scheme, gay people were not criminals subject to sociological and psychological studies, but writers of a distinct genre of literature and creators of a distinct culture."

In time, Rodwell would move to a bigger storefront, on Christopher Street, where he would host the likes of Tennessee Williams and Christopher Isherwood for readings. He'd get letters from people around the country and abroad seeking advice on starting their own LGBT bookstores. He'd receive letters from isolated gay teens in small towns and gay soldiers stationed in Vietnam who looked to him for advice on how to come out to their parents, how to live their lives. "If and when I tell them," wrote a high school student from Wesleyville, Pennsylvania, "I think it would upset them very bad. And that's why I feel that you can help me. I want to know something that can help keep us together." In general, Rodwell's advice was to "be firm with your family. *Insist* that they come to an understanding of you, that they read certain things, that they meet your friends. Insist that they love you as their son or daughter—which means that they know you!" The conviction that he was helping people who might otherwise feel very alone helped make up for the rocks tossed through the shop window over the years, the abusive phone calls, the "kill fags" graffiti scrawled on the building.

But in November 1967, it was just Craig starting something that even his friends thought would never fly. "Gay people," they told him, "weren't ready to support a legitimate bookshop." It was Craig putting himself out there, serious, unflinching, impatient, as always, with those who couldn't or wouldn't do their own version of the same. Not that he didn't have a playful side. He and his soon-to-be lover, a young man named Fred Sargeant, who came to work in the store with him, acquired a couple of schnauzers through the auspices of their friend Bob Kohler, a neighborhood fixture known for his own radical activism, his constant canine companion, Magoo, and his dedication to helping the street youth that hung out near the bar called the Stonewall Inn. The schnauzers were Magoo's brothers, Albert and Michael. Albert was gay, Craig liked to tell people, and very promiscuous.

CRAIG RODWELL HAD the sort of childhood that contained just the right elements in just the right proportions to make a lifelong rebel: plenty of brute institutional authority, and enough love to give him the mettle to confront it. He was born in Chicago on Halloween, 1940. His parents separated when he was a baby, and his mother, Marion, went to work as a secretary, leaving little Craig in the care of neighborhood women whom she paid to look after him. (Rodwell recounted these childhood travails in detail to the historian Martin Duberman, who interviewed him at length for his indispensable 1993 book about the Stonewall uprising.) One of them, a Mrs. Merkle, took in laundry and made the five-year-old Craig push sheets and pillowcases through the old-fashioned mangle—he was always terrified of getting his fingers caught between the rollers. She may have been harsh, but with her live-in husband and stay-at-home work, Mrs. Merkle was respectable. When she told Marion she wanted to adopt Craig to save him from growing up in a household with a single mother, Marion, panicked that the other woman might succeed, placed him in a boarding school for "problem" boys, where he went on scholarship.

The boys at the Chicago Junior School had "different problems,"

Craig told Duberman, "behavioral problems, weight problems, un-controllable, in some cases orphans, even a couple of displaced children from Germany." Though there were a few kindly house mothers, who slept in a room next to the dorm and told bedtime stories, the general regimen was harsh: 5 a.m. wake-up followed by Bible study; a march in formation to the dining hall; and a breakfast eaten in silence, perched on the front halves of the chairs for good posture. His own mother was permitted to visit once a month. Boys who got in trouble—as Craig often did for speaking with his incorrigible frankness, or neglecting to say "Sir," or fooling around under the bedclothes with other boys, a sin to which he readily admitted—were often set to work pulling up thick, tough burdock root that grew in the woods behind the school. One teacher preferred to beat the students with an electric cord.

Still, Craig, who remained at the school from the age of six till he was fourteen, remembered it fondly for the warm camaraderie he experienced with the other students, often in resistance to the school superintendent, and as the place where he first discovered his homoerotic feelings. He worshipped Bob, an older boy in his dorm who played the piano beautifully, and one very cold night, when Craig woke to find an extra blanket pulled over him, he just knew it was Bob, who "in the middle of the night had gotten up so concerned about me."

When he was twelve, Craig developed a crush on a boy named Tony, like him a fervent baseball fan. One day Tony managed to get them tickets for a Cubs doubleheader at Wrigley Field. They had permission to watch only the first game but they couldn't resist staying for the second. The two returned to school late that night, walking along the railroad tracks in the dark for the last three miles. The school superintendent, whom Craig hated, was waiting up for them, and not happy about it, but what seemed to upset the man most was when Craig provided his favorite detail of that memorable night: that he and Tony had been holding hands as they made their way home in the moonlight. The superintendent's wife, indulging what Craig recalled as her "faggot phobia," offered some "really nasty comments . . . making fun of us," and to Craig's sorrow, he and Tony were kept apart thereafter, in separate dorms.

From an early age, Craig seems to have suffered no compunction, and even less doubt, about his homosexuality. Living back at home with his mother and her new husband, a former prizefighter and a mean drunk, Craig began going out at night after dinner in search of other gay men. One evening at the dinner table, his stepfather, Hank, demanded to know where he was going. You know, Hank said, when I was your age, we used to go down to Diversey Parkway "to beat up queers." Craig looked him in the eye, and said, "Oh, you big brave man." Then he headed out the door.

Despite—or because of—his teenage bravado, he sometimes ran into trouble. One night, when Craig was in high school, he went home with an older Italian American guy named Frank who worked as a dishwasher. Back in Frank's room at an SRO, a room Craig would remember for the tiny sink in the corner with a bar of delightful-smelling soap, Craig got a blow job from him. Afterward, Frank was walking Craig to the subway when three or four police cars converged on them. At the station, the plainclothesman interviewing Craig pounded his fist on the table and said, "We've called your mother and stepfather: they're on their way down here. You might as well tell me the truth right now!" He didn't know with whom he was dealing. The teenager told the cop *exactly* what had happened, that it was consensual despite the age difference, and that Frank was a very sweet man. He said the same thing before a grand jury, and later at Frank's trial for sex with a minor, explaining again and again that Frank hadn't paid him for it. "I just told the truth, all the time," he recalled. "And I thought if I told the truth, everything would come out all right for him and for me both."

It was the first of many lessons Craig would undergo in his life, that for other people, and especially those in power, truth was not the redemptive force it was for him. Frank was sentenced to five

years in prison. The judge wanted Craig dispatched to a reforma-
tory, but his mother "cried and begged," he recalled, "and said she'd
do anything if they wouldn't send me away." In the end, the judge
agreed to put him on probation for two years, if Marion took him
to a psychiatrist at her own expense.

Since 1952, the *Diagnostic and Statistical Manual of Mental Dis-
orders* (DSM) had classified homosexuality as a mental disorder.
(The American Psychiatric Association would not remove it from
the DSM until 1973.) At the time, most therapists regarded same-
sex attraction as an abnormal adjustment for which overindulgent
or overbearing mothers could often be blamed. It was a pathology
to be rooted out; the more progressive therapists among them said
"cured."

A 1968 article in the *New York Times* with the boosterish headline "A Quiet Revolution in Mental Care" proclaimed that while
Freudian psychotherapy had admittedly proved a bit of a bust in
transforming legions of gay men and women into happy heterosexual householders, developments in behavioral therapy offered new
hope with the sheen of real science. "Some male homosexuals have
been successfully treated by subjecting them to electric shocks
while they viewed a picture of an attractive man," the newspaper
reported. "When the shocks were stopped, a picture of a female
was flashed. The homosexuals gradually learned to associate the
male figure with punishment and the female figure with reward."
(Problem solved!)

The psychiatrist Craig saw didn't recommend anything as sa-
distic as shock therapy. Marion had either chosen well or gotten
lucky. In fact, he seemed, while being careful not to say so directly,
supportive of Craig's identity. The psychiatrist informed Craig's
probation officer in his weekly reports that his young patient was
progressing nicely, even passing along Craig's claims to be dating
girls now. Craig was sure the shrink wasn't persuaded by the con
job he was pulling, but wanted to help him—he even told Craig
about how homosexuality was accepted among the ancient Greeks.

Still, Craig came out of the whole experience enraged, particularly by what had happened to Frank. Eventually, he would find a political outlet for his sense of righteous anger, a movement on which he left an indelible imprint. But Craig in his late teens and early twenties was a spinning top, colliding here and there with power, sparks flying off of him as if he were heated metal, never quite igniting the uprising he envisioned.

DETERMINED TO MOVE to New York, the city he'd heard was chockablock with queer people, especially in "Green-witch Village," Craig took summer jobs as an office boy and a mail-room clerk all through high school, walked to school to save money, and hoarded his birthday and Christmas cash. After a brief stint in Boston, which his mother thought might be safer, and where he lived in a rooming house she found for him—"Six little old ladies and me and one bathroom"—he made it to New York in 1958. By day, he studied at the American School of Ballet; by night, he ran the streets with a tough and flamboyant crew of young queer men—Puerto Rican, white, and Black.

When they went out at night, they wore false eyelashes or mascara and eyeliner for a doe-eyed effect, calling it "full-face." They shrunk their blue jeans to be extra-tight, washing them repeatedly in hot water. It wasn't really Craig's look, but he happily adopted it for the adrenaline rush of camaraderie the costume gave him when he and his new friends went out "wrecking"—doing their light-hearted but serious-minded best to discomfit the straights around them. It might include casually holding hands, that simple gesture that had gotten Craig in so much trouble back at school. But sometimes it was more performative: queens forming Rockette-style kick lines in the middle of the street, for instance. Craig sometimes brought along his Siamese cat, wearing a sequined collar. "We [used] to go in the subway and ride around for all hours, all over the city, and sing and be outrageous," Craig recalled. "I remember sitting right on the cement at the Times Square Station, a whole group of us just sitting down, thinking of falsetto songs from the *The Sound of Music.* 'Raindrops on Roses.' It would echo. And half of us would be in full-face." Craig was thin and pale, and his large brown eyes dominated his face. Under the sallow light of a street lamp, or when he hadn't had a good meal in a day or two, maybe especially when he was wearing one of the striped T-shirts he favored, he could look a bit like an elfin waif in a Keane painting. But out with his larky band of gender benders, he felt fearless, larger than life.

Besides, he'd always had an inherent stroppiness that seemed to deliver the surges of righteous indignation he needed at certain moments. Sometimes it was directed at more privileged gay men. His innate sense of bodily autonomy and personal dignity could strike others as arrogant, sometimes priggish—*Who did he think he was?*—but it contained a feminist streak that put him ahead of his time. Once, at a gay bar called the Tic-Toc, the actor Farley Granger swatted Craig on the butt as he walked by, murmuring some line about how good it looked, and Craig threw a glass of wine at him. "He thought it was a compliment. But I've never to this day enjoyed being treated that way," Rodwell told Duberman. "It's the way the stereotyped straight men treat women. . . . It's a way of putting people down, essentially."

Sometimes Craig's defiance put him in danger. Like many gay men and women, Craig liked to spend time sunbathing and cruising at Riis Park, a crowded stretch of beachfront that had been a queer hangout since the 1940s, and had the added appeal of being accessible by public transportation. The writer and scholar Joan Nestle remembered the rare pleasures it offered her as a young lesbian: "the wonder of kissing on the hot blanket in the sunlight, the joy" of laying her head in her lover's lap. Yet, "whenever I turned away from the ocean to face the low cement wall that ran along the back of our beach," Nestle wrote, "I was forced to remember that we were always watched, by teenagers on bikes, pointing and laughing, and by more serious starers who used telescopes to focus in on us."

Men enjoying the beach at Riis Park were subject to an arbitrary rule—their bathing suits had to cover their navels—that the police invoked at their discretion. One day on the boardwalk, the cops stopped Craig, and he told them off: they were just using this stupid rule to harass homosexuals, he declared, and it was wrong. They promptly arrested him. Along with a bunch of other guys, he was carted down to the criminal court building on Centre Street, still in his navel-baring swim trunks, barefoot and in handcuffs. A judge sent him home and told him he'd likely have to pay a small fine—perhaps ten or fifteen dollars. Two weeks later when he came back for his trial date, he found he'd been charged with inciting a riot and resisting arrest.

Craig tried his usual approach, telling the truth as he saw it: the antiquated bathing suit law dated from 1903 and was disproportionately used against homosexuals, he explained to the new judge. The judge's face had been "very blank and nondescript" up till that point, but now as he realized that the unusually confident, well-spoken young man before him was one of those very homosexuals, he flushed bright red, "banged his gavel down as hard as he could, and threw the book" at him—for a minor, as Craig was, that meant three days in jail or a $25 fine. Craig had exactly $17 with him.

In a holding cell at the Brooklyn House of Detention, one cop who didn't like the fact that Craig was refusing to answer questions punched him in the side of the head. "I remember he took my wallet and took my identification papers and whatever papers were in my wallet—probably pictures of my mother—and just threw them on the floor. 'Pick them up, faggot.'" The guards put him in what they called "the queens' tank" with trans sex workers and other queer denizens of the streets. That group was given none of the commissary privileges or recreation that other prisoners had, so after the first day, Rodwell decided to teach ballet lessons. When he wasn't trying to get his new pupils *en pointe*, he was trying to educate them about the unjust laws that were oppressing them.

And he simmered, thinking about all the indignities he'd put up with because of who he was, couldn't help but be, was *glad* to be. Cops on Greenwich Avenue "would stop and search our bags just walking down the street. Looking for drag so they could arrest you," or "come up and poke you in the side with their sticks. 'Keep moving, faggot. Keep moving.' They wouldn't allow you to stand or sit on a car hood or anything. Which we would do when they weren't around." The attitude was, "any homosexual standing still on the street must be hustling or procuring."

Craig was soon to enter the bleakest period of his life. He and Harvey Milk broke up—in the end not over politics. One evening, Harvey took Craig out to dinner at an Italian restaurant and though he was usually very playful and lively, he was somber that night. He told Craig he'd been diagnosed with gonorrhea, and that he must have caught it from him. Harvey hadn't slept with anyone else and Craig had to admit he had. The relationship faded out over four or five months, a slow peeling away that Craig found agonizing. Harvey, who used to wake his young lover up every morning with a phone call and a goofy joke, gradually called less and less and then not at all.

Craig gave up ballet, fell into a deep depression, and began to think about suicide. "I decided that's it. I don't have a career; I've lost the love of my life." He gave notice at his clerical job, found homes for his two cats, left a note for his roommate, Collin, an aspiring Broadway dancer, that instructed him to tell Craig's aunt first, so she, and not the police, could break the news to Marion. Then he downed a fistful of pills one night when Collin was out at the movies. Luckily, Collin wasn't interested in the second film on the double bill, and came home early. He took one look at the unconscious Craig, and called an ambulance. Craig was rushed to the hospital, where, to his enormous chagrin, the first person he saw when he awoke after having his stomach pumped was his least favorite category of public servant, a cop. He was so enraged he broke the straps that were holding him down, then passed out again.

Craig would spend a horrible month confined to the Bellevue psychiatric ward. "Just shuffling around the halls, and you could hear it all day long, the shuffle of the hospital slippers." To Craig, it was like living in *The Snake Pit*, that disturbing movie with Olivia de Havilland as a woman trapped in an asylum, and he was Olivia de Havilland. He remembered lining up in the hallway for pills he learned to hold under his tongue and not swallow. His mother arrived and got him transferred to a private hospital; even his elusive playboy father showed up to help her out. At St. Luke's, the mise-en-scène was a lot cheerier—there were televisions, a game room, nice bedspreads—but Craig couldn't stand the homophobic psychiatrist, and kept fearing he'd be selected for electroshock therapy. (He wasn't.) Harvey visited Craig once in the hospital, according to Milk's biographer, Randy Shilts: "Ever the pragmatist, Harvey suggested an afternoon tryst." Craig told Shilts, "I was still so madly in love with him. I got such a thrill out of saying no."

Maybe it was the whoosh of freedom or the sense that he'd been given a second chance, but after Craig got out of the hospital, he began to pour more and more of his fractious energy into activism. "My mind always worked overtime," he told Duberman, "trying to think of things to make us more visible."

While he was still with Harvey, Craig had joined the New York affiliate of the Mattachine Society, an organization founded in 1950 by the Los Angeles labor activist Harry Hay and his friends to promote the welfare of homosexual men. (It was named after a secret fraternity of unmarried men in medieval France, who entertained townspeople while wearing masks.) Hay and his group were leftists, but Mattachine New York strove particularly hard for respectability, a source of growing frustration for Craig. A Mattachine Society leaflet he picked up made the model gay man sound like a Golden Retriever: "Although he is harmless, the law considers him a criminal. . . . Although he is among the most friendly and companionable, he is ostracized and shunned as if he carried the plague." If the street queens Craig ran with were disruptive without being strategic, the Mattachine men were strategic without being disruptive. He appreciated that they were meeting together at all, and he knew it was one of the very first "homophile" organizations in the United States. But the scene at most of their gatherings— older men in business suits politely listening to lectures from sympathetic experts—wasn't exactly his vision of a movement. Craig felt patronized—he didn't need these long-winded, beard-stroking visitors to confer value on his life or tell him he wasn't crazy. The society had its headquarters on the fourth floor of an office building in midtown Manhattan, open only in the evenings for meetings. "We weren't accessible to the community at all," Craig recalled. "I wanted us to be out."

CRAIG FOUND HIMSELF looking to the civil rights movement and early demonstrations against the Vietnam War for inspiration. His sympathies were already there. He wrote to the Chicago Board of Education protesting a plan for mobile schools he thought was a cover for segregation, and to his congressman in New York calling upon him not to support the all-white Mississippi delegation to the 1964 Democratic convention at the end of Freedom Summer. In 1965, he attended one of the first big rallies against the Vietnam War, at Madison Square Garden. And in April of that year, he participated in several picket lines at the White House organized by a few different homophile organizations, including branches of the Mattachine Society and the Daughters of Bilitis, to protest job discrimination against gays and lesbians in the federal government. He was thrilled that the groups had decided to do something more public.

Sitting in the booth of a greasy spoon with a few of the other marchers afterward, Craig felt restless and excited. He couldn't bear the thought that no future actions were planned, so on the spur of the moment he came up with the idea for what he called the Annual Reminder—a picket line that would assemble every year on July 4 outside of Independence Hall in Philadelphia to remind fellow citizens that the nation's promises of liberty and the pursuit of happiness had not yet been extended to lesbians and homosexuals.

Frank Kameny, the head of the Mattachine Society of Washington, DC, loved the idea. An astronomer who'd been fired from the Army Map Service in 1957 after an arrest for cruising, Kameny launched a tireless crusade against rules that denied gay men and women the security clearances required for many federal government jobs. He rejected the orthodoxy that homosexuality was a mental illness, and invented the slogan "Gay is Good" to help counter it. In the words of two journalists who covered his activities over the years, Kameny had "the confidence of an intellectual autocrat, the manner of a snapping turtle, a voice like a foghorn, and the habit of expressing himself in thunderous bursts of precise and formal language." The Annual Reminder might not have been his idea, but he would be running it, thank you.

Craig took the bus from New York to Philadelphia, on a blazing-hot July 4, 1965, with fellow marchers singing "The Homophile Freedom Song" to the tune of the "The Battle Hymn of the Republic":

Mine eyes have seen the struggles of the Negroes and the Jews
I have seen the counties trampled where the laws of men abuse
But you crush the homosexual with anything you choose
Now we are marching on.

About forty people showed up—men and women. They carried neatly lettered signs whose slogans ("The Pursuit of Happiness Is an Alienable Right for Homosexuals," and "First Class Citizenship for Homosexuals") drew on what the historian Simon Hall calls "patriotic protest"—the natural rights language of the Declaration of Independence, the notion of an unfinished revolution that had left minorities behind. Kameny made the rules. The Annual Reminder would not "be an occasion for the assertion of personality, individuality, age, rebellion, generalized non-conformity or anti-conformity. . . . People are much more likely to listen to, to examine, and hopefully, to accept new, controversial, unconventional, unorthodox, or unusual ideas and positions, if these are presented to them from sources bearing the symbols of acceptability, conventionality, and respectability, as arbitrary as those symbols may be."

Men were supposed to wear suits, white shirts, and ties; and women, dresses or skirts and heels. Men "will have recent haircuts and fresh shaves; the wearing of beards will be discouraged." The wording of all signs was to be approved in advance; all inquiries from the press were to be referred to Kameny. Picketers were not to smoke or to exchange words with passersby.

At first, Craig fell in line. "Let me assure you," he told Kameny, "that if anyone does show up at the bus dressed in sneakers, blue jeans, or outlandish clothing, we will promptly return their $5.00 and remind them that participants in such a demonstration are not there to assert their individual egos, but rather as representatives of millions of homosexual citizens." After all, nobody else was out there proclaiming a gay identity the way this crew was. It took guts. The picketers could be fired from their jobs, disowned by their families. Besides, the Annual Reminder had been Craig's dream-child and he wanted to see it succeed. They may have "looked like a Sunday School group," but for those initial marches, Craig got Frank Kameny's point: "We didn't want to startle people by our appearances," Craig told Duberman. "We wanted them to hear our message"—namely, that gay people were citizens, too, entitled to the same rights and protections as everyone else.

Over time, though, Craig began to bridle at the tight structure of the Annual Reminder events—which occurred every July 4 from 1965 to 1969—and he wasn't the only one. The growing impatience was largely generational. Younger picketers set less store by the respectability politics Kameny was pushing. They took notice of the way the civil rights movement was shifting from demands for desegregation to the assertion of Black Power. The more that gay activists were involved with other movements—civil rights, anti-war, women's liberation—the more they perceived the focus, tactics, older membership, and steady politeness of once pioneering groups like Mattachine and Daughters of Bilitis as too narrow and modest. As a young radical, the lesbian scholar and activist Karla Jay came up with her own dismissive nickname for the DOB: the Daughters of Bursitis.

Craig told Duberman, "I can remember Frank saying, if we want to be employed by the federal government, we have to look employable by the federal government. I would say to Frank, well, but that's not all we're fighting for, to be employed by the federal government. That's your particular schtick, fine. That's not my schtick and other people's schtick."

CRAIG WASN'T THE only protester in Philadelphia who chafed under Kameny's ironfisted command. A young lesbian named Martha Shelley participated in the 1968 Annual Reminder—and hated it. It wasn't like she minded getting out there and taking a risk. Martha was a talkative, forthright New Yorker who'd grown up in a working-class Jewish family in Brooklyn, the kind in which "never cross a picket line" was a catechism. She'd felt different for as long as she could remember—at least since she was a kid in elementary school, when the girls would draw blond brides and the boys would draw fighter planes, and Martha's pictures, of octopuses and tropical fish, or cactuses and birds, seemed to show the world she didn't belong to either group. Martha attended the selective, public Bronx High School of Science, where one of her friends was a Black, gay nerd who would later emerge as the brilliant science fiction writer and social critic Samuel Delany. Martha wasn't exactly out, but she wasn't exactly conventionally feminine, either. Her father was supportive, but her mother would say things like, "I wish this was the old country, I would have arranged a marriage for you when you were twelve." *Thank God it's not the old country,* Martha thought.

In 1960, when Martha was a student at the City College of New York, she took an all-female judo class at the YWCA and met a married woman with whom she embarked on a passionate affair. The first time Martha kissed her, she knew that it was "totally different from kissing boys . . . the intensity of the feeling . . . and I went home, and I thought, *I'm a lesbian. This is what it is.* . . . It was like, I had just been given a vision of my destiny." Later, when she joined the Daughters of Bilitis, some of the older members told her she should adopt a pseudonym, to avoid harassment. (Her legal name was Martha Altman.) She picked "Shelley" because it had been her married lover's nickname for her, a reference to Martha's habit of showering the woman with romantic love poetry. Her naturally expressive nature often had to be clipped and constrained to fit the times. Once, when she was in the passenger seat next to an older girlfriend who was driving, Martha had reached out to hold the woman's hand. Though they were alone in the car, her girlfriend would not take Martha's hand; she was afraid someone would see, and she would lose her job.

Martha's own attitudes were a harbinger of things to come: an assertive gay liberation movement that demanded much more than mere tolerance from mainstream America and that allied with other radical movements for social transformation. "Older homophile organizations mostly wanted a piece of America's pie," she recalled. "They just want America to accept us as nice, middle-class people who are just a little bit different. But we were antiwar, we were feminists—the guys included—we were antiracist. We were socialists." She hated the preapproved signs at the Annual Reminders in Philly, and the fact that the women weren't allowed to march in pants (though she dutifully donned a white blouse, demure skirt, and punishing nylons for the occasion). Martha wore her dark, curly hair short; she had glasses and a winning gap-toothed grin, and when she wasn't at her office job, as a secretary at Barnard College in New York, she preferred plaid shirts and jeans.

Most of all she hated the fact that at the Independence Hall protest there were "tourists staring at us like they were at the zoo looking at the animals. I'll never forget one kid in his late teens licking an ice cream cone and just staring. It didn't feel right. It felt really bad." The DOB had chosen Martha to speak in abnormal psychology classes, a living demonstration that not all lesbians were *so* abnormal. That had been weird, but at least she was allowed to talk.

In later years, she would acknowledge the bravery and the importance of the pickets. "It showed the world, I suppose, that there were some people who were courageous enough to stand up in public and say, 'We are homosexuals.' And that was an important first step." But at the time, Martha was thinking about the civil rights movement, and how Black activists had grown more confrontational. "It had become very clear at that point that no matter how hard Black people tried to be nice, there were an awful lot of white people" who weren't going to let systemic racism be dismantled. Women, too, were easy to ignore when they were merely polite and accommodating. A Malvina Reynolds song she'd heard Joan Baez sing said it perfectly: "It isn't nice to block the doorway / it isn't nice to go to jail / there are nicer ways to do it / but the nice ways always fail."

In the year or so after her experience in Philadelphia, Martha became more countercultural, more free in heart and mind. She had an affair with a gay man, an activist like her, mainly just to mess with people's neat expectations and categories. "We were being young brats. And the gay movement couldn't really throw us out because we were perfectly willing to stand up in public and be on TV and say we were gay, even if we were having an affair with each other or whoever else we wanted." Her scandal-raising boyfriend turned her on to LSD one night in his dorm room, and something in the way she saw the world shuddered and shifted; doors unlatched. By the end of the year, she had quit her secretarial job and moved from the Upper West Side to the Lower East Side to become a full-time movement organizer.

Kiyoshi Kuromiya, an architecture student at the University of Pennsylvania, participated in all five Annual Reminders, but he too bristled at the rules. Kiyoshi would live his life as an avatar of what would later be called intersectionality, an activist who contained multitudes as a gay man, a Japanese American (he was born in a Wyoming internment camp to which the US government ordered his family during World War II), and a close ally of Black movement leaders. (He babysat for Martin Luther King Jr.'s children in the week after King's assassination.) Kiyoshi joined the civil rights movement in 1961, when he was eighteen, and participated in a series of sit-ins at restaurants and other public accommodations along Route 40 between Washington, DC, and Philadelphia. Trying to avoid international embarrassment, the Kennedy administration had successfully pushed these segregated establishments to start providing service for African dignitaries who had occasion to travel between embassies in Washington and the United Nations in New York. Black American patrons were still being turned away, however, and the contrast in treatment became galvanizing, with CORE (the Congress of Racial Equality) organizing sit-ins.

At one Maryland diner, Kiyoshi and a group of Black CORE protesters waited six hours without being served. He had a puckish side that proved useful when he got involved with the Yippies and their theatrical political protests later in the decade. At the Maryland diner, he and his friends played "God Bless America" over and over again on the jukebox, until the manager got fed up and unplugged the damn thing. The manager got even madder when a *New York Times* reporter covering the event shared his grilled cheese sandwich with Kiyoshi, who tore it into small pieces and passed them along to the other hungry protesters.

In 1965, Kiyoshi took part in the civil rights marches from Selma to Montgomery, Alabama. While leading a group of Black high school students to the capitol in Montgomery, he was clubbed by a posse of volunteer sheriffs and had to be hospitalized. A kind nurse—a gay man, as it happened—wheeled him out into the hall so he could call his parents and tell them he was alive. At some point, an FBI agent showed up at his bedside, but Kiyoshi had already acquired enough bitter knowledge to understand that nothing particularly helpful to him or the cause was likely to come of that visit. He and his fellow activists certainly could not count on the protection of local law enforcement, and they probably couldn't count on the protection of the US government, either. A frightening thought. But also a liberating one.

As a member of Students for a Democratic Society, the leading New Left group, and an antiwar activist, Kiyoshi was inventive. He once advertised an action on the University of Pennsylvania campus at which he threatened that a mysterious organization called "Americong" would napalm a dog. He had no intention of harming a hair on a canine head, but almost two thousand horrified students, veterinarians, and pet owners showed up at the appointed time and place on the Penn campus. Kiyoshi handed out leaflets that read, "Congratulations anti-napalm protest! You have saved the life of an innocent dog. Now your efforts should turn to protesting Dow Chemical and the U.S. Government's continued use of this genocidal weapon against the civilian population of a tiny country 10,000 miles away."

In 1968, Kuromiya designed a poster that simply said "Fuck the Draft" below a photograph of a young man burning his draft card. It became a national sensation. He distributed the poster by mail, advertising it with the slogans like "Buy five and we'll send a sixth one to the mother of your choice." Lady Bird Johnson was one suggestion. The ad brought Kuromiya to the attention of the FBI, which detained him, charging him with using the US Postal Service for distributing lewd and indecent materials. Undaunted, he took two thousand posters to that summer's Democratic National Convention in Chicago. Wearing a suit and tie so he could move around without attracting undue attention, he scattered them in all the downtown hotels hosting delegates.

Kiyoshi Kuromiya was one of those creative, questing, and emotionally attuned activists produced by the 1960s—many of whom rose to prominence in gay and women's liberation—who believed that the values of patriarchal power took root in people's psyches, as well as in political structures, and needed to be confronted within as well as without. So while the rebellious young Kiyoshi went to the Annual Reminders every year, knowing it was then the only game in town, he also "thought it was absurd, Frank Kameny telling me we couldn't hold hands in the picket line. That we couldn't loosen our ties or take off coats. . . . You couldn't wear slacks if you were a woman. . . . It was the idea that this is the first event of its kind and we want the press to concentrate on the fact that we look and act like everybody else, not like a caricature, whatever that meant to him, of what people thought we were."

Craig gave Kiyoshi a ride to the first Annual Reminder, picking him up in a Falcon convertible with placards crammed into the back seat. Like Craig's, Kiyoshi's hair was freshly cut—he wasn't yet sporting the ponytail that became his signature—and they both wore suits and ties. The two young gay liberationists exchanged looks of commiseration, maybe even an eye roll or two, on the orderly picket line. He could tell Craig felt the same way he did.

IN APRIL 1966, the spring after the first Philly protest, Craig participated in a demonstration that felt more like the civil rights sit-ins for which he had so much respect. Dubbed a "sip-in," the action was organized by the New York Mattachine Society to challenge the State Liquor Authority's policy of revoking the liquor licenses for establishments that knowingly served gays and lesbians. (Their mere presence supposedly turned a bar or restaurant into "a disorderly house.") To challenge the policy, Craig would go out on the town at 11 a.m. with two other Mattachine members, Dick Leitsch and John Timmons, trailed by the newspaper reporters they'd apprised of their plan. They were terrified. "We didn't announce we were going to storm the bar or anything," Craig recalled. "But we were going to occupy it and demand to be served." And that was the first time gays had done anything like that.

It was a courageous plan, but as it played out, also a little comical. First, they headed for the Ukrainian-American Village bar on St. Marks Place, which seemed a good bet for a showdown since it had a hand-lettered sign reading, "If you are gay, please stay away." Alas, it was closed. So was the place across the street with a similar sign, the Dom. As Lucy Komisar reported in a *Village Voice* piece entitled "Three Homosexuals in Search of a Drink," the whole entourage then piled into a car and headed to a Howard Johnson's on Sixth Avenue and Eighth Street. There, Craig, described as "a sober, serious young man," slid into a booth with his compatriots, while the reporters settled "discreetly at the next table under one of Howard Johnson's white and gold crystal chandeliers." Craig handed the manager a statement that read, "We, the undersigned, are homosexuals. We believe that a place of public accommodation has an obligation to serve an orderly person, and that we are entitled to service as long as we are orderly." If they were denied, the letter said, they would appeal to the State Liquor Authority.

But at Howard Johnson's, the amiable, silver-haired manager on duty, one Emil Varela, was only too happy to serve them. In fact, he gave everybody, including the reporters, drinks on the house—most took bourbon and water. "Why shouldn't they be served a drink?" he asked the reporters. "They look like perfect gentlemen to me," adding, "It's pretty ridiculous that anybody should determine what anybody's sex life is."

At the dimly lit, thatched-roofed Waikiki bar, with its abundant hanging coconuts, the trio was thwarted yet again—drinks all around. Finally, at Julius's on West Tenth Street, where they were joined by a fourth activist, Randy Wicker, the bartender obliged. "You can't serve us if we're homosexuals?" Leitsch asked him. "No," the man replied, he couldn't. For the three who'd been at this quest since 11 a.m., this was not only a strategic breakthrough but a personal relief: they weren't sure how much more alcohol they could take in the middle of the day. (Craig might still have been serious, but he was no longer sober.)

The State Liquor Authority was not moved by the Manhattan sip-in—as the *New York Times* headline put it, "S.L.A. Won't Act on Deviate Bans." But the chairman of the city's Commission on Human Rights, William H. Booth, a Black Republican lawyer appointed by the moderate Republican mayor, John Lindsay, was. Booth announced that his commission would take action against any establishments if homosexuals filed discrimination complaints against them.

IT WAS THE Oscar Wilde Memorial Bookshop, though, that became the headquarters for Craig's vision of liberation. Almost from the start, it projected the community center vibe Craig had in mind. Soon after opening day in 1967, Rodwell created a bridge to the radical student scene at nearby New York University, and to women customers, by hiring two young lesbians, Ellen Broidy, a New Yorker who was studying classics and Near East languages at the campus, and her girlfriend Linda Rhodes, an architecture student, to work in the store, along with himself and Fred Sargeant. People were sometimes hesitant about entering the shop, Ellen recalled, but the staff tried to be as welcoming and affirming as possible. The proximity of NYU provided handy cover for some patrons. "I encountered so many people coming in the door saying they were doing a paper on sociology," Ellen recalled. "They had to have some explanation of why they were there."

By the late sixties, the Village had become a roiling hub of antiwar and New Left activity. The United Methodist Church on

West Fourth Street, known as the "peace church," offered asylum and counseling to draft resisters, and meeting space for various left-wing groups, including the socialist-feminist Redstockings, who held their abortion speakout there in 1969. Behind the fanciful brick Jefferson Market library loomed the eleven-story, Art Deco–style Women's House of Detention, known colloquially as the House of D. Located squarely in the middle of the Village, like a "combination Bedlam and Bastille," as one writer put it, the House of D exerted a politicizing effect on some downtowners, making it hard to ignore questions of who was incarcerated and why. Passersby could get an earful from inmates who shouted obscenities and complaints about the House of D's notorious conditions from behind the mesh-covered windows. The writer Grace Paley recalled steering her children along the sidewalk "through whole families calling up—bellowing, screaming up to the third, seventh, tenth floor, to figures, shadows behind bars and screened windows. . . . Mami, mami, you like my dress? We gettin' you out, baby. New lawyer come by." In the late 1960s and early '70s, the usual cast of detainees—sex workers, vagrants, drug addicts—was often joined by political protesters, including, at various points, Paley herself, Angela Davis, and Andrea Dworkin.

Ellen Broidy was already political and out when she went to work at the Oscar Wilde (her mother claimed she knew her daughter was a lesbian from the time she was three). But in the heady atmosphere of the Village, Craig opened her "eyes basically to the whole concept of pride. Of not only being who you are but being damn proud of who you are." She sometimes thought that his commitment to working with lesbians was more political than personal—in his heart, he was all about the boys—but she appreciated it anyway. He had an "absolute passion to uncover things that reflected our experience back to us in ways that were not mediated by the church, the medical profession, or the criminal law establishment."

Homophobes were always accusing gay people of "recruiting"

for their "lifestyle." Craig thought maybe they ought to be. As he told a newspaper interviewer in the early seventies, "Homosexuality is even preferable to heterosexuality because it stresses what is common between two people, rather than what separates them. Heterosexuality, in a way, stresses dichotomies, separateness, a breakdown in human possibilities."

THE STONEWALL INN was the kind of establishment that ticked Craig off. It opened on Christopher Street in 1966 under organized-crime-affiliated ownership, like the majority of gay bars in the city. Since it had no liquor license, the owners paid off the police to avoid being shut down permanently. They made a profit in part by serving watered-down drinks. Some employees seem to have dabbled in the blackmailing of customers. The police regularly conducted raids, tipping off the management in advance. All the lights would go on, and patrons would stop whatever they were doing—flirting or shimmying or catching up with friends—and run for it. It was an annoying, often humiliating, sometimes terrorizing ritual, to which heterosexual bar-goers were not subjected.

"Since practically the only social outlet gay people had in New York City was bars, it infuriated Rodwell that these places were controlled by the Mafia and not by the gay community," wrote David Carter in *Stonewall: The Riots That Sparked the Gay Revolution.* "They like our money and hated our guts," Craig told him. "There was that collusion between the cops and the mob, and we were, like, caught in the middle all the time." In the first issue of a publication Craig started called *The Hymnal* (the "hym" part stood for Homosexual Youth Movement), he took on Mafia control of bars and homed in on the Stonewall, which he called the "tackiest joint in town." All night long, bartenders rinsed patrons' glasses in the same tub of water, which turned dingier with each passing hour, then reused them. Craig charged that the place was risking an outbreak of hepatitis. And it lacked a fire exit.

Yet the Stonewall did have its fierce adherents. Most of its patrons identified as men, and most were white, though the crowd was mixed: Black and Puerto Rican customers hung out there, too. "There was a significant and visible presence of genderqueer people," writes the historian Marc Stein, "some of whom identified as butches, drags, queens, transsexuals or transvestites." For all of those patrons, one of the joys of the place was that it generally allowed them to dance together.

The writer Edmund White would go the Stonewall and "drink three or four vodka tonics to get up the nerve to ask John Stipanela, a high school principal, to dance." In those days, White and his friends were skinny as greyhounds and hippie-adjacent. They had "long, dirty hair and untrimmed sideburns and hip-huggers and funny black boots that zipped up the side and denim cowboy shirts with pearlescent pressure-pop buttons." They smoked all the time and didn't work out, and got the clap a lot "since no one but paranoid married men used condoms." AIDS was still more than a decade away.

The Stonewall's dance area had a raw concrete floor that was often wet and dank-smelling because rain poured in the place somehow. Still, how exhilarating it was to be able to dance with whomever you wanted to! The regulars incorporated finger-snapping into their own distinctive Stonewall Inn style.

Outside, in and around Sheridan Square, there were always queer street kids hanging out, in close proximity to what the artist Thomas Lanigan-Schmidt, who was one of them, christened "Mother Stonewall." He recalled, "We lived in cheap hotels, broken down apartments, abandoned buildings, or on the streets. . . . Some were able to get menial jobs. Some of us were on welfare. Some of us hustled. And some of us panhandled. . . . Many of us had gotten thrown out of home before finishing high school. WE WERE STREET RATS. Puerto Rican, black, northern and southern whites, 'Debby the Dyke' and a Chinese queen named 'Jade East.' The sons and daughters of postal workers, welfare mothers, cab drivers, mechanics, and nurse's aides (just to name a few). Until properly introduced it was de rigueur argot to call everybody 'Miss Thing,' (after this it was discretionary usage.)"

The street kids had their own names for the cops who came by to raid the bar or move them along: Lily Law, Betty Badge, and The Devil with the Blue Dress On. Often, the youths in drag tugged at the skirts of Mother Stonewall, and she shooed them away, since even the $3 it took to get in the door was a golden ticket beyond reach. But there were other times when all it took was to "find an empty beer can, so the waiter would think you'd bought a drink, and the night was yours. . . . The jukebox played a lot of Motown music. We DANCED. The air conditioners seemed not to work at all because the place was always so crowded. We were happy. This place was the 'ART' that gave form to the feelings of our heartbeats. Here the consciousness of knowing you 'belonged' nestled into that warm feeling of finally being HOME."

In the early morning hours of June 28, 1969, Seymour Pine of the New York City Vice Squad Public Morals Division initiated a raid on the Stonewall that was supposed to go pretty much like all the other raids, everybody playing their assigned roles in the Kabuki. Pine had four other officers with him; two male and two female undercover police officers were stationed inside the bar. The lights flashed on and off, everybody trooped outside; in the normal course of events, as many of them as possible would slip away into the night, maybe quietly cursing Betty Badge or Lily Law. But that night the usual scenario began, fairly quickly, to unravel. Some patrons—for example, those who lacked proper ID—were usually arrested during the raids, and paddy wagons were supposed to take them away. But the police vans were late arriving. A crowd began to grow on the sidewalk outside, swelled by the ranks of queer street kids, and by passersby, many of them skeptical of the police. "Don't you know these people don't have anywhere else to go?" one woman demanded of an officer.

Craig and Fred were walking home across Sheridan Square after playing cards at a friend's apartment. Seeing the crowd and a patrol car, they figured there was a raid going on. Craig picked up on something more, "a feeling in the air that something was about to happen." The Stonewall Inn "had no harsher critic than Rodwell," wrote David Carter. "Yet when he saw the bar being raided, he reacted with anger." Bounding to the top of the highest nearby stoop he could find, Craig saw the first prisoners being led out and loaded into the waiting paddy wagon. The crowd wasn't loud but it felt like it had been plugged into some invisible new energy source. From his vantage point atop the stairs, Craig was moved to shout "Gay Power!" A few people took up the chant, but others giggled at its unfamiliar audacity and at Craig's intensity.

Like a number of aspects of that night at the Stonewall, the question of who threw the first rock or brick or punch, who, in other words, might have fatefully riled the crowd, is contested—so much so that it's become a meme, with increasingly arch and ridiculous candidates for the answer. Madonna threw the first brick, or Beyoncé, or God. It was a chaotic situation with eyewitnesses who could not have realized at the time how eagerly their witness would be called upon in the decades to come. Most accounts do agree that at one point the police led a butch lesbian out of the bar and tried to put her in a squad car, but she kept sliding across the seat, scrambling out the opposite door and scuffling with them. After an officer picked her up and tossed her in, she yelled out, "Why don't you guys do something?" The effect was to turn up the rage, tipping what had been an unusually chaotic and obstreperous raid into a full-out uprising. The crowd responded, booing and yelling and throwing coins—to symbolize the police payoffs—and later bottles, beers cans, and other makeshift projectiles.

The identity of the butch lesbian has never been definitively established, but multiple accounts contend that it was Stormé DeLarverie, a mixed-race entertainer originally from New Orleans, who was the drag king emcee of the Jewel Box Revue, the first integrated drag show of its kind. DeLarverie, who also worked as a bouncer, and was known as the "guardian of lesbians in the Village," died in 2014. As she got older, she began telling people it had indeed been her, and that she had punched the cop she was fighting with, after seeing him get rough with some of the young patrons he was hauling out of the bar.

At some point, Inspector Pine decided he and the officers under his command had no choice but to barricade themselves inside the bar for safety. A reporter from the *Village Voice*, Howard Smith, hunkered down inside with them, and later wrote a dispatch about it. The crowd got the door open at one point and hurled in beer cans and bottles. Some in the crowd turned a trash can and a parking meter into battering rams to try to break down the door. To Craig, it seemed medieval, like the Stonewall was a castle, and the people were trying to cross the moat and reclaim it. "We'll shoot the first motherfucker that comes in through the door," shouted one of the cops. "Pine glances over toward me," Smith wrote. 'Are you all right, Howard?' I can't believe what I'm saying. 'I'd feel a lot better with a gun.'"

The New York City Police Department had to dispatch the Tactical Police Force to extract Pine and his contingent from the Stonewall. It was a nice irony for those who stopped to think about it—the cops trapped inside the gay bar while the gays they had forced out ran wild in the streets, whooping and hollering and smashing car windows. The TPF formed a phalanx and set about trying to clear the riled-up Stonewall patrons and their reinforcements from the neighborhood. It took until about four in the morning.

"It was an interesting sidelight on the demonstrations," wrote Dick Leitsch, the Mattachine veteran who had been part of the sip-in, "that those usually put down as 'sissies' or 'swishes' showed the most courage and sense during the action. Their bravery and daring saved many people from being hurt, and their sense of humour and camp helped keep the crowds from getting nasty or too violent."

The cops "gave up on the idea of taking prisoners"—in the end there were only thirteen arrests, including several bar employees and the (straight) folk musician Dave Van Ronk, who had headed over from the nearby watering hole the Lion's Head Inn when he heard the commotion—and concentrated on clearing the area. They rushed both ways on Greenwich, forcing the crowds into 10th Street and 6th Avenue, where the people circled the blocks and re-entered Christopher.

More familiar with the labyrinthine downtown streets than the police were, the queens and street kids led their pursuers on a merry, Keystone Kops–style chase. Periodically they broke into choruses of "We are the Stonewall girls / we wear our hair in curls / we wear no underwear / we show our pubic hair" to the tune of the Howdy Doody song. The cops then "formed a flying wedge, and with arms linked, headed down Greenwich, forcing everyone in front of them into side streets. . . . They made full use of their night sticks, brandishing them like swords. At one point a cop grabbed a wild Puerto Rican queen" who, as the cop was about to club her, demanded to know, "How'd you like a big Spanish dick up your little Irish ass?" That stunned him into pausing, nightstick poised in the air, allowing his quarry to escape.

It is always a challenge to try to determine why certain protests take fire and others fizzle out. Why did this particular raid not end as so many others had, with some arrests, some resentful patrons skulking home, the bar reopening for business often that same night? The possible reasons range from the meteorological to the sociological. It was a hot, muggy Friday night in early summer; there was a full moon. The management did not seem, for some reason, to have gotten their usual warning and were taken aback by the raid, which also occurred later in the course of the night's revelry—1:20 a.m.—than such actions generally. (More of the patrons might have been fortified by the Dutch courage of multiple drinks.) There had been a spate of recent raids including one on the Stonewall itself earlier that week, as well as an event a few days earlier in which ax-wielding vigilantes had cut trees down at a neighborhood park in Kew Gardens, Queens, where gay men went to cruise.

Beyond such immediate triggers, there was the work that homophile organizations had been quietly but persistently doing that was making at least some gay people less willing to endure persecution quietly. The examples of other social movements—especially civil rights and Black Power—were in the air, along with the intoxicating pull of a rebellious, youthful counterculture. The particular alchemy of the street kids with a nothing-to-lose attitude who gathered outside the Stonewall, and the loyal regulars inside, created a charge that would not have existed had the Stonewall been in a less trafficked part of town or a less racially and economically diverse city. But any uprising is also a call and response between the crowd and individual actors in it. The patrons flushed out of the bar who decided to sashay and bow and generally camp it up like they were on some red carpet perp walk, instead of hurrying away with their heads down, infused the crowd with exuberant defiance. Stormé DeLarverie—or whoever the butch lesbian was—offered a dramatic display of resistance. Local denizens of the streets whom everybody more or less knew—like the trans sex worker and community activist Marsha P. Johnson—cheerfully steered people toward the gathering crowd, crying out the news of the gay rebellion like saucy Paul Reveres in drag. Craig's "Gay Power!" war cry provided the inchoate insurgency with a slogan.

People gathered near the closed Stonewall Inn to protest for the next several nights. But by the dawn's early light that first morning, the mood was already different, defiant, unfamiliar. When eighteen-year-old Martin Boyce headed down to Sheridan Square in his usual gender nonconforming "scare drag"—he identified as a boy but wore makeup—a sanitation worker gave him a Black Power salute. Another man told him, "You people look different." Perhaps he meant what the gay poet Allen Ginsberg did when he said that homosexuals "lost that wounded look" that night.

Sheridan Square and its environs presented a tableau Boyce

would never forget: "Broken windows and burnt things, and burnt ash can, and shops were smashed, and very gay in the sense . . . that you saw, sometimes, the little piece of pink or green tulle." The street was strewn with glass that shimmered when it caught the morning sunlight. "There it was," he thought, the glittering testimony of resistance—"All broken but beautiful."

THERE WERE PEOPLE at the Stonewall that uproarious night who might have felt, even then that it constituted a turning point. Certainly, as the years went by, Stonewall—the bar became a metonym for the event—was increasingly invoked as the originating event of the modern LGBTQ movement. As Edmund White put it, "Up till that moment we had thought that homosexuality was a medical term. Suddenly we saw that we could be a minority group—with rights, a culture, an agenda." But June 28, 1969, was not the first time queer people had refused to bow down before a police raid, and it wouldn't be the last.

In August 1966, for example, when the police started cooperating with the management of Compton's Cafeteria in San Francisco's Tenderloin district to ban the transgender customers who congregated there, the customers rioted, and came back the next day to picket. On New Year's Eve of that year, vice squad officers forced their way into a festively decorated gay bar called the Black Cat Tavern in Los Angeles's Silver Lake district, and according to an account from an LA gay newspaper, *Tangents*, "started beating patrons to the floor about 5 minutes after midnight." People who were kissing beneath the balloons and twinkly Christmas lights were arrested for public indecency. In February, activists organized a protest against the Black Cat raid and police brutality, and some four hundred people showed up—"Negroes, Mexican Americans and Sunset Strip Youths," according to the alternative *Los Angeles Free Press*.

"What made Stonewall distinct and different was not what happened there," said Ellen Broidy, "but what happened after. This was a moment that became a movement." The turning point had to be fashioned into one, and to a great extent it was Craig who was responsible for doing so. He became the skilled historical craftsman who helped ensure Stonewall's resonance.

Craig started calling the newspapers in the early hours of June 28 to make sure they knew what was happening at the Stonewall. Much of the coverage that resulted was less than respectful—"Homo Nest Raided, Queen Bees are Stinging Mad," the *New York Post* headline read—but at least, thought Craig, people could see that homosexuals, whom society expected to "be passive, docile," were capable of standing up for themselves. He made up leaflets and with his bookshop team—Ellen, Fred, and Linda—distributed them in the Village on Sunday morning, June 29: "The nights of Friday, June 27th, 1969, and Saturday, June 28th, 1969, will go down in history as the first time that thousands of Homosexual men and women went out into the streets to protest the intolerable situation which has existed in New York City for many years—namely the Mafia (or Syndicate) control of this country's gay bars in collusion with certain elements in the Police Dept. of the City of New York."

The July 4 Annual Reminder in Philadelphia was scheduled for less than a week later. It would be the last one. This time, Craig put an ad for the event in the *Village Voice*, which attracted a new contingent of long-haired, jeans- and sandals-wearing young people to the march, who didn't know Frank Kameny's rules and wouldn't be inclined to respect them if they had. That was exactly what Craig counted on. This time, one female couple boldly held hands, and an irate Kameny came up behind them and swatted their hands apart. "You can't do that! You can't do that! No talking or chanting!" he shouted, red in the face. "Walk in single file!"

Craig took his group aside and urged them to march holding hands—about twenty of them did. For the first time someone other than Kameny—Craig—went over to talk to the press. He said, "Did you hear what's going on in New York, and the riots last week?" In his own words, he "ranted and raved," saying "we're tired of not being able to hold hands, and the leadership of our demonstration has to change." On the way back in the bus, Craig and his group were still keyed up, talking animatedly about a whole new spirit of gay liberation. Craig decided then and there that he wanted to turn the Annual Reminder into something bigger and bolder: a march, to be held in June, to commemorate the resistance at the Stonewall.

The historian Lillian Faderman points out that the older homophiles and the younger radicals may have wanted many of the same things—the repeal of sodomy laws, an end to the harassment and entrapment of gay people in bars and on the streets, laws prohibiting discrimination in employment. But "in style and substance, 'gay power' seemed to be beyond the understanding" of the Mattachine veterans. They did not see themselves allying with other movements—the Black Panthers, the Young Lords, women's liberation—as the new generation of activists sought to. (When a student at Virginia Tech wrote to Craig asking for advice on how to get a gay movement going on his campus, Craig told him, "If there is a women's Lib on campus, align yourselves with them. Women's Lib and Gay Lib are the vanguard in the struggle against sexism in all its forms.") The homophile organizations were less confrontational, more circumspect, more incrementalist. They weren't so sure about embracing the raffish street queens. They didn't imagine some root-and-branch transformation of society along egalitarian, socialistic lines. They worried about how the melee at the Stonewall would make them look.

Craig drafted a resolution and in early November 1969, Ellen stood up and presented it at the Eastern Regional Conference of Homophile Organizations (ERCHO). In order to make the Annual Reminder "more relevant, reach a greater number of people, and encompass the ideas and ideals of the larger struggle in which we are engaged—that of our fundamental human rights," the resolution called for moving it to "the last Saturday in June in New York

City to commemorate the 1969 spontaneous demonstrations on Christopher Street."

As Martin Duberman points out in his account of Stonewall, nationally, this was a fraught political moment. It was just a few weeks after millions of Americans had halted their daily routines for the October 15, 1969, Moratorium against the Vietnam War, and a few weeks before a massive antiwar mobilization in Washington, DC, on November 15. The Weather Underground had split off from SDS and the rest of the student left, and would accidentally blow up a townhouse turned bomb-making factory in the Village several months later, killing three of their own. The Black Panthers and the women's liberation movements were vigorously charting their own courses. Radical ideas seemed to be ascendant.

The event Rodwell and his friends proposed would be called Christopher Street Liberation Day. There would be no dress or age regulations. "Our thought was to take that kernel of that demonstration," Ellen recalled, "and turn it from a demonstration about rights into a demonstration about liberation and pride to which anybody and everybody was welcome." They "encouraged groups that were growing up all over the country to do the same thing." Martha Shelley was one of a number of younger activists in attendance who got behind the resolution. It passed unanimously, with only members of New York Mattachine abstaining. At the bookstore, the Christopher Street Liberation Committee began to meet and plan for a whole new kind of action.

CRAIG, WHO HAD been imagining liberation for a long time, wanted to involve as wide a spectrum of gay organizations and identities as he could in the commemoration of that boisterous night at the Stonewall. But he had no idea how legendary the New York City march, planned for June 28, 1970, would become. The Gay Liberation Front—an exuberant new radical group whose founders included Martha Shelley, Kiyoshi Kuromiya, and Ellen

Broidy—was enthusiastic right away. Short-lived but vibrant and diverse, the GLF formed alliances with other groups on the left, including the Black Panthers and the Young Lords, as well as with transgender street activists who got themselves organized under the GLF umbrella and soon formed their own mutual aid association. The GLFers put on a series of dances—theirs was, like Emma Goldman's, the kind of revolution you could dance to— that successfully wrested some of young gay social life away from the Mafia-controlled bars. Martha Shelley would never forget the time she and other GLFers took over the dance floor at a Mafia-owned establishment where lesbians had recently been harassed. "Do you know who we are? We are the GLF!" five foot, four inch Martha announced, knees shaking, to the big toughs running the joint. Exuberant GLFers had taken to the streets after Stonewall passing out leaflets that said things like, "Are we a load of scream-ing queens? YES!" and "Do you think Homosexuals are revolting? You bet your sweet ass we are." And they would go on to protest negative depictions of gays in national media, picketing outside the Time-Life headquarters, for example. To Kiyoshi Kuromiya, who was involved with the GLF in Philadelphia, the new, young gay movement was enthralling because it was more racially diverse, and also more countercultural, even Dionysian, with an emphasis on breaking down boundaries between people, sometimes through drug-fueled soul-searching, and plenty of talking and dancing.

Rodwell loved the GLF's spirit and knew he could count on it. Ellen, Linda, and Fred—who were all still working at the Oscar Wilde Memorial Bookshop and deeply involved with the Chris-topher Street Liberation Committee—got book browsers psyched for the march. Craig won over Foster Gunnison, a cigar-smoking Mattachine activist from a wealthy, WASPy background, who usu-ally took a more cautious tack. To Gunnison, Craig exerted an ef-fect that "was almost like a spirit sitting in the room—quiet but forceful."

When Craig spoke at planning meetings, he didn't go on and on.

If the meeting wandered off into theoretical byways, David Carter wrote, "Craig would let the discussion go on for a while before raising a practical point with a remark such as 'Who's going to take these leaflets up to the Bronx?'"

On the morning of June 28, Ellen woke up "full of anticipation," and "though I would never have admitted it to myself at that moment," full of fear, too. Would the marchers be jeered at by homophobic spectators? Would the police block their way or give them trouble? Would gay people even show up? The sky was a clear, cloudless blue—that, anyway, augured well.

Though focused, detail-oriented Craig had tried to think of everything, he could not control the fact that by the morning of June 28, the Christopher Street Liberation Committee still had not been granted a parade permit from the police. To his flustered relief, it arrived by mail just before he had to leave the apartment. The march was to start in the Village at 2 p.m., and make its way up Sixth Avenue to Central Park for a "gay-in." When Craig arrived at the assembly point on Washington Place, between Sixth and Seventh Avenues, he felt a wave of dismay. "There were only maybe less than a thousand people," he recalled, and he had been hoping for more. Still, he had "made it a long march on purpose." His idea was that the younger people—the GLF types, the committed ones who were primed to reject secrecy and claim their place in the light—would turn out at the start, and as they marched along, more people would find the courage to join in. And that, in fact, is what happened. Every time Craig looked behind him, he could see the crowd growing. "As we rolled up Sixth Avenue it just ballooned and ballooned and got more and more thrilling. Half the people were in tears."

"Two four six eight, gay is just as good as straight," the marchers chanted, and "Gay Power!" and "Out of the closets and into the streets!" In the echoing cavern created by the tall buildings on either side, with bemused spectators massed on the sidewalks, the slogans resounded. There were shirtless hippie boys with Afros or long-flowing hair, women in jeans and T-shirts carrying signs that said "I am a Lesbian and I am Beautiful" or "Smash Sexism / Gays Unite Now." There were trans people like the emerging activist Sylvia Rivera and her friends, some in miniskirts and go-go boots and glitter. Some of the marchers strode up Sixth Avenue arm in arm, three or four across; some practically danced, spinning around, half delirious, half determined, between knots of old friends and people they'd just met.

By the time they got to the Sheep Meadow at Central Park, the mood of the parade was jubilant. Two men lay down and tried to break the heterosexual record for the longest kiss. Marchers broke out weed, and Frisbees, and picnic lunches. People of all gender identities took one another's hands and skipped in big, ragged circles like Matisse's dancers come to life in the New York sunshine.

It was the first celebration of the annual liberation spectacle that would become known worldwide as the Pride March. And the historic event was the brainstorm of one very determined bookshop owner.

In the years to come, Craig Rodwell would continue to operate the Oscar Wilde Memorial Bookshop as a social refuge and a political crucible, as well as a hub for gay writers and readers. In 1973, he moved the shop to a brick townhouse on Christopher Street. The staff was multiracial. Young queer people found information and affirmation there. The novelist Dorothy Allison remembered "wandering in there as a sort of baby dyke and being closely observed by the gay man behind the counter. I was concerned that he thought I was a shoplifter but actually he was admiring my leather jacket. That was a tiny but wonderful bookstore." Without it and the other gay and lesbian bookstores that sprang up after it, she "would never have found my people, my community, never had the encouragement and commentary of other gay and lesbian writers. I would not be who I am without those voices, those closely watching eyes, those critical and understanding perspectives."

During the AIDS crisis, Craig mobilized to educate the community. The Oscar Wilde, like many of the LGBTQ bookshops whose owners Craig generously advised and encouraged, stocked pamphlets and other information about the facts of the disease when the federal government, under Ronald Reagan, was slow to provide it. Still, some people who knew him then thought Craig in the 1980s seemed lonely—he was single for many years—and angry. The assassination of Harvey Milk and the ravages of the AIDS epidemic weighed on his mind. Like all independent bookstores, especially in an expensive city like New York, the Oscar Wilde was a constant challenge to keep afloat. Kim Brinster, who became the store's manager in 1996 and bought it in 2003, knew Craig in his later years, and found him irascible. She wondered if he might have been in physical pain. In 1993, at the age of fifty-two, Rodwell died of stomach cancer. His mother, who moved to New York to be close to him—she even lived in his apartment building—survived him, as did his only sibling, a brother. Brinster would turn out to be the last of the store's owners. Slow sales and competition from online retail forced her to close it in 2009.

But on that late June day in 1970, as Craig marched uptown in a parade that would become an indisputable landmark of LGBTQ history—an event that assured the Stonewall uprising would have long-term meaning—he was grinning and crying at the same time. He just felt so much joy. Newspapers estimated the crowd that day at as many as fifteen to twenty thousand people, a remarkable turnout for that historical moment. In 2019, on the fiftieth anniversary of Stonewall, nearly five million people marched in New York City's pride parade alone—millions more in cities across the country and around the world. By then, same-sex marriage was legal in the United States, and LGBTQ people were increasingly visible in almost every facet of American life.

"I used to dream about, daydream even, about millions of homosexuals marching through the streets, openly and everything," Craig Rodwell said in 1989. "And that's come to pass in my life. So it was more than a dream. It was almost a vision, in a way, of the future."

We All Shine On

John Lennon, Yoko Ono, and the Politics of Stardom

Unlike John Lennon and Yoko Ono's "bed-ins for peace" in Amsterdam and Montreal hotel suites—which attracted frenzied media swarms in 1969—this revolution was not televised. But once again, the celebrity couple made a big bed their political headquarters. This time it dominated the bedroom in a modest two-room apartment on the top floor of a three-story brick townhouse in Greenwich Village. John Lennon and his wife—and essential collaborator—Yoko Ono would live there from mid-October 1971 to February 1973, when they bid farewell to their freewheeling West Village days and moved uptown to the Gothic fortress known as the Dakota. This was John and Yoko's radical New York City interlude. With the exception of the movie star Jane Fonda, no popular artists became as closely associated with the revolutionary uprisings of the time. And no entertainer of John Lennon's status struck deeper fear and loathing into Richard Nixon's paranoid presidency and its repressive security machinery. The ballad of John and Yoko still illustrates the wild possibilities of celebrity activism, and its dark pitfalls.

The Lennons' walk-up apartment at 105 Bank Street, which had an iron staircase spiraling to the rooftop, was leased to them by Joe Butler, the drummer for the Lovin' Spoonful, another chart-topping rock group that had disbanded in 1969, the same year as the Beatles. The boyishly handsome Butler—who cowrote some of his group's songs and sang lead on a few of its most heart-tugging, like "Full Measure" and "Butchie's Tune"—was eclipsed by the Lovin' Spoonful front man, John Sebastian, who sported Lennon-like wire-rimmed glasses. But he used his rock fame to land a role in the Broadway musical *Hair*, and his small fortune to invest in Manhattan real estate.

Butler continued living in the apartment for a couple of weeks after John and Yoko moved in—they had been so eager to decamp from the gilded luxury of the St. Regis Hotel to the bohemian enclave in the West Village that Butler hadn't had time to move out. The trio often padded around the apartment nude, since performing in *Hair* made Butler comfortable with his natural state and the famous couple had already flaunted their bare selves on the cover of their experimental 1968 album *Two Virgins* (with the FBI's perverse old prude J. Edgar Hoover taking note). Butler couldn't help notice that Lennon "was amazingly flabby . . . he didn't seem to have any muscle tissue." Yoko was trying to restore Lennon's health with a proper diet, after years of drug excess and indolence. They spatted like any couple and John "still did dominate the relationship," Butler recalled, but "they were two people who really loved each other."

It was a kind of honeymoon idyll for the couple, temporarily shielded from the media glare and the public venom that had been aimed at them since their 1969 wedding. In the artsy environs of the West Village, they were just another creative couple—not "this Japanese witch [who's] made him crazy" and her "bananas" husband, as Lennon characterized their depiction in the especially vicious British press. "The racism and sexism were overt," he later wrote. "I was ashamed of Britain."

But on Bank Street, they were among their kind. Yoko knew their next-door neighbors—the avant-garde musician John Cage and his lover and collaborator, choreographer Merce Cunningham—from the early-sixties New York art scene. A steady parade of artists and activists marched upstairs to the Lennons' apartment, where they gathered around the couple's bed, passionately discussing politics, art, and religion—and how they could wake America from its dark Nixonian spell.

Poet Allen Ginsberg hobbled by, nursing a broken leg, and demonstrated how he meditated while lying on the floor like a corpse. Lennon, who was disenchanted with religion ever since the Beatles' 1968 trek to the opportunistic Maharishi's compound in the lower Himalayas, took a dim view of Ginsberg's spirituality. "John asked me if I believed in God," Ginsberg later recalled. "I said yes. He challenged me on that. My meditation at that time was, alas, somewhat theistic—schmaltzy, sentimental. He was nontheistic, which was pretty smart; he was ahead of me there."

One day, the Black Panther leader Bobby Seale paid a visit and ended up talking with the couple for hours. They were curious about the Panthers' Free Breakfast for Children efforts, free health clinics, and other community programs. Movie stars like Fonda and Marlon Brando had rallied around the Panthers. But talking with Lennon, Seale felt "we could have been very close, much closer than I've been with other celebrities. . . . See, John went out for us. He wanted to really do something."

Seale made a point of dropping by Bank Street. "Whenever I hit New York, I'd go by and see John Lennon. I must have visited him and Yoko Ono four or five times. He'd say, 'We got this song—"Give Peace a Chance."' And I'd say, 'Sounds good.' Because I related to artists—I was an artist in my own right. I was on stage way before the party was ever started."

The feminist writer and Redstockings collective veteran Kate Millett was also a frequent visitor. Her 1970 book *Sexual Politics*—a scathing, polemical work of philosophy and literary criticism (one of her academic advisers said reading it was like "sitting with your testicles in a nutcracker")—had become an unlikely bestseller. At a time when fierce feminist debates attracted a surprisingly wide audience, the book shared that distinction with Shulamith Firestone's *The Dialectic of Sex* and Germaine Greer's *The Female Eunuch*. Millett's intellect was formidable, but she did not intimidate John or Yoko. Wending her way through knots of assistants, Millett found her way to the bedroom, where a large-screen TV played silently at the foot of the bed and clouds of dope smoke filled the air. Meeting John, she was "terribly charmed and impressed," Millett later recalled. "He was lovely. Delightful. So intelligent and so funny and so busy." She felt painfully stupid telling him how much she admired him and adored his music.

Yoko appreciated it when visitors also focused their attention on her, and Millett did. "She was tough," said the writer. "We'd talk about what we ought to do [as feminists] . . . delightful pie-in-the-sky stuff. But a lot of it was serious, too."

But the Lennons' closest companions during the early Bank Street days were Yippie activists Jerry Rubin and Stew Albert. Rubin and his even more colorful sidekick Abbie Hoffman were America's leading radical pranksters. Creating chaos at the New York Stock Exchange by showering the trading floor with dollar bills, running a pig for president in 1968, the Yippies had mastered the art of media manipulation, combining Marx with the Marx brothers. The group injected some much-needed madcap humor into the heavy-browed New Left. Watching Rubin, Albert, and a pack of other Yippies turn upside down the talk show of stuffy English TV host David Frost, John and Yoko were delighted. Lennon called the Yippies "political Beatles" and the couple allowed themselves to become the anarchists' captives when Rubin and Hoffman swept the celebrities into their whirl soon after John and Yoko moved from England to New York in 1971.

Albert was in awe of the man whose music had been the soundtrack of his life. He would've been content to sit at the foot of Lennon's bed "while we dreamed of an impossible utopia, reveling in sparkling visions that were supported by firm decisions—and forgotten in moments. The grass was good and enlightening; guests dropped in and out. . . . By the early '70s, I was fairly blasé about hanging out with household names. . . . But a Beatle is a Beatle is a Beatle. And while I was able to control my awe most of the time, I did occasionally hear my inner voice say to me, 'I am sitting beside John Lennon. He is playing his guitar and singing a new song that he wrote—and he wants my opinion. Can you live on this planet and get any luckier?'"

But Rubin had bigger plans for the Yippies and John Lennon. As Albert ruefully observed, "By 1971 there really wasn't much left of the Left." Like Jane Fonda, John Lennon was late to the political war in America. The movement was splintering into factions, with some militant leaders going underground as President Nixon ratcheted up the repression. And by taking steps that year to end the draft, while converting Vietnam from a ground to an air war, his administration was weakening mass opposition. But Rubin "looked at John and Yoko as countercultural royalty," Albert observed. The Yippie leader believed that their proven ability to rivet the media's attention imbued them with magical powers.

"Jerry believed that if John made the right moves with us at his side, he could single-handedly resurrect the American protest movement," Albert later wrote in his memoir. "With a treasure such as John Lennon backing us, it could all come to life again."

Lennon was not simply a stooge of cunning radical leaders like Rubin, though. "John was more radical than I was in this period," the Yippie leader later recalled. "He would joke about [his and Ono's] earlier projects, saying, '*She's* the one who's into peace and love.' He was angry, really angry. He ranted and raved about the police. Yoko would tell him, 'You should have love for the pigs. All pigs are victims.'"

Coming out of the Beatles, which he described during this early breakup phase as a marriage "more stifling than my domestic life" with his first wife, Cynthia, John was on fire to tell the truth, no matter how searing, to trash all convention and protocol. In one of his earliest, post-Beatles, soul-baring interviews—with Tariq Ali and Robin Blackburn, publishers of the radical English newspaper *Red Mole*—Lennon traced his fury back to his Irish English working-class roots in Liverpool. Scathing wit was a treasured survival mechanism among the laboring class of the rough port city— particularly for a boy who had been rejected by both parents. (His stern but doting aunt, Mimi Smith, who raised him in a proper lower-middle-class English home, would take issue with John's version of his origin story.)

"I've always been politically minded, you know, and against the status quo," Lennon told the *Red Mole* journalists in January 1971. "It's pretty basic when you're brought up, like I was, to hate and fear the police as a natural enemy and to despise the army as something that takes everybody away and leaves them dead somewhere. I mean, it's just a basic working-class thing."

Brian Epstein, the bespoke manager who had carefully crafted the Beatles' wholesome image (while painfully hiding away his homosexuality), tried to steer his four lads clear of controversial topics like the Vietnam War. But Lennon couldn't be easily controlled. He made a pact with his bandmate, George Harrison, who was younger but also a seeker of truth on a more spiritual plane. "When [the US press] asks next time, we're going to say we don't like that war and we think they should get right out," he recalled in *Red Mole*. "At that time this was a pretty radical thing to do, especially for the Fab Four."

Lennon had already created a furor in March 1966 when he told a London newspaper on the eve of what would be the final Beatles tour of America that the band was "more popular than Jesus." The remark set off an incendiary response among outraged residents of the Bible Belt, who organized boycotts and made bonfires of Beatles albums. So when the Beatles were asked at a British press conference how they would respond if reporters in the US inquired about the Vietnam War, you could immediately see the consternation in the four young men's faces. This was no longer the playful give-and-take of earlier Beatles interviews, like the one following the Beatles' first, euphoric American tour in 1964. (British reporter with plummy accent: "Tell me, how did you find America?" Lennon, in his best Liverpudlian drawl: "Turn left at Greenland.")

It was John, of course, who took the bait in reply to the Vietnam question. "You can't just keep quiet about anything that's going on in the world—not unless you're a monk," he said. Trying to avoid another controversy in Christendom, Lennon instantly added, "Sorry, monks, I didn't mean it"—while the look on the face of the more cautious Paul McCartney melted into wry admiration for his witty bandmate.

In July 1969, Lennon wholeheartedly embraced the growing antiwar movement, releasing a song that would almost instantly become its anthem, "Give Peace a Chance." The song was shouted out—perhaps most famously by folk singer Pete Seeger and a half million protesters gathered on the Washington Mall in November of that year. "Are you listening, Nixon?" Seeger taunted the president as masses of people sang and swayed in unison. Lennon later said, "In me secret heart I wanted to write something that would take over 'We Shall Overcome'"—the anthem of the civil rights movement. But the truth is both songs would grace the robust songbook of the era's protest music.

During the fiery George Floyd protests in 2020, civil rights veteran Bernard Lafayette, who had accompanied Martin Luther King on his fateful trip to Memphis in 1968, mourned the disappearance of strong leadership and powerful protest music—both of which, he argued, are essential to sustain dissident movements.

"We need music, OK?" Lafayette declared in June 2020. "Once you get those artists singing songs about change and the movement, that helps to stimulate people and bring them together. There is nothing like music to bring people together."

Lennon agreed with this sentiment. "Why doesn't somebody write something for the people now?" John stated in the midst of the antiwar tumult. "That's what my job and our job is."

By 1971, Lennon had broken completely free from the constraints of pop stardom. "I don't believe in Beatles," he had concluded after similarly rejecting a list of other deities and idolatries in his song "God." "The dream is over." The musician released an astonishing barrage of introspective songs the previous year, beginning with the single, "Instant Karma (We All Shine On)," in February 1970. "Why in the world are we here?" asked John in that song, which reached the top 5 in the British and US charts—an age-old philosophical question never before asked by a rock star. "Surely not to live in pain and fear." But that's exactly what drove his creativity, he confided in another remarkably candid interview, with *Rolling Stone* publisher Jann Wenner in 1970. "Creating is a result of pain," said Lennon. "I have to put it somewhere and I write songs."

His first solo album, *John Lennon/Plastic Ono Band*—released in December 1970—is still shocking in its self-revelation more than a half century later. In addition to "God," the LP contained "Mother"—his howling, therapeutic song about his late mother, Julia ("Mother you had me, but I never had you")—and "Working Class Hero," his rant about the psychological injuries of class.

But after relocating to America in fall 1971, Lennon turned his fury outward. His song "Imagine," released as a single in October of that year, would be embraced over the years as a sweet expression of Lennon's idealism. But as he often pointed out, the song was actually much more radical, urging people to imagine a world without countries, war, religion, greed, or hunger. The song, which Lennon recorded in May 1971 at his Tittenhurst Park mansion near Ascot, owed a lot to the visionary poetry of Ono's 1964 book *Grapefruit*. ("Imagine the clouds dripping. Dig a hole in your garden to put them in.") Lennon later said he should have cocredited the composition to his wife, "but in those days I was a bit more selfish, a bit more macho, and I omitted her contribution, but it's right out of *Grapefruit*."

By the time John Lennon settled in Greenwich Village, he was singing "power to the people" and was ready to declare war on all authorities that were suffocating human freedom. In street protests, concerts, songs, and TV interviews, the man who was the most bravely outspoken—and perhaps most talented—musician in the rock pantheon of his time began taking on the Nixon administration, the FBI, the CIA, the Vietnam War, government drug trafficking, corporate exploitation, and the political apathy of young people. His plainly stated goal was to revolutionize America—which he saw as the imperial Rome of its day.

And he was joined in his vast dream by Yoko Ono, whose underground artistic background—and maybe her family privilege as the daughter of a Japanese banking dynasty—gave her similar confidence in their mission. "With my presentation of performance art, I was always aware that I wanted to inspire people and stir people, so that they can wake up," she observed.

John and Yoko were a powerful combination, a force larger than their individual talents; larger than their marriage; merging radical politics, music, and art. The couple's December 1969 "War Is Over! If You Want It" billboard campaign, which appeared in twelve cities around the world—from Times Square in New York to Toronto to Tokyo—had burst from Ono's artistic imagination. But she had envisioned only New York street posters. It was Lennon, with his Beatles-size audience expectations, who insisted on a grander, global scale for their peace campaign.

There was a breathtaking ambition to John and Yoko's enterprise. No celebrity couple with their combined political and creative vision had crossed the line of privilege into such dangerous territory. And the couple was attempting this American revival at a point when the nation was soul-sickened by assassinations, riots, and government surveillance, in a political atmosphere clammy with fear and violence.

But huddled in their Bank Street apartment with fellow troublemakers, Lennon and Ono were happily unaware of the hostile forces that were about to be released on them. Their campaign to liberate America would naturally start with a free concert, to be staged in Ann Arbor, Michigan, on December 10, 1971. First this college town in middle America, then the entire nation, and then the world.

IN EARLY DECEMBER 1971, Peter Andrews, an events director at the University of Michigan, and Leni Sinclair, the wife of John Sinclair, a radical countercultural hero who was serving a stiff sentence in a Michigan state prison for giving two marijuana joints to an undercover cop, showed up at 105 Bank Street, where John and Yoko were expecting them. Leni Sinclair—a petite woman who had taken over her imprisoned husband's leadership role at the Rainbow People's Party along with his brother David—had miraculously arranged to get John Lennon to headline a benefit concert on behalf of her husband. (Jerry Rubin had intervened on her behalf.) The concert, which was to take place at the recently constructed Crisler Arena on the U-M's Ann Arbor campus, was to feature rising hometown hero Bob Seger and a few middling acts like Commander Cody and His Lost Planet Airmen, as well as a slew of political speakers. Concert promoter Andrews was a friend of the jailed radical hippie, but he was initially reluctant to take over the John Sinclair Freedom Rally because he thought the underwhelming stage lineup would make the event "a total bomb."

But John Lennon appearing onstage in the United States for the first time since the breakup of the Beatles? Now that was a different story. Andrews needed to be certain that Lennon was committed, however, so he and Leni Sinclair made the trek to John and Yoko's West Village apartment. "They greeted us, they were very friendly, very, very nice," Andrews recalled years later. "I had Lennon sign a contract for $500 to appear, and he crossed it out and put, 'To be donated to the John Sinclair Freedom Fund.'"

Armed with a cassette tape on which Lennon confirmed he would be performing at the Sinclair rally, Andrews and Leni Sin-

clair held a press conference as soon as they returned to Ann Arbor.
Tickets (priced at $3) for the show at the fifteen-thousand-seat
arena sold out immediately. No paid advertising was necessary; the
announcement of John Lennon's name was enough to ensure the
event wouldn't be "a total bomb."

In the months before the concert, Leni and David Sinclair had
worked diligently to enlist other celebrities and radical leaders on
behalf of their imprisoned loved one, including Jane Fonda, Allen
Ginsberg, Tom Hayden, Jerry Rubin, and Abbie Hoffman—who
had even briefly seized the stage at Woodstock to publicize Sinclair's plight. (Hoffman later denied being cracked on the head by
the Who's guitar-wielding Pete Townshend.) But after two years,
Sinclair was still languishing in prison. Then John and Yoko came
to town.

On the afternoon of December 10, Andrews picked up the couple at the Detroit airport in a borrowed limousine and deposited
them at a suite in Ann Arbor's Campus Inn. John had brought a
ragtag band with him, including David Peel, a proto-punk Puerto
Rican guitarist from the Lower East Side whom Lennon had befriended, and some other New York street musicians. But the buzz
grew louder as Lennon and his crew started jamming in his suite
and continued backstage at the concert, which began in the late
afternoon and dragged late into the night. The crowd applauded
politely for the political speakers—getting the most pumped up
for Bobby Seale, who tied the environmental cause, which he knew
was taking off in campus communities like Ann Arbor, to the
struggle against war, racism, poverty, assassination, and fascism.
"The only solution to pollution is a people's humane revolution!"
Seale shouted in conclusion, to loud cheers from the mostly white,
youthful audience.

But the highlight of the concert before Lennon, who was scheduled to close out the marathon show, was surprise musical guest
Stevie Wonder. Raised in nearby Motown, Wonder electrified the audience, many of whom started dancing in the aisles. He also excited

Lennon, who'd never seen Wonder play live before. For security reasons, Andrews didn't want Lennon to watch Wonder's performance from the rear of the stage, where he could be recognized from the audience. But Lennon insisted. "Peter, don't you understand?" Lennon told the promoter. "Stevie Wonder is my Beatles." Wonder made clear that he was not there simply to entertain, telling the crowd that "we are in a very troublesome time today in the world." It was a time when a man could "get twelve years in jail for possession of marijuana" while the man who ordered the killing of "four students at Kent State [can] come out free. . . . What kind of shit is that?" added Wonder, to a roar from the packed arena.

Finally, at almost three a.m., John Lennon walked onstage with his haphazard group, which included Rubin on congas and Ono on backing vocals. The crowd was dazed and exhausted. "It had been a twelve-hour concert," recalled David Fenton, a young Ann Arbor activist at the time who was in charge of publicizing the show, which was televised statewide. "There were pounds of marijuana being distributed to the crowd." But despite the late hour and the purple haze, the audience jumped to its feet as Lennon came strolling onstage. There he was—in his round dark glasses, nonchalantly chewing gum, the personification of a carefree and creative spirit that now seemed lost in suffering America.

Like Wonder, Lennon immediately announced he had come to Ann Arbor for a serious reason. He was there to replug the dormant radical movement. "We came here not only to help John [Sinclair] and to spotlight what's going on, but also to show and to say to all of you that apathy isn't it, and that we can do something. OK, so flower power didn't work. So what? We start again."

We start again. It was like the words whispered to a sleeping princess to rouse her from her poisoned slumber. At that moment, it seemed that only someone with the shimmering aura of John Lennon had the power to break America's dark spell.

Then Lennon, playing only an acoustic guitar, launched into the angry protest song he had written for the occasion. The press later quoted the liberation chant from "John Sinclair" but it was a stanza in the middle of the song that revealed the ex-Beatle's growing radicalism. In it, Lennon denounced the US soldiers "shooting gooks in Vietnam" and getting away with their atrocities, like those who had massacred some five hundred unarmed men, women, and children at My Lai. He also called out the CIA for "selling dope and making hay"—another scathing reference to exposés in the alternative press about the spy agency's Southeast Asia drug trafficking (which would culminate in the explosive 1972 bestseller *The Politics of Heroin* by Yale graduate student Alfred W. McCoy).

In the late, twilight hour, John Lennon was kicking off his new revolutionary mission. He hoped to use his special powers as a former Beatle to rally America's youth, who had just been granted the eighteen-year-old vote, to defeat President Nixon's reelection bid in November 1972. There would be a nationwide concert tour to get out the youth vote, with Lennon being joined by Bob Dylan and even (in a "battle of the bands") by his estranged ex-partner Paul McCartney and Paul's new group Wings. The tour would culminate in August in a massive "political Woodstock" (in Rubin's words) at the Republican National Convention, which was originally planned for San Diego and then moved to Miami. After vanquishing the most fearsome war machine on the planet, John and Yoko would then take their peace campaign around the world. Lennon didn't lay out the bold plan during the concert, but it was already being discussed at Bank Street. Ann Arbor was the dress rehearsal for the 1972 youth revolution.

Jerry Rubin came closest to broadcasting the plan when he excitedly exclaimed onstage at Crisler Arena, "All these people are saying the revolution is over. It doesn't look that way to me. Fifteen thousand people demanding freedom for John Sinclair. . . . It shows that right now we can really unite music and revolutionary politics and really build the movement all across the country." Rubin also called on members of the youthful audience "to turn up at the Republican Convention to humiliate and defeat Richard Nixon."

Two days after Lennon's Ann Arbor performance, the Michigan Supreme Court released Sinclair from prison. The justices claimed they were simply acting in accordance with a newly passed state law reducing penalties for marijuana possession. But to the Sinclair family—and the movement that had been built around his legal cause—it was clear that John Lennon's fame had won the radical longhair's freedom.

Young activists weren't the only ones who recognized Lennon's power. Unknown to John and Yoko, undercover FBI informants were embedded at the Ann Arbor concert, taking detailed notes about everything from the crowd size, to the cost of renting the university arena ($4,000—"Paid for in cash and in advance"), to the song lyrics and political speeches onstage (some of which were transcribed in full). Hoover—the FBI's aging, reactionary director—was not well-informed about rock culture, but he knew enough to understand the political threat posed by an alliance between a former Beatle (the most outspoken and controversial one) and the radical leaders who had disrupted the 1968 Democratic National Convention in Chicago. Lennon had been joined onstage in Ann Arbor not only by Rubin and Seale, but by New Left leader Rennie Davis—all of whom were Chicago Eight defendants—and by a taped message from William Kunstler, one of the radical group's lawyers.

The FBI's practice under Hoover was to work with repressive machinery on Capitol Hill to target political enemies. The bureau tipped off Senator Strom Thurmond, the notoriously racist and far-right senator from South Carolina, about the Sinclair rally. In February 1972, Thurmond, in turn, alerted the Nixon White House and Attorney General John Mitchell. Thurmond, who urged administration action "at the highest level," attached a memo from the internal security subcommittee of the Senate Judiciary Committee—both of which he served on—that flagged the political danger represented by an influential rock star like Lennon as the 1972 presidential election approached.

A cell of New Left leaders was convening in the New York area to plot a campaign to "dump Nixon" in November 1972, the memo informed top administration officials. This radical group "intend[s] to use John Lennon as a drawing card to promote the success of the rock festivals and rallies" aimed at mobilizing the youth vote against Nixon. Relaying the FBI's alarm, the Senate subcommittee urged the Nixon White House to terminate the British musician's visa as "a strategy counter-measure."

So began the Nixon administration's war on John Lennon, a relentless campaign to "neutralize" (in the FBI's chilling terminology) or silence the outspoken star—a government crusade that would outlast the Nixon presidency and end only in 1976, when Lennon, after a long, costly legal battle with the Immigration and Naturalization Service, finally won his green card. Chronicled in three hundred pages of FBI documents—most of which were finally released after a lengthy Freedom of Information Act battle waged by historian Jon Wiener—the confidential memos reveal what Wiener called an epic "abuse of power, a kind of rock 'n' roll Watergate" against a man whose only crime was imagining a peaceful world.

"Give peace a chance—who could be opposed to that?" asked George McGovern, who ran against President Nixon in 1972. "The administration was." So deep was the government animus against Lennon that some believe it shadowed him until the day he died.

From the Ann Arbor concert to the day he was gunned down at the entrance of the Dakota nine years later, John Lennon had to balance his drive to express himself politically with his desire to keep himself and his family safe. From his Bank Street days on, he was the target of aggressive government surveillance. His phones were tapped, as well as those of his political allies and immigration lawyer; he was followed by government agents; and his personal life and finances were pored over.

"It was our perspective on Lennon that most of the time he was walking around stoned—whacked out of his mind. But he was a high-profile figure, and so his activities were being monitored," coldly remarked G. Gordon Liddy, one of the most sinister Nixon operatives. "They wanted me to know—to be scared," Lennon said. "And I was scared."

EARLY IN THE evening of December 17, 1971—a week after the John Sinclair Freedom Rally—a troupe of four Black Panthers showed up at 105 Bank Street, on the order of the party's defense minister, Huey Newton, to escort John Lennon uptown to the legendary Apollo Theater in Harlem. Among them was William "BJ" Johnson, a former heroin dealer and addict whose life had been turned around at the Malcolm X Cultural Center in New York City, which then became a Black Panther office. Lennon had agreed to join Aretha Franklin and other marquee musicians that night at a benefit concert for the families of prisoners massacred at upstate New York's Attica Correctional Facility in September by National Guard soldiers, state troopers, and sheriffs. The *New York Times* had rushed to blame the murders of ten guards on the savagery of the rebellious prisoners, but it soon was revealed that nearly all of the guards and thirty-two inmates were killed in the frenzy of gunfire unleashed by Governor Nelson Rockefeller. Three months after the Attica bloodbath, the emotional tempest in New York City was still billowing. Huey Newton knew, Johnson later recalled, that since Lennon "was going to Harlem with all those black people, if he had some Panthers with him, nothing was going to happen to him."

At Bank Street, Lennon made the Panthers feel at home, and when Jerry Rubin offered Johnson a hit off "the biggest joint I'd ever seen in my life," he didn't hesitate. "Hell, yeah!" Johnson exclaimed. After taking a drag from the thick doobie, Johnson asked Lennon to play one of his Beatles songs, but the musician declined. "I forgot that shit," he said.

But later, backstage at the Apollo, R&B singer/songwriter Don Covay ("Mercy, Mercy," "Chain of Fools") collared Lennon and they sang a duet of "Eleanor Rigby," with John playing acoustic guitar. Other musicians were sticking their heads out of their dressing rooms and shouting, "John Lennon's here!" Johnson, who later became a road manager for a soul group called the Variations, never forgot the electricity of the evening at the Apollo.

"Finally, we got to Aretha Franklin's room," Johnson recounted. "She said, 'Hey, John!' They were hugging and making small talk. John Lennon turned away, getting ready to leave. I grabbed John by the shoulder and said, 'John, you forgot the phone number.'"

Lennon was not only performing at the Apollo that night, he was also on a mission for the Black Panthers—to get Aretha Franklin's home number for Huey Newton, so he could arrange for her to headline a Panther benefit. Reminded of his political task, Lennon whispered in Franklin's ear. "She calls to her bodyguard, 'Gimme a pen!' She writes down her number, gives it to John, John hands it to me."

Later, onstage, Lennon had some hard acts to follow, but his new protest song "Attica State," which he sang with Ono, provoked loud cheers from the capacity crowd of 1,500 people, particularly the lines, "Media blamed it on the prisoners / But the prisoners did not kill / 'Rockefeller pulled the trigger' / That's what the people feel." Though not one of his memorable compositions, it was another remarkably radical song by the ex-Beatle, even advocating "revolution"—a subject on which he had once famously equivocated. ("You can count me out . . . in" went a version of his song "Revolution.")

Lennon told the families of the slain prisoners that it was "an honor to be here at the Apollo and for the reasons we're all here." Then, after apologizing for not yet having an electric band, he said, "I'll just have to busk it," and sang a moving, solo version of his recently released "Imagine," armed only with his acoustic guitar. It was a beautiful and anguished highlight of the evening.

After the show, Lennon insisted on taking his Black Panther escorts to a Harlem restaurant for a late-night dinner. Johnson and his fellow soldiers had been strictly instructed by Omar Barbour, the top Panther that night, not to order "anything too extravagant. Just get coffee and donuts." But Lennon opened the menu and insisted that Johnson pick his favorite dish. "Well, I'd love some steak and eggs," he offered tentatively, trying to avoid Barbour's eyes. "Waiter!" shouted Lennon. "Bring him some steak and eggs." The other Panthers quickly followed suit.

"Like I said," BJ Johnson remembered, "we had a lot of fun."

Following the night at the Apollo, John Lennon continued to act like a man on a political mission. He and Ono joined a protest march in Manhattan after British troops opened fire on Northern Irish demonstrators, killing thirteen. Lennon commemorated "Bloody Sunday" at the protest with an angry new song, "The Luck of the Irish," venting his Celtic rage at British "genocide." That same month, Lennon quietly donated a large sum to the Attica Defense Fund, an estimated $10,000. He gave as much as $75,000 to the radical leaders planning to block Nixon's reelection—the equivalent of a half million dollars in 2020. And he walked around Manhattan wearing a button urging "Indict Rockefeller for Murder."

Most of the media ignored Lennon's appearance at the Apollo Theater, even though it was only his second US performance as a solo artist. But John and Yoko took their music and politics to the airwaves, turning American TV shows—where he was a welcome guest because of his Beatles fame—into their political platforms. On a US broadcast of the *David Frost Show* in January 1972 (recorded the previous month), the couple sat on the edge of the stage and performed "Attica State," backed by street musicians David Peel and the Lower East Side. Ono also discussed a Vietnam antiwar art film she produced and sang a feminist song, "Sisters, O Sisters." Then the couple plunged into a heated discussion with Frost's studio audience about the Attica rebellion and prisoner rights, with the divided crowd equally booing and cheering them. The Attica song "glorifies" criminals, one woman shouted. "We're not glorifying them," Lennon patiently but emphatically responded. "This song will come and go. But there will be another Attica tomorrow."

Lennon's give-and-take with the crowd demonstrated how much thought he had given to the prickly subject of crime and punishment. "I understand that society hasn't worked out what to do with people who kill and violent people," he said at one point. "But there are a lot of people in jail who aren't violent, who don't kill, and they're in there for no reason at all, and then they go mad in jail."

Before the show ended, John and Yoko brought the chief of the Onondaga nation in upstate New York onto the stage to explain his people's battle against a highway expansion planned through tribal land. And then the couple and their band performed the "John Sinclair" freedom song and discussed the cruelty of drug laws. It was a remarkable mainstreaming of deeply controversial subjects, and only the Lennons had the star power and the revolutionary innocence to commandeer entire TV talk shows like this. Lennon, in particular, was able to talk with wit, candor, and self-deprecating humor about issues that bitterly divided the American people. He had a knack for cutting to the emotional heart of causes, whether it was peace in Vietnam or the rights of prisoners, Native Americans, Blacks, and women.

In February 1972, John and Yoko took their radical act directly to the American heartland, appearing as weeklong cohosts on the *Mike Douglas Show*, a nationally syndicated daytime talk show that originated in Cleveland before moving to Philadelphia. The program featured an entertainment lineup as wholesome as its star, a genial former big-band singer who'd scored a top-40 hit with a song called "The Men in My Little Girl's Life." Roger Ailes, the dark genius who later created Fox News, got his first big break in television as a producer on the show, which reached over six million viewers each day, many of them housewives. John and Yoko were determined to introduce some of their insurrectionary friends to middle America that week and show that they didn't have horns.

"There's such a gap between the young generation and the old generation now," Ono explained at the time. "Because this is a show that really communicates more with the older generation, we wanted to reach our hands out to them and say, 'Don't be afraid of us. And we shouldn't be too hostile to you either. Let's work it together, because we have to work it together.'"

Lennon proved himself a skillful interviewer throughout the week, and consumer advocate Ralph Nader and even Bobby Seale—who stressed the Black Panthers' self-defense philosophy and community service programs—came across as sympathetic figures. Lennon was especially smooth at drawing out Nader on the importance of registering young people to vote—even when the choice between candidates sometimes seemed like nothing more than a "Tweedledum and Tweedledee distinction," in Nader's words. (The thirty-seven-year-old Nader's endorsement of the two-party system, despite its limitations, now seems ironic in light of his later third-party runs for president.)

With the November 1972 presidential election in view, Lennon made a strong pitch for getting out the youth vote. Young people in England and "movement" activists in the US had made a mistake, said the musician, by rejecting the ballot box as "irrelevant." But even just "an inch of breathing space" between liberal and conservative candidates can be crucial for people, Lennon remarked. "A lot of movement people are deciding that voting *is* relevant because it's the only chance they're gonna get. If you want to beat the Establishment, you gotta know how it works."

Jerry Rubin was a less crowd-pleasing guest on the show. Nervous and given to angry and self-righteous eruptions, Rubin turned off many in the studio audience and the smiley-faced host himself. The movement is quieter now, he argued, "because the repression is so heavy that anyone who does anything gets arrested, jailed, killed." There was truth about Nixon's America in Rubin's statement, but as usual, his tone tended toward the shrill and bombastic. An exasperated Mike Douglas shot back, "This is the only country in the world where a man can say something like this on television."

Lennon guided Rubin away from his doomsday rhetoric to concrete plans for election year action. Young people should vote "as
a bloc . . . to get Nixon out of the White House," the Yippie leader
declared. He then urged young Americans to descend on the Republican National Convention "and nonviolently make our presence felt."

"Nonviolently," Lennon stressed.

But Rubin wouldn't moderate his flaming rhetoric. "Because
if we do anything any other way, we'll be killed. That's the kind
of country we live in." The audience booed him. Again, there was
truth to what Rubin charged—Nixon security forces *were* prepared
to crush RNC protests with bloody force. But Rubin came off as
arrogant and self-righteous, despite John and Yoko's best efforts to
humanize him.

As historian Jon Wiener later observed, Lennon was drawn to
movement celebrities when he resettled in America, working with
Chicago Eight radical leaders he later derided. "They were picked
for [leadership] roles not by the movement, but first of all by the
government prosecutors and then by the media," Wiener wrote.
"Rubin in particular had been sharply criticized by many sections
of the New Left. But if they were not legitimate movement representatives, that wasn't John's fault. That was the responsibility of
the American left itself, disorganized and represented by super-
stars almost by default. John was working with the movement as it
existed, for better or for worse."

In *Skywriting by Word of Mouth*, his 1978 journal doodlings,
Lennon would later put down these former comrades from his Bank
Street days. "We even got them on the *Mike Douglas Show*, but none
of them knew how to talk to the people—never mind lead them!"

The FBI, ever observant of movement schisms it could exploit,
was aware of the tensions between Lennon and radical leaders. But
it was most concerned with the plan announced by Rubin—first
at the Sinclair concert and now on the *Mike Douglas Show*—to
rally America's youth to defeat Nixon. Hoover's bureau obviously

believed that electorally opposing Richard Nixon was an "un-American activity," and FBI agents who monitored and recorded John and Yoko's weeklong appearance on the talk show classified Rubin as an "extremist" and Lennon as "SM-NL" (Security Matter–New Left). The ability of the ex-Beatle to inject rebellious ideas into the American mainstream was clearly disturbing to the Nixon administration, and equally to the country's sprawling security apparatus.

The FBI widely distributed its reports on Lennon and the anti-Nixon campaign to other federal and military security agencies, including the Secret Service and US naval intelligence. The CIA also put the musician under observation as part of its CHAOS program, the agency's illegal domestic spying operation started under director Richard Helms in 1967 and overseen by the notorious counterintelligence chief James Jesus Angleton.

Taking guidance from Attorney General John Mitchell—a Nixon stalwart who had prioritized his longtime friend's reelection—the Immigration and Naturalization Service revoked Lennon's visa and began deportation proceedings against him on March 6, 1972. But when Lennon retained the counsel of top immigration lawyer Leon Wildes and delayed his deportation, the FBI resorted to additional extralegal measures. In a memo about Lennon sent to the FBI's New York bureau, Hoover wrote that "subject is heavy narcotics user," and suggested that he be set up in a drug bust, giving the INS further ammunition to deport him.

Lennon was feeling the full heat of the US government in ways that few celebrities have ever endured. Aware their phones were tapped, John and Yoko began going next door to John Cage and Merce Cunningham's apartment to make sensitive calls. At the urging of attorney Wildes, Lennon reluctantly canceled plans for the national, anti-Nixon concert tour, going on the *Dick Cavett Show* in May to announce that he and Yoko had no intention of appearing at the tumultuous GOP convention, which had been moved from San Diego to Miami for security reasons. Lennon was wracked by guilt,

fearing he had caved to "Tricky Dick," as he scathingly referred to
Nixon on "Gimme Some Truth," a song of brilliant fury on his 1971
album, *Imagine*.

None of Lennon's friends held the cancellation against him, at
least in public, though New Left militants like Rubin who were pin-
ning their hopes for a radical revival on the famous musician were
obviously bitterly disappointed and kept pressuring the couple in
private. It was clear, however, that John and Yoko were "headed for
trouble," as John Sinclair sympathetically declared. "Canceling the
tour plan was wise."

The Lennons did not just fear deeper immigration troubles if
they headlined an anti-Nixon concert in Miami. As Yoko explained
years later, they feared lethal violence. "If we had gone to the Republican convention," she firmly stated, "we would've been in danger of our lives."

Years after the 1972 Republican convention, Lennon was still
bitter about how "the 'leaders' of the movement wanted another
[riotous 1968] 'Chicago.' And we were to be the bait, only we said
no." Venting in acerbic Lennon fashion in *Skywriting by Word of
Mouth*, he railed, "The thing that bothered most of our revolutionary brothers was the fact that we weren't *against* anything, just *for*
things, you know, like peace and love and all that naïve crap. . . .
The biggest mistake Yoko and I made in that period was allowing
ourselves to become influenced by the male-macho 'serious revolutionaries.' . . . We should have stuck to our own way of working
for peace: bed-ins, billboards etc."

But it wasn't only the New Left that was trying to exploit John
Lennon's star power. Yoko thought of New York as her "hometown" because of her time in the 1950s and early '60s as a Sarah
Lawrence College student and underground performance artist.
But by the 1970s, New York was becoming the overheated capital
of celebrity culture. Artist Andy Warhol, always looking for ways
to extend his fifteen minutes of fame, astonished John and Yoko by
asking them to stage a public wrestling match in Madison Square

Garden, which he would film. "Just to show the great 'peace and love' people having a fight onstage," marveled John at Warhol's commercial cynicism.

The truth is that John and Yoko wanted to be masters of their own celebrity power. And Lennon himself was being cynical or disingenuous when he wrote that all he and his media-savvy wife were trying to do was naively promote peace and love. The Lennons always had a more sophisticated, radical agenda than that. And even under growing pressure from the Nixon administration in spring 1972, they continued to perform heated protest songs and speak their minds. On the *Dick Cavett Show* in May, while declaring surrender to Nixon on the Republican convention, they still sang "Woman Is Nigger of the World"—a song banned on radio because of the word alone. The couple felt forced to solicit the support of prominent African Americans like comedian Dick Gregory and Representative Ron Dellums, chairman of the Congressional Black Caucus, to help explain the political context of the heavily loaded word. (Gregory once warned Lennon, "If you start meddling in real business, they'll reduce you down to a nigger. They'll make you act the way niggers are supposed to act—very quiet, behaving themselves.")

On the Cavett show, John, backed by Yoko and Elephant's Memory—a tight New York band featuring wailing sax player Stan Bronstein—ripped into a ferocious version of the banned song, whose title came from an Ono interview in a British magazine. Lennon's passionate performance of the song left no doubt about his conversion to feminism under the influence of Ono—or how his own damaged childhood had made him deeply empathetic with the "niggers" of the world. John obviously related to the gender victim in the song, made to "paint her face and dance."

On the same show, Yoko made an impassioned plea for Children's Medical Relief International, which aided young victims of the US war in Vietnam. As she urged viewers to contribute to the fund, John held up a photo of a Vietnamese boy who had been badly scorched by a white phosphorus grenade. "War was not an abstraction to [Ono]," Elliot Mintz, a close friend of the Lennons, later remarked. "She experienced it first-hand. . . . She came from an extremely privileged background—a banking family. Then the sky opened up and the bombs fell." During their World War II childhood, Yoko and her younger brother were evacuated from Tokyo to the countryside during the devastating US air attacks on Japan. Scorned by the rural families, she and her brother suffered hunger and deprivation during the war.

In May 1972, the same month as John and Yoko's Cavett show appearance, J. Edgar Hoover died suddenly of a heart attack at his home in Washington. "Jesus Christ! That old cocksucker!" President Nixon responded uncharitably to the news. Nixon had feared that the aging FBI autocrat would "pull down the temple with him, including me." But the Nixon regime would slouch on for another two years. And the end of Hoover did not mean the end of John Lennon's troubles—he continued to be mercilessly hounded by the FBI, INS, and other government agencies.

Feeling harassed and hectored from all sides, the Lennons decided to escape New York that month and light out for California. They bought a new green Chrysler Town & Country station wagon, outfitted it with a portable turntable to play 45-rpm singles since the vehicle lacked a stereo, and with their assistant Peter Bendry at the wheel, hit the highway heading west. They had personal as well as political reasons for going to California. The far coast would be a temporary sanctuary for the couple.

BY 1972, JOHN LENNON had begun taking control of his drug mania—channeling much of his demonic energy into political combat—but his addictive tendencies still bedeviled him. John began popping pills when he was seventeen, and drinking hard in art school. Taking uppers was the only way that he and the other Beatles could maintain their frantic, late-night work pace at Hamburg clubs in their early years. "I've always needed a drug to *survive*," he told *Rolling Stone* magazine's Jann Wenner in his astonishingly confessional interview in December 1970. "The others too, but I always had *more*. I always took *more* pills and *more* of everything, 'cause I'm *more* crazy." As the Beatles' musical career progressed, the pills gave way to marijuana and—especially for Lennon—to LSD. "I must have had a thousand [acid] trips," he told Wenner. "I used to just eat it all the time."

Lennon credited his LSD journeys with some of his strangest, most beautiful compositions, including "Tomorrow Never Knows" and "She Said She Said"—but *not* "Lucy in the Sky with Diamonds," he always insisted. (It was actor Peter Fonda who gave Lennon the disturbing line "I know what it's like to be dead" during a bad acid trip at a Los Angeles house party.)

To the end of his life, Lennon extolled the magic of LSD, which he felt had the power to open "the doors of perception," in the words of novelist and psychedelic proponent Aldous Huxley. In one of his final interviews, with *Playboy* magazine reporter David Sheff, Lennon commented on the irony of LSD's origin as a CIA-sponsored mind-control drug. "We must always remember to thank the CIA and the army for LSD, by the way," the musician wryly remarked. "Everything is the opposite of what it is, isn't it? They brought out LSD to control people, and what they did was give us freedom. Sometimes it works in mysterious ways, its wonders to perform. But it sure as hell performs them."

Lennon was also a rock pioneer in the use of heroin, which took him on a much darker path. He began experimenting with heroin in 1968, snorting the drug, and got more deeply ensnared while holed up with Ono in their upstairs sanctum at Tittenhurst Park, their white Georgian mansion set serenely on a seventy-two-acre estate. Soon Yoko was addicted to heroin too, because they did everything together. (Lennon would always feel guilty for turning Brian Epstein on to pills, a habit that eventually killed the Beatles manager.) The couple succeeded in kicking heroin in late summer of that year, although it proved even more of an ordeal for Lennon, as he characteristically revealed in his purgation of a song, "Cold Turkey." ("The temperature's rising / The fever is high / Can't see no future / Can't see no sky.")

Lennon later explained his heroin use as an effort to block the pain—from the breakup with the Beatles, his only true family, and from the unrelenting hostility directed at his union with Yoko from his bandmates, his aunt Mimi, and the world at large. On the *Dick Cavett Show* in September 1971—chatting up a TV host with whom the musician felt sympatico (and who secretly suffered his own psychological demons)—Lennon turned philosophical when the subject of drugs was raised. "The basic thing nobody asks is why people take drugs," commented Lennon. "And that question has to be resolved first before you ask, 'Well, what can we do for the poor drug addict?' . . . People take drugs and drink so they don't feel what's going on around them."

What John and Yoko didn't reveal in their otherwise forthright interviews during this period was that they were still addicted—to methadone, the drug they had used to get off heroin, an addiction that they felt was much more difficult to kick. One reason they came to California was to find an alternative treatment for their methadone dependency. They also were searching for Yoko's young daughter Kyoko, who had been whisked away by her father, Ono's ex-husband Tony Cox, in violation of their custody order. The Lennons had pursued the hunt for Kyoko from Europe to the United States, enlisting teams of lawyers and private detectives along the way. They now had word that Cox was hiding out with the child somewhere in Southern California. So, in early June, John and Yoko settled into a rented house in the remote, artsy town of Ojai. Huxley resided in Ojai, and spiritual leader Jiddu Krishnamurti had opened a meditation center in the lush valley, located close to the Pacific coast.

While there, the couple tried to promote their new collection, *Some Time in New York City*. But the double album—which contained "Woman Is Nigger of the World" and "Attica State," as well as a live performance featuring underground masters Frank Zappa and the Mothers of Invention—was their most politically charged and artistically weak release, and it met with stiff resistance from radio stations. Elliot Mintz, then a popular Los Angeles DJ, was one of the only radio personalities to play the challenging album in its entirety without commercial interruptions. After Mintz finished spinning the double album, he was promptly fired. But the Lennons rescued him, sweeping him up in their nonstop life drama.

At their secluded Ojai residence—an early-century Craftsman house seemingly "in the middle of nowhere," in Mintz's memory—Lennon drew the DJ into a bathroom, turned on the faucets, and whispered that the rental might be bugged by the FBI. "I was petrified," Mintz recalled.

John and Yoko stayed in Ojai less than a month, heading for the San Francisco Bay Area after they were informed that Tony Cox and Kyoko had been spotted in Sausalito. Lennon believed he belonged in San Francisco, in some ways, more than in New York. The Big Apple was Yoko's city. "She can stay in New York 365 days a year," Lennon once mused. But he had mixed feelings about the city, as he did about America itself. "It wore me out, New York," he said after a visit not long before moving there. "I love it, I'm just sort of fascinated by it, like a fucking monster. . . . I'm too *frightened* of it. It's so much and people are so *aggressive*." But San Francisco reminded him of his hometown Liverpool, a cool, gray port city, with people of "Irish descent and blacks and Chinamen, all sorts there." The Haight-Ashbury cultural revolution happened in San Francisco for a reason, said Lennon—because, like Liverpool, it was a "poor" and "tough" labor town with a mix of cultures and an openness to new music from underground caverns.

In the Bay Area, John and Yoko recruited Craig Pyes, a twenty-four-year-old alternative journalist, to drive them around in his VW Beetle. Pyes had founded *SunDance* magazine with Ken Kelley, a brilliant, eccentric journalist. They envisioned their magazine to

have radical values, but to be slickly designed, editorially sophisticated, and capable of attracting "the George McGovern–type de-
mographic we saw emerging" at the time. Introduced to Lennon
by Jerry Rubin at Bank Street the previous year, Pyes told the rock
star about the idea for his magazine. Pyes's timing was perfect—he
had trashed *Rolling Stone* in the underground press as a "hip capitalist magazine," and John shared his dim view of Jann Wenner's
avarice after the rock publisher turned the "Lennon Remembers"
Rolling Stone interview into a quickie, bestselling book without his
permission.

"I said [to Lennon], 'Why don't you write a column for *Sun-
Dance?*'" Pyes recalled. "And he said, 'Why should I do that? Magazines like *Esquire* have offered me a lot more money than you can
pay.' My political language wasn't very sophisticated at the time. I
just said, '*Esquire* is a pig magazine.' And John said, 'Well, OK, I'll
do it.'"

SunDance was indeed a special publication, an oversize, artfully
designed compendium of investigative journalism, political analysis, and counterculture coverage—including the column that was
actually written by Yoko, but featured illustrations by John. Produced out of an office on Fillmore Street, it was another unique—
and as it turned out, short-lived—artifact that could have emerged
only from San Francisco.

Pyes, Kelley, and their crew managed to publish only three
issues, and their final, most memorable one in December 1972
featured a cover story about Nixon and his ties to the Mafia by
investigative reporter Jeff Gerth (who later had a mixed career at
the *New York Times*). They were able to pay for this last issue only
because Pyes grudgingly asked Lennon for a handout. "*SunDance*
turned out to be more of an art project than a publishing business,"
Pyes said years later. "By the last issue, we were totally broke. We
had this big cover story on Nixon and the Mafia but we couldn't
afford to have it printed. I'd never hit up John for money before,
but I was forced to beg to get the issue out. It was humiliating."

Lennon also financed the publication of perhaps the first "deep state" feature on the Watergate break-in at the Democratic Party's headquarters, which had taken place six weeks before John and Yoko arrived in San Francisco. Paul Krassner, a friend of Yoko from their old New York days and a cofounder of the Yippies, published *The Realist*, an underground publication known mainly for its obscene political satire. Now based in San Francisco, Krassner realized that the Nixon White House's explanation for the break-in smelled of a cover-up, and he commissioned conspiracy researcher Mae Brussell to look deeper at the bungled burglary.

Brussell's article typically went too far, predicting a Nixonian coup in 1972 and the imposition of "a Fascist dictatorship." But her *Realist* article, published two months before Bob Woodward and Carl Bernstein began breaking their Watergate stories in the *Washington Post*, was the first to make provocative connections between the heavily Cuban burglary team, the CIA's anti–Fidel Castro operation, and the assassinations of the Kennedy brothers. The deep dive into Nixon's machinations would not have been printed if Lennon hadn't footed the printer's bill.

After John and Yoko read the galleys of Mae Brussell's article, they and Krassner "went to the Bank of Tokyo [in San Francisco] and they withdrew five thousand dollars in cash," the underground publisher later related. "I remember as the issue came off the press, I got melodramatic and called John . . . and said, 'I can die happy now.' He just said, 'Tut, tut.' He was humble, he knew his power, but he didn't take himself as seriously as his causes."

Driving the streets of San Francisco, where John and Yoko were considering buying a mansion, and across the Golden Gate Bridge to Sausalito, where Tony Cox was rumored to now be hiding out with Kyoko, Craig Pyes also came to see his celebrity passengers as regular folks. "You sort of fall in love with them," said Pyes, conjuring his feelings from those days. He enjoyed the full range of his conversations with Yoko, who rode shotgun in the VW bug, and with John, who sat directly behind him, once breaking into perfect harmony on Bill Withers's "Lean on Me" when it came on the car radio. "John was becoming more political, but they were mainly artists. They operated on lots of different levels. To put them only in a political box would be a mistake—you'd miss the full architecture of their thoughts."

Pyes traversed a wide spectrum of Bay Area life with the celebrity couple. "We hung out in San Francisco for a couple of months. I was living in a little student apartment in Berkeley and here I suddenly was going around with a real estate agent looking for a Pacific Heights mansion for John and Yoko to live in. I asked John what kind of house he wanted. And he said, 'White.'"

The Lennons were staying at the Miyako Hotel in San Francisco's Japantown (now the Hotel Kabuki), an elegant high-rise which featured traditional Japanese suites and gardens. But they would soon move to more modest quarters in the suburb of San Mateo, about twenty miles down Highway 101 from the city. It was Pyes who connected John and Yoko to a Chinese American acupuncturist who lived in San Mateo, after they confided they were still hooked on methadone and desperate to try alternative therapies to break their addiction. Born in Shanghai, Yuan Bain Hong was a practitioner of Chinese herbal medicine and acupuncture at a time when the needle treatment was still illegal in America. At first Hong was reluctant to take on the case. But his English was poor, and he changed his mind when he thought that Pyes said John was an important "senator" instead of "singer."

John and Yoko stayed with Hong; his wife, Betty; and their two young daughters for a week or two, sleeping on a living room couch in the simple, two-bedroom, pink stucco house. Hong assured them that if they meticulously followed his prescribed health regimen, they would not only be cured of their addiction, they would be able to create a child. ("So I get an assist for Sean Lennon," Pyes chuckled.)

John and Yoko ate Mrs. Hong's home cooking and rarely left the house. "They were totally integrated into the family," Pyes said. "There were chickens running around in the backyard." Mrs. Hong was convinced that John was her husband's illegitimate son because he had worked on the Liverpool docks in the early 1940s. "One day we were all standing in the Hongs' backyard, and John started singing 'Imagine' for us a cappella. The song was on the radio all the time, and there he was singing it for us in flesh and blood. Amazing moment." But since the Hongs had no TV or radio in their house, they had only a dim sense of John's musical stature, which was just fine for the Lennons.

The couple left Hong's home cured of their methadone addiction, as he had predicted. And three years later, on October 9, 1975—John's thirty-fifth birthday—Yoko gave birth to their son, Sean. But Yuan Bain Hong suffered from his own addiction, to alcohol, and while his daughters were still growing up, he drank himself to death. Afterward, the Lennons sent Betty Hong checks, some for thousands of dollars, until both of her girls reached adulthood. "The support made a big difference in our lives," Emily Hong, one of the daughters, later said.

By August 1972, John and Yoko were back on Bank Street in New York. They never again seriously considered moving to San Francisco. But in December 1980, the final days of John's life, the couple agreed to return to San Francisco to join a demonstration of workers who were striking three major Japanese food importers for higher wages. Shinya Ono, one of the strike leaders, was a cousin of Yoko. Known as "a kind of Japanese-American Woody Guthrie," Shinya Ono came out of the New Left, serving as an editor of the movement's first publication, *Studies on the Left*, and joining the Weather Underground faction of Students for a Democratic Society in 1969 and '70. John issued what would be his last political statement on behalf of the strikers. He and Yoko then bought three plane tickets to San Francisco, where they planned to join the labor rally "because John had a son who was half Oriental," Yoko later stated. "So he was envisioning carrying Sean" at the march. The plane tickets went unused.

IF JOHN AND Yoko had moved to a San Francisco mansion, their lives would not have been politically serene. Federal agencies would surely have continued to stalk him. And the radical movement in the Bay Area was descending into its own hell, with the rise of the mysterious Symbionese Liberation Army in 1973, a series of terrorist bombings, the racially motivated Zebra murder spree, and the cult catastrophe of Jonestown—a wave of madness culminating in the assassinations of San Francisco mayor George Moscone and gay supervisor Harvey Milk in 1978. But back on Bank Street, the Lennons were soon caught up again in their Nixonian political maelstrom.

Despite the couple's repeated public denials about showing up at the Republican convention—which started on August 21, 1972—FBI agents scoured the Miami area during convention week, in an elusive search for the rock star, whom they suspected might be hidden among the thousands of protesters descending on President Nixon's coronation ceremony. A memo from FBI headquarters to the bureau's Miami office again suggested that Lennon could be the target of a drug bust, which would make him "immediately deportable."

While John and Yoko wisely avoided Miami, they were far from silent during the presidential campaign, urging young voters to support Democratic presidential candidate George McGovern and cast Nixon out of the White House. In their *SunDance* column, the couple used the radical rhetoric of the day, calling on Nixon's working-class base to rise against him: "To the hard-hats who think that they don't have the power to free themselves from the tyranny and suppression of the capitalists, it's not their power or money that is controlling you. Their power depends on your fear and apathy. . . . REMEMBER TO VOTE."

But John Lennon's true power came through his music. On August 30, nearly a week after the Republican convention, he marched on stage at Madison Square Garden in New York with his band Elephant's Memory, and gave what would be the last full-scale concerts of his life, performing once in the afternoon and again in the evening. The concerts were a benefit for the young mental patients at a Staten Island institution whose notorious conditions were exposed by TV newsman Geraldo Rivera. But Lennon used the stage at the sold-out shows in the cavernous arena to deliver a strong political message. His playlists for the two concerts were heavily loaded with songs from his radical playbook, including "Power to the People," "Woman Is Nigger of the World," and "Give Peace a Chance." He sang only one of his Beatle songs, "Come Together," but he turned some of its lyrics into a rousing anthem: "Come together / Stop the war / Right now!" The huge crowd roared at the song's revised message. Surely the federal agents watching Lennon's Madison Square Garden shows breathed a sigh of relief that he had felt compelled to cancel his anti-Nixon national tour.

The fall polls in the presidential race were discouraging for the Nixon opposition, but Lennon kept hoping for an upset. All such pipe dreams were crushed on the November 7 election night, when Nixon swept to a landslide victory, winning over 60 percent of the vote and claiming every state except Massachusetts and the District of Columbia—the biggest Republican presidential triumph in US history. By the time John and Yoko got to the election viewing party at Jerry Rubin's New York apartment, Lennon was fuming. "He came into the house screaming," Rubin recalled, "crazy with rage."

The musician began lashing into Rubin and his guests, a collection of Yippies and Elephant's Memory bandmates. "This is it? This is *it*?" he shouted, coldly surveying the room. "I can't believe this is fuckin' *it*! I mean, here we are—*this* is the fuckin' revolution. Jerry Rubin, John and Yoko and accessories. This is the fuckin' middle-class bunch that's gonna protect *us* from *them*."

Sax player Stan Bronstein suggested that instead of wailing, Lennon could work harder at organizing people. "Yeah, organize people," someone else seconded. "They'll listen to you." But Lennon was in no mood to discuss long-term strategy that night. With Nixon's massive victory, it was more likely now that John would be deported before he could ever join another rally. Besides, he no longer had any confidence in his political power. "Listen to me? Man, where have you been?" Then he circled the room, like the angry young man of his Liverpool and Hamburg days, shoving and taunting people as if he wanted to fight.

Finally, after the dispirited party had dwindled to a handful of people, Lennon approached a young woman "and started fondling her in front of everybody," Rubin recalled. "Then he took her into my bedroom. It was a humiliation for Yoko—total humiliation. I'd never seen him do anything like it before. He was totally out of it on drugs. Their relationship ended right there—even if they did live together for a few more months. That's what broke John and Yoko up."

In December 1972, after Nixon's decisive reelection, the FBI declared victory over John Lennon and officially closed his case. But the INS would keep trying to deport him for over three more years. In a letter to the immigration service, the couple's old friend Kate Millett—one of many intellectuals and artists who pled on their behalf—wrote that what made Lennon and Ono "so crucial to our contemporary culture is their refusal to live only in the world of art. Instead, they have reintegrated art with the social and political facets of life and offered us something like moral leadership with their committed pacifism."

But Lennon's ongoing immigration battle trapped him in a Kafkaesque legal labyrinth that made him wary of politically expressing himself or even performing in public. Even after the downfall of Richard Nixon, who resigned his presidency in scandal in August 1974, Lennon told journalist Pete Hamill that he was "nervous about commenting on politics, they've got me that jumpy these

days." His immigration battle, he said during his June 1975 interview with Hamill, was "like a toothache that wouldn't go away."

Lennon again lashed out at Jerry Rubin and Abbie Hoffman—
seeming to blame the radical pranksters for his troubles with the
government. "I'm sick of being in crusades because I always get
nailed up before I'm even in the crusade." His militant activism in
the early seventies had a damaging effect on his music, Lennon also
stated. "It almost ruined it, in a way. It became journalism and not
poetry."

Yoko Ono was John Lennon's political lodestar. Without her
guidance, he tended to fall into despair and cynicism. In October
1973, she kicked him out of their home—by then the sprawling,
two-floor apartment complex in the Dakota. This was the start
of Lennon's roughly eighteen-month "lost weekend," as he called
it—an extended period of debauchery in Los Angeles with equally
dissolute musical companions Harry Nilsson, Keith Moon, and
Bobby Keys. Ono, always Lennon's minder even in separation, asked
their twenty-three-year-old assistant May Pang to accompany her
husband to Los Angeles as his mistress and surrogate caretaker.
"Mother" was John's term of affection for Yoko—an imprint of his
lifelong search for the missing parent.

Yoko was used to being "an artist and free and all that," she later
explained, but she had begun feeling suffocated by John's titanic
public persona and personal needs. "I lost the freedom. And also,
both of us were together all the time—24 hours a day."

Politically committed celebrities always have a tortuous time
on their own navigating between activists' constant and conflicting
demands, sniping from media and fans and, sometimes, government surveillance. In her 2005 memoir, Jane Fonda wrote that she
felt like a strung-out "lone ranger" after she plunged into radical
politics, speaking at antiwar rallies and military bases before she
had found her public voice. She was anorexic, bulimic, popping
speed—a legacy of her lifelong struggles with body image that grew
worse in her political turmoil—and "I must have weighed all of

one hundred pounds" on the glittery night in 1972 when she won the Best Actress Academy Award for *Klute*. "I was betwixt and between. Was I a celebrity? An actor? A mother? An activist? A 'leader'? Who was I?" But later that same year, when she and New Left leader Tom Hayden became a romantic and political couple, Fonda finally began putting herself together. They would become one of the most formidable couples in American politics.

"For me he was the white knight who had arrived in my life just in the nick of time to set everything straight and save me from chaos," Fonda wrote. "Poor Tom. . . . No mortal man could possibly live up to that."

Hayden always had a troubled relationship with Fonda's fame, which outshone his own and filled him with feelings of resentment and awe. He also realized his wife's political potential as a fundraiser and magnet for public fascination. "It's animal, it's an instinct," Hayden once remarked about his wife's ability to glide easily through a staring crowd, naturally averting her eyes when someone locked on her.

But Hayden's political organizations—first the Indochina Peace Campaign and then the Campaign for Economic Democracy—gave Fonda a structure that John Lennon lacked. The handpicked New Leftists in the Hayden-Fonda network—many of whom had worked with Hayden before or deeply admired his antiwar leadership—became neighbors and friends of Fonda, and in the case of Bruce Gilbert, who had lived with Hayden in Berkeley's Red Family commune, her film producer. The activists in Hayden and Fonda's orbit were smarter and more disciplined than the anarchic Yippies with whom Lennon fell in.

Even on the left, Hayden once observed, celebrities like his wife were targets for hustlers and opportunists. "They were basically saying, 'You shouldn't be a movie star, dear, you should give all your money to us!' Their real solution for her would have been to give everything to them and commit suicide. And she was headed in that direction."

John, too, could have benefited from forming a political alliance with Hayden's organization during his Los Angeles exile. Musicians like Linda Ronstadt, Jackson Browne, Bonnie Raitt, and the Grateful Dead had been drawn into Hayden and Fonda's antiwar and solar energy causes, playing benefit concerts and speaking out for them. But Lennon was too drunken and dissolute—and discouraged about politics—to get involved while he was living in California.

Hayden was acutely aware of Lennon's outspoken efforts on behalf of peace in Vietnam and Northern Irish independence. But the two never worked together politically. Years later, he "eagerly agreed" when Yoko Ono asked him to contribute to an essay collection she published in 2005 titled *Memories of John Lennon*. "His greatest qualities were as an artist, of course," wrote Hayden, "but he would have been a different artist without the rebellious, nonconformist and subversive spirit of the 1960s. Revered by all as a great musician, John also became an enemy of the state, which future generations of fans need to remember."

John Lennon lacked Jane Fonda's politically sophisticated mate and organization. But he did have Ono. When they reunited in 1975, Lennon seemed to regain his center. He was able to begin speaking about the 1960s and their activism again with a sense of charity and even renewed purpose. Yoko was not a political leader like Hayden—she was an artist who often acted on intuition, even superstition, consulting mystics before she made major decisions and when she and John traveled. She was heavily into numerology. But Yoko had solid instincts about people and causes and a steady moral compass. She also described herself as "an endless optimist," a strong antidote to John's chronic darkness.

And when she took over Lennon's deeply muddled finances, which had been the blasted terrain of armies of lawyers and crooks since the Beatle years, Ono succeeded in sorting them out. By 1980 their fortune was estimated at $150 million (the equivalent of over a half billion dollars in 2020). Making the transition from artist to business manager proved remarkably easy for Yoko, who described the financial world as "a chess game. And I love chess." His wife's business wizardry also liberated John to devote himself first to raising their son, Sean, and then after a five-year withdrawal from the music business, to reenter it on his own terms in 1980.

Earlier in his musical career, Lennon told *Playboy* interviewer David Sheff that he had squandered his wealth through bad management and profligate spending (including impulsive political contributions). "Subconsciously it was because I was guilty about having money," John said, a holdover from his working-class upbringing in Liverpool. "Because I thought money was equated with sin.

"But," John continued, "having a lot of money is no longer a problem for me," noting that he and Yoko practiced tithing, donating 10 percent of their wealth each year to causes and charities. "What is it? The Zen thing? One bowl, one cloak. For me to do that would be pretty crazy—to just walk away from it all."

Yoko's mastery of "the money game" gave her a new power in her relationship with John, who in the final days of his life expressed his respect for her in euphoric terms. "I learned everything from her," Lennon exclaimed. "It *is* a teacher-pupil relationship. That's what people don't understand. . . . I'm the famous one who's supposed to know everything, but she's my teacher. She taught me everything I fucking know. She was there when I was nowhere, when I was the *nowhere man.*"

ON OCTOBER 7, 1975 a federal judge overturned the deportation order against John Lennon and ordered the INS to reconsider John's application for permanent residence. The following year, in July, the immigration service finally granted him permanent residence, after he duly confirmed he had never belonged to an organization that attempted to overthrow the United States government. Afterward, Lennon was thronged by the press and supporters outside the New York courthouse. His Washington tormentors were gone—with Attorney General Mitchell and White House clandestine operator Gordon Liddy among those sentenced to prison for their roles in the Nixon scandals. But Lennon's wit was still acid-tipped.

"Do you hold a grudge" against Mitchell and the other government officials "for putting you through all this for all these years?" a reporter asked him.

"No," he replied, with a steely glint. "I believe time wounds all heels." Then he broke into a goofy, celebratory grin for the cameras, as in the old Beatles days.

Four years later, when he came out of hibernation after his much-chronicled time as a househusband and father (albeit with a full staff), John was eager to give lengthy interviews again. He and Yoko "haven't communicated outside for a long time and we're gonna enjoy it and have fun with it," he enthused to *Playboy*'s Sheff.

Lennon and Ono did their final interviews mostly as a team, emphasizing their collaboration on what would be his final album, *Double Fantasy*. Dave Sholin of the RKO Radio syndicate conducted what would be the last interview with the couple, on the afternoon of December 8, 1980. "I was afraid they were going to fight like a cat and dog," Sholin recalled years later. "But it was really and truly a dialogue. They had a strong chemistry, glancing back and forth at each other as they talked, like we weren't even there. In his eyes she could walk on water. We talked about everything—politics, their relationship. They were definitely not pulling back from politics. Their message was: we made a difference in the world—and we can still do that."

Looking back at their most militant period, on Bank Street, Lennon's attitude was now much more generous than he'd been a few years before. "In the early seventies," John told Sholin, "politics was in the air in those days and you couldn't avoid it. And being artists, when we get into something, we *get into it*—you know what

I mean? We wanted to be right there—down on the front lines. But, as we always said to everybody, with flowers. But I still mean right down there—we wanted to go all the way with it."

Yoko jumped into the conversation at this point, making clear that their message of peace and love was just as vital in 1980. "Love is a very powerful political weapon," she said. "And if we go on like this, we'll just be used by the capitalist society and all be components of capitalist society—and finally be replaced by the computers. Or we'll just stand up and have a human renaissance. Just say, 'We're human again and we want to reach each other and become human again.'"

Later that afternoon, after completing the three-and-a-half-hour interview with John and Yoko, Sholin and his radio crew encountered Mark David Chapman on the sidewalk outside the Dakota. Chapman talked briefly with Sholin's sound engineer, and then—spotting John emerge from the building—approached him for an autograph, clutching his copy of the newly released *Double Fantasy* album. Chapman later said he could have shot Lennon then. But the musician had been so obliging, readily signing his album and asking, "Is that all you want?" Chapman "had expected a brush-off, but it was just the opposite. . . . And I said, 'I can't shoot him like this.' I wanted to get the autograph." Chapman would wait until nearly 11 that night before his next chance, when John and Yoko returned home from the Hit Factory recording studio, where they were completing Ono's song, "Walking on Thin Ice."

As John emerged from the limousine and walked toward the Dakota doorway, Chapman dropped into a combat stance and—squeezing the trigger of his Charter Arms "Undercover .38 Special," a snub-nosed revolver popular with detectives and murderers because it was easy to hide—he fired five extremely destructive hollow-point bullets at Lennon's back. Branded a crazed fan by the media, the twenty-five-year-old Chapman pled guilty to Lennon's murder, never went to court, and was sentenced to twenty years to life, beginning his sentence—ironically—at the Attica state penitentiary.

Lennon was the type of star—hugely confessional and empathetic—who attracted more than his share of emotionally distraught acolytes. He made time to talk with many of them, explaining to them that he was no divinity but just another suffering mortal like themselves. But there was something immediately puzzling about Chapman, and because he was never put on trial or deeply investigated by the press, questions still linger about the man convicted of killing John Lennon.

Lennon himself feared assassination—a fear that went back to the Beatles' 1966 tour of America and the tempest he had created with his glib "more popular than Jesus" remark. John later said he had to be persuaded by his bandmates and Brian Epstein to go ahead with the US concerts. "I thought they'd kill me—'cause they take things so seriously there. . . . I was scared stiff." At the Beatles' Memphis show, police were instructed to look out for snipers.

Assassination was again on Lennon's mind in 1969 after he and Yoko staged their bed-ins for peace, because he knew that the spectacles—as politically inoffensive as they seemed—were still fomenting strong passions in Vietnam-mired America. They aimed to be "humorists," Lennon told BBC Radio 1. "We're Laurel and Hardy, that's John and Yoko. And we stand a better chance under that guise 'cause all the serious people like Martin Luther King and Kennedy and Gandhi got shot."

As Nixon's offensive against Lennon had grown more aggressive, John's paranoia deepened. When the Lennons were visiting with Paul Krassner during their 1972 California trip, the underground publisher recalled, "I remember John said to me at one point, 'If anything happens to me or Yoko, it was not an accident.'" But writing in his journal in 1978, Lennon mocked the rampant fears of Krassner, who even warned John that his fellow Yippies Rubin and Hoffman were CIA double agents. Lennon also wrote dismissively of Mae "They're Coming Through the Windows!" Brussell—one of the commentators who later alleged that the musician was assassinated because he was a "threat" to the forces of war and repression within the incoming Reagan administration.

Many remained puzzled by the enigma of Mark David Chapman. Fenton Bresler, an English lawyer and legal correspondent for the *Daily Mail* and *Sunday Express* of London, spent eight years researching his 1989 book *Who Killed John Lennon?*, raising questions about the mysterious funding sources for Chapman's global travels (including his stays in upscale New York hotels), his apparent training as a skilled shooter, and his inexplicable behavior after being taken into custody.

Bresler interviewed Arthur O'Connor, who oversaw the New York Police Department detectives at the 20th Precinct station where Chapman was booked after his arrest. He was one of the police officers who first questioned the shooter that night. "It's possible Mark could have been used by somebody," O'Connor told Bresler. "I saw him the night of the murder. I studied him intensely. He looked as if he could have been programmed—and I know what you are going to make of that word!"

Chapman also proved a conundrum to Dr. Naomi Goldstein, a staff psychiatrist at Bellevue Hospital, who was the first mental health professional to interview the shooter. Goldstein, who spoke with Chapman several more times over the following days, told reporter Jack Jones that "she never had a more elusive case than the one that sat before her on the evening of December 9, 1980." The psychiatrist noted that Chapman's speech was "coherent, relevant and logical" and found no evidence of "hallucinations or delusions." Chapman knew with certainty that he had shot John Lennon, but he was vague about why he had killed the man whom he had idolized since childhood. At the end of her first interview, Goldstein wrote that her diagnosis of Chapman would have to be "deferred."

Some assassination researchers have also raised questions about José Perdomo, a Cuban refugee who worked as a Dakota doorman at the time of the shooting. According to Chapman, he conversed at length with Perdomo in the days when he was staking out the building, with the Cuban émigré talking about the CIA's failed Bay of Pigs invasion in 1961 and the assassination of President John F. Kennedy, which Perdomo blamed on Cuban leader Fidel Castro. According to government documents released under the JFK Records Collection Act of 1992, a José Sanjenis Perdomo played a nefarious role in the Bay of Pigs invasion, as a leader of Operation 40, a team of assassins that was supposed to eliminate political enemies in Cuba if the invasion had been successful. According to the government documents, Perdomo had been an enforcer for deposed Cuban dictator Fulgencio Batista and was described as a "shady character [with] a gangster background."

After Chapman shot Lennon and dropped his gun, he recalled, Perdomo kicked it away and told him, "Get out of here, man!" But Chapman stood meekly at the crime scene. "Where would I go?" he asked the doorman forlornly. When police cars arrived at the Dakota, it was Perdomo who identified Chapman as the shooter. The doorman disappeared after the shooting, and no researcher has ever proved he is the José Sanjenis Perdomo identified as a Cuban hit man.

By the time Sean Lennon, who was five when his father was murdered, came of age, he believed that Mark Chapman was only part of the story. In April 1998, the twenty-two-year-old Lennon told the *New Yorker* magazine, "Anybody who thinks that Mark Chapman was just some crazy guy who killed my dad for his personal interests is insane, I think, or very naïve, or hasn't thought about it clearly. It was in the best interests of the United States to have my dad killed. . . . [My father] was a counterculture revolutionary, and the government takes that kind of shit really seriously historically. He was dangerous to the government. If he had said, 'Bomb the White House tomorrow,' there would have been 10,000 people who would have done it. These pacifist revolutionaries are historically killed by the government."

After his bold (and unsupported) comments to the *New Yorker,* Sean Lennon stopped speaking to the press about his father's violent death. He didn't answer a request to be interviewed for this book. No reporter or investigator has so far produced conclusive evidence of a conspiracy in John Lennon's murder.

IN ONE OF his final statements—during an interview with *Rolling Stone*'s Jonathan Cott, with whom the rock star had been conversing off and on since his Beatle days—Lennon summed up his life philosophy, as if he were preparing his own eulogy: "I'm not claiming divinity. I've never claimed purity of soul. I've never claimed to have the answers to life. I only put out songs and answer questions as honestly as I can—but *only* as honestly as I can, no more, no less. I cannot live up to other people's expectations of me, because they're illusionary. I cannot be a punk in Hamburg and Liverpool because I'm older now. I see the world through different eyes now. But I still believe in peace, love and understanding, as Elvis Costello said. What's so fucking funny about peace, love and understanding? It's fashionable to be a go-getter and slash thy neighbor with a cross, but we're not one to follow the fashion."

In death, Lennon was made by millions around the world into a deity, despite his ghostly admonitions. As for Yoko Ono, she has tried to keep her husband's message alive without resurrecting him from the dead or turning him into a saint. There would be no funeral for her slain husband, only a silent ten-minute vigil six days after his murder which was observed by mourners all over the world. The largest gathering—about a hundred thousand people— took place on a cold, windy afternoon in New York's Central Park, and included Tom Hayden and Jane Fonda, who stood solemnly and undisturbed in the throng. Kyoko, Ono's long-lost daughter, was among those who contacted her after John's death, sending her a telegram of condolence. John and Yoko had abandoned their hunt for Kyoko, deciding their pursuit only made the girl's life more painful and turbulent. But years after Lennon's death, the mother and daughter finally reunited.

Yoko still trumpets the cause of peace, sometimes buying full-page newspaper ads with messages like "Imagine Peace" or "Give Peace a Chance." But she's assumed a more modest political posture, only occasionally using her celebrity for causes she embraces. In 2014, she helped lead a successful campaign to ban fracking in the state of New York—a ban that the state legislature and governor made permanent in 2020. "We organized a press junket—filled a bus with reporters and drove them to Pennsylvania," said David Fenton, whom Yoko hired to lead the anti-fracking media campaign decades after his PR role at the John Sinclair concert. "We showed the press how people's drinking water was filthy and catching fire. We won—we pushed Governor [Andrew] Cuomo to ban fracking in New York."

But Yoko never had the same public impact that she and John did with their unified imagination. In 2012, Jonathan Cott caught up with her in Stockholm. Cott had known her since 1968, when he dropped by the London basement flat she was sharing with John. Now Yoko was pushing eighty, and the longtime friends were eating breakfast together on a hotel veranda overlooking the Old Town and the Royal Palace. Ono was preparing a sweeping exhibit of her life's artwork at Stockholm's Moderna Museet, and he was impressed by her indefatigable energy. But there was a wistful tone in her voice when she talked about the impossible enterprise she had undertaken with John.

Cott brought up her old image as a Japanese witch who had cast a dark spell over the brilliant Beatle. He told her that a recent newspaper article asserted "that without doubt you were the most hated woman in the world." Decades later, she was still being reminded of those poison arrows, but she had stopped flinching.

"It's true," Yoko said, she did feel the most reviled woman on Earth in those days. "But I was living in a different world. I thought it was very important for all of us to do our best to keep the world floating and not sinking." And for a time, she and John Lennon did.

The Great Escape

Dennis Banks, Madonna Thunder Hawk,
Russell Means, and the Warriors of Wounded Knee

In the winter of 1973, the living could hear the dead at Wounded Knee. They could hear their moans and cries at night, in the wind that swept the bleak, snowy South Dakota prairie. They could hear their plaintive Ghost Dance Songs. It was a mournful chorus rising on moonless nights from the ravine where—eight decades earlier, on December 29, 1890—as many as three hundred members of Chief Big Foot's Lakota tribe were massacred by the US 7th Cavalry. The men, women, and children were torn apart by a storm of rifle and Hotchkiss cannon fire—merciless fusillades fired by soldiers so crazed with liquor and a fury to avenge the 7th Cavalry's disastrous defeat under the command of General George Armstrong Custer that they shot fleeing mothers in the back and the infants who were strapped to their bodies. They even killed fellow US cavalrymen in a mad frenzy of cross fire. The smoke from the ceaseless barrage was so thick over the killing field that Big Foot's fleeing tribespeople—even those not yet dead or wounded—looked spectral in the thick haze.

"There was no wind to clear [the smoke] away. It hung like a pall over the field," remembered Joseph Horn Cloud, one of the survivors of the Wounded Knee massacre. "Women who were wounded and had babies [dug] hollow places in the [creek] bank and placed the little things in them for safety. . . . Some women were found lying dead with dead infants on their breasts; one mother lay dead, her breast covered with blood from her wound, and her little child was standing by her and nursing."

Now, in February 1973, over two hundred Lakota Indians and American Indian Movement (AIM) warriors had returned to Wounded Knee, to protest the corrupt and brutal regime in control of the Pine Ridge Reservation as well as the long history of US government perfidy and broken treaties that kept Native Americans in colonized misery. It was a breathtakingly bold action, and the AIM leaders were acutely aware of its enormity. "Be prepared to defend this position with your life!" shouted Dennis Banks, the cofounder of AIM, after the band of resisters seized control of the site. "The feds will be coming soon. What is at stake here at Wounded Knee is not the lives of a few hundred Indian people, but our whole Indian way of life."

The warriors were standing on haunted and hallowed ground, next to the trench where the bodies of their ancestors had been unceremoniously dumped by the 7th Cavalry. Many years had passed since the massacre, but the creased, scrub-brush terrain bordering Wounded Knee Creek still echoed with the unforgettable past. The activists who occupied the deeply symbolic Wounded Knee site in 1973 were returning to an unquiet place where the dead still demanded justice.

The memory of Wounded Knee had become contested territory as soon as the smoke had cleared from the bloody field. Colonel James Forsyth, commander of the 7th Cavalry, immediately framed the massacre as a heroic "battle" between his cool and disciplined troops and "fanatical" Indians under the dangerous spell of the Ghost Dance craze then sweeping much of the Lakota nation, with its desperate dream of deliverance from white extermination through feverish dancing and hallucination.

The US War Department officially endorsed Colonel Forsyth's Wounded Knee cover-up at a court of inquiry held the year following the massacre, even awarding twenty Medals of Honor to 7th Cavalry soldiers for gallantry. This desecration of the truth was reinforced by subsequent official investigations and even by an action-packed, silent Western film produced by William "Buffalo Bill" Cody in 1913. *The Indian Wars* depicted Wounded Knee as a thrilling victory by unflinching US cavalry soldiers over an army of heavily armed savages on horseback.

But the reality was that Chief Big Foot, a well-known peacemaker and diplomat, was desperately trying to find a refuge for his weary and hungry tribe after a long, bitter-cold journey to the Pine Ridge Reservation. With their chief suffering from pneumonia, and surrounded by over five hundred heavily armed troops, the Lakota tribespeople found it hard to sleep the night before their doom. Some began singing Death Songs even before the 7th Cavalry unleashed their rain of fire.

If Wounded Knee was memorialized as a noble military victory in American history, Native people knew the truth, passed down from generation to generation in searing family stories. Survivors of the massacre like Joseph Horn Cloud and his brother Dewey Beard fought for decades to persuade Washington officialdom to hold honest investigations, and when they were thwarted by federal authorities, they found sympathetic ears among a few white journalists and amateur historians who dutifully recorded their nightmarish oral histories.

So it was the restless ghosts of Wounded Knee who brought the American Indian Movement's two charismatic leaders—Dennis Banks and Russell Means—back to the Pine Ridge Reservation in winter 1973. The two men would lead the most courageous and sustained Native American uprising in the twentieth century, an occupation of the historic site that withstood the firepower of the US government and lasted a full seventy-one days. This time, the Wounded Knee story would not end in gory tragedy. This time,

Wounded Knee—which had gone down in history as the final Indian defeat, the final calamity of the Old West—would become synonymous with heroic resistance. And this time, the chief of this resistance would not be captured or executed. He and his top warriors would live to fight another day.

"What Wounded Knee told the world was that John Wayne hadn't killed us all," as Means described the significance of the Native American action in his 1995 memoir. "Essentially, the rest of the planet had believed that except for a few people sitting along highways peddling pottery, there were no more Indians. Suddenly billions of people knew we were still alive, still resisting."

Looking back in his own 2004 memoir, Banks agreed, recalling the lengthy, armed confrontation between the Indian activists and the modern-day US cavalry as "the greatest event in the history of Native America in the twentieth century. It was our shining hour, and I am proud to have been a part of it."

The fact that the two dynamic leaders of the American Indian Movement lived long enough to write their memoirs was a victory in itself. The Native American heroes they called to mind—Sitting Bull and Crazy Horse—had both been assassinated while being taken into federal custody near the end of the sprawling Plains Indian Wars in the nineteenth century. Those wars between the US Army and the tribes of the northern plains—including the Lakota, Cheyenne, Crow, Blackfoot, Arapaho, and Ojibwe—comprised the longest military conflict in American history, pitting horsed tribal warriors whom some US Army officers considered the most skilled fighters in the world against a ruthless foe with overwhelming firepower. The Wounded Knee action conjured these historic battles for many of the activists who took a stand on the Pine Ridge Reservation in 1973.

For some, particularly those AIM activists who had recently served in combat, the siege also called to mind the Vietnam War. The men, women, and children who occupied the forlorn Wounded Knee hamlet—including a trading post, a church, and a few ramshackle dwellings—instantly found themselves surrounded by a growing army of heavily armed FBI agents, federal marshals, Bureau of Indian Affairs police officers, and assorted ranchers and vigilantes under the command of the Pine Ridge Reservation tribal chairman, Dick Wilson, who kept threatening "all-out war" on the Wounded Knee protesters. The federal siege was enforced by over a dozen tanklike armored personnel carriers, a swarm of low-flying jets and helicopters, and a fearsome arsenal of war weaponry.

At one point, the FBI even brought in the US Army colonel in command of the 82nd Airborne—a unit trained to put down civil disturbances in President Richard Nixon's tumultuous America. The colonel was asked to draw up plans for a military invasion to overrun the small, diverse tribe holding Wounded Knee, who wielded only a motley collection of weapons. Military personnel disguised in civilian clothing illegally visited the siege site to advise FBI agents. It was as if this sudden demonstration of Indian fortitude had resurrected all the raging demons from the Old West, including the massive military overkill that had obliterated Chief Big Foot's tribe.

The federal forces arrayed against the Native American activists regarded them the same way the US military viewed the Vietnamese enemy. "They called us 'gooks'—the racist language they used in Vietnam," recalled Madonna Thunder Hawk, a cousin of Means and one of the women who emerged as a leader at Wounded Knee. "The federal marshals all wore the same blue jumpsuits and they all looked the same—tall, blond, with buzz cuts. They looked like cyborgs, fresh back from Vietnam. People say today, 'Oh the police are so militarized.' But we knew that back in the seventies."

Banks understood that taking Wounded Knee would provoke a strong official reaction. "But I didn't know how far they would go."

INITIALLY, DENNIS BANKS had been reluctant for AIM to undertake the Wounded Knee occupation. He was not a member of the Lakota tribe—though his wife, Kamook, and Means were—and in its early years AIM did not have strong roots on reservation land. The Native rights group originated in the inner cities where Indians had emigrated, not on reservations like Pine Ridge. By 1970, nearly half of the Native American population was living in cities, drawn by a federal relocation program and the promise of better economic opportunities than existed in desperately poor tribal territory. But these urban ghettos held their own woe and terror, and Banks and his AIM cofounders originally banded together in summer 1968 to fight police brutality in the grim bars and streets of Minneapolis, inspired by the Black Panthers' resistance against police harassment in Oakland, California.

But as AIM grew, Banks—an Ojibwe Indian born on the Leech Lake Reservation in northern Minnesota—felt a spiritual pull back to Native land. He and Means, a member of the Lakota nation's Oglala subtribe who was raised partly on Pine Ridge, realized that what distinguished their movement from other liberation struggles in 1970s America was the Indian peoples' land base. Even though their original homelands had been drastically reduced in size by invasion, property theft, and US government betrayal, many tribes were still rooted in ancestral lands. And so the AIM battleground shifted in the seventies to protect Native American land rights and the civil rights of reservation tribespeople.

The young men and women activists who flocked around Banks and Means were drawn by their daring leadership and by AIM's willingness to directly confront injustice after decades of officially ignored or sanctioned abuse of Native people. Banks, who had survived a brutal childhood in one of the notorious Indian boarding schools, later joined the air force but returned home from duty in Japan to the predictably bleak options that faced young Natives in Minneapolis. He wound up doing time for burglary in the Stillwater prison in Minnesota, where a disproportionate share of the convicts was Native. Locked in solitary for nine months of his two-and-a-half-year prison stretch, he read stacks of books about Indian history, the Vietnam War, and the civil rights battles sweeping America. Like many liberation movements, AIM was born in the dark holes of the penal system.

Means too had a criminal background. He had grown up in Bay Area housing projects and reservation poverty, becoming a drug dealer, a hard-drinking barroom brawler, and an Indian dancer for white tourists before resuming his education and finding work in a Cleveland antipoverty program, where Banks recruited him into AIM's leadership. "Dennis practically glow[ed] with charisma," Means recalled about their first meeting. "I asked him, 'How do I join AIM? He said, 'You just did.'" Means too had a shining aura. "He was a spellbinding speaker," declared Banks. "Women adored him."

As they grew their hair long, tying it in braids, and took to wearing traditional Native clothes, Banks and Means became the movie-star faces of the new Native power movement. Holding forth at rallies, press conferences, and in courthouses, the AIM leaders inspired passionate devotion from a new generation of Natives hungry for justice and dignity, and equally strong reactions from white citizens and authorities for whom Old West animosities had never died.

Led by Banks and Means, the AIM warriors came riding into reservations and white-ruled border towns where Indians had been abused, raped, and even murdered for years with impunity. They were flaming arrows of justice, insisting that red lives mattered and demanding that authorities take action against whites who victimized Native men and women. "Our motto was, 'Anytime, Anywhere, Any Place'—and that was the most important job that we could do," said Banks. "To be anywhere there was injustice, and to confront it."

In January 1973, a month before AIM seized Wounded Knee, the group grabbed headlines in a South Dakota cow town appropriately named Custer, after the war criminal who, as an AIM bumper sticker put it, "Had It Coming" when he met his doom at Little Bighorn. At the request of local Oglala Lakota tribespeople, Banks and Means led a protest caravan of some two hundred Native men, women, and children to Custer, the county seat. The AIM group demanded that a white man who had stabbed to death an Oglala named Wesley Bad Heart Bull, after loudly vowing in a bar to "get that red son of a bitch," be charged with premeditated murder, instead of the lenient manslaughter charge that county law officials had filed against him.

Arriving in Custer, Banks and Means met with the county attorney inside the courthouse, while their AIM followers, including the murder victim's mother, Sarah, waited outside in a blizzard. But the county attorney was unbending, airily dismissing the eyewitness testimonies about the murder that Banks and others had painstakingly compiled. The AIM protesters knew where this train was headed—they had seen how the most brazen crimes against Indians in cowboy country were routinely downplayed or dismissed. And this time their fury couldn't be contained. Enraged by the county attorney's obvious contempt and by the fifty state troopers massed in full riot gear, the AIM band began fighting with the troopers in hand-to-hand combat. The brawl quickly escalated until the courthouse was in flames, the snow outside was stained with blood, two police cars were torched, and twenty-two people were arrested, including Sarah Bad Heart Bull.

Frontier law still held sway in South Dakota: Wesley Bad Heart Bull's murderer was later acquitted of all charges by an all-white jury, and did not spend a single day in jail, while Sarah Bad Heart Bull was convicted of "riot with arson" and served five months in prison.

THIS WAS THE fraught atmosphere in South Dakota in February 1973 when Oglala Lakota tribespeople on the Pine Ridge Reservation urgently requested that AIM come to their rescue. Dick Wilson, a mixed-race reservation politician, already had a reputation for corruption and thuggery when he narrowly won the 1972 election as tribal chairman. As tribal leader, he quickly established an authoritarian reign, maintaining his iron grip on Pine Ridge with graft, favoritism toward his mixed-race base, and violent intimidation. The thickly built tribal strongman, whose dark shades added to his menacing swagger, terrorized his critics with a private militia whose members proudly called themselves GOONS (Guardians of the Oglala Nation). Pine Ridge residents at first turned to federal authorities for help. Finding no sympathy from official quarters, which were aligned with Wilson's rule, tribespeople turned to a warrior whose father had grown up on their reservation, Russell Means.

Means had spent much of his youth on South Dakota tribal land, including the Yankton Reservation, where his formidable maternal grandmother, Mabel Arconge, lived. He came from a long line of Native resistance fighters on his mother's side, and as a boy he and his cousins would spend long summer afternoons playing Indian war games in the tall grass and rolling hills by the roaring Missouri River, before it was dammed above the reservation by the Army Corps of Engineers. His maternal cousins were like sisters to young Means, in keeping with their tribe's matrilineal tradition. And one of these cousins was Madonna Thunder Hawk. Years later she remembered the endless military campaigns that her "brother" Russell commanded.

"When we were kids, Russ would stage epic wars in the grasslands near our grandmother's house—they would sometimes last a week," she recalled. "At the end of the day, we all went home and ate dinner and then, *boom*, we would hit the door. Russ was always the general, and it was never cowboys versus Indians, it was always Indians fighting Indians over territory. He was a leader even then, and he was teaching us to strategize and be strong."

But it was Thunder Hawk and other women warriors in AIM and on the embattled Pine Ridge Reservation who convinced Banks and Means to seize Wounded Knee. The dramatic community meeting where the occupation was debated took place in a crowded church basement in Calico, a hamlet five miles from the Pine Ridge tribal center. All the Oglala Lakota tribal elders were there, along with the reservation's younger civil rights activists who had been trying to legally remove Wilson from power. Under his control, the Oglala Lakota homeland—a desolate place of widespread disease, malnutrition, alcoholism, shabby housing, and 70 percent unemployment—seemed destined for worse.

Anticipating an uprising by his desperate people, Wilson turned the tribal government center into a heavily fortified bunker, with .50-caliber machine guns mounted on top of the building, and dispatched his heavily armed goon squad throughout the reservation to shoot up the homes of opponents, beat people, and spread terror throughout Pine Ridge. Meanwhile, federal agencies continued to pour funds into Wilson's coffers, little of which reached the impoverished people of Pine Ridge, while FBI agents and US marshals flocked to Pine Ridge and reinforced his despised regime.

During the Calico meeting, Banks and Means remained silent while one after the other tribal leaders stood up in the church basement and described their plight. But it wasn't until women warriors took the floor that AIM's top men knew they had to act. "They shamed us men," Banks would later recall in his memoir. A Lakota activist named Ellen Moves Camp was the first woman to speak out that evening. Banks had seen her in battle at Custer and other AIM actions, and he took her seriously. She pointed a finger directly at the AIM leader and said, "Dennis Banks, what are you going to do?"

"Her words stung me," Banks wrote later. "I felt as though I had been stabbed with a knife."

Then a woman elder drove the knife in even harder. "You AIM people . . . you are supposed to be warriors," lashed out a Lakota tribeswoman named Gladys Bissonette. "If you men can't do it, then we women will. Even as I speak, the FBI and marshals are taking over our schools, hospitals, and sacred places." Then switching to Lakota in words so passionate they made her fellow tribespeople weep, Bissonette concluded, "We must take action today, not to-morrow."

A male elder pointed out that it would be suicide to try taking the Pine Ridge tribal council building, since Wilson's goons would mow them down with their machine guns. But a Lakota woman warrior named Lou Bean had another idea. "We'll fool them," she suggested. "Instead, let's go to Wounded Knee and make our stand there."

Banks immediately understood the ancestral power of her words. Wounded Knee was the most sacred place for the Lakota. "I felt chills running down my spine. . . . My adrenaline surged at the thought of what we were about to do."

Thunder Hawk immediately began helping organize the AIM caravan to Wounded Knee. "I knew we were making history for our people—[our story] didn't [end] in the 1800s. We were still fighting in the modern day. That's how I felt, that it was a continu-ation. And that's why I was *not* afraid. I was not afraid."

As the fleet of vehicles, most of them old and limping, slowly made their way to Wounded Knee in the dead of night, Thunder Hawk looked back at the long line of cars and pickups whose head-lights were cutting through the darkness. "I felt we had strength in numbers. We were all together, we were a movement of our people. There were families and children with us. I even had my ten-year-old son with me. This wasn't a planned operation. The people of Pine Ridge had pleaded for our help and we responded."

But as soon as they approached their destination, Thunder Hawk and the others realized the great risk they were taking. "By the time we got near to Wounded Knee, we could hear gunfire." As people began parking and getting out of their vehicles, someone shouted, "Hit the dirt!"

For the next ten weeks, the Wounded Knee protesters would be subjected to frequent fusillades from the hostile forces that quickly surrounded them, including federal officers and Wilson's militia. Much of the withering fire came from military-grade weaponry, and would total over five hundred thousand rounds of ammunition during the occupation.

AT DAWN ONE morning early in the siege, Russell Means listened to an alarmist news report on the radio about the "Indian uprising" at Wounded Knee, and then walked outdoors to gather his shaken thoughts, where he was joined by two other warriors. "We probably won't get out of this alive," he told the others. Means's fellow warriors nodded. "It was a sobering moment," he later wrote. "The three of us stood in the cold looking into the misty eastern sky, waiting for the sun to come up, each lost in his own thoughts."

Dennis Banks rose from his pillow early another morning with the same cold stab of fear. "Some droning sound woke me up and Stan Holder [a Vietnam veteran in charge of security at the Wounded Knee camp] said, 'Listen, guys, I've heard that noise before.' It sounded to him like the rumble of armored vehicles he'd seen in Vietnam. And sure enough, as the early morning fog began to lift, we could see about fifteen APCs, mounted with .50-caliber machine guns, on the ridge in the distance. I was beyond frightened at that moment. But then, it kind of inspired me. If they were going to go that far to crush us, that showed how formidable we were. And that's what I said at that day's meeting with all our camp people—'If they are mobilizing this kind of war machine to crush us, then I want all of you to rise to the occasion.'"

Banks then asked the women if they would like to leave the camp with the children while they still could. "One lady stood up," he recalled. "And she said, 'I came here to fight. I brought my children here and my grandchildren. We're not afraid of the FBI. If we have to, I'll fight them with my fists.'

"And one by one, the other women started to speak. And the last one I think was Madonna Thunder Hawk. And she said, 'If you men want to leave, sure, you can get on that bus and leave. We'll stay here.'"

Banks smiled and shook his head at the memory. "I thought, *Man, that's some courage.*"

Holder, a Wichita Indian, quickly assumed the role of military commander at Wounded Knee and began overseeing the construction of bunkers along the camp perimeter, picking other veterans who had served in Vietnam to anchor the front lines. The Native warriors were vastly outgunned and in constant danger of being tear-gassed and having their posts overrun by federal forces and armored vehicles. But they stood their ground during the firefights, which often erupted in the deep gloom of night, when the feds used tracers and night-vision goggles to target them, just like in Vietnam. Federal sharpshooters and vigilantes even took shots at women and children as they sprinted to the outhouse, and at medics treating wounded warriors. But AIM's thin line of defense gave enough protection to the Wounded Knee occupiers to allow them to build a remarkably resilient community during the siege.

Over time, the Wounded Knee encampment became a unique blend of Pine Ridge residents, AIM warriors, volunteers from more than a dozen tribes, and a scattering of racially mixed supporters from all over the country. A powerful sense of solidarity was forged between the protesters because of the common dangers they faced every day. The warriors in the forward bunkers spoke with special passion of these bonds.

During the siege, Holder described his band of brothers and sisters. "There's no discipline in this warrior society except self-discipline. I don't raise my voice at the [warriors] that I supposedly command. We haven't had any trouble with this because people realize that once there is a breakdown in this trust we have, there will be no independent Oglala Nation. So it's an army of love, an army born purely out of love for the Indian race and not hate for the white race."

An apocalyptic mood hovered over the Wounded Knee camp, a sense they might soon be joining their doomed ancestors. "One day I walked over to that gully and I picked up some sage and I went and washed myself and I prayed to those ancestors who were buried there in that gully," said AIM warrior Carter Camp. "And I said to them, 'We're back.'"

"AIM was preparing itself to make a real final stand," recalled Banks. "A final stand that said, 'No more abuse and no more killing and no more ripping off of our land and resources.'"

Means, who was given to heated rhetoric, was later accused by media critics of a militant flamboyance that invited catastrophe. Two weeks into the siege, he announced that Wounded Knee was now a sovereign nation, and he threatened to execute any US agent caught within the village's borders "like any spy at a time of war." But the truth is that this bold defiance was shared widely throughout the Wounded Knee camp, a deep and bitter belief that the Native people of America had nothing left to lose. Means was cheered by fellow Wounded Knee warriors when he shouted his war cry into a loudspeaker.

The goals of the Wounded Knee occupiers were eminently reasonable: an end to Dick Wilson's violent tyranny, true self-determination for the people of Pine Ridge, and a commitment by the Nixon administration to redress the government's long record of broken treaties with Native tribes. But the AIM leaders knew from grim experience that unless they were willing to risk everything, including their lives, Washington would never take their demands seriously. Banks and Means had to ride their tribe all the way to the cliff's edge to force the Nixon administration into negotiating mode—while stopping short of plummeting into the deep canyon below. In doing so, they worked out a careful choreography of joint leadership. "Russell would come to me and say, 'Listen, DJ [Banks's nickname], I'm going to take a hard stand and be the bad ass. You be the diplomat.' My relationship with Russell was cemented at Wounded Knee."

The two AIM leaders were deeply aware of the many lives of all ages that were now their responsibility. It would take all of their leadership skills—and the courage of all those whose lives were entrusted to them—to avoid another Wounded Knee disaster.

Banks and Means knew that their people's survival was based partly on the heroism of the warriors on the front lines, even though they were outgunned and outnumbered by the modern cavalry surrounding them. Stan Holder's warriors only had one battlefield weapon among them, an AK-47 assault rifle taken home from Vietnam as a souvenir. But the roar of that one gun, the North Vietnamese weapon that was helping defeat the mighty US military, was enough to unnerve the federal forces at Wounded Knee. They imagined a swarm of Indian braves with the most lethal weaponry.

Like the Black Panthers, American Indian Movement warriors were not opposed to arming themselves; but also like the Panthers, Banks always insisted that their guns were used only in self-defense. AIM was "confrontational but not violent," Banks wrote in his memoir. "AIM walks with the Canupa, the sacred pipe of peace. If we were to put the pipe away and only carry the gun, our movement would come to nothing."

Nonetheless, the Wounded Knee resisters overwhelmingly embraced the idea that their weapons prevented the massive forces mobilized against them from storming their camp. Don Cuny, an Oglala Lakota security chief also known as "Cuny Dog," still emphatically held this view years later. "My position at Wounded Knee was OK, you could pray and all of that. But as a warrior, I have a right to carry a gun and defend my people. If you're going to use guns against my people, we'll use them against you too."

The images of AIM warriors with rifles raised defiantly in the air would come to define Wounded Knee and the militant "red power" movement, inspiring a new spirit of resistance but also attracting heavier government repression for many years.

In addition to their armed defenses, Banks and Means were aware that their embattled camp was protected by the massive media presence at Wounded Knee. The Wounded Knee takeover soon became national and even international news, attracting TV crews from all three US networks at the time and reporters from major newspapers around the globe.

One tense afternoon, Means stood on a grassy hill as gunfire crackled in the distance, and scolded a group of his warriors for their hostile attitude toward the swarming press. "You guys get so uptight and down on the press," he said. "Hell, we *want* them to film this bullshit. When they open up on us with automatic weapons, we got to get that filmed. And we only got .22s in our hands against APCs. So don't be jumping on the press."

The Wounded Knee resisters also felt enfolded by the spirits of Chief Big Foot and his ghostly tribe. As much as the federal forces wanted to put a swift end to the AIM occupation with a massive military-style assault, they feared the deep stain of another bloodbath on the very site of the 1890 massacre. Even some FBI agents and federal marshals were haunted by the shadows of Wounded Knee. "The feds in their bunkers had heard the ghosts too, and it had shaken them up," Banks recalled. "Some of the marshals said later that an Indian on a horse had ridden through their camps and then suddenly dissolved into a cloud, into nothingness."

Ancestry and tradition were powerful unifying forces in the Wounded Knee camp. Leonard Crow Dog, AIM's spiritual leader, and several other revered medicine men played prominent roles during the occupation. The daily routine at the camp included prayers and sweat lodge ceremonies. "Everything we did was preceded by prayer, and by smoking of the sacred pipe—everything," recalled Clyde Bellecourt, one of the fellow Ojibwe activists who had cofounded AIM with Banks. All newcomers who hiked in to join the Wounded Knee camp had to first meet with one of the medicine men for a spiritual orientation.

Realizing that many original AIM members had grown up like him in Indian boarding schools and urban environments, where Native traditions had been erased, Banks had traveled in 1969 to Lakota reservations where he thought the spiritual roots were deeper, seeking guidance from legendary medicine men. With the help of religious figures like Crow Dog, AIM began incorporating ceremonial rituals into its worldly activism. "People often forget that AIM is not so much a political organization as it is a spiritual one," Banks would later write in his memoir.

As the siege dragged on, and the camp's morale began suffering under the incessant gunfire, Crow Dog decided to revive the Ghost Dance tradition. The Ghost Dance ceremony had been passionately embraced in Lakota territory in 1890, with its promise of uniting the living with the spirits of the dead and peacefully driving out the white invaders who had destroyed the traditional way of life. The marathon, hallucinatory dancing deeply mystified white authorities and colonists, filling them with fear.

At dawn one morning, some forty Wounded Knee warriors followed Crow Dog down into the gully where their Lakota ancestors had been slaughtered, and began slowly dancing as a flurry of snow drifted over them. "Some of the dancers fell down in a trance, some had visions," Banks recalled. "Four full days the Ghost Dancers danced. Some of those dancing and praying were descendants of the people from Big Foot's band. And we had a sign. A lone eagle circled overhead. . . . We were becoming what we once had been."

At one point in the ceremony, Means spoke to the Ghost Dancers: "The white man says that the 1890 massacre was the end of the wars with the Indians, the end of the Indians, the end of the Ghost Dance. Yet here we are at war, we're still Indians, and we're Ghost Dancing again."

DURING ONE FIERY assault on the camp, a Native warrior was hit and lay crumpled in an open field. Means's younger brother Bill was astonished to see Lorelei DeCora, an eighteen-year-old AIM medic, crawl out to help him, but in the process she was pinned down by a storm of gunfire. "We had to get on the radio [to federal agents]," he remembered. "'Halt your fire! There's a woman trying to help the wounded!'" DeCora was unable to move for over an hour while AIM warriors frantically tried to negotiate safe passage for her and the wounded man.

"They gave us ten minutes for one person with a white flag to go rescue her. 'If anyone opens fire,' they told us, 'that man is dead.' We were worried. She'd stopped moving—we thought she was hit. But when we crawled out there, she was asleep, she'd been out there so long. Everybody teased her about that—she could even sleep through a Wounded Knee [firefight]."

In spite of AIM's hypermasculine, martial reputation, women played a central role at Wounded Knee. They made up the majority of the resisters there—managing the community kitchen, but also standing guard in the front-line bunkers, discussing peace terms at the negotiating tables, running food and ammunition in daring missions through enemy lines—and, like DeCora, risking their lives as medics under fire.

"We women didn't need to make a big deal out of everything we did," said Madonna Thunder Hawk years later, shrugging. "The media wanted a stoic chief on horseback with a headdress. Yada, yada, yada. In reality we knew who was calling the shots. We didn't need to be constantly tapping people on the shoulder and whining, 'The women are here, the women are here.' We didn't need to do that because everybody knew that already."

Thunder Hawk, who was a thirty-three-year-old mother of three young children at the time of Wounded Knee, ran the makeshift medical clinic with DeCora, who was still a teenager when recruited by AIM. Thunder Hawk was older and more experienced than most of the AIM warriors and she was respected as a big sister. DeCora would become a registered nurse and renowned Native health activist, but at the time neither woman had medical training, much less combat experience. Their heroism under fire became legendary during the Wounded Knee ordeal.

DeCora felt inexorably drawn to Wounded Knee. Her great-grandmother had survived the massacre there as a seven-year-old-girl, and later insisted that she had miraculously been led to safety by her uncle and baby brother, even though both of them had been killed earlier in the 7th Cavalry onslaught. DeCora's great-grandmother grew up and gave birth to a small tribe of children. For the rest of her life, she could see spirits, and sometimes gazing out the window of her home, she would see her long-dead uncle.

"Women like DeCora and Madonna were the backbone at Wounded Knee," said Cuny Dog. "They had the power, and we just had to listen to them."

Life at the besieged camp flowed unstoppably on—there was a marriage ceremony, a birth (in the midst of a ferocious firefight) and, toward the end, a funeral. Community life was carefully organized, with committees in charge of security, sleeping quarters, and village kitchens. Each night there was a general meeting in the trading post to debate strategy and make announcements. Banks also printed a Wounded Knee bulletin on a mimeograph machine, to keep warriors informed about the outside world and to reinforce their sense of solidarity.

"It was my job to boost [people's] spirits," recalled Banks. "Every night I handed out news bulletins and distributed mail that had been smuggled in by our runners. Many times I played psychiatrist to people with troubled minds. I also arranged for people inside to get word to their families and friends on the outside via our underground railroad."

The men and women at Wounded Knee had a clear sense of the global news impact they were making, at least until the Nixon administration decided to block media access to the camp. One day, before the camp phone lines were cut, Banks received a long-distance call from a group of Indians serving in Vietnam who "wished they were with us at the Knee [and told us] that the real war was happening in America, not in Southeast Asia."

"During one [camp] meeting," Banks later wrote, "I read aloud no less than seventy telegrams from supporters." If the Wounded Knee community was not the sovereign nation that Means proclaimed it to be, it was certainly a vivid political drama.

Antiwar, civil rights, and other liberation groups collected food and donations for the Native resisters. The liberal senators George McGovern and James Abourezk came to the camp to help negotiations with the government—although McGovern turned out to be surprisingly hostile to the AIM leaders, reflecting the prejudices of his white South Dakota constituents. Civil rights leaders including the Reverend Ralph Abernathy, and radical heroes such as Angela Davis and Dick Gregory, turned up at Wounded Knee, as well. Activist-comedian Gregory slipped through the government lines to entertain the Wounded Knee warriors. His routine had the assembled Natives "in stitches," recalled Means. "Dick risked his life to make us laugh and I, for one, will always be grateful."

Hopes soared and crashed at Wounded Knee as the Nixon administration negotiators switched tactics, shifting abruptly back and forth between intransigence and compromise. The administration was represented at Wounded Knee by a changing cast of Justice and Interior Department officials, in part because the White House staff was increasingly distracted by the deepening Watergate scandal. As the air war in Vietnam escalated along with the militance of radical opposition, Wounded Knee's spectacle of intractable resistance, led by people of color, became more of an irritant to the administration.

On day 8 of the occupation, government officials suddenly issued a grim ultimatum to the AIM and tribal leaders: send out the women and children "before darkness falls" two days later because federal forces were going to storm the camp. But the warriors stood firm. "I told Dennis to burn [the government order]," said Oglala Lakota activist Regina Brave, who lived on Pine Ridge. "We prepared for the final stand."

The occupiers smeared red war paint on their cheeks. Banks told them if they died in battle wearing paint, they would "go to the spirit world with great honor."

"I had this little bitty bag—I had one bullet in there," recalled Brave. "And I had a semiautomatic and I put my one bullet in there. And I said, 'If I'm going, I'm taking somebody with me.'"

But two days later, Banks's car came screeching down the dusty road into the village. He was beaming and waving a red flag. Government officials had blinked and backed down from their deadly ultimatum.

The battlefield pressure on the Wounded Knee camp eased for the next three weeks. But on day 32, a new hardline Justice Department official named Kent Frizzell took over at Pine Ridge with a White House mandate to shut down the occupation. The electricity and water lines to the camp were cut. The roadblocks were reinforced, making it harder for runners to slip into camp with food and supplies. And most ominous, all reporters and TV news crews were suddenly barred from entering Wounded Knee.

BY NOW, THOUGH, the Native activists had won the hearts of millions of Americans. A national poll taken around this time revealed that a majority of the country supported the Wounded Knee action. Among these supporters was actor Marlon Brando, who would use the Academy Awards ceremony, held on the evening of March 27 that year at the glittering Dorothy Chandler Pavilion in Los Angeles, to shine a global spotlight on the beleaguered Natives at Wounded Knee. Brando, who won the Best Actor Award that year for his career-pinnacle performance in *The Godfather*, boycotted the ceremony, sending in his place a twenty-six-year-old actress-activist named Sacheen Littlefeather, who was an Apache Yaqui Indian on her father's side. Littlefeather read a message onstage from Brando explaining that, as a protest against Hollywood's treatment of Native Americans, and in recognition of "recent happenings at Wounded Knee," he would not be accepting his Oscar.

Littlefeather's brief speech drew loud boos from the audience, and the film industry reaction only grew more outraged afterward. The actor John Wayne, Hollywood's leading avatar of contempt for Native Americans, was not alone in dismissing Littlefeather's on-stage appearance as a publicity stunt, declaring that Brando himself should have made the statement "instead of taking some little unknown girl and dressing her up in an Indian outfit."

Littlefeather's budding acting career immediately foundered. "I was redlisted," she said years later, "not blacklisted." Seeing no future in Hollywood, Littlefeather pursued a new career in Native American healthcare and AIDS education. But she never regretted the stand she took that night for Native rights and Wounded Knee.

"I agreed to make that appearance on behalf of Marlon because I knew how the media blackout was putting the Wounded Knee camp in extreme danger," recalled Littlefeather. "The FBI was getting ready to go in and take all of the AIM leaders and cage them someplace like Guantanamo where they'd never be heard from again. In order to foil the FBI plans, Brando used the Oscars ceremony to shine the media spotlight again on Wounded Knee."

Though it was widely portrayed then and since as a sensational ploy by a narcissistic star, the Brando no-show had actually been carefully planned with AIM, and the Wounded Knee occupiers were elated by it. "We watched the whole show on TV that night," remembered Banks, smiling broadly at the memory. Brando, who remained boldly supportive of American Indian struggles until his death in 2004, went on the *Dick Cavett Show* soon after the Oscars and eloquently explained how reading about the true, blood-soaked history of the Old West had left him reeling: "I realized that everything we're taught about the American Indian is wrong . . . and our schoolbooks are hopelessly lacking. When we hear, as we've heard throughout our lives, that we are a country that stands for freedom, for rightness, for justice for everyone—it simply doesn't apply to those who aren't white. And we were the most rapacious, aggressive, destructive, torturing, monstrous people, who swept from one coast to the other, murdering and causing mayhem among the

Indians. But that isn't revealed because we don't like that image of ourselves. We like to see ourselves perhaps as John Wayne sees us."

With the Brando action focusing new public attention on Wounded Knee, Nixon officials grew more conciliatory. On day 37, Native leaders and government negotiators signed a tentative peace pact. The Nixon administration agreed to investigate tribal government corruption at Pine Ridge, to call for congressional hearings on Indian treaty rights, and to hold a White House meeting to discuss other Native grievances. That night the Wounded Knee camp celebrated with drums and dancing. The warriors elected four leaders to represent them at the historic White House meeting, including Means and Crow Dog. "We really thought we won," said Carter Camp. "And not only that, we thought we had survived."

But when the Wounded Knee delegation arrived in Washington, they discovered that once again Native warriors had been tricked by a US president. White House officials demanded that the Wounded Knee camp surrender all its arms before the meeting was held. "That wasn't our deal—that's bullshit," Means angrily told a press scrum that was following him around the nation's capital. The Native resisters knew all too well how this ugly story went. "We told the feds that the last time we did that—[disarmed under pressure] at Wounded Knee in 1890—our ancestors had been massacred," Means commented.

Blocked by federal forces from returning to Wounded Knee, Means embarked on a national speaking tour to spread the word about AIM and raise funds for the Pine Ridge occupation. After speaking on the UCLA campus, Means was being driven to the airport on the freeway when six carloads of Los Angeles police officers pulled over the Volkswagen bug he was riding in and ordered him to get out. Emerging from the VW, Means heard a "chorus of metallic clicks": a circle of guns cocked and pointed at him. A cop struck the unresisting Means on the head with a baton and he crumpled to his knees. Just when it looked like the AIM leader might become another Native victim of police violence, two FBI cars screeched up, and the agents jumped out, shouting frantically, "Stop, stop . . . we're taking this man!"

Means later mordantly remarked: "They were obviously afraid the cops were going to do something irreversible that might embarrass the Nixon administration."

Russell Means would spend the rest of the Wounded Knee siege behind bars in Sioux Falls, South Dakota, where federal agents transferred him. With their White House meeting ploy, Nixon officials had successfully extracted one of the Wounded Knee camp's most visible and effective leaders—and shut him down. Meanwhile, back at Pine Ridge, the government vise was tightening, and conditions in the besieged village were badly deteriorating.

IN THE FIRST weeks of the siege, nearby Pine Ridge Reservation supporters and teams of backpackers kept the Wounded Knee camp well supplied. Banks organized nightly backpack caravans, teams of Native runners who knew the rolling hills and arroyos of the area by heart and could elude the night-vision government snipers and trained attack dogs. The runners carried backpacks as heavy as fifty pounds—filled with food, medicine, toiletries, and ammunition—during their exhausting, several-mile treks. They found they could throw the police dogs off their scent by pissing a trail of urine that ended in a mound of hot chile pepper. "Once their noses connected with the pepper," Banks noted, "the dogs were useless for hours."

But after the promised discussions in Washington collapsed, Frizzell, the lead federal negotiator at Wounded Knee, announced, "The fun and games so far as I'm concerned are over." Government forces tightened their encirclement around Wounded Knee, Banks observed, so "that hardly a mouse could get through." At one well-traveled stretch of the camp's underground supply trail, the feds positioned several APCs with mounted machine guns.

By April, the Wounded Knee occupiers were down to two meals

a day. A week later it was one meal a day. "And then a week after that, we had to get by with one meal every other day with a bowl of thin soup in between," Banks later wrote. The sparse meals mostly consisted of pinto beans, although AIM warriors did once succeed in rustling a stray cow from a nearby ranch. City-bred young men, they had to rely on a white reporter with a rural background to show them how to butcher it.

"Hunger—for the first time in my life I knew what hunger was," Thunder Hawk recalled. "That was the only thing that really worried me because I had my ten-year-old son." As their food supply grew short, a man carrying a fifty-pound sack of calf feed showed up in the community kitchen one day, and the cooks made pancakes from it like it was flour. "It was all we had to eat," said Thunder Hawk.

Medical volunteers at the camp first noticed the signs of malnutrition among the children. Respiratory and intestinal diseases were also spreading among the kids, whose immunity was low, and among many of the elderly. The clinic was of little help because it had run out of medical supplies. A bleak feeling settled over the camp as the icy South Dakota winter dragged on and people walked around camp coughing, bundled in blankets against the wind and sleet.

The FBI used another tactic to weaken resistance at Wounded Knee—one whose sinister effects lasted much longer than the ten-week siege. As part of its counterintelligence program, known as COINTELPRO, the FBI began inserting infiltrators in the camp, a tactic the bureau had been using very effectively since the 1960s to sow discord and suspicion within many dissident groups. It was a spore of paranoia that would wreak terrible psychic damage on AIM, which became riddled with undercover agents and informers during the seventies—including, to Banks's great distress, his personal bodyguard Douglas Durham and eventually even his ex-wife Kamook Nichols. From 1973 to 1976, the FBI official in charge of South Dakota told a journalist covering AIM, the bureau ran an astonishing 2,600 agents through the Pine Ridge Reservation. "There was a lot going on that made the paranoia believable," Banks said years later. "It became impossible to trust anybody."

One victim of this rampant suspicion in the warlike atmosphere of Wounded Knee was Ray Robinson, a Black civil rights activist from Alabama, who showed up in the camp one night in April after backpacking successfully through federal lines. Robinson's ability to somehow slip through the tightened government stranglehold must have raised doubts about his identity. When the newcomer later reportedly got into a fight in one of the front-line bunkers and brandished a knife, an AIM member shot him in the knee, and he bled to death. The FBI pinned the murder on unnamed AIM militants, but decades later the bureau refused to fully disclose its information to Robinson's widow, Cheryl, and her lawyers, who suspected the federal agents were still trying to conceal the names of AIM informants.

Another terrible casualty of this billowing cloud of fear and distrust was Anna Mae Pictou Aquash, a young Canadian Indian who had also backpacked into Wounded Knee. Aquash was an ardent Native rights activist, but she aroused resentments when she became romantically involved during the siege with Banks, whose marriage to Kamook, a Lakota woman, was one way the Ojibwe Indian had cemented relations with the Pine Ridge tribe. After Wounded Knee, the FBI took actions that were seemingly designed to increase suspicions about Aquash within the tense AIM community. "The government set the stage for anybody in the movement to think that Anna Mae was a fed," observed Banks.

In February 1976, three years after the Wounded Knee occupation, Aquash's body was found dumped in a ravine on the edge of Pine Ridge, with a bullet in the back of her skull. Many years later two marginal AIM players would be convicted of her murder, but the bullet that killed Aquash also tore through the organization, ripping apart former allies and leaving a wound that was impossible to heal. Aging AIM leaders would forever be haunted by the knowledge that in the fury of their life-and-death struggle with the US government, they had condemned one of their own.

The idea that his lover and fellow AIM warrior had become a victim of the organization's FBI-manufactured paranoia was overwhelming for Banks. Author Peter Matthiessen, a deep sympathizer with the Native rights movement, interviewed Banks for his 1983 book *In the Spirit of Crazy Horse*, during which the Native leader revealed he called off an internal investigation into Aquash's death because "if it was true that AIM was involved, it would crush the movement."

Anna Mae's violent death would continue to disturb Banks until the end of his own life. Many years after Aquash's murder, Paul DeMain, publisher of the independent newspaper *Indian Country News*, met Banks at a protest march and began talking about his long journalistic investigation of her death. "When I started talking about [the murder] with him," DeMain recalled, "he welled up and couldn't speak for a while. . . . And he said, 'You've got to keep asking questions, keep searching.'" Banks encouraged DeMain's journalistic quest, even though he undoubtedly knew where his investigation was going—and that it was likely to turn up high-ranking AIM suspects.

SICK, HUNGRY, COLD, and losing their spirit, the Wounded Knee warriors were given one more miraculous boost on April 17, day 50 of the siege, when three single-engine planes came swooping over the village at dawn, dropping 1,500 pounds of food and supplies by parachute. The daring air mission was led by Bill Zimmerman, a thirty-two-year-old antiwar activist with a pilot's license, who had only days to organize the relief squadron. This was the same radical leader who would go on to run Tom Hayden's 1976 Senate race.

The sophistication of Zimmerman's operation—which involved raising funds, recruiting three flight crews and renting three planes, training for the dangerous mission, evading government surveillance, and expertly coordinating the actual air drop—demonstrated not only how well organized the Vietnam peace movement was becoming by 1973 but how much solidarity was being forged between antigovernment groups with very different cultural identities.

When Zimmerman was discreetly contacted by a Wounded Knee sympathizer about undertaking the audacious airlift, he was working in the Boston office of Medical Aid for Indochina, a peace group that sent medical equipment to the war-ravaged peoples of Vietnam, Laos, and Cambodia. His initial reaction to the request was, understandably, skeptical. "Do you know what you're asking?" Zimmerman exclaimed. "I could get shot doing that!" Zimmerman was also worried about putting his antiwar group and those whose help he would need at legal risk.

But Zimmerman soon realized he could not say no. "I was put on the spot. It was not possible to say no," he later wrote in a dramatic recounting of the Wounded Knee relief mission. "The request was made to *me*, and my answer would say something about my life and how I chose to live it. . . . If I refused to take the risk, then surely my own life would be diminished and robbed of some of its meaning."

The diverse makeup of Zimmerman's flight crews and their support network reflected how widely antigovernment sentiments were spreading during Nixon's presidency. They included an African American pilot named Billy Wright who had served in Vietnam, who told his fellow flight crew members, "This is probably the most important thing I've ever done." The three Piper Cherokee planes were secured for the mission by Zimmerman's former flight instructor, an ex-cop who also recruited his next-door neighbors in Chicago—white, ethnic, working-class women—to stay up all night sewing the big duffel bags to hold the relief goods. And Tom Oliphant—the young *Boston Globe* reporter who volunteered to cover the risky mission as a passenger in Zimmerman's small plane—went so native that by the time the small squadron flew over Wounded Knee, he was working frantically as a cargo handler,

pushing the heavy bags of food out the dangerously open cargo
hatch of the Cherokee.

The remarkable fact about the Wounded Knee airlift is that even
though none of the flight crews or the dozens of men and women
actively supporting the operation were Native American, they all
sympathized strongly enough with the Indians' struggle to risk their
freedom, and even their lives, to help them. Wounded Knee was
a striking example of the personal and political webs that by the
early seventies were bonding people from all over the country,
despite their different ways of life, in common cause to radically
transform America.

As the three small planes approached the Wounded Knee village, flying as low and slow as possible so the heavy duffel bags could
be pushed out of the open hatches and parachuted within the AIM
camp perimeters, Zimmerman's flight teams feared they would be
greeted by gunfire from below, particularly from Dick Wilson's assault rifle–wielding goons. From the air, the area looked like a war
zone. "We had flown out of the United States and into [Vietnam],"
marveled Zimmerman, who spotted rows of sandbagged trenches
and hulking, tanklike vehicles surrounding the Indian camp on all
sides. But gliding over Wounded Knee shortly after 5 a.m., the relief squadron caught Nixon's forces and Wilson's militia off guard.
By the time the feds began firing their M-16s at the planes, they
were safely out of reach.

Zimmerman's airborne courage was tested further when one of
the big duffel bags sheared off part of his airplane's tail as the cargo
went plummeting out the rear. Keeping the Cherokee in the air
until he was safely far away from militarized Pine Ridge took all
of his flying skill. As gusts of wind buffeted his damaged single-
engine plane, Zimmerman struggled to keep control. "It was more
like riding a rodeo horse than flying an airplane," he later recalled.
When he finally brought the broken plane down in a harrowing
landing—at a tiny airport in South Sioux City, Nebraska, some 340
miles from Wounded Knee—the air mechanic who inspected the

Cherokee shook his head and said to Zimmerman and his crew-mates, "You know, you three fellas shouldn't be alive."

But the forty seconds he flew over Wounded Knee made it all worth the risk, Zimmerman felt. As the food containers billowed to earth, Zimmerman could see dozens of Indians on the ground erupting with joy and sprinting to free the cargo from the big puddles of parachutes. Banks later remembered the celebratory rush that people in the camp felt as the planes dropped their precious cargo. "Our people were jumping up and down, yelling, '*Food, food!*'

"I thought, *Goddamn! Somebody cares! They care if we survive or not, and they knew how to deliver this manna from heaven! Plus, the planes were called* Cherokees! It was almost too good to be true."

Men, women, and children began hauling the food into the community kitchen, rejoicing at the culinary pleasures they hadn't enjoyed for weeks: bags of rice, carrots, raisins, onions, cornmeal, flour, cheese, coffee, sugar, salt, and cans of ham. There were even urgently needed toiletries like tampons and toilet paper. But the camp's elation was short-lived. As a family that lived in Wounded Knee—including several young children—began carrying some of the food bags to the kitchen, a military helicopter suddenly hovered over the camp and began firing at them, forcing all of them to dive into a ditch for cover. Several AIM warriors protected the family by quickly returning fire at the helicopter, hitting the craft and forcing it to flee.

This brief exchange of gunfire sparked a massive fusillade on the camp that was the beginning of the end at Wounded Knee. Humiliated by the surprise food drop, FBI officials at the siege radioed to Washington that the duffel bags contained guns and ammunition, not food. This false report gave federal forces the green light to unleash a barrage of gunfire at the Indian resisters, a withering storm that totaled four thousand rounds of ammunition within a little over two hours.

People huddled wherever they could find shelter, but the military-grade firepower struck six camp members, one of them severely. Frank Clearwater, an Apache, had hiked into Wounded Knee only the night before with his pregnant wife Morning Star, a Cherokee. They were not AIM members but they wanted to help in any way they could. Clearwater was sleeping inside the white, clapboard Catholic church on a knoll in the center of the village when a bullet tore through a wall and blew off the rear of his skull.

"They literally tore that church apart with .50-caliber bullets," recalled Banks. "Great big holes the size of softballs going in one side and coming out the other as big as a washtub. . . . They sure intended to tear us apart, too."

Accompanying her wounded husband as he was evacuated, Morning Star was arrested by FBI agents. She would be stuck inside an overcrowded Pine Ridge Reservation jail as Frank Clearwater lay dying in a Rapid City hospital.

The first fatality at Wounded Knee devastated many of the re-sisters, including DeCora, the teenage medic, who struggled vainly to keep Clearwater alive as his head gushed blood in the church. "The whole top of his head was blown off," she recalled. "I had my hands on top of his head trying to hold the pieces together. Every-thing up to that point was fun, but when I saw that, I thought, *This man just gave his life, so this better be worth it.* My whole perception of Wounded Knee changed at that moment, and I wondered, *What are we accomplishing here?*"

On April 26, nine days after the food drop, Dick Wilson's goons provoked what would be the final and most fierce firefight of Wounded Knee by shooting in the direction of federal forces. Mistaking it for AIM fire, FBI agents and marshals began blasting away at the camp, igniting a battle that would rage for two days. This firefight would claim the second fatality of Wounded Knee, a beloved thirty-one-year-old Pine Ridge resident and Vietnam War veteran named Buddy Lamont, who was struck through the heart by a sniper's bullet. Lamont was also the uncle of Banks's wife, Kamook, who rushed to the fallen warrior and cradled his body in her arms, sobbing, "Buddy, Buddy, Buddy."

Banks realized that Lamont's death was the end of the Wounded Knee struggle: He had been so deeply part of Lakota life on Pine Ridge that his loss was like a bullet through the community's own heart. Hundreds of people, including all the Lakota chiefs and tribal elders, came to mourn Lamont's death. Defying federal orders, the crowd descended on Wounded Knee for his funeral. He was laid to rest by the creek, in the gully where his ancestors had been buried in 1890. Someone reached into his open casket before Lamont's body was lowered into the ground and placed a sacred eagle feather in his hair.

A defiant Banks and his fellow AIM warriors wanted to keep resisting at Wounded Knee. But the Lakota elders could feel their people's sorrow and fatigue, and anxious to avoid perhaps even more catastrophic bloodshed, they began a final round of peace negotiations with government officials. They won some vague government promise to discuss broken treaties in the future and to investigate Wilson's violent, corrupt Pine Ridge regime. To AIM, the agreement seemed as transparently fake as a long line of previous Washington duplicities. Banks knew he had to accept the tribal will. But he and Carter Camp—the other AIM political leader still at Wounded Knee—refused to sign the final agreement with the feds, he recalled, "because we did not want to put our names on a document of surrender."

The Lakota elders were wise to sue for peace when they did, because by late April President Nixon's troops had blood in their eyes. FBI forces at Wounded Knee, pushed by the increasingly belligerent Wilson militia, were itching to crush the camp. Federal agents had been deeply embarrassed by the ambitious air relief mission and feared that even more antiwar movement support for the Wounded Knee resistance would materialize in late spring when college campuses across the nation disgorged their students.

In an interview for this book near the end of his life, Banks recalled a remarkable meeting he had with H. R. "Bob" Haldeman and John Ehrlichman in 1974. According to Banks, the sit-down was requested by the former top Nixon aides, who by then had resigned from the White House and were awaiting trial on charges related to the Watergate scandal, and took place at the Los Angeles home of Marlon Brando. Haldeman and Ehrlichman told the AIM leader that in the later days of the Wounded Knee siege, FBI officials had met with Nixon in the White House and presented a plan to terminate the protest by invading the camp with overwhelming force. "Nixon's men told me that the FBI wanted to lay down a blanket of gas from helicopters," Banks recalled. "And then they were going to come in with arms and retake it."

The president was outraged by the FBI plan, reported his former aides. "They said Nixon was very angry," recalled Banks. "The president said, 'You mean to tell me that a group of ragtag Indians has got the whole Justice Department and the FBI and the US marshals running scared? That you want to use gas and bullets to end this? Not on my watch.'"

By 1973, Nixon and his aides were deeply estranged from the FBI and CIA, suspecting the agencies were sabotaging his administration. Indeed, W. Mark Felt, the FBI's number-two official during the Nixon presidency, later revealed himself to be "Deep Throat," the *Washington Post*'s Watergate whistleblower. Haldeman and Ehrlichman might have been acting on their anti-FBI animus by telling Banks that the bureau had a shock-and-awe plan to destroy the Wounded Knee camp, and were stopped from acting on it only by a more temperate President Nixon. Still, there's little doubt that the Wounded Knee occupiers had stirred frustration and rage in the national security elite.

But if the Lakota tribal elders were right to end the Wounded Knee stand when they did, Dennis Banks was right to reject the final peace document, which called for him and other AIM leaders to hand themselves over to government agents. Banks suspected that his peaceful surrender, like the federal arrests of Sitting Bull and Crazy Horse many years earlier, would result in his quick and violent death. By plotting his dramatic escape from Wounded Knee on the last night of the occupation, Banks avoided the tragic end that had befallen so many of the Indian leaders who had come before him. He and many of his warriors would live to fight another day.

EARLY ON THE morning of May 8, the 150 people or so still at the Wounded Knee camp emerged from their bunkers and living quarters and lined up to be processed by a small army of federal officials, as called for by the peace plan. The Lakota elders and medicine men who had negotiated the agreement with the government were deeply worried about another 1890 massacre, which had been set off when 7th Cavalry soldiers began roughly seizing the guns from Chief Big Foot's terrified, surrounded tribe and a stray shot went off, triggering the slaughter. The tribal negotiators won assurances that a group of defense lawyers would be allowed on the scene to monitor the surrender. With the powerful Hotchkiss cannons in mind that had torn apart Big Foot's tribe, the Lakota leaders also insisted that the feds' machine-gun-mounted APCs be withdrawn from the nearby Wounded Knee perimeter. Finally, they secured a government pledge that Pine Ridge strongman Dick Wilson's dangerous thugs would be kept away from the camp that day.

In short, both sides at the negotiating table agreed that the surrender should be conducted in the most peaceful and dignified manner possible. But little of this carefully worked-out choreography was actually followed by federal officials that morning.

As the Wounded Knee resisters were searched, fingerprinted, and loaded on buses to be taken to a government processing center, FBI agents quickly plucked out the two AIM leaders they could find: Carter Camp and medicine man Leonard Crow Dog. The two men were slapped in handcuffs, chains, and leg irons, and swiftly bundled onto a military helicopter and flown to a jail in Rapid City.

Then, while most of the resisters were still in custody at the camp, they were forced to watch a humiliating "victory" ceremony performed by their militarized captors. A group of federal marshals, led by a gung-ho type whom the Indians identified as an ex–Green Beret, tore down the AIM flag hanging over the camp and raised the Stars and Stripes in its place, as they shot off volley after volley of rifle shots to commemorate the occasion.

When a Wounded Knee warrior from Oklahoma named Arvin Wells complained that the Natives were not supposed to be subjected to this kind of Old West display, which he said added "insult to injury," the Green Beret veteran got in his face and shouted angrily, "Boy, don't ever say anything about that flag. . . . Or I'll knock your fucking head off." The marshals then boasted that the Indians were their POWs.

"It was really a pitiful sight," recalled Wells. "Man, I don't think we should have ever surrendered. I don't give a damn whether they'd have come in there and killed us, man, because it was really humiliating the way they treated us all through that whole day."

The Wounded Knee captives were forced to endure one more round of indignities, as the feds broke another promise and allowed Wilson's goon squad to go rampaging through the village, looting property and wrecking homes.

But there was one big missing piece that day in the federal forces' victory party. The modern US cavalry failed to grab the man they thought of as the "Big Chief"—Dennis Banks—and as many as sixty of his top warriors. Banks was supposed to be their main war trophy, shackled like Camp and Crow Dog, and paraded before the news cameras. These crushing images would have announced to all who dared think of resistance in America: *See, this is what happens to Indian braves who defy the authorities. It ends in shame and defeat.* But Dennis Banks was nowhere to be found that final day at Wounded Knee.

Of course, Banks's fate could have been worse if he'd been caught that day; he might well have ended up in a morgue instead of a jail cell. Rumors of his imminent death swept Wounded

Knee in the final days of the siege. Tribal elders warned Banks
that armed federal officials would precipitate a firefight during the
stand-down and use it as an excuse to assassinate the AIM leader,
claiming later that he had resisted arrest. The fear was buried deep
in the Plains Indians' memories. This is the way that other tribal
heroes had been killed while being taken into federal custody.

"The women elders were especially vehement," recalled AIM
warrior Lenny Foster. "They said, 'You've got to get Dennis out
of here or they're going to kill him.'" If the feds didn't gun down
Banks, many in the Wounded Knee camp believed, Wilson's goons
would. The Pine Ridge chairman's threats against AIM had grown
increasingly violent during the siege, as he branded Banks a "clown,"
"a hoodlum," and "a dangerous Communist" who should not be
allowed to escape unscathed. "AIM will die at Wounded Knee,"
Wilson vowed.

Banks's deputies told him that his humiliation—or assassination—
would not be only a personal tragedy; it would gravely wound the
movement. "Generals don't surrender." That's how Foster put it.

LENNY FOSTER WAS surprised when Dennis Banks summoned him to his little log cabin two or three days before the
scheduled surrender at Wounded Knee. Offering him a cup from
the last coffee rations, Banks asked Foster if he intended to surrender on May 8. "Hell no, I'm not going to surrender—I'm going to
sneak out of here," Foster announced.

"I tell you what—I want you to lead me out of here," Banks
told him.

Foster was stunned by Banks's request. He was just a twenty-
five-year-old AIM "dog soldier," as he described himself at the time.
Banks, more than a decade older, was Foster's deeply respected
commander-in-chief. The younger man had observed Banks closely
in a number of excruciatingly tense actions, even before Wounded
Knee, and grew to trust his leadership. "He was stern and very

intelligent," Foster recalled. "He was kind and sensitive to the people around him, and he listened to people. But when he made a decision, he'd stand by it and he wanted things done."

Though he was surprised by the trust that Banks was placing in him, Foster didn't hesitate to answer. "I just said, OK, I'll walk point for you." To Banks's bodyguard, Henry Wahwassuck, Foster was even more fervent. "I'll protect him with my own life," the young man vowed.

Banks's choice of Foster to lead his daring escape mission was a wise one. The young AIM warrior had long made an impression on Banks and the group's other leaders. Lenny Foster grew up in Arizona, on the vast Navajo nation, one of five children of a World War II hero who had served as a legendary code talker in the bloodiest battles of the South Pacific. Skilled in sports, young Foster played outfield for his Colorado State University baseball team, where he was scouted by the Los Angeles Dodgers. But he dropped out to join the Native liberation movement, first hitchhiking to San Francisco to take part in the Indian occupation of Alcatraz Island in 1970 and then signing up with the Denver chapter of AIM later that year.

The American Indian Movement felt like the answer to Foster's prayers. All his life, he had heard and read about—and personally experienced—"The extreme racism and aggression of the United States government. The colonization of our mind and body and spirit through white schools, churches, and corrupt tribal governments on our reservations. All the ways we were made to feel ashamed of who we were as Indians, to do away with our ceremonial practices and beliefs. We were on the brink of extermination as a culture. And then AIM came along. It was a reaction against all of that. They took a powerful stand against this attempt to kill us once and for all."

To the young Navajo, AIM leaders like Dennis Banks, Russell Means, Vernon and Clyde Bellecourt, and Madonna Thunder Hawk were the messiahs who had been prophesied in Native spirituality.

"I call them Red Giants—that's how I look at them. Red Giants walked the earth at one time."

And now young Lenny Foster was being given the grave task of keeping alive one of these giants.

Foster served all seventy-one days of the Wounded Knee occupation in perhaps the most dangerous station—the Little Bighorn bunker on the front lines of the camp. Bordering the Wounded Knee Creek bank, where the ghosts of 1890 could be heard at night, Foster's bunker was the one closest to the armored war vehicles, and withstood some of the most terrifying federal barrages. The young AIM warrior was armed only with a .45-caliber M-1 carbine, which he soon found out was no match for the assault-rifle fire aimed at Little Bighorn. During one lull in a firefight, when Foster quickly stuck his head out of the trench, it was nearly shattered by a bullet that went whizzing past him so closely he could feel the vibration.

Foster said that his courage under fire during the long siege came from spiritual strength. Before he left his home on the Navajo reservation for Wounded Knee, he spent time at a remote sheep camp with his grandfather, a traditional man who did not speak English. The older man gave Lenny a small medicine pouch, filled with corn pollen and an arrowhead, which he had blessed. "When I woke up each morning at Wounded Knee, I would take that medicine pouch out of my pocket, and open it, and make offerings to the east, west, north, and south. And after praying with it, I put it away."

His grandfather had given Foster's father and uncle similar spiritual gifts before they shipped out with the marines for the South Pacific, which the family believed had protected the young soldiers from the horrors of Iwo Jima and Okinawa.

During the Wounded Knee occupation, in addition to his morning prayers, Foster was also sometimes observed at sweat lodge ceremonies, which reinforced his image in the camp as a serious young man of spiritual discipline. In fact, the day before he was to lead

Banks's escape mission, Foster suggested that their small team—
including three other young AIM warriors—undergo a sweat ritual
with medicine men Leonard Crow Dog and Wallace Black Elk so
that their dangerous trek would have a spiritual shield.

"We prayed and we sang and we smoked a pipe," Foster remembered. "And then Crow Dog told us, 'By doing this, these prayers
and songs will make you invisible at night.'" Later, Foster wanted
to talk about Crow Dog's stunning blessing with the other young
men on Banks's escape team—his deep sense that the ancient ritual
would indeed "somehow protect us." But the sweat ceremony did
not sink into them the same way it did for Foster. They were eager
for action, for the following night to come.

They set off from the Wounded Knee camp the next night
around 9 p.m. Banks's escape team was a cross-tribal alliance, led
by Navajo Foster, and including the AIM leader's bodyguard Henry,
a Potawatomi from Kansas; Percy Casper, a Shuswap from British
Columbia; and Frank Black Horse, a Lakota.

It seemed to Foster that the night was unusually dark, but he
knew the pitch blackness would soon be periodically lit up by a
federal light show, including sweeping searchlights, and flares fired
into the sky attached to little parachutes. The escape party also
had to beware of trip wires, which if stumbled upon in the darkness would set off a loud racket and shoot off more flares. If the five
men attracted any attention during their escape, they would soon
be hunted by heavily armed FBI agents and federal marshals with
snarling German shepherds—and, even more ominously, by Wilson's vigilantes. The AIM warriors would have to slip through an
iron circle that was reinforced by APCs and other military vehicles
stationed at intervals around the perimeter, and by security forces
equipped with night-vision goggles.

Banks's team decided to head north toward Porcupine, a reservation town eight miles away whose residents were stalwart supporters of the Wounded Knee occupation, despite constant harassment
by Wilson's goon squad. They were wearing light backpacks, and

they were also carrying rifles because Banks feared they might have to use them. Lou Bean, the Pine Ridge activist who had dramatically proposed that AIM seize the Wounded Knee site, and a group of other women warriors staged a loud distraction on the southern flank of the camp as the escape party ran into the night in the opposite direction. "Big flood lights . . . were suddenly trained on that area," Banks recalled, where Bean's group was creating "a tremendous racket. We grabbed our opportunity to sneak out. I will never forget the brave women [of Wounded Knee]."

Foster ran twenty or thirty yards ahead of the others, skillfully avoiding the trip wires and scouting the terrain to make sure it was safe. He kept the group out of federal vision by cresting hills as quickly as possible and running in deep gullies. Because the ravines "zigzagged all over the place" instead of following a straight line, this made their escape especially arduous. "It took maybe two hours to cover a mile and a half," Banks recalled.

Foster knew that one false step on the rugged escape route could mean his doom and that of the "Red Giant" who had entrusted his life to the young warrior. But, he later insisted, he felt no fear. "I used the darkness. I used my belief, my prayers, and the pipe. I truly believed we *were* invisible."

By the still-dark early morning, Foster had painstakingly guided the group through the federal encirclement. But they were still two miles or so from Porcupine and they knew they faced random dangers in the darkness. Suddenly, Foster, still walking point, spotted an owl sitting in a shadowy tree. "That kind of spooked me, because the owl is a bad omen in our tradition. I began talking to the owl and I decided in my mind that the owl was there for a reason. To warn me about something up ahead, that I had to be very careful."

Sure enough, Foster soon spied a parked car on the road. Approaching the vehicle very stealthily, using a nearby tree line as cover, he saw it contained two federal marshals armed with assault rifles. Foster ran back to tell the others they would have to widely circumvent the feds' car. But just then Frank Black Horse ran across the road, immediately attracting the marshals' attention. "I thought, *Oh man, what the hell is he doing?*" recalled Foster. To this day, he doesn't know for sure what motivated Black Horse, but he has his suspicions.

Suddenly the feds were calling for backup, and another patrol car soon skidded to the scene, carrying more lawmen and a police dog.

"I told Dennis, 'Go on—take off! You run along the ridge by the tree line and go north. We'll stay and protect the rear and we'll meet up with you later.' And that's what he did—he ran into the night."

Led by their search dog, the feds soon closed in on Foster and the remaining escape team, as they crouched in the tree cover. The Natives cocked their rifles in anticipation. Just then, a pack of reservation dogs—the bony, vicious breed that typically roams the rez—appeared from nowhere. "It was divine intervention," Foster declared. "They were sent by the Spirit to run interference, to allow us to get away." As the reservation dogs leapt on the German shepherd in a snarling tangle of fangs and fur, the marshals had to devote all their attention to saving their animal. "And we did get away, because of those dogs."

When they reached Porcupine, Foster and the others were taken in by a Lakota named John Attacks Them, a friend of Casper, who regarded the AIM warriors as heroes—a sentiment widely shared on the Pine Ridge Reservation. Waiting until the cover of next nightfall, Attacks Them then drove the group to the reservation town of Rosebud, where the fleeing Banks had been warmly received by another Pine Ridge resident. Desperately knocking on this stranger's door, as the feds were pursuing him, Banks was taken in by "a kind, stout-hearted lady" who instantly recognized him. "Come inside quick!" she told Banks. "Don't worry. I won't let these pigs into my house."

Reunited in Rosebud with Banks, the group laughed together late into the night as they relived their remarkable escape. The next day, they went their separate ways, never again to repeat such a breathtaking mission together.

LENNY FOSTER NEVER fell into law enforcement's grip. "I realized even then that you never wanted to surrender," he said many years later. He was telling his story as a sixty-nine-year-old man, still physically robust and ruggedly handsome, with his long, white hair tied in a braid. He was wearing wire-rim glasses, a turquoise Navajo amulet around his neck, a crisp white shirt, and dark jeans. "If they captured you, they'd fingerprint you and take your mug shot. They'd always have you in their system, and they'd hound you the rest of your life. Instead, I escaped that night and blended back into the community. That was always one of the best moments of my life—being able to escape with our leader, and to live another day. To escape with my pride and my dignity."

Ironically, Foster wound up serving much of his life in prisons—nearly a hundred of them across the country. But he was a spiritual adviser, not an inmate, working for the Navajo tribal government to bring traditional Native rituals to incarcerated American Indians.

While a young AIM warrior, he had observed firsthand the deep effects that bringing the pipe and prayer could have on despairing Native prisoners, particularly when these shorn and uniformed convicts saw the ceremonies being led by medicine men with traditional long braids and clothing. Until he retired in 2017, Foster worked for thirty-six years as the director of the Navajo Nation Corrections Project, providing spiritual counseling to Indians from all tribes, including those in some of America's most brutal maximum-security dungeons and on death rows.

To Foster, the penal system was just a more intensive version of the way that Native peoples were treated in America. "Our country is shaped along the same lines. Our system can't tolerate human rights, human dignity. They're intent on destroying the essence, the psyche of a man by putting him in cages, humiliating him, and subjecting him to psychological warfare."

Foster's mission—and he said it began with AIM—was to fight for his people's humanity. He did this not only with prison prayer, suing prisons for the right to build sweat lodges within their walls, but also by testifying against inhumane prison conditions and the death penalty before the US Senate and the United Nations Human Rights Commission. Late into his life, Foster remained active in AIM as a member of the organization's Grand Council, speaking at conferences and marching in protests.

Like Foster, Madonna Thunder Hawk also decided to escape on the final night of the Wounded Knee occupation rather than surrendering to federal officials. Thunder Hawk and a "whole crew" of male and female AIM warriors slipped past the siege forces to freedom. "Hell, no, we weren't going to surrender," she said, looking back years later. "You're thinking of your ancestors, you know? What if they all surrendered? We wouldn't be here."

In the years following Wounded Knee, Thunder Hawk was at the forefront of Native liberation, starting a "survival school" for the children of AIM warriors ensnared by the criminal justice system after the occupation. She then cofounded Women of All Red Nations in 1974 to fight the scourge of abuses suffered by Indian women, including forced sterilization, domestic violence, government theft of children, and other assaults on tribal family life. And in 1979, Thunder Hawk helped organize the Black Hills Alliance, a groundbreaking "cowboy and Indian coalition," as she described it, between white ranchers and Native activists to oppose a Union Carbide uranium mining project on sacred Lakota territory that was contaminating the area's water supply.

Thunder Hawk lived an overflowing life as a "warrior woman," taking her children with her as she traveled the globe so her lives as a mother and activist would never be separated. In the late 1980s, she was visiting indigenous tribes in Central America to share lessons about their mutual battles for survival. One day she trekked into a remote jungle village. An older woman holding a grandchild stared at Thunder Hawk after hearing her name, and then touched her arm. "Wounded Knee," the elderly woman said.

"I was just stunned—I didn't know what to say," recalled Thunder Hawk. "Even out there in the jungle. Wounded Knee was an awakening in our people, everywhere. It was a global rising."

Thunder Hawk was treated as a heroic elder in early 2016 when she showed up at the Standing Rock Reservation in North Dakota to protest the construction of an oil pipeline underneath tribal waterways—the most dramatic Native rights action since Wounded Knee. These two protracted stands galvanized remarkably brave, diverse coalitions, and their reverberations were felt around the world. But in conventional political terms, both protests ended in defeat, as their powerful enemies shut down the Native resistance camps without making any tangible concessions.

Still, the outcomes of these historic battles didn't dispirit Thunder Hawk. She explained her philosophy over lunch one day in a San Francisco Mission district Mexican restaurant, during a 2017 visit from her home on the Cheyenne River Reservation in South Dakota. At age seventy-seven, wearing jeans and cowboy boots, with a flowing gray ponytail and a face creased with life, Thunder Hawk was still fighting on the front lines of freedom, calling herself a "warrior woman" and a "granny"—which her grandson proudly expanded to "original gangsta granny."

It's all about living to fight another day, Thunder Hawk said. "It's a continuous struggle—the war will never be won. As long as we have a land base in this country, we will be constantly in battle. We're not going anywhere. It's our home. Were we going to stop that major energy pipeline? Come on, we're not that naïve. We've been at this a long time—long before my lifetime. So it's all about fighting and gaining some ground here and there, you know?

"Someday soon, I'll be gone. And we're only responsible for our life span, what we do while we're here. We did the hard work, we stood our ground like our ancestors. And now it's your turn, your time—our children and grandchildren. We had our time. We did the best we could. They can read about me in your book. And then they'll go, 'Here's what she did—now what should *we* do?'"

AFTER ESCAPING FROM Wounded Knee, Dennis Banks was forced to keep fleeing "to the end of the world" as he put it, including the frozen northern reaches of Canada. Nearly all of the blood spilled at Wounded Knee was by the Native resisters. There was only one casualty on the federal side, an agent who was shot and paralyzed—and AIM leaders strongly suspected he had been wounded by "friendly fire" from Wilson's trigger-happy militia. Still, the US government was intent on making an example of Banks and his fellow AIM leader Means.

By the time Banks turned himself in to face the Wounded Knee charges of assault and conspiracy, he and Means had assembled a formidable legal team. The AIM leaders mounted a dramatic defense in their 1974 trial, invoking the squalid treatment of Indians throughout US history and presenting evidence of government criminality during and after the siege. The surprisingly sympathetic federal judge in the St. Paul, Minnesota, courtroom finally dismissed the government's case, scolding prosecutors for their misconduct, including their blatant evidence-tampering.

Despite his Wounded Knee courtroom victory, Banks continued to be relentlessly pursued by a lawman named William Janklow, the attorney general and later governor of South Dakota, who was determined to punish the AIM leader for the fiery protest in Custer. Janklow, whose morbid obsession with Banks surpassed Inspector Javert's single-minded pursuit in *Les Misérables*, kept the AIM warrior on the run for nine years. "He publicly said the best thing to do with Dennis Banks was to put a bullet through his head," the AIM leader recalled. "I was Janklow's favorite man to hate."

But AIM had developed so much political support in liberal states that Banks was able to win sanctuary in California from Governor Jerry Brown, who rejected South Dakota's extradition requests on the very justifiable basis that Banks feared for his life in that state. Later, in 1983, when Governor Brown was replaced by a Republican, Banks was granted sanctuary on a reservation in upstate New York by Governor Mario Cuomo. By the time Banks finally turned himself in to face the old Custer charges, Janklow was out of office, and he ended up serving only fourteen months behind bars.

Some histories of the American Indian Movement have portrayed the organization as a tragic victim of its own militance and government harassment. It's true that Banks, Means, and hundreds of other AIM activists were often tied up in lengthy legal battles or in flights from the law—and that like many other groups on the left, AIM sometimes fell victim to a corrosive paranoia bred from real government infiltration. But Banks managed to flourish as an activist, educator, and father of a sprawling new generation of sons and daughters. Over the years, he served as chancellor of Deganawidah-Quetzalcoatl (D-Q) University, a small college for Indians in Davis, California; supervised an addiction treatment program on the Pine Ridge Reservation; and organized cross-country treks of Indians and environmental activists that he called "Sacred Runs" for the Earth. In 2016, he ran on a socialist and feminist platform for vice president, sharing a Peace and Freedom Party ticket headed by Gloria La Riva. Running as a symbolic, single-state ticket in California only, they won sixty-six thousand state votes. In his later years, buoyed by a rising wave of Native entrepreneurial energy, Banks launched a successful wild rice and maple syrup business on his Leech Lake homeland, fighting agribusiness efforts to merchandise genetically engineered rice.

Even next-generation critics of AIM, like Ojibwe-raised scholar and author David Treuer—who argues that the organization was plagued by "ineffectiveness, violence and chauvinism"—acknowledges its lasting accomplishments, including "schools and job-training programs and housing" in cities like Minneapolis where AIM enjoyed political leverage. More broadly, Treuer affirms that "Indian life had become Indian again, due in no small part to" AIM's militant activism.

This vibrancy of Native life was on full display at Standing Rock Reservation in 2016, which grew from a local protest against the Dakota Access Pipeline—an oil line from the Bakken shale fields that was planned to snake under the tribe's main water source—into an inspiring community model of how an emerging American resistance can be organized. Dozens of colorful flags fluttered over the sprawling protest camp, denoting the many tribes that had sent representatives. Their ranks were swelled by thousands of environmental and human rights activists from all over America and the world. The Standing Rock crusade to protect water—the source of all life—struck a deep global chord.

Contrary to Treuer's criticism of AIM, the Standing Rock protest's strong organization and internal discipline echoed the Wounded Knee resistance. Both epic actions were defined by female-heavy leadership; daily camp meetings; tightly run committees to oversee food preparation, medical care, legal aid and other essential services; a savvy media operation; a wide network of outside supporters; rigorous security precautions; and a strong spiritual foundation.

Like Madonna Thunder Hawk, Dennis Banks was greeted as a hero when he came to Standing Rock, where he spent a total of ten weeks. Nearing eighty, he still was a riveting figure and a passionate speaker, given to wearing a mix of traditional Indian clothing and jewelry with modern touches like dark, round shades and stylish hats. Banks recognized how Wounded Knee had both inspired the thrilling festival of resistance at Standing Rock, and been superseded by it. "I sense a much stronger [Indian] nation this time," he told a reporter at Standing Rock in October 2016. Banks and Thunder Hawk were reunited with many of their fellow Wounded Knee warriors at Standing Rock, and were also joined by many of their children and grandchildren. Young water protectors on the front lines at Standing Rock—who were being tear-gassed, beaten, and hit by rubber bullets fired by the militarized forces surrounding their camp—gained courage from listening to Banks's stories of the Wounded Knee resistance.

As Banks admiringly noted, Standing Rock was explicitly organized on nonviolent principles, with guns strictly banned at the camp. But not all Wounded Knee veterans agreed with the Standing Rock strategy. AIM security chief Cuny Dog, who participated in both actions, ruefully observed that following President Donald Trump's inauguration in January 2017, the astonishingly vibrant Standing Rock camp was swept away overnight by the energy consortium's militarized forces. "If we had told the other side at Standing Rock that we have warriors that are armed and dangerous, it would've been a whole different thing," Cuny asserted.

And yet, in July 2020, an environmental lawsuit filed by the Standing Rock tribe against the pipeline again put the "black snake," which by then was funneling over five hundred thousand barrels of crude oil a day, at risk of being legally shut down. The presidential election of Joe Biden later that year sank the controversial pipeline in even deeper jeopardy. Again, the Indians lived to fight another day. "We're in it for the long haul," Madonna Thunder Hawk declared about the environmental battle.

IN LATER YEARS, Russell Means pursued a successful acting career in Hollywood and was sometimes drawn into eccentric political adventures, like joining pornography mogul Larry Flynt's presidential ticket in 1984. The often-abrasive Means alienated many of his old AIM comrades. But Banks stayed close to him, visiting him at his ranch on the Pine Ridge Reservation in 2012, as his longtime friend was wasting away from the esophageal cancer that would kill him at age seventy-two. Means had cut off his braids soon before his cancer diagnosis, in a traditional Lakota gesture meant to release his teeming memories into the spirit world.

Means said he didn't fear death, because he didn't believe it was the end. "Indigenous people know that there is no beginning and no end," he wrote. "If the rest of the human race would accept that, feel that, live that, they would no longer fear the unknown, they would no longer fear the darkness called death."

Means felt only pride in what he had accomplished with AIM. "Just about every admirable quality that remains in today's Indian people is the result of the American Indian Movement's flint striking the white man's steel. . . . We lit a fire across Indian country."

But despite his brawling ways and sometimes violent rhetoric, Means came to a surprising conclusion near the end. "I have swallowed my share of official violence, and I now feel that real change cannot come except through nonviolence," he declared.

A younger Native activist joined Banks and Means as they were having their final conversation in Means's study. "Within minutes," the activist said afterward, laughing, "these guys were planning their next action, giving me instructions and all the rest."

Dennis Banks died of complications from open-heart surgery at age eighty, in October 2017, almost exactly five years after Means's death. Before Banks died, his former scout Lenny Foster, who had stayed in touch with the AIM leader ever since Wounded Knee, bid him farewell on his next journey into the night.

Acknowledgments

This book is a family enterprise. It was coauthored by a brother and sister, David and Margaret Talbot, with help from journalist and author Arthur Allen—Margaret's husband—who wrote the chapter on Cesar Chavez, Dolores Huerta, and the United Farm Workers. The book also benefited from the astute editorial advice of Camille Peri, David's wife and another author in the family. We couldn't have done it without you two.

We're grateful to our siblings, Stephen Talbot, a documentary filmmaker and veteran of the Vietnam antiwar movement; and Cindy Talbot, a doctor who worked in the women's health movement, for their own memories and observations of the political, social, and cultural transformations we write about here. And to our children, Joe Talbot, Nat Talbot, Ike Allen, and Lucy Allen, and to their friends, for helping keep us attuned to current ones.

We're also grateful for the assistance of Karen Croft, Josie Abugov, Annie Rosenthal, Caroline Hunter Wallis, and Talia Weinreb.

We want to thank Jennifer Barth, our HarperCollins editor,

who conceived this book idea and whose firm belief in the enterprise sustained us through years of unforeseen upheaval. David's agent, Sloan Harris of International Creative Management, was also a steady source of counsel and support.

Most important, we express our gratitude to the archivists and activists who thought to record and preserve some of the important stories of the second American Revolution, and a special appreciation to the participants in this turbulent history who shared their stories directly with us over the years: Tom Hayden, Jane Fonda, Anne Weills, Robert Scheer, Bill Zimmerman, Fred Branfman, Steve Wasserman, Bobby Seale, Kathleen Cleaver, David Weir, Kate Coleman, Stephen Shames, Heather Booth, Judith Arcana, Jeanne Galatzer-Levy, Amy Kesselman, Eleanor Oliver, Abby Pariser, Vivian Rothstein, Martha Scott, Sheila Smith, Dolores Huerta, Luis Valdez, Marshall Ganz, Eliseo Medina, Fred Ross Jr., Kim Brinster, Ellen Broidy, Ed Hermance, Fred Sargeant, Martha Shelley, David Fenton, Craig Pyes, Dennis Banks, Madonna Thunder Hawk, Lenny Foster, Sacheen Littlefeather, and Don Cuny.

We're also pleased the book includes the on-the-scene photography of Stephen Shames, more of whose work can be found in *Power to the People: The World of the Black Panthers*; David Fenton, whose collection is titled *Shots: An American Photographer's Journal, 1967–1972*; and Kevin McKiernan, maker of the documentary film *From Wounded Knee to Standing Rock*.

David: This book marks a full circle in a career as a journalist and historian dedicated to chronicling America's epic drama. As an activist from the 1960s on, and as a writer, I've long grappled with the dark mysteries of US democracy and the flawed heroes who fought to breathe life into the American myth. I worked on some of their radical campaigns, I came to know some of them personally, and I interviewed some in depth for this book. Their unfinished crusades illuminate our nation's tragedy, and its hope.

Margaret: As the youngest in a family of four, who came of age a little too late to be an eyewitness or participant in the movements chronicled here, working on this book was a reminder of all the ways I've benefited from them. In particular, women's liberation's fight for reproductive freedoms, less constricting gender roles, and more egalitarian relationships has made my life, like many other people's in my generation and my children's, more fulfilling in so many ways.

Notes

Introduction

1   Turned "America into the most liberal": Gordon S. Wood, *The Radicalism of the American Revolution* (New York: Vintage, 1993), 6–7.

2   "America never was America to me": Langston Hughes, "Let America Be America Again," Poetry Foundation, https://www.poetryfoundation.org/poems/147907/let-america-be-america-again.

3   "I would never have drawn my sword in the cause of America": Gary B. Nash, *The Unknown American Revolution: The Unruly Birth of Democracy and the Struggle to Create America* (New York: Penguin Books, 2006), 434.

3   "Eighty years later": Nash, *The Unknown American Revolution*, 435.

4   "remember the ladies": Alan Taylor, *American Revolutions: A Continental History, 1750–1804* (New York: Norton), 452.

4   "our Struggle has loosened the bands of Government": Nash, *The Unknown American Revolution*, 127.

4   his famous Independence Day address: David W. Blight, *Frederick Douglass: Prophet of Freedom* (New York: Simon & Schuster, 2018), 229–36.

6   "Well, I am tired": Raoul Peck, "James Baldwin Was Right All Along," *The Atlantic*, July 3, 2020.

10 "certain people" were "crazy" enough: *Soundtracks: Songs That Defined History* documentary, CNN, April 2017.

11 "Why America May Go to Hell": Martin Luther King Jr., *The Radical King*, ed. Cornel West (Boston: Beacon, 2015), ix.

11 almost universally denounced: David J. Garrow, "When Martin Luther King Came Out Against Vietnam," *New York Times*, April 4, 2017.

12 "Martin was preparing to not just march": Interview with David Talbot.

13 "emotional and moral plain-speaking": Maurice Isserman and Michael Kazin, *America Divided: The Civil War of the 1960s* (New York; Oxford, U.K.: Oxford University Press, 2015), 171.

14 "Simply put, an ambitious, active left": Jamelle Bouie, "If Biden Wants to Be Like F.D.R., He Needs the Left," *New York Times*, November 20, 2020.

14 "Someday soon, I'll be gone": Interview by David Talbot.

The Purity of Protest and the Complexity of Politics: Tom Hayden, Jane Fonda, and the Red Family

17 after interviewing a "courteous, gentle" Martin Luther King Jr.: Tom Hayden interview, Activist Video Archive, https://activistvideoarchive.org/archive-library-1/2018/6/8/tom-hayden.

17 A "golden age" that glowed with the heroism: Hayden interview, Activist Video Archive.

17 These three epic blows "permanently derailed what remained of the hopes": Tom Hayden, *Writings for a Democratic Society: The Tom Hayden Reader* (San Francisco: City Lights, 2008), 386.

19 "a medieval torture chamber": "The Chicago 7 Go On Trial": History, September 22, 2020, https://www.history.com/this-day-in-history/the-chicago-seven-go-on-trial.

19   Hayden always cited homegrown populists: Hayden, *Writings*, 417–18; and interview, Activist Video Archive.

19   Dylan (who attended one or two early SDS meetings): Hayden, *Writings*, 378.

20   "Tom and I went to Fred's apartment": Interview by David Talbot.

21   "You are going to jail": Hayden, *Reunion: A Memoir* (New York: Collier, 1988), 370.

21   the group's "sinister attraction": Hayden, *Reunion*, 359.

21   "Anne and I were not the same people": Interview by David Talbot.

22   "He just totally identified with it": Interview by David Talbot.

22   "The fatalist in me": Hayden, *Reunion*, 371.

23   The Flint gathering was feverish: Arthur M. Eckstein, *Bad Moon Rising: How the Weather Underground Beat the FBI and Lost the Revolution* (New Haven, CT: Yale University Press, 2016), 78–80.

23   "Dig it, they murdered those pigs": Eckstein, *Bad Moon Rising*, 78.

24   Weather's dark catacombs: Interview by David Talbot.

24   "My high school mates cut each other": Steve Wasserman, "Remembering Tom Hayden," *The Nation*, October 26, 2016.

25   "everything around me continued to decay": Hayden, *Reunion*, 415.

25   "We were involved in some serious things": Interview by David Talbot.

25   "One of the things I loved most": Interview by David Talbot.

26   Hayden later labeled "a fanatic dreamer": Eckstein, *Bad Moon Rising*, 18.

27   "so obstinate no man is ever going to want you": Interview by David Talbot.

27   "They decided to do this just as women": Interview by David Talbot.

28   "Hayden's collective": Hayden, *Reunion*, 424.

28 "I don't think Bob ever really loved Tom": Interview by David Talbot.

28 the "complexity . . . is always denied": Interview by David Talbot.

28 Hayden found these meetings to be "torture sessions": Hayden, *Reunion*, 421.

29 "whose parents subscribed to the idiotic view": Interview by David Talbot.

30 "I was drawn to the Berkeley collective": Hayden, *Reunion*, 424.

30 "wanting to be the great white hero": Interview by David Talbot.

31 Hayden "reacted angrily and defensively": Hayden, *Reunion*, 425.

32 Berkeley radicals were skeptical of Scheer's plunge: Interview by David Talbot.

32 "We even made a document that I found years later": Interview by David Talbot.

32 The "self-imposed failures": Hayden, *Reunion*, xv.

33 "I didn't want to be bothered with being Tom Hayden": Hayden, *Reunion*, 427.

33 "It was like the monkey is off my back!": Interview by David Talbot.

34 "a tiny Marxist splinter group": Hayden, *Reunion*, 426.

34 eventually writing a book: Tom Hayden, *The Love of Possession Is a Disease with Them* (New York: Holt, Rinehart and Winston, 1972).

34 he too had lost his "mooring": Hayden, *Reunion*, 428.

35 "No matter how hard and honest I tried to be": Hayden, *Reunion*, 432.

37 "I had come full circle": Hayden, *Reunion*, 439.

37 A lifetime of "men defining me": Jane Fonda in *Jane Fonda in Five Acts* documentary, produced by Susan Lacy, HBO, 2018.

37 returning home from France "to be with my people": Jane Fonda in *Five Acts*.

37 He found her "shrill": Hayden, *Reunion*, 440.

38 "He was a movement hero": Jane Fonda in *Five Acts*.

38 he was wearing rubber sandals: Speech by Jane Fonda at Tom Hayden memorial service, UCLA, February 19, 2017.

39 "Tom came to see me in Berkeley": Interview by David Talbot.

39 arrested on trumped-up drug smuggling charges: "Jane Fonda Spent a Night in Jail in 1970. Her Mug Shot Defined Feminist Rebellion," *Washington Post*, November 22, 2019.

40 Hoover tried to discredit Fonda by authorizing a fake letter: "'70 Effort by Hoover to Discredit Jane Fonda Described in Memo," *New York Times*, December 16, 1975.

40 Fonda was also the target: Donald R. Katz, "Jane Fonda Is a Hard Act to Follow," *Rolling Stone*, March 9, 1978, https://www.rollingstone.com/movies/movie-features/jane-fonda-is-a-hard-act-to-follow-45410/.

40 "It was Tom's idea to go to the grassroots": Jane Fonda in *Five Acts*.

40 "Rather than withdrawing into personal happiness": Hayden, *Reunion*, 448.

42 One visitor remembered a Fourth of July gathering: Interview with Stephen Talbot, by David Talbot.

42 "I would come home [from school]": Jane Fonda in *Five Acts*.

43 "walked into a starry Washington night": Hayden, *Reunion*, 460.

44 "We need to resist the military occupation of our minds": Tom Hayden, *Hell No: The Forgotten Power of the Peace Movement* (New Haven, CT: Yale University Press, 2017), 11.

44 "allow me to change my status": Hayden, *Reunion*, 467.

45 "I thought a Senate campaign would impose a discipline": Interview by David Talbot.

45 "We've seen many candidates come and go": Hayden, *Reunion*, 468.

46 "I figured I didn't know anything": Interview by David Talbot.

47 Like Zimmerman: Bill Zimmerman, *Troublemaker: A Memoir from the Front Lines of the Sixties* (New York: Doubleday, 2011).

50 "Big bump, and my brain exploded": Interview by David Talbot.

51 "I covered Tom's Senate campaign": Interview by David Talbot.

52   Even "dismissive" of the Hayden race: Interview by David Talbot.

52   Described as an "intersectional" feminist: Maggie Doherty, "The Fighter," *New York Review of Books*, November 5, 2020.

53   "I will never forget his answer": Branfman memoir, 526.

53   "I was not from California": Interview by David Talbot.

55   Branfman had been "in awe" of "Jane of Arc": Branfman memoir, 543.

55   "We're not interested in being protesters": David Talbot and Barbara Zheutlin, *Creative Differences: Profiles of Hollywood Dissidents* (Boston: South End Press, 1978), 138.

56   "To put it simply, . . . Jane was kept in her place": Branfman memoir, 561.

56   "I received a call from a colleague": Branfman memoir, 564.

56   "neither Tom or I were very big": Jane Fonda in *Five Acts*.

57   "You're living with someone who": Jane Fonda in *Five Acts*.

58   "There were few people in the New Left": Interview by David Talbot.

59   "I still feel I owe him a great deal": Branfman memoir, 589.

59   "What was effective about Tom": Interview by David Talbot.

60   "It took Tom and I years to get friendly again": Interview by David Talbot.

Revolution Has Come, Time to Pick Up the Gun: Bobby Seale, Huey Newton, Eldridge Cleaver, and the Black Panthers

61   comfortable with guns: Interview by David Talbot.

61   he called it "unjust": Bobby Seale, *Seize the Time* (New York: Vintage, 1970), 5.

62   another African American teenager: Interview by David Talbot.

62   "more sense than that": Interview by David Talbot.

62   Seale's air force service . . . was tempestuous: Interview by David Talbot; Seale, *Seize the Time*, 7–11.

63   "If you want to fire me": Seale, *Seize the Time*, 11–12 .

64 "I was stupid": Seale, 12.

64 Seale went to hear the Reverend Martin Luther King Jr.: Interview by David Talbot.

65 "one-man riot": Stephen Shames and Bobby Seale, *Power to the People: The World of the Black Panthers* (New York: Abrams, 2016), 22.

66 stabbing a man with a steak knife: Joshua Bloom and Waldo E. Martin Jr., *Black against Empire: The History and Politics of the Black Panther Party* (Oakland: University of California Press, 2016), 30.

66 "don't know enough about their history": Shames and Seale, *Power to the People*, 22.

67 "Huey was something else": Seale, *Seize the Time*, 83.

67 his "bravery was sometimes just spontaneous and stupid": Interview by David Talbot.

67 Newton "didn't believe he could die": Seale, *Seize the Time*, 16.

68 "I ran up behind Huey as he was charging": Interview by David Talbot.

68 "See that Bank of America over there": Interview by David Talbot.

69 On the night of October 5, 1957, Williams organized a group of men: Charles E. Cobb Jr., *This Nonviolent Stuff'll Get You Killed* (New York: Basic Books, 2014), 111.

69 "This nonviolent stuff ain't no good": Cobb, *This Nonviolent Stuff'll Get You Killed*, 7.

69 described King's parsonage as "an arsenal": Cobb, 7.

70 "The claim that armed self-defense": Cobb, 1.

71 an animal that "moves back until it is cornered": Bloom and Martin, *Black against Empire*, 42.

71 "while Bobby and I were rapping": Bloom and Martin, 44.

71 "There was absolutely no difference": *The Black Panthers: Vanguard of the Revolution*, directed by Stanley Nelson, PBS, 2016.

71 John Reading, summoned the city council: Bloom and Martin, *Black against Empire*, 38.

72 the Community Alert Patrol complained that police so often harassed them: Bloom and Martin, 39.

72 "We're not just doing self-defense for its own sake": Interview by David Talbot.

74 "Huey! Huey! A block away, a police car is on the right": Shames and Seale, *Power to the People*, 25.

75 "Everyone was trained how to hold their guns": Interview by David Talbot.

75 "Them ain't no sticks, Jimmy": Shames and Seale, *Power to the People*, 25.

76 "I would pace around": Interview by David Talbot.

76 "A California State Supreme Court ruling states": Shames and Seale, *Power to the People*, 25.

76 "Some sister was standing on the sidewalk": Interview by David Talbot.

77 "Ladies and gentlemen, my name is Bobby Seale": Interview by David Talbot.

77 "We were not thugs": Interview by David Talbot.

78 "we might not ever come back home one day": Seale, *Seize the Time*, 91.

79 "I'm with you, Huey": Seale.

79 "OK, you big, fat, racist pig": Seale, 128.

79 In April, the Panthers raised the stakes with police: Bloom and Martin, *Black against Empire*, 52–57.

80 "to handle any press in case something went wrong": Shames and Seale, *Power to the People*, 27.

80 He delivered a powerful, prepared statement: Bloom and Martin, *Black against Empire*, 59.

81 "As far as I'm concerned it's beautiful that we finally got an organization that don't walk around singing": Bloom and Martin, 62.

82 *Work out, soul brother!*: Bloom and Martin, 50.

83 "We shall have our manhood": Eldridge Cleaver, *Soul on Ice* (New York: Delta, 1999), 16.

83 "I'll beat him to death with a marshmallow": Nelson, *The Black Panthers.*

83 "He was like Richard Pryor as a Communist": Interview by David Talbot.

84 "Huey P. Newton was a gun-toting gangster": Eldridge Cleaver interview, *Frontline*, PBS, 1997, https://www.pbs.org/wgbh /pages/frontline/shows/race/interviews/ecleaver.html.

84 "He'd be writing things in the newspaper": Interview by David Talbot.

86 "He was studying for his role in *Burn!*": Interview by David Talbot.

86 "One day Brando called me up": Interview by David Talbot.

87 "We saw ourselves as providing backbone": Cleaver interview, *Frontline.*

87 "'I'm very honored that you're calling'": Interview by David Talbot.

89 "I will tell anybody that that was the first experience of freedom": Cleaver interview, *Frontline.*

89 "I was already squeezing the trigger": Cleaver interview, *Frontline.*

89 "That could've been my son lying there": "Marlon Brando Eulogizes Black Panther Bobby Hutton (1968)," San Francisco Bay Area Television Archive, Intelligent Channel, https://www .youtube.com/watch?v=1g05Sb9CcnE.

90 "There was no discipline": Shames and Seale, *Power to the People*, 51.

90 "I never saw the evil Eldridge": Interview by David Talbot.

92 the breakfast program became an immediate success: Bloom and Martin, *Black against Empire*, 182.

93 "One of the ironies of the Black Panther Party": Nelson, *The Black Panthers.*

93 "I was very young but I realized I had to step forward": Interview for Oakland Museum of California exhibition All Power to the People: Black Panthers at 50, October 2016.

93 "steaming platters of fried chicken and soul food": Interview for OMCA exhibition.

93   "the Black Panther Party, without question, represents the greatest threat": Bloom and Martin, *Black against Empire*, 210.

94   "No aspect of the Black Panther program was of greater concern to the FBI": Bloom and Martin, 211.

95   "Never had I experienced so much death": Interview for OMCA exhibition.

96   "Abbie Hoffman and Jerry Rubin were great. . . . John [Lennon] got in touch with me": Interview by David Talbot.

97   He was targeted by an FBI disinformation campaign: Joe Street, "The Shadow of the Soul Breaker: Solitary Confinement, Cocaine, and the Decline of Huey P. Newton," *Pacific Historical Review* 84, no. 3 (August 1, 2015), 333–63.

97   Newton ventured outside: Elaine Brown, *A Taste of Power: A Black Woman's Story* (New York: Anchor Books, 1994), 282.

98   "It appears Newton may be on the brink of mental collapse": Street, "The Shadow of the Soul Breaker."

98   "When he was sober, Huey Newton was brilliant": Interview by David Talbot.

99   "There was a big difference before and after he went to jail": Interview by David Talbot.

100   "It is inconceivable that incarceration had no [psychological] impact on Newton": Street, "The Shadow of the Soul Breaker."

100   "Niggers on the street don't like 'pretty niggers'": Brown, *A Taste of Power*, 252.

100   Newton called Cleaver a "coward": "Huey P. Newton vs. Eldridge Cleaver," *AM* (talk show), https://www.youtube.com/watch?v=XHHcUQuZzw4.

101   House Committee on Internal Security: Bloom and Martin, *Black against Empire*, 339.

101   "Huey didn't want any other strong leaders": Interview by David Talbot.

102   "You didn't get these [Panther] brothers from revolutionary heaven": Nelson, *The Black Panthers*.

102 "At dawn every day, Bobby pushed us onto the streets": Brown, *A Taste of Power*, 324.

103 "He hid his shit from me": Interview by David Talbot.

103 Seale received a tip: Interview by David Talbot.

103 "I would've gotten rid of Huey": Interview by David Talbot.

104 "You've been believing your own lies too long, Bobby": Brown, *A Taste of Power*, 350.

105 "Huey and Elaine never threatened me": Interview by David Talbot.

106 Huey Newton was long gone: "Police Arrest Suspect in Newton Killing," Associated Press, August 25, 1989.

106 "I'm telling you after I ran into the Egyptian police": Cleaver interview, *Frontline*.

107 Cleaver finally publicly acknowledged the truth: Kate Coleman, "Souled Out," *New West*, May 19, 1980.

107 "The Black Panther Party appeared like a comet": Quoted in All Power to the People OMCA curatorial statement.

108 "Ladies and gentlemen, my name is Bobby Seale": Interview by David Talbot.

Sisterhood Is Blooming: Heather Booth and the Women of Jane

109 Jeanne Galatzer-Levy's story and quotes: Interview with Jeanne Galatzer-Levy by Margaret Talbot, June 2020.

110 "stewardess with a radical feminist consciousness": Interview with J.P.A., 1980, Jane Collective Archive Interviews, Special Collections, University of Illinois, Chicago.

113 Sheila Smith's story and quotes: Interview with Sheila Smith by Margaret Talbot, June 2020.

113 "it was alright to be, you know, sleeping with somebody": Redstockings Abortion Speakout, Washington Square Methodist Church, New York City, March 21, 1969, https://archive.org /details/RedstockingsAbortionSpeakoutNewYork1969March21 /Part+3+-+Redstockings+Abortion+Speakout+New+York+1969 +March+21.m4a.

113 "a very fine clinic": Redstockings Abortion Speakout.

114 "It is absolutely essential that we conduct sufficient investigation": UPI, "Women Activists Called 4-Year Target of Hoover," *New York Times*, February 7, 1997; for broader discussion of the FBI targeting of the women's movement, see Ruth Rosen, *The World Split Open: How the Modern Women's Movement Changed America* (New York: Penguin Books, 2006), 239–60.

116 "These are the police": Interview with Jeanne Galatzer-Levy by Margaret Talbot.

117 "inclusive, reasoned, humorous, and egalitarian": Amy Kesselman with Heather Booth, Vivian Rothstein, and Naomi Weisstein, "Our Gang of Four: Friendship and Women's Liberation," in *The Feminist Memoir Project: Voices from Women's Liberation*, edited by Rachel Blau Duplessis and Ann Snitow (New York: Three Rivers, 1998), 36.

117 "The people who were too this or too that," and Heather Booth's childhood, high school, and college years: Interviews with Heather Booth by Margaret Talbot, January 2019, July 2019, and June 2020, and with David Talbot, September 2017; see also *Heather Booth: Changing the World*, directed by Lilly Rivlin (Women Make Movies, 2016).

119 "These students bring the rest of the country with them": Josh Zeitz, "The Tragic Success of Freedom Summer," Politico, June 19, 2014.

119 "an intellectual and creative vacuum in the lives": "Charlie Cobb," SNCC Digital Gateway, https://snccdigital.org/people/charlie-cobb/.

120 "unbigoted turn of mind," and details of Casey Hayden's upbringing: Casey Hayden, "Fields of Blue," in *Deep in Our Hearts: Nine White Women in the Freedom Movement* (Athens: University of Georgia Press, 2002), 335–40.

120 a "Southern voice so soft it would not startle a boll weevil"; "What are you doing in there, Henry?"; "the ability to think morally": Harold L. Smith, "Casey Hayden: Gender and the Origins of SNCC, SDS, and the Women's Liberation Movement," in *Texas Women: Their Histories, Their Lives*, ed. Elizabeth Hayes Turner, Stephanie Cole, and Rebecca Sharpless (Athens: University of Georgia Press, 2015), 364–65.

121   Watching film of white sheriff, and "We cried over you in the staff meeting": Elizabeth Martinez, ed., *Letters from Mississippi: Reports from Civil Rights Volunteers & Poetry of the 1964 Freedom Summer* (Brookline, MA: Zephyr Press, 2007), 8.

122   "this case, like so many others that have come before": *Freedom Summer,* directed by Stanley Nelson, *American Experience,* PBS, 2014.

122   "how much it takes to make a child"; "I thought of how much it took to make a Herbert Lee": Martinez, ed., *Letters from Mississippi,* 170.

123   Bob Moses, speech: Martinez, ed., 36–37; see also interviews with Marshall Ganz, Heather Booth, and Pam Allen in *Freedom on My Mind* documentary, directed by Connie Field and Marilyn Mulford (Clarity Films, 1994).

124   "Well, boys, you've done a good job": Howard Ball, *Murder in Mississippi* (Lawrence: University Press of Kansas, 2004), 62.

125   John Dittmer tally: John Dittmer, *Local People: The Struggle for Civil Rights in Mississippi* (Urbana and Chicago: University of Illinois Press, 1995), 251.

125   "sad, angry, and guilty;" "believing that the police were your friends": Wesley C. Hogan, *Many Minds, One Heart: SNCC's Dream for a New America* (Chapel Hill: University of North Carolina Press, 2007), 173.

125   "Last night I was a long time before sleeping": Martinez, ed., *Letters from Mississippi,* 169.

126   Heather's inability to speak at all for several days when she came home: Interview with Margaret Talbot, June 2020.

127   "I guess if I'd had any sense": DeNeen L. Brown, "Civil Rights Crusade Fannie Lou Hamer Defied Men—and Presidents—Who Tried to Silence Her," *Washington Post,* October 6, 2017.

127   "conveyed a moral core"; "that if you organize, you can change the world"; "There are sometimes unjust laws": Interviews with Heather Booth by Margaret Talbot, July 2019 and June 2020.

129   Heather's initial contacts with Dr. Howard: Interviews with Heather Booth by Margaret Talbot, January 2019 and July 2019; for more on Dr. Howard, see David T. Beito and Linda Royster

Beito, *Black Maverick: T.R.M. Howard's Fight for Civil Rights and Economic Power* (Urbana and Chicago: University of Illinois Press, 2009).

130   "The subject was present": Red Squad Collection, Research Center, Chicago History Museum, file cards on Heather Booth.

131   "they needed to talk alone together and get their act together": Interview with Heather Booth by Margaret Talbot, July 2019; the incident is discussed in detail in Sara Evans, *Personal Politics: The Roots of Women's Liberation in the Civil Rights Movement and the New Left* (New York: Vintage, 1980), 162–63.

131   "Cool down, little girl": Evans, *Personal Politics*, 199; Jo Freeman aka Joreen, "On the Origins of the Women's Liberation Movement from a Strictly Personal Perspective," in DuPlessis and Snitow, eds., *Feminist Memoir Project*, 180.

132   "Women must take control of our bodies": Susan Brownmiller, *In Our Time: Memoir of a Revolution* (New York: Dell Publishing, 1999), 57; the incident is also recalled in "She's Beautiful When She's Angry."

132   "We were smart, we were dedicated": DuPlessis and Snitow, eds., *Feminist Memoir Project*, 35.

132   the women "were always there and were respected": Evans, *Personal Politics*, 109.

133   the Westside Group: See Kesselman, Booth, Rothstein, and Weisstein, "Our Gang of Four: Friendship and Women's Liberation," in DuPlessis and Snitow, eds., *Feminist Memoir Project*, 25–53; and Joyce Antler, *Jewish Radical Feminism: Voices from the Women's Liberation Movement* (New York: New York University Press, 2018), 31–70.

133   "The best part of the group was that we all took each other seriously": DuPlessis and Snitow, eds., *Feminist Memoir Project*, 38.

133   "Jackie Kennedy our sister or our enemy"; "when a movement starts": DuPlessis and Snitow, eds., *Feminist Memoir Project*, 40.

134   Vivian Rothstein's uniform idea: Email from Vivian Rothstein to Margaret Talbot, June 2020.

134   "steer a generous course away from": DuPlessis and Snitow, eds., *Feminist Memoir Project*, 42.

135 "Knowledge is power," and WITCH zaps: Interview with Heather Booth by Margaret Talbot, July 2019; interview with Amy Kesselman by Margaret Talbot, June 2020; and "Episode 8: WITCH in Action" podcast, Jewish Women's Archive, October 27, 2016, https://jwa.org/podcasts/canwetalk/witch-in-action.

135 "was one of the few New Left men who took me seriously": Email from Vivian Rothstein to Margaret Talbot, June 2020.

137 *If he can do this, and do it well:* Interview with Judith Arcana by Margaret Talbot, June 2020.

138 the baby they already had "made too much noise": "She Said," from Judith Arcana, *What if Your Mother* (Goshen, CT: Chicory Blue Press, Inc., 2005), 85

140 "might be held at a women's center": Michelle Murphy, "Immodest Witnessing: The Epistemology of Vaginal Self-Examination in the U.S. Feminist Self-Help Movement," *Feminist Studies* 30, no. 1 (Spring 2004), 115–47; for more on the women's health movement, see Wendy Kline, *Bodies of Knowledge: Sexuality, Reproduction, and Women's Health in the Second Wave* (Chicago: University of Chicago Press, 2010); for feminist interpretation of women's health history, see, for example, Deirdre English and Barbara Ehrenreich, *Witches, Midwives, and Nurses: A History of Women Healers* (New York: Feminist Press, 2010).

141 "People who had post-partum depressions": "Our Bodies, Ourselves Collective," website of the film *She's Beautiful When She's Angry*, http://www.shesbeautifulwhenshesangry.com/obos.

141 "abortion is a safe, simple, relatively painless": Abortion Counseling Service, *Abortion: A Woman's Decision, A Woman's Right*, reprinted in *Jane: Documents from a Clandestine Abortion Service, 1968–1973* (Baltimore: Firestarter Press, 2004), 8.

141 "we always tried to get away from thinking of women as objects": Interview with Jody Parsons, one of the key figures in Jane, interview with J.P., Jane Collective Archive Interviews, Special Collections, University of Illinois, Chicago.

142 "Lorry" anecdote: Interview with Lorry, November 26, 1992, Paula Kamen Collection, discussed in Leslie J. Reagan, *When Abortion Was a Crime: Women, Medicine, and Law in the United*

States, 1867–1973 (Berkeley: University of California Press, 1997), 226.

142   "like a twenty-year-old poor person": Interview with Jeanne Galatzer-Levy by Margaret Talbot, June 2020.

142   "wanted to be there for women to see": Laura Kaplan, *The Story of Jane: The Legendary Underground Feminist Abortion Service* (Chicago: University of Chicago Press, 1997), 211.

143   "revolutionary strength lies in the fact that we outnumber the pigs": Sherie M. Randolph, *Florynce "Flo" Kennedy: The Life of a Black Feminist Radical* (Chapel Hill: The University of North Carolina Press, 2015), 180.

143   "to raise the issue of abortion": Linda Averill interview with Nina Harding, "How We Won Abortion Rights," April 2004, Freedom Socialist Party, https://dev.socialism.com/fs-article/how-we-won-abortion-rights/.

143   "too far removed from a cultural past where Black women were": Randolph, *Florynce "Flo" Kennedy*, 182.

144   "big mouths, just like me": Kaplan, *Story of Jane*, 212; "laid-backness, the closeness of the one-to-one": Kaplan, 211–12.

144   When the detectives started casing, and subsequent details of the bust, and the seven women's release from jail, and of Judy Pildes's (Judith Arcana's) story leading up to it: Interviews with Judith Arcana, Jeanne Galatzer-Levy, Abby Pariser, Martha Scott, and Sheila Smith by Margaret Talbot, June 2020; also Kaplan, *Story of Jane*; "Diary Entry 45, Judith, 71," The Abortion Diary podcast, August 2014, https://soundcloud.com/theabortiondiary/diary-entry-45-judith-71-chicago-il-1974; and contemporary news accounts including Associated Press, "Abortion Clinic Raided," May 4, 1972; "Drive Started to Get Funds to Aid 7 Accused in Abortions," May 6, 1972, *Chicago Tribune*; "Defense Fund Forming to Aid Accused Abortionists from Area;" May 10, 1972, *Hyde Park Herald*; "Abortion 7 Case Sent to Grand Jury," *Hyde Park Herald*, August 16, 1972.

147   "We never resolved it as a group": Email from Martha Scott to Margaret Talbot, July 20, 2020.

148 "never spent more than five minutes with his clients": Email from Eleanor Oliver to Margaret Talbot, July 1, 2020.

148 Comparable to those at licensed medical facilities," and "unable to trace any to actions of the collective": Charles R. King, "Calling Jane: The Life and Death of a Women's Illegal Abortion Service," *Women and Health* 20, no. 3 (1993): 88–89.

150 "It is indicative of our "'system of justice'": King, "Calling Jane," 77.

151 The Janes who'd been arrested tried to hang together; "Prevention is a hell of a lot easier than abortion"; "We didn't want to be made into martyrs": Interviews with Judith Arcana, Jeanne Galatzer-Levy, Abby Pariser, and Sheila Smith by Margaret Talbot, June and July 2020.

152 "Queen of the Hopeless," and other details about Joanne Wolfson: Interview with Judith Arcana by Margaret Talbot, June 2020; see also Paula Zekman, "Husband, Wife Defend Courtroom Underdogs," *Chicago Tribune*, December 10, 1970; Jack Star, "Wolfson and Wolfson for the Defense," *Chicago Tribune Magazine*, June 26, 1975; Robert Enstad, "Order Brach Boyfriend to Answer Questions," *Chicago Tribune*, June 15, 1979.

153 the mood "was more subdued than jubilant": Kaplan, *Story of Jane*, 275.

154 searching for absolute truths: Interview with Vivian Rothstein by Margaret Talbot, June 2020.

154 Jo Freeman's "The Tyranny of Structurelessness" and "On Trashing" have been much reproduced and debated over the years. They can be found, among many other places, on her website: https://www.jofreeman.com/joreen/tyranny.htm, https://www.jofreeman.com/joreen/trashing.htm.

154 "The rage against women who stood out in any way": DuPlessis and Snitow, eds., *Feminist Memoir Project*, 51–52.

154 "so acrimonious that she no longer recruited": DuPlessis and Snitow, eds., *Feminist Memoir Project*, 51.

155 "Building an Enduring Democratic Majority": https://prospect.org/power/building-enduring-democratic-majority/; for more on Heather Booth's subsequent activist career, see, for example, *Heather Booth: Changing the World.*

The Martyr Complex: Cesar Chavez, Dolores Huerta, and the Righteousness of La Causa

157   hands of twenty strikebreakers: "Scabs Beat Hirsch," *El Malcriado*, Farmworker Movement Documentation Project (FMDP), February 21, 1968, https://libraries.ucsd.edu /farmworkermovement/ufwarchives/elmalcriado/Dalzell /February%2021,%201968_001.pdf.

157   which was not unusual: Dolores Huerta interview with David Talbot.

158   "value them more": Miriam Pawel, *The Crusades of Cesar Chavez* (New York: Bloomsbury, 2014), 157.

159   bowls of pasta: "Fred Hirsch 1967–1968," FMDP, https:// libraries.ucsd.edu/farmworkermovement/essays/essays/040%20 Hirsch_Fred.pdf.

160   "We lived in barracks": Luis Valdez, interviewed in *Huelga!*, directed by Skeets McGrew (New York: National Educational Television, 1966), https://libraries.ucsd.edu/farmworker movement/medias/videos/.

160   "You get a very lost feeling": Luis Valdez interview.

162   "This is good!": Gilbert Padilla, oral history, "Founding of the National Farm Workers Association (NFWA) 1962," FMDP, https://libraries.ucsd.edu/farmworkermovement/media/oral _history/music/Gilbert%20Padilla%20part%203.mp3.

162   message like a virus: Fred Ross Jr. interview with Arthur Allen, June 25, 2020.

162   on a red background: Gilbert Flores interview with LeRoy Chatfield, December 9, 2008, FMDP, https://libraries.ucsd.edu /farmworkermovement/media/oral_history/jan09/Gilbert%20 Flores.mp3.

163   "do seemed impossible": Richard W. Etulain, ed., *Cesar Chavez: A Brief Biography with Documents* (Boston: Bedfords, 2002), 41.

163   around the valley: Wayne C. Hartmire, "Wayne 'Chris' Hartmire 1962–1989: Support for the Unionization of Farmworkers: Approximately 1961 through 1967," FMDP, https://libraries. ucsd.edu/farmworkermovement/essays/essays/006%20 Hartmire_Chris.pdf.

164   growers and legislators: Marshall Ganz interview with Arthur
      Allen, July 10, 2020.

164   Chavez's brother Richard: Mario T. Garcia, *A Dolores Huerta
      Reader* (Albuquerque: University of New Mexico Press, 2008),
      xvi–xvii.

164   from field organizers: Marshall Ganz, *Why David Sometimes
      Wins: Leadership, Organization, and Strategy in the California
      Farm Worker Movement* (London: Oxford University Press,
      2010), 190–91.

165   return to Delano: Hartmire, "Support for the Unionization of
      Farmworkers."

165   "Alfredo Acosta Figueroa 1965–1979," oral history, FMDP,
      https://libraries.ucsd.edu/farmworkermovement/essays
      /essays/021%20Figueroa_Alfredo.pdf.

165   "as an activist": Luis Valdez interview with David Talbot.

166   "no mysticism, no *chingaderas*": Etulain, *Cesar Chavez: A Brief
      Biography*, 88.

166   sheriff Leroy Gaylen: Larry Tye, "RFK, Cesar Chavez and
      Unfinished Business," *Sacramento Bee*, August 11, 2016, https://
      www.sacbee.com/opinion/op-ed/article94893182.html.

167   pilgrimage through the San Joaquin: Pat Hoffman, "Impact of
      Farmworker Movement on Churches and Church Leaders," oral
      histories, 1985, https://libraries.ucsd.cdu/farmworkermovement
      /medias/oral-history/ (audio) and https://libraries.ucsd.edu/
      farmworkermovement/media/oral_history/INTRO%20TO%20
      AUDIO%20INTERVIEWS.doc.pdf (introduction).

167   biggest agricultural producer: Pawel, *The Crusades of Cesar
      Chavez*, 132–40.

167   in the union election: Ganz, *Why David Sometimes Wins*,
      195–98.

168   "move right in": Peter Matthiessen, *Sal si Puedes (Escape if You
      Can): Cesar Chavez and the New American Revolution* (Berkeley;
      Los Angeles: University of California Press, 2016), 158–59.

168   Meanwhile, DiGiorgio was: Pawel, *The Crusades of Cesar
      Chavez*, 157.

168   a UFW picket line: Frank Bardacke, *Trampling Out the Vintage: Cesar Chavez and the Two Souls of the United Farm Workers* (London: Verso, 2011), 293–94.

169   Ibid., 295.

169   "white" seats in a movie theater: Matthiessen, *Sal si Puedes*, 32.

169   "submarines" into the fields: Matthiessen, *Sal si Puedes*, 34.

169   union cars were common: Bardacke, *Trampling Out the Vintage*, 286–90.

169   "the essence of peace": Cesar Chavez, "We Are Accused," *El Malcriado*, February 21, 1968, FMDP, https://libraries.ucsd.edu /farmworkermovement/ufwarchives/elmalcriado/Dalzell /February%2021,%201968_001.pdf.

170   "assassination of Martin": Miriam Pawel, *The Union of Their Dreams* (New York: Bloomsbury, 2010), 40–42.

170   Huerta said years later: Dolores Huerta interview with David Talbot.

170   "zoomed up": Miriam Pawel, *The Crusades of Cesar Chavez*, 158–59.

170   "went to Toronto": Elaine Woo, "Jessica Govea Thorbourne," 58; "Organizer for UFW Sounded Alarm on Pesticides," *Los Angeles Times*, February 2, 2005, https://www.latimes.com/archives /la-xpm-2005-feb-02-me-thorbourne2-story.html.

171   "acts of any of us": Pawel, *The Crusades of Cesar Chavez*, 159–60.

171   to his organization: Etulain, *Cesar Chavez: A Brief Biography*, 43.

172   "emotions and elicits action": "Bonnie Burns Chatfield 1965–1973," FMDP, https://libraries.ucsd.edu/farmworkermovement/ essays/essays/014%20Chatfield_Bonnie%20Burns.pdf.

172   "part of the Mexican culture": Etulain, *Cesar Chavez: A Brief Biography*, 42–43.

172   all had to stop: Jerry Cohen, "Gringo Justice: The United Farm Workers Union, 1967–1981," February 2008, 14, FMDP, https:// libraries.ucsd.edu/farmworkermovement/essays/essays/Gringo justice.pdf.

173   would change his mind: Cohen, "Gringo Justice," 15–16.

173   Richard Chavez collected: Pawel, *The Crusades of Cesar Chavez*, 160–63.

173   as Communist subversion: Chris Hartmire interview with Rev. William Dew, FMDP, https://libraries.ucsd.edu/farmworker movement/media/oral_history/music/BillDew%20Chris Hartmire.mp3.

173   remain in Delano: Mark R. Day, "Mark R. Day 1967–1970: My Time with the UFW," FMDP, https://libraries.ucsd.edu /farmworkermovement/essays/essays/043%20Day_Mark.pdf.

174   "The episode came": Pawel, *The Crusades of Cesar Chavez*, 199.

174   Their intransigence: Hartmire, "Support for the Unionization of Farmworkers."

174   "I did more organizing": Matthiessen, *Sal si Puedes (Escape if You Can): Cesar Chavez and the New American Revolution* (Berkeley; Los Angeles: University of California Press, 2016), 178–92.

174   "Cesar's eating right now": Cohen, "Gringo Justice," 12.

175   "But for the pervasive": Hirsch essay, FMDP.

175   "over a pass": Jacques E. Levy, *Cesar Chavez: Autobiography of La Causa* (Minneapolis: University of Minnesota Press, 2007), 261.

175   "looked like puppies": Cesar Chavez interview with Charlie Rose, November 25, 1992, https://charlierose.com/videos/12078.

176   "blew the court away": Pat Hoffman interview with Jerry Cohen, 1985, "Impact of Farmworker Movement on Churches and Church Leaders," FMDP, https://libraries.ucsd.edu/farm workermovement/medias/oral-history/.

176   took him seriously: Bardacke, *Trampling Out the Vintage*, 305–6.

176   one witness recalled: Chatfield essay, FMDP.

177   "suffer for others": Wallace Turner, "Head of Farmworkers Union Ends 25-Day Fast in California," *New York Times*, March 11, 1968, https://libraries.ucsd.edu/farmworkermovement/ufwarchives/nyt /AA%201965%20-%201969/022%20MARCH%2011,%201968 %202.pdf.

177   "spent himself like": Cohen, "Gringo Justice," 17.

177   "Lenten period of 1966": Pawel, *The Crusades of Cesar Chavez*, 157.

177 "transformational," said Marshall: Ganz, FMDP, https://libraries
.ucsd.edu/farmworkermovement/media/oral_history/music/new
/MarshallGanz.mp3.

178 "at a key moment": Medina interview with Arthur Allen.

178 as one writer put it: Nat Hentoff cited in Ilan Stavans, foreword,
Matthiessen, *Sal si Puedes*, xlv.

178 "he is, simply, a man": Matthiessen, *Sal si Puedes*, lvi, 315–16.

179 in the South: Fred Ross Jr. interview with Arthur Allen.

179 Celebrities like Leonard Nimoy: Daneen Montoya, "Daneen
Montoya 1968–1973," FMDP, https://libraries.ucsd.edu
/farmworkermovement/essays/essays/050%20Montoya_Daneen
.pdf.

179 "mayor Joseph Alioto": Dick Meister, "Nixon Attacks Boycott,"
San Francisco Chronicle, 1968, https://libraries.ucsd.edu
/farmworkermovement/ufwarchives/meister/16%20Nixon%20
Attacks%20Boycott.pdf.

179 sinister influence: Fred Ross Jr. interview with Arthur Allen.

180 "Vermont, and Syracuse, New York": Richard Chavez,
"California State University Northridge (CSUN): Farmworker
Movement Oral History Project—1995," Chicano Labor History
Project, March 13, 1997, FMDP, https://libraries.ucsd.edu
/farmworkermovement/media/oral_history/music/CSUN%20
TAPES/Chavez,%20Richard.mp3.

180 troops in Vietnam: "Grapes of War," unsigned document, FMDP,
https://libraries.ucsd.edu/farmworkermovement/ufwarchives
/RogeroPitt/02/DEFENSE%20DEPT%20GRAPE%20
PURCHASES.pdf.

180 red letters, "Why?": Levy, *Cesar Chavez*, 290–93.

180 data gathered by the: Jerry B. Brown, "Jerry Brown 1966–1970:
Impact of the Grape Boycott," FMDP, https://libraries.ucsd.edu
/farmworkermovement/essays/essays/029%20Brown_Jerry.pdf.

181 signed the grape contracts: Pawel, *The Crusades of Cesar Chavez*,
214.

181 "get a gut punch": Marshall Ganz interview with Arthur Allen.

181 "Jerry Cohen noted": Cohen, "Gringo Justice," 22.

182   eager for a fight: Marshall Ganz interview with Arthur Allen; Pawel, *The Crusades of Cesar Chavez*, 219.

182   "cause for justice": "Rey Huerta 1968–1975: The Most Memorable Times of Our Lives," FMDP, https://libraries.ucsd.edu /farmworkermovement/essays/essays/053%20Huerta_Rey.pdf.

183   the price doubled: Pawel, *The Crusades of Cesar Chavez*, 218.

183   ordered him released: Pawel, *The Crusades of Cesar Chavez*, 220–26.

183   build a new one: Chavez, television interview, December 1970, diva.sfsu.edu/collections/sfbatv/bundles/190205.

184   "dime an hour": Pawel, *The Union of Their Dreams*, 43–45.

184   "on a broader scale": Pawel, *The Crusades of Cesar Chavez*, 195–96.

184   *"sacrificios"* and *"beneficios"*: Doug Adair, "Doug Adair 1965–1971, 1975–1977," FMDP, https://libraries.ucsd.edu/ farmworkermovement/essays/essays/017%20Adair_Doug.pdf.

185   an "unapproachable father": Bardacke, *Trampling Out the Vintage*, 453.

186   led to neglected administration: Cohen, "Gringo Justice," 22.

186   means to that end: Pawel, *The Union of Their Dreams*, 83–90.

186   opportunity for corruption: Matthiessen, *Sal si Puedes*, 24–25.

187   read people's "auras": Larry Tramutola, "UFW 1975–1980: The New Law, New Challenges, the Game, the Purge," FMDP, https://libraries.ucsd.edu/farmworkermovement/essays/essays /Tramutola%20Larry.pdf.

188   Cohen wrote in 2009: Cohen, "Gringo Justice," 28.

188   "I should have fought": Huerta interview with David Talbot.

189   *Si, se puede!*: Randy Shaw, *Beyond the Fields: Cesar Chavez, the UFW, and the Struggle for Justice in the 21st Century* (Berkeley: University of California Press, 2010), 5–6.

189   "don't regret a minute of it": Medina interview with Arthur Allen.

189   home care workers: Colleen Shalby, "Dolores Huerta Is Arrested Once Again, This Time During Protest to Help Fresno Home Care Workers," *Los Angeles Times*, August 20, 2019.

190   "an American hero": Nathan Heller, "The Rise and Fall of Cesar
       Chavez," *New Yorker*, April 7, 2014.

Liberation Day: Craig Rodwell and the Making of Pride

191   Rodwell's duties at the Fire Island Hotel: Craig Rodwell
       Papers, Manuscripts and Archives Division, New York Public
       Library, Martin Duberman interview with Rodwell for Martin
       Duberman, *Stonewall: The Definitive Story of the LGBTQ Rights
       Uprising That Changed America* (New York: Dutton, 1993),
       161–63.

191   the first three months of rent on a storefront near Washington
       Square: From *The Gay Crusaders*, quoted in Craig Rodwell,
       "Craig Rodwell," *The Stonewall Reader*, ed. The New York Public
       Library (New York: Penguin Books, 2019), 89.

192   Christian Science reading room as a model for the Oscar Wilde
       Memorial Bookshop: Fred Sargeant interview by Margaret
       Talbot, September 2020.

192   Rodwell adamant that Oscar Wilde bookshop would not sell
       porn magazines: Fred Sargeant interview by Margaret Talbot;
       also see, for example, *The Gay Crusaders* excerpt in New York
       Public Library, ed., *The Stonewall Reader*, 90–92.

193   Cruising and "wanted for murder in Kansas or something":
       "Stonewall 50—Minisode 4—Craig Rodwell," *Making Gay
       History: The Podcast*, June 28, 2019, https://makinggayhistory
       .com/podcast/stonewall-50-minisode-4-craig-rodwell/; Craig
       Rodwell Papers, Martin Duberman interview.

193   Harvey Milk: "an enveloping kind of personality," Craig Rodwell
       papers, Martin Duberman interview; "In San Francisco in the
       1970s": Lillian Faderman, *Harvey Milk: His Lives and Death*
       (New Haven, CT: Yale University Press, 2018), 48; "Yes, Harvey,
       you've got a great job": Randy Shilts, *The Mayor of Castro Street:
       The Life and Times of Harvey Milk* (New York: St. Martin's,
       1982), 26.

194   "being myself, being free, being a whole person": "Stonewall
       50—Minisode 4—Craig Rodwell," *Making Gay History:
       The Podcast*; "I can't let it out," Shilts, *The Mayor of Castro
       Street*, 26.

194 "I'm not a censor": Craig Rodwell Papers, newspaper clipping, "The Maturing Craig Rodwell."

195 "One salesman couldn't really believe": New York Public Library, ed., *The Stonewall Reader*, 92.

195 Personal ad that offended Rodwell: "Vito Russo's Our Time: Episode 6: Writers": https://www.youtube.com/watch?v=bbb9jfunymw.

196 How Rodwell stocked the bookstore: Interview with Ellen Broidy by Margaret Talbot; he avoided carrying "books with certain key words": New York Public Library, ed., *The Stonewall Reader*, 91; "There's just a lot more published for": New York Public Library, ed., 92.

197 "the first time in American history that literature had been organized under the subject heading of 'gay culture'": Jim Downs, *Stand by Me: The Forgotten History of Gay Liberation* (New York: Basic Books, 2016), 69.

197 "If and when I tell them": Crag Rodwell Papers, letter from high school student.

197 "be firm with your family": New York Public Library, ed., *The Stonewall Reader*, 93.

197 "kill fags" graffiti: New York Public Library, ed., *The Stonewall Reader*.

198 "weren't ready to support a legitimate bookshop": Craig Rodwell Papers, letter from Craig Rodwell, "Dear Gay Brothers & Sisters," February 1972.

198 Bookstore schnauzers: Interview with Fred Sargeant by Margaret Talbot; "very promiscuous": New York Public Library, ed., *The Stonewall Reader*, 91.

199 "different problems, behavioral problems, weight problems": Craig Rodwell Papers, interview with Martin Duberman.

200 "you big brave man"; Frank incident; "I just told the truth, all the time": Interview with Martin Duberman.

201 "A Quiet Revolution in Mental Care": *New York Times*, May 19, 1968, found in Craig Rodwell Papers.

202 "wrecking": Craig Rodwell Papers, interview with Martin Duberman; described in Duberman, *Stonewall*, 82–83.

203 "He thought it was a compliment": Craig Rodwell Papers, interview with Martin Duberman.

203 Riis Park: "Riis Park Beach," NYC LGBT Historic Sites Project, 2017, https://www.nyclgbtsites.org/site/beach-at-jacob-riis -park/; Christina B. Hanhardt, "Making Community: The Places and Spaces of LGBTQ Collective Identity Formation," National Park Service, 2016, https://www.nps.gov/articles/lgbtqtheme -community.htm.

204 "whenever I turned away from the ocean to face the low cement": Joan Nestle, *A Restricted Country* (Ithaca, NY: Firebrand Books, 1987), 36–37.

204 "very blank and nondescript"; "I remember he took my wallet"; "would stop and search our bags just walking down the street": Craig Rodwell Papers, interview with Martin Duberman.

205 "I decided that's it"; "Just shuffling around in the halls"; "My mind always worked overtime": Craig Rodwell Papers, interview with Martin Duberman.

206 "I was still so madly in love with him": Shilts, *The Mayor of Castro Street*, 28.

207 "Although he is harmless": Craig Rodwell Papers, Mattachine Society brochure.

207 "We weren't accessible to the community at all": Craig Rodwell Papers, interview with Martin Duberman.

207 Chicago Board of Education: Craig Rodwell Papers.

208 "the confidence of an intellectual autocrat": Dudley Clendinen and Adam Nagourney, *Out for Good: The Struggle to Build a Gay Rights Movement in America* (New York: Simon & Schuster, 2001), 113.

208 "Homophile Freedom Song": Eric Cervini, *The Deviant's War: The Homosexual vs. the United States of America* (New York: Farrar, Straus and Giroux, 2020), 233.

209 "patriotic protest": Simon Hall, "The American Gay Rights Movement and Patriotic Protest," *Journal of the History of Sexuality* 19, no. 3 (September 2010), 536–62.

209 "occasion for the assertion of personality, individuality": "Regulations for Picketing," Committee on Picketing and Other

Lawful Demonstrations, Mattachine Society of Washington, Craig Rodwell Papers; for general tenor of the annual reminders, see short film by Lilli Vincenz, *The Second Largest Minority*, 1968, https://blogs.loc.gov/now-see-hear/2014/06/lilli-vincenz/.

209 "Let me assure you": Cervini, *The Deviant's War*, 233.

210 Daughters of Bursitis: Interview with Karla Jay by Gwen Shockey, March 8, 2018, "Addresses Project: Oral History Archive," Gwen Shockey, http://gwenshockeyfineart.com/oral-history-archive/karla-jay.

210 "I can remember Frank saying": Craig Rodwell Papers, interview with Martin Duberman.

211 "I wish this was the old country": Voices of Feminism Oral History Project, Sophia Smith Collection, Smith College, Martha Shelley interviewed by Kelly Anderson, 2003, 13, https://www.smith.edu/libraries/libs/ssc/vof/transcripts/Shelley.pdf.

211 "totally different from kissing boys": ibid., 19.

211 "Older homophile organizations": Interview with Martha Shelley by Margaret Talbot.

212 "tourists staring at us like": Interview with Martha Shelley by Margaret Talbot.

212 "It showed the world, I suppose, that": *Stonewall Uprising: The Year That Changed America*, directed by Kate Davis and David Heilbroner, *American Experience* (PBS, 2020); interview with Martha Shelley.

212 "We were being young brats": Ibid.

215 Kiyoshi Kuromiya activism history: Interview by Marc Stein; Liz Highleyman, "Kiyoshi Kuromiya: Integrating the Issues," in *Smash the Church, Smash the State! The Early Years of Gay Liberation*, ed. Tommi Avicolli Mecca (San Francisco: City Lights Books, 2009), 17–21; Douglas Martin, "Kiyoshi Kuromiya, 57, Fighter for the Rights of AIDS Patients," *New York Times*, May 28, 2000, https://www.nytimes.com/2000/05/28/us/kiyoshi-kuromiya-57-fighter-for-the-rights-of-aids-patients.html; Steve Vaughan, "The Defiant Voices of S.D.S.," *Life*, October 18, 1968.

215 "thought it was absurd, Frank Kameny telling me": Interview by Marc Stein, June 17, 1997, "Kiyoshi Kuromiya, June 17, 1997,"

Philadelphia LGBT History Project, 2009, http://outhistory.org
/exhibits/show/philadelphia-lgbt-interviews/interviews/kiyoshi
-kuromiya.

216 "We didn't announce we were going to storm the bar": Craig
Rodwell Papers, interview with Martin Duberman.

216 "Why shouldn't they be served a drink?": Jay Levin and Normand
Poirier, "Three Test Law That Bars Drinks for Homosexuals,"
New York Post, May 4, 1966, found in Craig Rodwell Papers.

217 "I encountered so many people coming in the door": Interview
with Ellen Broidy by Margaret Talbot.

218 "combination Bedlam and Bastille": John Strausbaugh, *The
Village: 400 Years of Beats and Bohemians, Radicals and Rogues*
(New York: Ecco, 2013), 169.

218 "through whole families calling up": Strausbaugh, *The Village*,
170–71.

218 "an absolute passion to uncover things that": Interview with Ellen
Broidy by Margaret Talbot.

219 "Homosexuality is even preferable to": "The Maturing Craig
Rodwell."

219 "Since practically the only social outlet" and "They like our
money and hated our guts": David Carter, *Stonewall: The Riots
That Sparked the Gay Revolution* (New York: St. Martin's Press,
2004), 78.

220 "There was a significant and visible presence": Marc Stein, *The
Stonewall Riots: A Documentary History* (New York: New York
University Press, 2019), 3.

220 "drink three or four vodka tonics": Edmund White, "City Boy," in
New York Public Library, ed., *The Stonewall Reader*, 155.

221 "We lived in cheap hotels, broken down apartments": Thomas
Lanigan-Schmidt, "1969 Mother Stonewall and the Golden
Rats," New York Public Library, ed., *The Stonewall Reader*,
105–6.

222 "had no harsher critic than Rodwell": Carter, *Stonewall*, 265.

223 "We'll shoot the first motherfucker that comes in the door":
Howard Smith, "View from Inside: Full Moon over the

Stonewall," *The Village Voice*, July 3, 1969, in New York Public Library, ed., *The Stonewall Reader*, 110.

223 "It was an interesting sidelight on the demonstrations": Dick Leitsch, "The Hairpin Drop Heard Around the World," *New York Mattachine Newsletter*, in New York Public Library, ed., *The Stonewall Reader*, 102–3.

226 "Broken windows and burnt things": Martin Boyce, "From Oral History Interview with Eric Marcus," New York Public Library, ed., *The Stonewall Reader*, 150.

226 "Up till that moment we had thought": Edmund White, "City Boy," New York Public Library, ed., *The Stonewall Reader*, 156.

226 "started beating patrons to the floor": Mike Davis and Jon Wiener, *Set the Night on Fire: L.A. in the Sixties* (London and New York: Verso, 2020), 169.

227 "What made Stonewall distinct and different": Interview with Ellen Broidy by Margaret Talbot.

228 "we're tired of not being able to hold hands": Craig Rodwell Papers, interview with Martin Duberman; Lillian Faderman, *The Gay Revolution: The Story of the Struggle* (New York: Simon & Schuster, 2015), 189.

228 "in style and substance": Faderman, *The Gay Revolution*, 190.

228 "If there is a women's Lib on campus," Craig Rodwell Papers, letter from Rodwell to Jeffrey S. Schall, April 25, 1971.

229 "more relevant, reach a greater number": Elizabeth A. Armstrong and Suzanna M. Crage, "Movements and Memory: The Making of the Stonewall Myth," *American Sociological Review* 71, no. 5 (October 2006), 724–51.

229 "Our thought was to take that kernel of that demonstration": Interview with Ellen Broidy by Margaret Talbot.

230 "almost like a spirit sitting in the room": Duberman, *Stonewall*, 271.

232 "would never have found my people": Jason Villemez, "Authors and activism: A History of LGBT bookstores," Out in New Jersey, September 28, 2019, https://outinjersey.net/authors-and -activism-a-history-of-lgbt-bookstores/.

233   Interview with Kim Brinster by Margaret Talbot.

233   "I used to dream about, daydream even": "Stonewall 50—
       Minisode 4—Craig Rodwell," *Making Gay History: The Podcast*.

We All Shine On: John Lennon, Yoko Ono, and the Politics of Stardom

236   leased to them by Joe Butler: Jon Wiener, *Come Together: John
       Lennon in His Time* (Chicago; Urbana: University of Illinois Press,
       1991), 176.

236   "this Japanese witch [who's] made him crazy": Interview by Dave
       Sholin, RKO Radio, December 8, 1980.

236   "The racism and sexism were overt": John Lennon, *Skywriting by
       Word of Mouth* (New York: It Books, 2010), 15.

237   Poet Allen Ginsberg hobbled by: Wiener, *Come Together*, 177.

237   "we could have been very close": Wiener, *Come Together*, 180.

237   "Whenever I hit New York, I'd go by and see John Lennon":
       Interview by David Talbot.

238   She was "terribly charmed": Wiener, *Come Together*, 176.

238   Albert was in awe of the man: Stew Albert, *Who the Hell Is Stew
       Albert? A Memoir* (Los Angeles: Red Hen Press, 2004), 181–82.

239   "By 1971 there really wasn't much left of the Left": Albert, *Who
       the Hell Is Stew Albert?*, 179.

239   "John was more radical than I was in this period": Wiener, *Come
       Together*, 178.

239   "more stifling than my domestic life": Lennon, *Skywriting*, 17.

240   "I've always been politically minded": *Red Mole*, March 8–22, 1971.

241   [Lennon] took the bait in reply to the Vietnam question: *The
       U.S. vs. John Lennon* documentary, directed and produced by
       David Leaf and John Scheinfeld (Lionsgate, 2006).

241   "In me secret heart": Jann S. Wenner, *Lennon Remembers*
       (London and New York: Verso, 2000), 93.

241   "We need music, OK?": Ellen Barry, "7 Lessons (and Warnings)
       from Those Who Marched with Dr. King," *New York Times*,
       June 17, 2020.

242 "Creating is a result of pain": Wenner, *Lennon Remembers*, 60.

242 "but in those days I was a bit more selfish": Radio interview by Andy Peebles, December 1980.

243 "With my presentation of performance art": Interview with Yoko Ono in *The U.S. vs. John Lennon*.

244 underwhelming stage lineup would make the event "a total bomb": Alan Glenn, *Ann Arbor Chronicle*, "The Day a Beatle Came to Town," December 27, 2009.

246 "It had been a twelve-hour concert": Interview by David Talbot.

246 "We came here not only to help John": *The U.S. vs. John Lennon*.

247 "All these people are saying the revolution is over": "It shows that right now we can really unite music and revolutionary politics": *The U.S. vs. John Lennon*; FBI transcript; Jon Wiener, *Gimme Some Truth: The John Lennon FBI Files* (Berkeley: University of California Press, 1999), 119.

248 FBI informers were embedded at the Ann Arbor concert: Wiener, *Gimme Some Truth*, 112–13.

249 the memo informed top administration officials: Wiener, *Gimme Some Truth*, 3–4.

249 "Give peace a chance—who could be opposed to that?": *The U.S. vs John Lennon*.

249 "It was our perspective on Lennon": *The U.S. vs. John Lennon*.

250 "They wanted me to know": *The U.S. vs. John Lennon*.

250 four Black Panthers showed up at 105 Bank Street: Bryan Shih and Yohuru Williams, eds., *The Black Panthers: Portraits from an Unfinished Revolution* (New York: Nation Books, 2016), 34–37.

252 Lennon continued to act like a man on a political mission: Wiener, *Come Together*, 199.

252 On a US broadcast of the *David Frost Show*: *The David Frost Show*, "John Lennon; Yoko Ono," Paley Center for Media, https://www.paleycenter.org/collection/item/?item=T:60182.

254 "There's such a gap between the young generation and the old": Jeff Giles, "When John Lennon and Yoko Ono Became TV Hosts," Ultimate Classic Rock, February 14, 2017, https://ultimateclassicrock.com/john-lennon-mike-douglas-show/.

254   Lennon was especially smooth at drawing out Nader: "John Lennon Interview Ralph Nader on *Mike Douglas Show* (Excerpt—1972)," https://www.youtube.com/watch?v =izEBez3pBn0.

254   Rubin was a less crowd-pleasing guest: Wiener, *Come Together*, 202–4.

255   "They were picked for [leadership] roles": Wiener, *Come Together*, 207.

255   "We even got them on the *Mike Douglas Show*": Lennon, *Skywriting*, 28.

256   "subject is heavy narcotics user": Wiener, *Come Together*, 231.

257   John and Yoko were "headed for trouble": Wiener, *Come Together*, 239.

257   "If we had gone to the Republican convention": *The U.S. vs John Lennon.*

257   "we were to be the bait": Lennon, *Skywriting*, 28.

258   "Just to show the great 'peace and love' people having a fight onstage": Jonathan Cott, *Days That I'll Remember* (New York: Anchor, 2013), 205.

258   Gregory once warned Lennon: Wiener, *Come Together*, 239.

259   "War was not an abstraction to [Ono]": Interview, *Above Us Only Sky* documentary, directed by Michael Epstein (2018).

259   "Jesus Christ! That old cocksucker!": Anthony Summers, *Official and Confidential: The Secret Life of J. Edgar Hoover* (New York: Putnam, 1993), 3.

260   "I've always needed a drug to *survive*": Wenner, *Lennon Remembers*, 57.

260   "We must always remember to thank the CIA": David Sheff, *The Playboy Interviews with John Lennon & Yoko Ono* (New York: Playboy Press, 1981), 99.

261   "why people take drugs": Josh Jones, "John Lennon & Yoko Ono's Two Appearances on *The Dick Cavett Show* in 1971 and 72," Open Culture, October 23, 2012, http://www.openculture.com/2012/10/watch_john_lennon_and_yoko_onos_two _appearances_on_the_dick_cavett_show.html.

261 John and Yoko settled into a rented house in the remote, artsy town of Ojai: "Some Time in Ojai Valley," *Ojai* magazine, March 10, 2015.

262 "She can stay in New York 365 days a year": Sheff, *The Playboy Interviews*, 71.

262 he had mixed feelings about the city: Wenner, *Lennon Remembers*, 145.

262 John and Yoko recruited Craig Pyes: Interview by David Talbot.

264 they and Krassner "went to the Bank of Tokyo": Wiener, *Come Together*, 247.

266 "The support made a big difference in our lives": Scott James, "Family Opened Up the Door to John and Yoko," *New York Times*, October 7, 2010.

266 "a kind of Japanese-American Woody Guthrie": Wiener, *Come Together*, 304.

267 the radical movement in the Bay Area was descending into its own hell: David Talbot, *Season of the Witch* (New York: Free Press, 2012).

268 "He came into the house screaming": Wiener, *Come Together*, 253.

269 what made Lennon and Ono "so crucial to our contemporary culture": "The John Lennon Deportation Proceedings: Letters to the INS—Kate Millett—Feminist," The John Lennon FBI Files (Jon Wiener website), 2003, https://lennonfbifiles.com /natl_comm_john_yoko/kate_millett.html.

270 Lennon told journalist Pete Hamill: Pete Hamill, "John Lennon: Long Night's Journey into Day," *Rolling Stone*, June 5, 1975, https://www.rollingstone.com/feature/john-lennon-pete -hamill-185277/.

270 Yoko was used to being "an artist and free": Sheff, *The Playboy Interviews*, 20.

271 "I was betwixt and between": Jane Fonda, *My Life So Far* (New York: Random House, 2006), 280.

271 "For me he was the white knight": Fonda, *My Life So Far*, 286.

271 "It's animal, it's an instinct": Katz, "Jane Fonda Is a Hard Act to Follow."

271 "They were basically saying": Katz, "Jane Fonda Is a Hard Act to Follow."

272 He "eagerly agreed": Hayden, *Writings*, 425.

273 "And I love chess": Sheff, *The Playboy Interviews*, 87.

273 "Subconsciously it was because I was guilty": Sheff, *The Playboy Interviews*, 85.

274 "time wounds all heels": *The U.S. vs. John Lennon*.

274 "I was afraid they were going to fight like a cat and dog": Interview by David Talbot.

275 "politics was in the air": RKO Radio interview, "Hear John Lennon's Final Interview, Taped on the Last Day of His Life (December 8, 1980)," Open Culture, March 12, 2015, http://www.openculture.com/2015/03/hear-john-lennons-final-interview-taped-on-the-day-of-his-death.html.

275 "Is that all you want?": James R. Gaines, "In the Shadows a Killer Waited," *People*, March 2, 1987.

276 "I thought they'd kill me": Jordan Runtagh, "When John Lennon's 'More Popular Than Jesus' Controversy Turned Ugly," *Rolling Stone*, July 29, 2016, https://www.rollingstone.com /feature/when-john-lennons-more-popular-than-jesus -controversy-turned-ugly-106430/.

276 "We're Laurel and Hardy": BBC radio interview transcript, The Beatles Ultimate Experience, http://www.beatlesinterviews.org /db1969.0508.beatles.html.

276 "I remember John said to me at one point": *The U.S. vs. John Lennon*.

276 Lennon mocked the rampant fears of Krassner: Lennon, *Skywriting*, 28.

277 Bresler interviewed Arthur O'Connor: Fenton Bresler, *Who Killed John Lennon?* (New York: St. Martin's, 1989), 19.

277 "she never had a more elusive case": Jack Jones, *Let Me Take You Down: Inside the Mind of Mark David Chapman, the Man Who Killed John Lennon* (New York: Villard Books, 1992), 74.

278 Chapman . . . conversed at length with Perdomo: Jones, 34.

278   José Sanjenis Perdomo played a nefarious role in the Bay of Pigs invasion: May 19, 1961 memo by R. W. Herbert for Western Hemisphere chief J. C. King to CIA director Allen Dulles, Mary Ferrell Foundation archives, https://maryferrell.org/pages/Archive.html.

278   "Get out of here, man!": Jones, 46.

278   "Anybody who thinks that Mark Chapman was just some crazy guy": "The Talk of the Town: Department of Legacies," *New Yorker*, April 20, 1998.

279   "I'm not claiming divinity": Cott, *Days That I'll Remember*, 194.

280   "We showed the press": Interview by David Talbot.

280   "It's true," Yoko said: Cott, *Days That I'll Remember*, 222.

The Great Escape: Dennis Banks, Madonna Thunder Hawk, Russell Means, and the Warriors of Wounded Knee

281   Chief Big Foot's Lakota tribe were massacred: David W. Grua, *Surviving Wounded Knee: The Lakotas and the Politics of Memory* (New York: Oxford University Press, 2016).

282   "There was no wind": Eli S. Ricker, *The Indian Interviews of Eli S. Ricker, 1903–1919, Voices of the American West, Volume 1* (Lincoln: University of Nebraska Press, 2005), 201.

284   "John Wayne hadn't killed us all": Russell Means with Marvin J. Wolf, *Where White Men Fear to Tread* (New York: St. Martin's Griffin, 1995), 277.

284   "the greatest event in the history of Native America": Dennis Banks with Richard Erdoes, *Ojibwa Warrior: Dennis Banks and the Rise of the American Indian Movement* (Norman: University of Oklahoma Press, 2004), 209.

285   The colonel was asked to draw up plans: Peter Matthiessen, *In the Spirit of Crazy Horse* (New York: Penguin Books, 1992), 72.

285   "They called us 'gooks'": Interview by David Talbot.

285   "But I didn't know how far they would go": *A Good Day to Die* documentary, directed by David Mueller (Kanopy, 2010).

287   "Dennis practically glow[ed] with charisma": Means, *Where White Men Fear to Tread*, 152.

287 "Our motto was 'Anytime'": *We Shall Remain*, episode 5, "Wounded Knee," directed by Stanley Nelson, *American Experience*, PBS, 2014.

288 the group grabbed headlines in a South Dakota cow town: Banks, *Ojibwa Warrior*, 152–56.

289 "When we were kids": Interview by David Talbot.

290 "They shamed us men": Banks, *Ojibwa Warrior*, 160–61.

291 "I knew we were making history": Nelson, *We Shall Remain*.

292 "We probably won't get out of this alive": Means, *Where White Men Fear to Tread*, 260.

292 "Some droning sound woke me up": Interview by David Talbot.

293 "There's no discipline in this warrior society": *Akwesasne Notes* editors, *Voices From Wounded Knee, 1973* (Mohawk Nation, 1974).

294 "One day I walked over to that gully": Nelson, *We Shall Remain*.

294 "AIM was preparing itself": *A Good Day to Die*.

294 he threatened to execute any US agent: Nelson, *We Shall Remain*.

294 "Russell would come to me and say": Interview by David Talbot.

295 "confrontational but not violent": Banks, *Ojibwa Warrior*, 105.

295 "My position at Wounded Knee": Interview by David Talbot.

296 "You guys get so uptight": Nelson, *We Shall Remain*.

296 "The feds in their bunkers": Banks, *Ojibwa Warrior*, 6.

296 "Everything we did was preceded by prayer": Nelson, *We Shall Remain*.

297 "People often forget that AIM": Banks, *Ojibwa Warrior*, 185.

297 The Ghost Dance ceremony had been passionately embraced: Peter Cozzens, *The Earth Is Weeping: The Epic Story of the Indian Wars for the American West* (New York: Vintage, 2016), 427–37.

297 "Some of the dancers fell down in a trance": Banks, *Ojibwa Warrior*, 186.

297 "The white man says that the 1890 massacre": *Akwesasne Notes* editors, *Voices from Wounded Knee, 1973*, 89.

298 "We had to get on the radio": *A Tattoo on My Heart: The Warriors of Wounded Knee, 1973* documentary, directed by Charles Abourezk and Brett Lawlor (Badland Films, 2005).

298 "We women didn't need to make a big deal": Interview by David Talbot.

298 DeCora felt inexorably drawn to Wounded Knee: Duane Noriyuki, "The Women of Wounded Knee," American Indian Movement website.

299 "Women like DeCora and Madonna": Interview by David Talbot.

299 "It was my job to boost [people's] spirits": Banks, *Ojibwa Warrior*, 189.

299 Banks received a long-distance phone call: Banks, *Ojibwa Warrior*, 190.

299 "During one [camp] meeting": Banks, *Ojibwa Warrior*, 190.

300 "Dick risked his life": Means, *Where White Men Fear to Tread*, 269.

300 "I told Dennis to burn": Nelson, *We Shall Remain*.

302 Littlefeather's brief speech drew loud boos: *Entertainment Weekly*, January 19, 2013.

302 "I was redlisted": Interview by David Talbot.

302 "We watched the whole show on TV": Interview by David Talbot.

303 "We really thought we won": Nelson, *We Shall Remain*.

303 "That wasn't our deal": Means, *Where White Men Fear to Tread*, 288.

303 a "chorus of metallic clicks": Means, 289.

304 "Once their noses connected with the pepper": Banks, *Ojibwa Warrior*, 189.

304 "hardly a mouse could get through": Banks, *Ojibwa Warrior*, 188.

305 "we had to get by with one meal every other day": Banks, *Ojibwa Warrior*, 188.

305 "for the first time in my life I knew what hunger was": Abourezk and Lawlor, *A Tattoo on My Heart*.

306 the bureau ran an astonishing 2,600 agents: Mike Mosedale, "Bury My Heart," *City Pages* (Minneapolis), February 16, 2000.

306 "There was a lot going on": Eric Konigsberg, "Who Killed Anna Mae?", *New York Times Magazine*, April 25, 2014.

306 "The government set the stage": Konigsberg, "Who Killed Anna Mae?"

307 "if it was true that AIM was involved": Matthiessen, *In the Spirit of Crazy Horse*, 438.

307 "When I started talking about": Mosedale, "Bury My Heart."

308 "Do you know what you're asking?": Bill Zimmerman, *Airlift to Wounded Knee* (Chicago: Swallow Press, 1976), 8.

308 "This is probably the most important thing": Zimmerman, *Airlift to Wounded Knee*, 245.

309 "more like riding a rodeo horse": Zimmerman, *Airlift to Wounded Knee*, 291.

310 "I thought, *Goddamn! Somebody* cares!": Banks, *Ojibwa Warrior*, 197.

311 "The whole top of his head was blown off": Noriyuki, "The Women of Wounded Knee."

311 Kamook . . . rushed to the fallen warrior: Banks, *Ojibwa Warrior*, 205.

312 "we did not want to put our names": Banks, *Ojibwa Warrior*, 208.

313 "Nixon's men told me": Interview by David Talbot.

315 they were forced to watch a humiliating "victory" ceremony: *Akwesasne Notes* editors, *Voices from Wounded Knee, 1973*, 240–44.

316 "The women elders were especially vehement": Interview by David Talbot.

320 "Big flood lights were trained": Banks, *Ojibwa Warrior*, 7.

321 Banks was taken in by "a kind, stout-hearted lady": Banks, *Ojibwa Warrior*, 10.

322 "I realized even then that you never wanted to surrender": Interview by David Talbot.

323 "Hell, no, we weren't going to surrender": Interview by David Talbot.

324 proudly expanded to "original gangsta granny": Elizabeth Castle, "'The Original Gangster': The Life and Times of Red Power Activist Madonna Thunder Hawk," in *The Hidden 1970s: Histories of Radicalism*, ed. Dan Berger (New Brunswick, NJ; London: Rutgers University Press, 2010), 279.

324 "It's a continuous struggle": Interview by David Talbot.

325 "He publicly said the best thing to do": Banks, *Ojibwa Warrior*, 213.

327 "ineffectiveness, violence and chauvinism": David Treuer, *The Heartbeat of Wounded Knee* (New York: Riverhead, 2019), 357.

327 "I sense a much stronger [Indian] nation this time": Interview by Abby Martin, *Empire Files*, October 2016.

328 "If we had told the other side at Standing Rock": Interview by David Talbot.

329 "know that there is no beginning and no end": Means, *Where White Men Fear to Tread*, 538.

329 "We lit a fire across this Indian country": Means, *Where White Men Fear to Tread*, 541.

329 "I have swallowed my share of official violence": Means, *Where White Men Fear to Tread*, 542.

329 "Within minutes, these guys were planning their next action": Interview with Robby Romero by David Talbot.

Image Credits

Page 10: photograph by Kay Tobin Lahusen, Manuscripts and Archives Division, New York Public Library (top); photograph by Diana Davies, Manuscripts and Archives Division, New York Public Library (bottom)

Page 11: photographs by Diana Davies, Manuscripts and Archives Division, New York Public Library

Page 12: Central Press/Stringer via Getty Images (top); copyright David Fenton Collection (bottom)

Page 13: John Rodgers/Contributor via Getty Images (top); Bettmann/ Contributor via Getty Images (bottom)

Page 14: Michelle Vignes/Contributor via Getty Images (top); Bettmann/ Contributor via Getty Images (bottom)

Page 15: photograph by Kevin McKiernan (top); courtesy of Lenny Foster (bottom)

Page 16: Hulton Archive/Stringer via Getty Images (top); courtesy of Bill Zimmerman (bottom)

Index

Abernathy, Ralph, 87, 300
Abortion Counseling Service of
  Women's Liberation. *See* Jane
  Collective
abortion rights, 2, 7–8, 10, 109, 112–
  18, 128–31, 136–37, 141–56, 218
abortions, 138, 139
Abourezk, James, 300
Abzug, Bella, 52
Acosta Figueroa, Alfredo, 165
Adair, Doug, 176, 185
Adams, Abigail, 4
Adams, John, 3–4, 6
Affordable Care Act, 155
AFL-CIO, 162, 175
AFSCME, 155
Agricultural Workers Organizing
  Committee, 162
AIDS crisis, 220, 232–33, 302
Ailes, Roger, 253
Albert, Stew, 24, 238–39
Alcatraz occupation, 317
Ali, Muhammad, 83
Ali, Tariq, 240
Alinsky, Saul, 161, 171
Alioto, Joseph, 179
Allen, Louis, 118
Allison, Dorothy, 232

"All Power to the People" exhibition,
  105
American Friends Service
  Committee, 130
American Indian Movement (AIM),
  2, 5, 9, 13–14, 282–329
American Prospect, 155
American Psychiatric Association, 201
Amin, Idi, 106
Andersson, Joan, 34–35, 47
Andrews, Peter, 244–46
Angleton, James Jesus, 256
Annual Reminders, 208–13, 215,
  227–28
Anthony, Susan B., 5
antiwar (peace) movement, 2, 7, 9,
  11–13, 16–17, 27, 34–47, 87, 112,
  114, 127, 130, 135, 170, 207, 210–
  11, 214, 229, 245, 252, 271–72,
  280, 300, 307–8, 312
Antle, Bud, 183
Apache, 311; Yaqui, 301
Aquash, Anna Mae Pictou, 306–7
Arapaho, 284
Arcana, Judith. *See* Pildes, Judy
Archerd, Army, 40
Arconge, Mabel, 289
Attacks Them, John, 321

Attica prison, 250–53, 262, 276
Avery, Paul, 90

Bad Heart Bull, Sarah, 288
Bad Heart Bull, Wesley, 288
Baez, Joan, 179, 212
Baker, Ella, 127
Bakunin, Mikhail, 86
Baldwin, James, 6
Bambara, Toni Cade, 143
Banks, Dennis, 9–10, 13, 282–307,
   310–22, 325–29
Barbour, Omar, 252
Bar Sinister, 35
Bay of Pigs invasion, 278
Bean, Lou, 291, 320
Beard, Dewey, 283
Beatles, 236–37, 239–42, 259–61,
   268, 272, 276
Beatty, Warren, 47
Bellecourt, Clyde, 296, 317
Bellecourt, Vernon, 317
Bendry, Peter, 259
Bergman, Lowell, 98
Berkeley Barb, 27
Berkeley Free Speech Movement,
   127
Berkeley People's Park, 21
Bernstein, Carl, 264
Bernstein, Harry, 182–83
Biden, Joe, 328
Big Foot, Chief, 281, 283, 285,
   296–97, 314
Bissonette, Gladys, 290–91
Blackburn, Robin, 240
Black Cat Tavern protests, 226
Black Elk, Wallace, 319
Blackfoot Indians, 284
Black Guerilla Family, 106
Black Hills Alliance, 323
Black Horse, Frank, 319, 321
Black Lives Matter, 5–6, 105, 106
Black Muslims, 82
Black nationalism, 62, 65, 83, 94, 143
Black Panther Party, 5, 7, 9, 12, 18,
   20, 25–26, 28, 39–40, 52–53, 58,
   65, 67–108, 152, 170, 228–30, 237,
   250–52, 254, 286, 295
Black Power, 2, 6, 71, 114, 126, 210,
   225
Blazing Star, 135

Bloom, Joshua, 94
Bond, Julian, 119
Booth, Dan, 130
Booth, Gene, 130
Booth, Heather, 9, 10, 13, 110, 117,
   119–37, 154–55
Booth, Paul, 13, 129–30, 135, 155
Booth, William H., 217
Boston Globe, 308
Boston Women's Health Collective,
   110, 140–41
Bouie, Jamelle, 14
Boyce, Martin, 225–26
Brando, Marlon, 13, 85–86, 237,
   301–3, 313
Branfman, Fred, 47, 51–56, 59
Brave, Regina, 300–301
Bread and Wine (Silone), 59
Brecht, Bertolt, 166
Bresler, Fenton, 277
Brewster, Kingman, Jr., 26
Brinster, Kim, 233
Broidy, Ellen, 217–18, 227–31
Bronstein, Stan, 258, 269
Brown, Edmund "Pat," 167
Brown, Elaine, 99–106
Brown, Jerry, 54, 326
Brown, Michael, 91
Brown, Rita Mae, 196
Browne, Jackson, 272
Brumfield, Steve, 61–62, 65
Brussell, Mae, 264, 276–77
Buckley, William F., 40
"Building an Enduring Democratic
   Majority" (Booth), 155
Bureau of Indian Affairs, 285
Burns, Bonnie, 171
Butler, Joe, 236

Cage, John, 236–37, 256
Calhoun, William, 71, 92
California Agricultural Labor
   Relations Board, 188
California Democratic primaries:
   (1968), 25; (1976), 44–52, 55
California state legislature, 52, 54,
   58–60, 80, 91, 96
California State Supreme Court, 76,
   183
Camacho, Epifanio, 168–69, 175
Camp, Carter, 294, 303, 312, 314–15

Campaign for Economic Democracy,
54, 56, 271
Camus, Albert, 19
Carmichael, Stokely, 71, 170
Carr, Billy John, 81
Carson, Clayborne, 93
Carter, Bunchy, 94
Carter, David, 219, 222, 231
Casper, Percy, 319, 321
Castro, Fidel, 23, 264, 278
Catechism of a Revolutionary, The
(Nechayev), 86
Cell 16, 133
Chaney, James, 121–22, 124–26
CHAOS program, 256
Chapman, Mark David, 275, 277–78
Chatfield, LeRoy, 163, 171–73, 175,
177
Chavez, Cesar, 8–10, 45, 53, 96,
157–90
Chavez, Helen Fabela, 158, 173, 177,
183
Chavez, Juana, 177
Chavez, Manuel, 169, 173–74, 176
Chavez, Richard, 158, 164, 171, 173
Chekhov, Anton, 77
Cheyenne, 284
Cheyenne River Reservation, 324
Chicago Board of Education, 207
Chicago Defender, 124
Chicago Eight, 13, 18–22, 26–27, 34,
40–41, 94–96, 248, 255
Chicago police: 17, 20, 34, 94, 109,
116–17, 146, 150, 152; Red Squad,
114, 130, 145–49
Chicago Women's Liberation Union,
133, 135–36, 139, 150–51, 154
Children's Medical Relief
International, 258
China Syndrome, The (film), 55
Chisholm, Shirley, 52, 143
Christopher Street Liberation Day
parade, 229–31
Central Intelligence Agency (CIA),
42, 243, 247, 256, 260, 264, 276,
278, 313
Civil Rights Act (1964), 6, 126
civil rights movement, 2, 6–7, 11,
16–17, 46, 64, 69, 118–29,158,
165, 170, 207, 210, 212–13, 215,
225, 241, 287, 300, 306

Civil War, 3–4
Clark, Mark, 150
Clay, Charity, 105
Clearwater, Frank, 311
Clearwater, Morning Star, 311
Cleaver, Eldridge, 9, 28, 82–92,
100–101, 106–7, 144
Cleaver, Kathleen, 83–86, 89, 106–7
Cobb, Charles E., Jr., 70, 119
Cody, William "Buffalo Bill," 283
Cohen, Jerry, 164, 174–76, 181, 188
COINTELPRO, 93–94, 114, 305–6
Cold War, 16, 35, 45, 128
Cole, Nat King, 73
Coleman, Kate, 88, 90
Coming Home (film), 55
Commander Cody, 244
Community Service Organization
(CSO), 161–63, 189
Compton's Cafeteria picket, 226
Congressional Black Caucus, 107,
258
Conspiracy, The, 27
Consumer Financial Protection
Bureau, 155
Continental Army, 2–4
Continental Congress, 4
contraception, 110, 112–13, 143, 152
Conyers, John, 107
CORE (Congress of Racial Equality),
118, 122, 213
Cory, Donald Webster, 196
Costello, Elvis, 279
Cott, Jonathan, 279–80
Coughlin, Father Charles, 19
Covay, Don, 250–51
Cox, Kyoko, 261–62, 264, 279
Cox, Tony, 261–62, 264
Coyote, Peter, 98–99
Crane, Hart, 196
Crazy Horse, Chief, 284, 313
Crow Dog, Leonard, 296–97, 303,
314–15, 319
Crow nation, 284
Cunningham, Merce, 237, 256
Cuny, Don "Cuny Dog," 295, 299,
328
Cuomo, Andrew, 280
Cuomo, Mario, 326
Custer, George Armstrong, 62, 281
Custer protests, 287–88, 290

Dakota Access Pipeline, 327
Daley, Richard, 17, 45, 135
Darnell, Nolan, 88
Daughters of Bilitis (DOB), 194,
 207, 210–12
David Frost Show, 252
Davis, Angela, 218, 300
Davis, Rennie, 34, 41, 95, 248
Day, Mark, 173–74
Days of Rage, 20–21, 26
Debs, Eugene, 130
Declaration of Independence, 1–3, 5,
 49, 209
DeCora, Lorelei, 297–99, 311
Dederich, Charles "Chuck," 186–87
Deferred Action for Childhood
 Arrivals, 155
Deganawidah-Quetzalcoatl (D-Q)
 University, 326
de Havilland, Olivia, 206
Delancey Street Foundation, 179,
 186
Delany, Samuel, 210
DeLarverie, Stormé, 222–23, 225
De Leon, Daniel, 130
Dellinger, David, 41–42, 258
Dellums, Ron, 107
DeMain, Paul, 307
Democratic National Convention:
 (1960, Los Angeles), 17; (1964,
 Atlantic City), 126–27, 207; (1968,
 Chicago), 16–18, 94–95, 114, 126,
 215, 248
Democratic Party, 22, 32, 52, 58,
 126
Diagnostic and Statistical Manual
 (DSM), 201
Dialectic of Sex, The (Firestone), 133,
 238
Dick Cavett Show, 256, 258–59, 261,
 302–3
Diggers, 98–99
DiGiorgio strike, 167–68
Dittmer, John, 125
Dohrn, Bernardine, 21, 22, 23
Dolores Huerta Foundation, 189
Double Fantasy (album), 274–75
Douglass, Frederick, 4–5
Dow Chemical, 183, 214
Dowell, Denzil, 79–80
Downs, Jim, 197

draft resisters, 129–30, 132, 214, 218
Drake, Jim, 163
Duberman, Martin, 198–99, 203,
 206, 209–10, 229
Duggan, John, 171
Durham, Douglas, 305
Dworkin, Andrea, 218
Dylan, Bob, 8, 19, 247

Eastern Regional Conference
 of Homophile Organizations
 (ERCHO), 228
Ehrlichman, John, 312–13
elections: (1960), 17; (1964), 126;
 (1966), 32; (1968), 25, 179; (1970),
 52; (1972), 36, 40, 52, 96, 247–49,
 252, 254, 257, 264, 267–69; (1974),
 43; (1976), 44–52; (1984), 328;
 (2008), 189; (2016), 326
Elephant's Memory, 258, 268
Ellington, Duke, 73
Ellsberg, Daniel, 36–37, 44
El Malcriado, 169, 185
El Teatro Campesino, 166
Emancipation Proclamation, 64
Emerson, Ralph Waldo, 120
environmentalism, 2, 114, 245, 328
Epstein, Brian, 240, 260, 276
Equal Rights Amendment, 134
Erikson, Erik, 97
eugenics, 143
Evers, Medgar, 129

Faderman, Lillian, 193, 228
Fanon, Frantz, 66, 84
farmworkers, 7, 10, 158–90
Federal Bureau of Investigation
 (FBI), 11, 20, 23, 33–34, 39–40,
 65, 70, 93–98, 101, 106, 114, 124,
 129, 150, 214, 236, 243, 248–49,
 255–56, 259, 262, 267, 269, 285,
 290, 292, 302–7, 310–14, 319
Felt, W. Mark "Deep Throat," 313
Female Eunuch, The (Greer), 238
Fenton, David, 246, 280
Ferguson, Missouri, protests, 91
Fire Drill Friday protests, 57
Firestone, Shulamith, 131, 133, 238
Flacks, Dick, 45
Flacks, Mickey, 45
Floyd, George, 6, 57, 106, 241

Flynt, Larry, 328
Fonda, Henry, 37, 48
Fonda, Jane, 9, 33, 37–44, 46–50, 53, 55–59, 235, 237, 239, 245, 270–72, 279
Fonda, Peter, 260
Forman, James, 46
Forsyth, James, 282–83
Foster, Lenny, 316–23, 329
Franklin, Aretha, 74, 250–51
Franklin, Benjamin, 3
Free Breakfast for Children Program, 92, 94, 237
Freedom of Information Act, 249
Freedom Summer, 13, 17, 70, 118–28, 158, 165, 207
Freeman, Jo, 131, 133, 154
Frey, John, 84
Friends of SNCC, 118
Frizzell, Kent, 301, 304
Frontline (PBS show), 89
Frost, David, 238, 252
Fun with Dick and Jane (film), 48
Furies, The, 133

Gain, Charles, 103
Galatzer, Barney, 111
Galatzer, Jeanne, 109–17, 139–40, 142, 144, 148, 150, 156
Galatzer, Milt, 111
Gandhi, Mahatma, 171, 175, 178, 180, 184, 276
Ganz, Marshall, 127, 165, 170, 177, 181–83, 187–88
Garity, Emmett, 34
Garity, Troy, 42, 56
Garrett, Jimmy, 131
Garry, Charles, 95
Gay Crusaders, The (Lahusen and Wicker), 195
Gaylen, LeRoy, 166–67
Gay Liberation Front (GLF), 229–30
Geer, Will, 50
George III, King of England, 3
Gerth, Jeff, 263
Ghost Dance, 281–82, 297
Gilbert, Bruce, 33, 42, 55, 271
Ginsberg, Allen, 225, 237, 245
Gitlin, Todd, 58
Giumarra Companies, 168–70, 175–76, 179, 181

Godfather, The (film), 301
Goldman, Emma, 230
Goldstein, Dr. Naomi, 277
Goldwater, Barry, 126, 193
Gollon, Abby, 144, 152
Goodman, Andrew, 121–22, 124–26
GOONS (Guardians of the Oglala Nation), 289
Govea, Jessica, 170
Granger, Farley, 203
Grant, Allan, 166
Grapefruit (Ono), 242
Grapes of Wrath, The (Steinbeck), 161
grape strike, 158, 163–81, 185
Gray, Victoria, 125
Green, Al, 74
Green New Deal, 54
Greer, Germaine, 238
Gregory, Dick, 119, 258, 300
Grogan, Emmett, 99
Guevara, Che, 45
Gumbo, Judy, 24
Gunnison, Foster, 230

Haber, Alan, 130
Hair (musical), 236
Haldeman, H.R. "Bob," 312–13
Hall, Simon, 208–9
Hallinan, Vincent, 22
Hallinan, Vivian, 22
Hamer, Fannie Lou, 127, 129
Hamill, Pete, 269–70
Hampton, Fred, 20, 23, 94, 150
Harding, Nina, 143
Harper, Frances E.W., 5
Harrison, George, 240
Hart, Peter, 48
Hartmire, Chris, 163, 171
Hawkins, Andrew, 123–24
Hawkins, Mary Lou, 123–24
Hay, Harry, 206
Hayden, Casey, 21, 119–21, 128
Hayden, Tom, 8–9, 13, 15–60, 90, 95–96, 119–20, 127, 135, 245, 271–72, 279, 307
Heller, Nathan, 190
Hell No (Hayden), 43–44
Helms, Richard, 256
Hilliard, David, 28
Hinckle, Warren, 21, 82

Hines, Earl "Fatha," 73
Hiroshima and Nagasaki, 81
Hirsch, Fred, 157, 159, 168–69, 171, 175–76
Hirsch, Ginny, 157, 159, 168, 171
Ho Chi Minh, 23, 45
Hoffman, Abbie, 27, 42, 95–96, 238, 245, 270, 276
Hoffman, Julius, 18–19, 95
Holder, Stan, 292–93, 295
Holiday, Billie, 73
Homosexual in America, The (Cory), 196
Hong, Betty, 265–66
Hong, Emily, 266
Hong, Yuan Bain, 265–66
Hoover, J. Edgar, 11, 23, 39–40, 93–94, 129, 236, 248, 255–56, 259
Horn Cloud, Joseph, 281–83
Horowitz, David, 90
Howard, Dr. T.R.M., 128–29, 137
Huerta, Dolores, 9–10, 57, 157, 161–65, 172, 176, 178–80, 188–89
Huerta, Rey, 182
Huggins, Ericka, 25–26, 93–95, 106
Huggins, John, 94–95
Hughes, Langston, 2
Hulett, John, 70
Hutton, Bobby, 72, 88–90
Huxley, Aldous, 260–61
Hyde amendment, 153
Hymnal, The, 219

Imagine (album), 257
"Imagine" (song), 242, 251, 266
Immigration and Naturalization Service (INS), 249, 256, 259, 269–70, 273
Indian Citizenship Act (1924), 5
Indian Country News, 307
Indian Wars, 34
Indian Wars, The (film), 283
Indochina Peace Campaign (IPC), 40–41, 43, 46–47, 271
Industrial Areas Foundation, 161
Ink Spots, 73
"Instant Karma (We All Shine On)" (song), 242
Interior Department, 300
International Workers of the World ("Wobblies"), 166

In the Spirit of Crazy Horse (Matthiessen), 307
Irish nationalists, 171, 175
Isherwood, Christopher, 197
Isserman, Maurice, 13
Itliong, Larry, 162, 164, 172–73

James, Etta, 74
Jane Collective, 9, 109–18, 128–30, 136–57
Janklow, William, 325
Japanese Americans, internment of, 213
Jarvis, Howard, 54
Jay, Karla, 210
Jefferson, Thomas, 3, 49, 50
Jensen, Richard, 88
JFK Records Collection Act (1992), 278
Ji, Guru Maharaj, 41
Jim Crow, 5, 64, 68, 73, 81
John Lennon/Plastic Ono Band (album), 242
John Sinclair Freedom Rally, 244–48, 250
"John Sinclair" (song), 253
Johnson, Lady Bird, 214
Johnson, Lyndon B., 12, 32, 126–27
Johnson, Marsha P., 225
Johnson, William "BJ," 250–52
Jones, Jack, 277
Jonestown, 267
Juarez, Benito, 169
Julius's bar, 216–17
Justice Department, 125, 180, 300–301, 313

Kameny, Frank, 208–10, 215, 227
Kazin, Michael, 13
Kelley, Ken, 262–63
Kennedy, Ethel, 183
Kennedy, Florynce, 143
Kennedy, Jackie, 133
Kennedy, John F., 17, 19, 180, 213, 264, 276, 278
Kennedy, Robert F., 17, 19, 25, 166–67, 176–80, 264
Kennedy, Robert F., Jr., 57
Kent State killings, 246
Kern County Superior Court, 175–76

Kesselman, Amy, 132–35
Keyes, Bobby, 270
King, B.B., 73
King, Martin Luther, Jr., 1–2, 6, 10–13, 17, 19, 46, 64–65, 69, 87–88, 92, 131, 170, 175, 178, 180, 213, 241, 276
King, Mary, 128
Kleindienst, Richard, 19
Klute (film), 38, 271
Koedt, Anne, 140
Kohler, Bob, 198
Komisar, Lucy, 216
Krassner, Paul, 264, 276
Krishnamurti, Jiddu, 261
Ku Klux Klan, 68–69, 124–25, 129
Kunstler, William, 19, 248
Kuromiya, Kiyoshi, 213–15, 229–30

Labor Department, 182
Ladder, The, 194
Ladner, Dorie, 127
Ladner, Joyce, 127
Lafayette, Bernard, 241
Lafayette, Marquis de, 3
Lahusen, Kay, 195
Lakota, 62, 281–96, 300, 312–15, 319, 321, 323, 329
Lamont, Buddy, 311–12
Lanigan-Schmidt, Thomas, 220
La Riva, Gloria, 326
Last Exit to Brooklyn (Selby), 196
Lee, Herbert, 118, 123
Leech Lake Reservation, 286, 326
Leitsch, Dick, 216–17, 223
Lenin, Vladimir I., 23
Lennon, Cynthia, 239
Lennon, John, 10, 13, 96, 235–80
Lennon, Julia, 242
Lennon, Sean, 265–67, 273, 278–79
"Letter from a Birmingham Jail" (King), 11
lettuce strike, 183, 185
Levy, Robert, 156
LGBTQ rights, 2, 7, 135, 191–233
Liberation, 69
Liberation School for Women, 135–36
Library of Congress, 197
Liddy, G. Gordon, 250, 274
Lifton, Robert J., 25
Lincoln, Abraham, 5, 64

Lindsay, John, 217
Lira, Agustín, 166
Littlefeather, Sacheen, 301–2
Lonely Rage, A (Seale), 107
Lord of the Rings (Tolkien), 123
Los Angeles Community Alert Patrol, 72
Los Angeles Free Press, 226
Los Angeles police, 71–72, 303
Los Angeles Produce Market, 163
Los Angeles Times, 33, 51, 173, 182–83
Los Angeles Watts riots, 71–72
Louisville protests of 2020, 9
Love of Possession Is a Disease with Them, The (Hayden), 34
Lowndes County Freedom Organization (LCFO), 70–71
Lumpen (band), 92
lynchings, 68, 129

Mabry, Esther, 74
Madison, James, 3
Mafia, 219, 227, 230, 263
Maher, John, 179, 186
Making the Future Ours (Hayden), 45
Malcolm X, 65, 79, 82
Malcolm X Cultural Center, 250
Manning, Bishop Timothy, 173–74
Manson, Charles, 23
Mao Zedong, 40, 175
Marshall, Thurgood, 70
Martin, Waldo E., Jr., 94
Marx, Groucho, 47, 238
Marx, Karl, 23, 66, 82, 238
Mattachine Society, 206–8, 210, 215–16, 223, 228–30
Matthiessen, Peter, 174, 178, 190, 307
May Day protests, 25–26, 46
McCartney, Paul, 241, 247
McCoy, Alfred W., 247
McGovern, George, 44, 249, 263, 267, 300
Means, Bill, 297
Means, Russell, 9, 10, 283–97, 303–4, 317, 325–26, 328–29
Meany, George, 175
Medical Aid for Indochina, 46, 308
Medical Committee for Human Rights, 128
Medina, Eliseo, 170, 177, 185–89
Memories of John Lennon (Ono), 272

Merkle, Mrs., 198
Merritt College (Oakland), 65–66, 72, 75, 105–6
methadone, 261, 265–66
Mexican Americans, 7, 159, 161–62, 166, 169
Mexican braceros, 182
Mexico City uprising, 130
Michigan Supreme Court, 248
Migrant Ministry, 163, 171
Mike Douglas Show, 96, 253–56
Mailer, Norman, 84
Milk, Harvey, 52, 193–94, 205–6, 233, 267
Miller, Isabel, 196
Millett, Kate, 13, 237–38, 269
Mills, C. Wright, 19, 24
Minneapolis police, 286
Minneapolis protests, 9, 106
Mintz, Elliot, 259
Mississippi Freedom Democratic Party, 126–27, 207
Mitchell, John, 180, 248, 256, 274
Monterey County jail, 183
Moon, Keith, 270
Moratorium against the Vietnam War, 229, 241
Moscone, George, 193, 267
Moses, Bob, 29–30, 46, 118–19, 123
Mothers of Invention, 262
Mount Vernon, 3
Moves Camp, Ellen, 290
Mulford, Donald, 80, 81
multiracial and cross-cultural coalitions, 11–13, 96, 178, 189
Murphy, Michelle, 140
Murrieta, Joaquin, 165
My Lai massacre, 247
"Myth of the Vaginal Orgasm, The" (Koedt), 140

Nader, Ralph, 254
napalm, 183, 214
Nash, Diane, 127
Nash, Gary B., 3
National Association for the Advancement of Colored People (NAACP), 68–70
National Conference for New Politics, 131
National Council of Churches, 163

National Farm Bureau, 179
National Guard, 250
National Labor Relations Act (1935), 161
National Organization for Women (NOW), 134, 151
Nation of Islam, 65, 78
Native Americans, 2–3, 5, 7, 9, 34, 38–39, 61–63, 81, 85, 165, 253, 281–323
Navajo nation, 317–19, 322
Navajo Nations Corrections Project, 322
Near, Holly, 40
Nechayev, Sergey, 86
Negroes with Guns (Williams), 70
Nestle, Joan, 203
Newark SDS antipoverty project, 16
New Deal, 19
New England Free Press, 141
Newfield, Jack, 18
New Left, 13, 15–18, 22, 51–52, 58, 90, 95, 129, 132–33, 135, 214, 217–18, 238, 249, 255, 257, 266, 271. *See also specific groups and individuals*
New Mexico state legislature, 163
Newton, Huey P., 9, 10, 12, 66–68, 70–85, 90–92, 95–106, 108, 250–51
New West, 88
New York City Commission on Human Rights, 217
New York *Daily News*, 136
New Yorker, 178, 190, 278
New York Police Department, 204–5, 227, 277; Tactical Police Force, 223; Vice Squad Public Morals Division, 221
New York Post, 227
New York Radical Women, 133
New York State, abortion legalized in, 137–38, 143
New York state legislature, 280
New York State Liquor Authority, 215–17
New York Times, 11, 36, 81, 201, 213, 217, 250
Nichols, Kamook, 286, 305–6, 311
Nilsson, Harry, 270
Nimoy, Leonard, 179

Nineteenth Amendment, 5
Nine to Five (film), 55
Nixon, Richard, 7, 10, 19, 21–23, 32, 34, 36, 39–43, 46, 50, 94–96, 98, 131, 179–80, 235, 239, 243, 247–50, 252, 254–59, 263–64, 267–69, 274, 276, 285, 299–300, 303–4, 308–9, 312–13
nonviolence, 69, 127, 164, 169–70, 172–75, 177–78, 182, 184, 328–29
Northern Ireland, 252, 272
North Korea, 106
North Oakland Anti-Poverty Center, 72
North Vietnam, 7, 16, 39, 43, 46, 135
nuclear freeze movement, 41

Oakland police, 10, 28, 71–81, 84–85, 88–89, 91–92, 97–98, 102–3, 105–6, 108, 286
Obama, Barack, 189
Occupy movement, 58
O'Connor, Arthur, 277
Odd Girl Out (Bannon), 195
Oglala Lakota, 286, 288–96, 300
Ojibwe, 284, 286, 296, 326
Oliphant, Tom, 308
Oliver, Eleanor, 145–47
Ondaga Nation, 253
Ono, Shinya, 266
Ono, Yoko, 10, 13, 96, 235–39, 242–49, 252–70, 272–76, 279–80
Operation 40, 278
Orendain, Tony, 171
Osborne, Walter, 176
Oscar Wilde Memorial Bookshop, 192, 194–98, 217–18, 230, 232–33
Our Bodies, Ourselves, 110, 140–41

Padilla, Gilbert, 162
Paine, Tom, 49–50
Paley, Grace, 218
Pang, May, 270
Panther 21, 103
Patience and Sarah (Miller), 196
Paul, Alice, 5
Peace and Freedom Party, 326
Peace Corps, 17
Peel, David, 245, 252
Pelican Bay prison, 59–60
Pentagon Papers, 35–36
Pepper, William, 12

Perdomo, José, 277–78
Piercy, Marge, 156
Pildes, Judy, 137, 144, 149–53, 156
Pildes, Michael, 144, 149–50
Pine, Seymour, 221, 223
Pine Ridge Reservation, 62, 282–316, 321, 326, 328
Place for Us, A (Miller), 196
Plains Indian Wars, 284
Planned Parenthood, 152
Playboy, 260, 273–74
Polanski, Roman, 23
police brutality, 23, 71–72, 98, 102, 170, 226. *See also specific police departments*
Politics of Heroin, The (McCoy), 247
Pontecorvo, Gillo, 85
Poor People's March, 11–12, 87
Port Huron Statement, 16, 17, 45, 130
Portland protests, 9
Potawatomi Indians, 319
Potter, Paul, 45
Power Elite, the (Mills), 24
Price, Cecil, 124
Pride March, first, 229–33
Proposition 13, 54
Pryor, Richard, 83
Pyes, Craig, 262–67

Quatrefoil (Barr), 196

racism, 12, 16, 212, 236, 245, 248, 317
Rackley, Alex, 95
Rainbow People's Party, 244
Raitt, Bonnie, 57, 272
Ramparts, 21, 28, 32–33, 79, 82, 88, 90
RAND Corporation, 36
rape, 135, 138, 155
Reading, John, 71, 101
Reagan, Ronald, 81, 83, 107, 180, 233, 277
Realist, The, 264
Rebellion in Newark (Hayden), 16
Red Family, 15, 27–33, 39, 42–43, 271
Red Mole, 240
Redstockings, 113, 133, 136, 218, 237
Republican National Convention (1972, Miami), 96, 247, 255–58, 267–68
Republican Ripon Society, 43

Reunion (Hayden), 22
Reyes, Rudy, 176
Reynolds, Malvina, 212
Rhodes, Linda, 217, 227, 230
Richmond police department, 79
Riker's Island jail, 103
Rivera, Geraldo, 268
Rivera, Sylvia, 232
Robbins, Terry, 26
Robinson, Cheryl, 306
Robinson, Ray, 306
Rockefeller, Nelson, 250–52
Rodwell, Craig, 10, 191–210, 215–19, 221–33
Roe v. Wade, 9, 153
Rolling Stone, 98, 242, 260, 263, 279
Ronstadt, Linda, 47, 272
Roosevelt, Franklin D., 19
Ross, Fred, 161–62, 164, 167, 170, 172, 179
Ross, Fred, Jr., 179
Rothstein, Vivian, 132–35, 154
Rubin, Jerry, 13, 27, 41, 47, 95–96, 238–39, 244–48, 250, 254–57, 263, 268–70, 276
Rubyfruit Jungle (Brown), 196
Russo, Anthony, 36
Russo, Vito, 195

Sacramento: Black Panthers protest at, 80–81; UFW march on, 167, 177
Sacred Runs for the Earth, 326
Salinas Valley, 181–83, 186
Saludado Magana, Maria, 165–66
same-sex marriage, 155, 233
Sanders, Bernie, 48–49, 58
San Francisco Board of Supervisors, 52, 193
San Luis Obispo prison, 91, 99
Sargeant, Fred, 198, 217, 221–22, 227, 230
Savio, Mario, 127
Scheer, Christopher, 15, 23, 28, 31
Scheer, Robert, 21–23, 26, 28–29, 32–33, 51, 59, 82, 88, 90–91
Schlesinger, Arthur, Jr., 17
Schwenk, Madeline, 144
Schwerner, Michael, 121–22, 124–26
Schwerner, Rita, 122
Scott, Martha, 138, 144, 146–47, 153
Scott, Norbert, 138

Seale, Bobby, 8–13, 18, 25–26, 28, 41, 52, 61–68, 70–90, 92–98, 101–8, 237, 245, 248, 254
Seale, George, 61–62
Sebastian, John, 236
Secret Storm, 135
Seeger, Pete, 241
Segal, George, 48
Seger, Bob, 244
segregation, 118–19, 207, 213
Seize the Time (Seale), 66–67
Selby, Hubert, 196
Selma-Montgomery March, 214
Seneca Falls convention, 5
"Sex and Caste" (Hayden and King), 128
Sexual Politics (Millett), 237
Shabazz, Betty, 79
Sheff, David, 260, 273–74
Sheinbaum, Stanley, 28
Shelley, Martha, 210–13, 229–30
Shilts, Randy, 206
Sholin, Dave, 274, 275
Shrum, Robert, 44
Shuswap, 319
Siegel, Dan, 34
Silone, Ignazio, 59
Silva mind control, 187
Sinatra, Frank, 167
Sinclair, David, 244–45
Sinclair, John, 244, 247–48, 255, 257, 280
Sinclair, Leni, 244–45
sip-in, 215–17, 223
sit-ins, 13, 120, 127, 129–30, 213, 215
Sitting Bull, Chief, 284, 313
Skywriting by Word of Mouth (Lennon), 255, 257
slavery, 2–3, 81, 120
Slim Jenkins Café, 73–74, 76
Smith, Howard, 223
Smith, Mimi, 240, 261
Smith, Sheila, 112–17, 138, 144, 146, 148–49, 152
Smiths, The, 196
Snake Pit, The (film), 206
solar energy, 48, 54, 272
solitary confinement, 286
Some Time in New York City (album), 261–62
Soul on Ice (Cleaver), 28, 82–83, 144

Soul Students Advisory Council, 65–67
South African apartheid, 189
Southern Christian leadership Conference (SCLC), 87
Spock, Dr. Benjamin, 131
spousal abuse, 111–12, 138
Standing Rock protests, 324, 327–28
Stanton, Elizabeth Cady, 5
Stein, Marc, 220
Steinbeck, John, 161
Stevens, Diane, 144, 149
Stillwater prison, 286
Stipanela, John, 220
Stonewall (Carter), 219
Stonewall uprising, 10, 198, 219–30, 233
Story of My Experiments with Truth, The (Gandhi), 184
Strange Sisters (Flora), 195
Street, Joe, 100
strikebreakers, 168–69, 183
Student Nonviolent Coordinating Committee (SNCC), 29, 46, 70–72, 83, 118–27, 131
Students for a Democratic Society (SDS), 13, 16, 19–20, 45, 58, 118, 129–32, 214, 229, 266
Studies on the Left, 266
SunDance, 262–63
Surgal, Ruth, 145, 150
Synanon, 179, 186, 187
Symbionese Liberation Army, 267

Talbot, David, 41
Taste of Power, A (Brown), 101–2
Tate, Sharon, 23
Teachers for Radical Change, 130
Teamsters Union, 163–64, 181, 183, 188
Tea Party, 58
Terrell, Mary Church, 5
Tet offensive, 170
Thoreau, Henry David, 19, 120
"Three Homosexuals in Search of a Drink" (Komisar), 216
Thunder Hawk, Madonna, 9, 10, 14, 285, 289–92, 298–99, 305, 317, 323–25, 327–28
Thurmond, Strom, 248
Tijerina, Reies, 170

Till, Emmett, 129
Timmons, John, 216
Title IX, 111
"To Be of Use" (Piercy), 156
Tobin, Jon, 123
Tolkien, J.R.R., 123
Townhouse Collective, 26
Townshend, Pete, 245
transgender people, 226, 232
"Trashing" (Freeman), 154
Treuer, David, 326–27
Trump, Donald, 57–58, 328
Truth, Sojourner, 5
Tunney, John, 44, 50–51
Two Virgins (album), 236
"Tyranny of Structurelessness" (Freeman), 154

Union Carbide uranium project, 323
United Auto Workers, 43, 163, 172
United Farm Workers (UFW), 2, 10, 45, 53, 57, 96, 127, 157–90
United Nations Human Rights Commission, 323
U.S. Air Force, 62, 286
U.S. Army, 284; Corps of Engineers, 289; 82nd Airborne, 285; Map Service, 208; 7th Cavalry, 281–83, 299, 314; Third Infantry, 12
U.S. Conference of Mayors, 43
U.S. Congress, 11, 12, 43, 47, 52, 153
U.S. Constitution, 1, 49, 124, 153, 167
U.S. House of Representatives, 43; Internal Security Committee, 101
U.S. Marines, 12
U.S. Marshals, 290, 313, 315, 319, 321
U.S. Navy, 73; intelligence, 256
U.S. Senate, 323; migratory labor subcommittee, 166; Judiciary Committee, 248–49
U.S. Supreme Court, 70, 153
urban riots, 12, 71–72, 170
US Organization, 94

Vacaville state prison, 99
Vadim, Roger, 37
Valdez, Luis, 160, 164–67, 174, 188
Van Ronk, Dave, 224
Varela, Emil, 216
Variety, 40

Vaughan, Sarah, 73
vegetable workers, 181–83, 186
Vietcong, 167
Vietnamese National Liberation
 Front (NLF), 21, 43
Vietnamese Women's Union, 135
Vietnam War, 7, 9, 11–12, 16, 18, 20,
 23, 29, 32, 34–44, 58, 63, 81, 87,
 97, 127, 170, 180, 183, 207, 239–
 41, 243, 247, 253, 258–59, 284–85,
 287, 293, 295, 299–300, 308
Village Voice, 216, 223, 227
voter registration, 118, 121–27, 189
Voting Rights Act (1965), 6, 126

Wahwassuck, Henry, 317, 319
Walters, Barbara, 56–57
War Department, 283
Warhol, Andy, 257–58
"War Is Over!" campaign, 243
Washington, George, 2, 3
Washington, Harold, 155
Washington Post, 264, 313
Wasserman, Steve, 24
Watergate scandal, 36, 43, 264, 269,
 300, 313
Wayne, John, 284, 302, 303
Weather Underground, 20–24, 26,
 35, 229, 266
Webb, Marilyn, 131–32
Weills, Anne, 15, 20–23, 25–35, 39,
 55, 59–60
Weinglass, Leonard, 20, 36
Weir, David, 98
Weisstein, Naomi, 133–34, 154
Wells, Arvin, 315
Wells, Ida B., 5
Wenner, Jann, 242, 260, 263
Westside Group, 133
White, Edmund, 220, 226
Who Killed John Lennon? (Bresler),
 277
Whose Streets? (documentary), 91
"Why American May Go to Hell"
 (King), 11
Wichita nation, 293
Wicker, Randy, 195, 217
Wiener, Jon, 249, 255
Wilde, Oscar, 196
Wildes, Leon, 256
Wild in the Streets (film), 22

Wilkins, Roy, 69
Williams, Barbara, 57
Williams, Robert F., 68–70
Williams, Tennessee, 197
Willis, Ellen, 132
Wilson, Dick, 285, 288–91, 294,
 309–16, 319, 325
WITCH, 134–35
Withers, Bill, 265
Wolfenden Report, The, 196
Wolfson, Jo-Anne, 152–53
"Woman Is Nigger of the World"
 (song), 258, 262
woman suffrage movement, 5, 171
Women of All Red Nations, 323
Women on Waves, 156
Women on Web, 156
women's health movement, 140–41
Women's House of Detention
 (Greenwich Village), 218
women's liberation (feminist)
 movement, 2, 7, 12–13, 16, 27–30,
 34–35, 52, 110–14, 127–56,
 210–11, 215, 218, 228–29, 237–38,
 252–53, 258
Wonder, Stevie, 245–46
Wood, Gordon S., 1
Woodward, Bob, 264
World War I, 5
World War II, 73, 75, 160, 213, 259,
 317–18
Wounded Knee: airlift, 307–10;
 massacre of 1890, 281–84, 296–
 99, 314, 318; siege of 1973, 8–9,
 13, 47, 281–319, 323–25, 327–28
Wretched of the Earth, The (Fanon), 66
Wright, Billy, 308

Yankton Reservation, 289
Yippies, 27, 42, 96, 213, 238–39,
 255, 264, 268, 271, 276
Young, Andrew, 10
Young Lords, 228, 230

Zacchino, Nardo, 51
Zappa, Frank, 262
Zarnow, Leandra Ruth, 52
Zebra murders, 267
Zhou Enlai, 98
Zimmerman, Bill, 13, 45–50, 52–55,
 307–10

About the Authors

David Talbot is the *New York Times* bestselling author of *The Devil's Chessboard: Allen Dulles, the CIA, and the Rise of America's Secret Government*; *Brothers: The Hidden History of the Kennedy Years*; *Season of the Witch: Enchantment, Terror, and Deliverance in the City of Love*; and, most recently, the memoir *Between Heaven and Hell*. He founded the pioneering online magazine *Salon* and was a senior editor of *Mother Jones* magazine and a columnist for the *San Francisco Chronicle*. His articles have appeared in *Rolling Stone, Time*, the *Washington Post*, the *Guardian*, and elsewhere. He posts frequently on the David Talbot Show (https://www.thedavidtalbotshow.com/).

Margaret Talbot has been a staff writer at the *New Yorker* since 2004, was a contributing writer at the *New York Times Magazine* and has written for the *New Republic*, the *Atlantic, National Geographic*, and the *Times Book Review*. She is a recipient of a Whiting Award in nonfiction and a New America foundation fellowship, among other honors, and is the author of *The Entertainer: Movies, Magic and My Father's Twentieth Century.*

Arthur Allen has reported and edited for the Associated Press from Europe, Mexico, and Central America, and for *Politico* and the Kaiser Health News from Washington, DC. He is the author of *The Fantastic Laboratory of Dr. Weigl: How Two Brave Scientists Battled Typhus and Sabotaged the Nazis; Ripe: the Search for the Perfect Tomato,* and *Vaccine: The Controversial Story of Medicine's Greatest Lifesaver.*